Underpaid and Unrecognized

OXFORD LABOUR LAW

General Editors: Alan Bogg, Professor of Labour Law at University of Bristol Law School; Anne Davies, Dean of the Oxford Law Faculty; Keith Ewing, Professor of Public Law at King's College London; and Mark Freedland, Emeritus Research Fellow in Law at St John's College and Emeritus Professor of Employment Law in the University of Oxford.

The *Oxford Labour Law* series (formerly known as the *Oxford Monographs on Labour Law* series) has come to represent a significant contribution to the literature of British, European, and international labour law. The series recognizes the arrival not only of a renewed interest in labour law generally, but also the need for fresh approaches to the study of labour law following a period of momentous change in the UK and Europe. The series is concerned with all aspects of labour law, including traditional subjects of study such as collective labour law and individual employment law. It also includes works that concentrate on the growing role of human rights and the combating of discrimination in employment, and others that examine the law and economics of the labour market and the impact of social security law and of national and supranational employment policies upon patterns of employment and the employment contract. Two of the contributing authors to the series, Lucy Vickers and Diamond Ashiagbor, have received awards from the Society of Legal Scholars in respect of their books.

ALSO AVAILABLE IN THE SERIES

Shaping Contracts for Work
The Normative Influence of Terms Implied by Law
Gabrielle Golding

Human Rights Due Diligence and Labour Governance
Ingrid Landau

Catholic Social Teaching and Labour Law
An Ethical Perspective on Work
Mark Bell

Structural Injustice and Workers' Rights
Virginia Mantouvalou

Reforming Age Discrimination Law
Beyond Individual Enforcement
Alysia Blackham

Putting Human Rights to Work
Labour Law, the ECHR, and the Employment Relation
Philippa Collins

Underpaid and Unrecognized

State-Induced Unfree Labour

KATIE BALES
Associate Professor of Law,
University of Bristol, UK

AMIR PAZ-FUCHS
Professor of Law and Social Justice,
University of Sussex, UK

OXFORD
UNIVERSITY PRESS

OXFORD
UNIVERSITY PRESS

Great Clarendon Street, Oxford, OX2 6DP,
United Kingdom

Oxford University Press is a department of the University of Oxford.
It furthers the University's objective of excellence in research, scholarship,
and education by publishing worldwide. Oxford is a registered trade mark of
Oxford University Press in the UK and in certain other countries.

Published in the United States of America by Oxford University Press
198 Madison Avenue, New York, NY 10016, United States of America.

British Library Cataloguing in Publication Data
Data available

Library of Congress Control Number: 2026934382

ISBN 9780197910436

DOI: 10.1093/9780197910467.001.0001

Printed and bound by
CPI Group (UK) Ltd., Croydon, CR0 4YY

The manufacturer's authorized representative in the EU for product safety is
Oxford University Press España S.A. of Parque Empresarial San Fernando de Henares,
Avenida de Castilla, 2 – 28830 Madrid (www.oup.es/en or product.safety@oup.com).
OUP España S.A. also acts as importer into Spain of products made by the manufacturer.

MIX
Paper | Supporting
responsible forestry
FSC® C013604

For those who labour at the margins and whose work
too often goes unrecognized

Series Editors' Preface

Historically, the subject of labour law was framed around a set of fundamental organizing concepts and categories. Perhaps the most important of these was the standard employment relationship, which presupposed a stable, open-ended employment contract of indefinite duration with a single employer. This standard employment contract was typically full-time, and the worker benefited from union representation and collective bargaining. It was supplemented by labour standards enacted by state institutions directed at the promotion of decent work. This was labour law's central case.

Other forms of work were located at the margins of the discipline. These included the multiplicity of 'atypical' variations reflected in non-standard work. At the most extreme edges of the periphery, there were forms of work that were scarcely recognizable to the labour lawyer: prison work, work in other forms of coercive detention such as asylum detention centres, and instances of modern slavery and forced labour. Although usually treated as invisible, even when it was grudgingly acknowledged, the periphery was treated as a moral problem. Culpable employers exploited the most vulnerable workers, and culpable workers engaged in illicit labour that was often tainted by criminality (especially in contexts of irregular migration). The worker's consent was of dubious legitimacy, in contrast to the standard employment relationship. In pushing for the standardization and formalization of these peripheral instances of work, activists often understood themselves as pushing at an open door of a willing state ready to eradicate exploitative work.

In this addition to the Oxford Labour Law series, the authors provide a powerful and arresting challenge to this conventional narrative. Each author is extremely well placed to make this challenge. Dr Bales's academic work has developed sophisticated socio-legal and Marxist feminist critiques of the carceral state in the regulation of migrants and asylum seekers. Professor Paz-Fuchs has a formidable scholarly reputation in his work on welfare, workfare, and the intersections between social security and work regulation. Taken together, these vantage points provide a structural perspective on the regulation of work. Work regulation has never just been about labour law. That is just the tip of the regulatory iceberg. Beneath it is the looming structural presence of migration law, welfare and social security law, prison law, criminal law, and family law. The rich interdisciplinarity on display in this book places it within the critical strand of a tradition that might now be described as 'the law of the labour market'.

The authors' central thesis is to challenge the familiar conventional narrative of the standard employment relationship and the role of the state—namely, the belief that labour unfreedom is exceptional and driven by private actors actuated by vice and greed. Against this, and through rigorous critical argument contextualized through case studies, the authors reveal unfree labour as structurally constituted by legal and political arrangements within liberal democratic states. It is not merely that exploitation persists despite the law; rather, law—through its concepts and modes of reasoning—is itself generative of unfreedom. Moreover, the law obscures and even conceals its own structural contribution through its claims to neutrality and corrective justice. This unfreedom exists on a continuum, disrupting the traditional legal category of valid consent that operates as a binary enquiry for legal officials.

The authors' argument is developed through careful socio-legal analysis and anchored in concrete case studies: prison labour, workfare, labour in immigration detention, and unpaid internships. Each type of work is facilitated and legitimated through state action, while labour law usually treats the work as not 'real' work subject to an enforceable contract. Yet for all its invisibility, created through law, these workers frequently perform economically productive labour while remaining excluded from core protections. This is because their work is frequently presented as rehabilitative, punitive, or a beneficial opportunity for the worker either to redeem themselves or to augment their 'employability'.

This book goes beyond doctrinal analysis of the law's formal categories. Without critical and historical perspectives, there is a risk that legal concepts become entrenched as naturalized and inescapable. Instead, through careful critical analysis of doctrines such as the employment contract, the law's role in creating and sustaining exploitative work can be subjected to scholarly scrutiny. It is therefore a vital counterpart to more doctrinally orientated studies.

This important book concludes with a powerful challenge to labour lawyers. Indeed, its message is revolutionary in import. For the kind of work that we have traditionally regarded as being at the periphery must now be repositioned as central. And we can no longer take the worker-protective claims of the liberal democratic state at face value. Emancipation is unlikely to be achieved through the specific adjustment of legal rules governing employment without a consideration of the structural totality. As the authors argue, this requires nothing less than a structural response, captured in their idea of 'power to the workers'. In this stirring call for the full democratization of work, the authors have set down a challenge to labour lawyers—indeed, to the very idea of labour law itself. The editors are delighted to welcome it to the series.

AB, ACLD, KDE, MRF

Acknowledgements

The writing of this book has been a long time in the making, and we owe an immense debt of gratitude to the many people who have inspired, guided, and worked alongside us during the book's gestation.

Katie: My thanks go first to Lucy Mayblin, whose influence was central to the early development of these ideas and who helped illuminate the sociological literature on labour unfreedom—a body of work that has profoundly shaped my understanding of the field. I am equally grateful to Katie Cruz, whose intellect and guidance have been invaluable, as has her generosity in reviewing and discussing my work.

Huge thanks to both Jon Burnett and David Whyte, who encouraged me to situate these questions beyond the sphere of immigration and challenged me to develop analyses of labour unfreedom across the diverse case studies explored in this book. A Leverhulme Trust Research Fellowship also afforded me the time and space to reflect on these ideas outside the demands of teaching.

I have been fortunate to work alongside extraordinarily generous and brilliant colleagues at the University of Bristol—Alan Bogg, Joanne Conaghan, Manoj Dias-Abey, and Tonia Novitz—each of whom has read and offered thoughtful feedback on drafts and chapter excerpts. I am also grateful to Bridget Anderson, Eileen Boris, Judy Fudge, Julie Greene, Paddy Ireland, Julia O'Connell Davidson, and Marlese Von Broembsen, all of whom have shaped and inspired my thinking in different ways in recent years.

Finally, my deepest thanks go to my family and support network—especially Lauren, Karen, and my mum—and to my children, Joss and Fenne, who inspire me every day to keep moving forwards and to do better.

Amir: In developing the arguments in this book, I have had the privilege of sharing ideas, receiving feedback, and being supported by colleagues and friends near and far. Special thanks go to Virginia Mantouvalou, Paula McDonald, and Maayan Niezna for ongoing conversations and deliberations over the substantive topics as well as their friendship and sound advice over the years. On the latter front, like Katie, I am also grateful to Alan Bogg and Joanne Conaghan, who somehow always seem to find the time and patience to help.

I have had the opportunity to present relevant chapters at the International Society for Labour and Social Security Law in Rome, the Labour Law Research

Network Conference in Bangkok, and the London Labour Law Discussion Group and am grateful to panel organizers, respondents, and discussants who have helped shape and refine my thoughts on the issues.

Finally, my father passed away during the writing of this book, and there is no day of personal, professional, or intellectual relevance that I don't miss sharing with him. And amidst a range of personal and professional challenges, my partner, Tilly, and our children—Nimrod, Amitai, and Hagar—are my touchstone for strength and support, and for which I am grateful beyond words.

Finally, our joint thanks extend to the team at Oxford University Press for their patience as this manuscript unfolded.

Brief Contents

Detailed Contents

Table of Cases

UNITED KINGDOM

EUROPEAN COMMISSION OF HUMAN RIGHTS (ECOMMHR)

EUROPEAN COURT OF JUSTICE

EUROPEAN COURT OF HUMAN RIGHTS (ECTHR)

UNITED KINGDOM TRIBUNAL

AUSTRALIA

CANADA

GERMANY

ISRAEL

UNITED STATES

Table of Legislation

UK STATUTES

NATIONAL INSTRUMENTS

Canada

United States

TABLE OF INTERNATIONAL INSTRUMENTS

1

Introduction

The State, The Market and Unfree Labour

1. The State and Unfree Labour: A Bird's Eye View

Unfree labour is neither a relic of pre-modern economies nor a peripheral concern within contemporary labour regulation. It is not confined to criminal enterprises or the illicit margins of the market. Rather, it is sustained, expanded, and legitimated by state institutions that claim to be its guardians. This book begins from the premise that the modern state does not merely tolerate unfree labour; it produces and profits from it.

There is a story about the role of the state with respect to free labour that goes something like this: at first, the state facilitated and perpetuated unfree labour. It instigated slavery, and enforced it, directly or through third parties (eg the East India Company[1]). However, at some point (which varies for different countries) the state took on an emancipatory role. Initially, that role was most clearly visible with the abolition of slavery *strictu sensu* (ie the legal ownership of people), but increasingly, it enacted a wider array of protections that enhanced *freedoms from the market* or from third party actions. Thus, the state, incrementally but consistently, legislated to safeguard health and safety, job protection, wages, a decent work–life balance, protection from unmerited discrimination, and so forth. Where the state was not successful or, alternatively, was slow to succeed, the explanation was that other forces—predominantly 'big business'—were more effective at mobilizing the political and legal resources to counter the benevolent forces and interests that the state advances. The state, therefore, is not just part of the *response* to unfree labour but, moreover, may even be construed as one of its victims.[2]

Two conclusions derive from this story. First, the state was always involved in the construction of freedom and unfreedom. We will endeavour to show

[1] William Dalrymple, *The Anarchy: The Relentless Rise of the East India Company* (Bloomsbury 2019).

[2] Genevieve LeBaron and Nicola Phillips, 'States and the Political Economy of Unfree Labour' (2018) 24 New Political Economy 1, 3, referring to International Labour Office (ILO), *Profits and Poverty: The Economics of Forced Labour* (2nd edn, ILO 2024) <https://doi.org/10.54394/JJJE9035>.

Underpaid and Unrecognized. Katie Bales and Amir Paz-Fuchs, Oxford University Press.
 DOI: 10.1093/9780197910467.003.0001

how this is indeed the case. But there is a second conclusion in this story, according to which it is a (Whig) story of linear progress, a move from unfreedom to freedom in which the state is a central actor. This conclusion leads many to considerable frustration when they find that the power of the state is used to restrict individual freedom rather than enhance it. But the reason for this disappointment is simple: high expectations. The linear progression story was always a false—or at least, a more complicated—one.

2. Fragmentation, Exclusion, and Exploitation

The capitalist labour market is notoriously fragmented, with over half the global labour force working in the informal economy, in which workers share one commonality: lack of legal and social protections.[3] Although the informal economy varies from country to country, informality is primarily associated with private labour relations that persist 'out of sight' of government agencies, remaining unmonitored and unregulated.

Generally, there are strong correlations between gender, class, and race relations, with certain demographics more likely to be impacted by vulnerabilities such as poverty, which increases the likelihood of informality and the risk of abuse and exploitation by 'unscrupulous employers' or third-party agents seeking to maximize surplus value extraction from their workforce. The 'unscrupulous employer' narrative is commonly harnessed by neoliberal policymakers who, instead of addressing the underlying structures leading to exploitative work (or increasing labour rights to redress bargaining power), lean on the criminal law as a solution to addressing labour exploitation. Within this neoliberal framing, the market is constructed through the simplistic lens of natural cause and effect, obfuscating the central role of law in the creation and maintenance of property as a structural relation granting the market its power.[4] Similarly, the imbalance of bargaining power that emanates from divergent property rights is mystified and naturalized. On this basis, designated laws and policies such as employment protections and welfare provision are ostensibly created to cushion the process of commodification and protect citizens from the vagaries of the market, though to what extent this is actualized is debatable, and, importantly, these protections are only afforded to a lucky few.

[3] Martha Alter Chen, 'The Informal Economy: Definitions, Theories and Policies' (August 2012) Women in Informal Employment Globalizing and Organizing (WIEGO) Working Paper No 1 <www.wiego.org/sites/default/files/publications/files/Chen_WIEGO_WP1.pdf> accessed 12 November 2025.

[4] Paddy Ireland, *Property in Contemporary Capitalism* (Bristol UP 2024).

Devoid of this material context, those working within the informal sector are constructed within law and policy as either criminals or victims—with little space in between to recognize the inherent complexities that drive or coerce individuals into low-waged and unregulated forms of work. Law both creates and validates this moral division through, for example, the criminalization of working without the correct immigration status (and thereby denying the 'right to work') while setting the benchmark for protection from exploitation at a high level, triggered only where instances of slavery, servitude, forced labour, and/or trafficking are identified. This threshold is implemented at both the domestic and international level, meaning that legal protections are only afforded to exploited workers in extreme circumstances, often where they lack consent or where their agency is overridden by threat of penalty, which is constructed in non-economic terms, ignoring poverty as a coercive force. As noted by O'Connell Davidson, 'the depiction of a world where people are either abject, passive objects and slaves or freely contracting subjects works to rescue the privileged Western audience from certain psychic anxieties'.[5] Such an imaginary serves to validate not only poor working conditions, such as low pay and long hours, but also the exclusion of large swathes of workers from formal legal protection, instead classifying their work under the law as informal, illegal, or irregular, effectively moralizing their choice to engage in exploitative work as 'voluntary'.

Against this background, there is a growing sector of workers who meet the criteria of informal work due to limited, or lack of, access to labour rights and protections. But rather than existing outside the purview of the state, their labour relations are instead initiated and organized by governments, creating a cheap and unregulated labour force from which numerous actors benefit. This includes those performing prison work, workfare, and work within immigration detention centres. To this we add the intriguing case of internships, in which the state operates in the background, creating the general and legal structure to facilitate and legitimize exploitation through the denial of rights. In contrast to the criminal/victim narrative that permeates the informal sector, exclusion from labour and employment protections in these scenarios is justified on different grounds: that the work performed is of a 'non-market', or 'non-economic' character. This distinction between market and non-market work is not new but, rather, has a long history of excluding particular populations from employment recognition and its associated rights, including women

[5] Julia O'Connell Davidson, *Modern Slavery: The Margins of Freedom* (Palgrave Macmillan UK 2015) 206.

performing domestic work within the home[6] and colonized populations, rendering the work 'invisible' and 'naturalized into non-existence'.[7] It is work that is initiated and facilitated by the state, directly or indirectly, that is the focus of this book, whereby workers are excluded from labour rights and paid less than the minimum wage for their efforts, with particular focus on the case studies of prison work, labour in immigration detention, workfare, and internships.

The first three case studies were initially selected because they share the commonality of state exploitation of particularly vulnerable groups from whom both the state and private corporations profit and are also sectors that have expanded over the past few decades to make them more accessible to capital. In addition, there are historical continuities in terms of the demography of workers performing this work that remains highly classed, gendered, and racialized. Internships, on the other hand, represent a very different worker demographic. We decided to extend our study to include internships to provide a contrasting account of labour unfreedom: while many of the structural vulnerabilities associated with the work of prisoners, immigration detention detainees, and those subject to the disciplinary apparatus of workfare are not present in the case of interns—or, at least, do not take the same form—the labour of this group is also excluded from recognition as formal, 'market' work, and they have no access to labour rights and protections, including the national minimum wage. In conceptualizing labour unfreedom, we therefore felt it was appropriate to take into account labour that, in many instances, may be considered 'decent work' but which remains at the fringes of informality and unfreedom. Such an analysis is timely as studies of informal and precarious work have been the subject of study and concern over the past two decades,[8] with particular focus on low wages,[9] agency work,[10] zero-hour contracts,[11] and

[6] Joanne Conaghan, 'Gender and the Labour of Law' in Hugh Collins, Virginia Mantouvalou, and Gillian Lester (eds), *Philosophical Foundations of Labour Law* (OUP 2018).

[7] Zoe Adams, 'Invisible Labour: Legal Dimensions of Invisibilization' (2022) 49 Journal of Law and Society.

[8] Bridget Anderson, 'Migration, Immigration Controls and the Fashioning of Precarious Workers' (2010) 24 Work, Employment and Society 300; Guy Standing, *The Precariat: The New Dangerous Class* (Bloomsbury 2011); Guy Standing, *The Precariat: The New Dangerous Class* (Special COVID-19 edn, IB Tauris 2019); Leah F Vosko, *Managing the Margins: Gender, Citizenship, and the International Regulation of Precarious Employment* (OUP 2011).

[9] LJB Hayes, 'Care and Control: Are the National Minimum Wage Entitlements of Homecare Workers at Risk under the Care Act 2014?' (2015) 44 Industrial Law Journal 492; Lydia Hayes, *Stories of Care: A Labour of Law: Gender and Class at Work* (Palgrave 2017); Zoe Adams, 'Understanding the Minimum Wage: Political Economy and Legal Form' (2019) 78 Cambridge Law Journal 42; Zoe Adams, *Labour and the Wage: A Critical Perspective* (OUP 2020).

[10] Alessio Bertolini, *Temporary Agency Workers in Italy and the UK: The Comparative Experience of Labour Market Disadvantage* (Palgrave Macmillan 2020).

[11] Zoe Adams, SF Deakin, and Institute of Employment Rights, *Re-Regulating Zero Hours Contracts* (Institute of Employment Rights 2014); Jo Grady, 'The State, Employment, and Regulation: Making

platform-organized services such as Deliveroo and Uber whereby private labour relations are scrutinized.[12] This book represents a departure from this literature as it centres upon the state as the primary actor in the control, organization, and/or facilitation of unfree labour practices.

3. State Exclusion from Labour Recognition and Rights

Jermaine, a prisoner aged eighteen, began his sentence in a youth prison where he was studying to qualify as a gym instructor. After being moved to an adult prison, he was told he could continue his studies; however, that promise was not kept. Instead, he was put to work in Workshop One of the prison, clipping wires for a private corporation.[13] *The minimum pay for prisoners is £4.00 per week.*[14] *The average varies depending on placement. In July 2022, the average full time weekly wage for prisoners at Her Majesty's Prison (HMP) Send was £13.93.*[15]

John was detained in Brook House Immigration Removal Centre from April to November 2018 after claiming asylum in the United Kingdom out of fear of returning to Jamaica. Outside of detention, John was paid £9.00 an hour as a specialist cleaner and decorator. Once detained, John began working as a cleaner for the detention centre. He worked seven days a week and cleaned throughout the day, whenever was needed, making it difficult to quantify just how much work he did. He was paid £1.00 an hour for this work and no more than £30.00 per week.[16]

Ann worked in admin after leaving college. She lost her job at an estate agents during the recession and had to go on to Job Seekers' Allowance. Despite her secretarial and organizational experience, she was sent to work in a supermarket for four weeks. She had no agency over the choice of placement as contesting

Work Not Pay' (2017) 39 Employee Relations 274; Anna Ginès Fabrellas, 'The Zero-Hour Contract in Platform Work: Should We Ban It or Embrace It?' (2019) 0 Revista de Internet, Derecho y Politica 29; Elise Dermine and Amaury Mechelynck, 'Zero-Hour Contracts and Labour Law: An Antithetical Association?' (2022) 13 European Labour Law Journal 339.

[12] Jeremias Adams-Prassl, *Humans as a Service: The Promise and Perils of Work in the Gig Economy* (1st edn, OUP 2018).

[13] Jenna Pandeli, Michael Marinetto, and Jean Jenkins, 'Captive in Cycles of Invisibility? Prisoners' Work for the Private Sector' (2019) 33 Work, Employment and Society 596.

[14] HM Prison Service (2020) 'Prisoner's Pay': Prison Services Order 4460 [2.1.1].

[15] Inside Time, '"Prisoners Need a National Pay Scale"' (*Inside Time Reports*, 22 March 2023) <https://insidetime.org/newsround/prisoners-need-a-national-pay-scale> accessed 12 November 2025.

[16] John, 'Working for a Pound an Hour: An Immigration Detainee's Perspective' (*Futures of Work*, 30 September 2019) <https://futuresofwork.co.uk/2019/09/30/working-for-a-pound-an-hour-an-immigration-detainees-perspective> accessed 12 November 2025.

it would lead to loss of her benefit payment. At the end of the placement, she was told there was no job available for her as she didn't have enough 'retail experience'.[17]

Natasha (now an established writer) started her first internship at the age of eighteen, which involved writing five to seven stories per day at a rate of £25.00 per week. From a low socio-economic background, Natasha's parents were unable to support her during her internship, so she also worked at Topshop and used this money to fund accommodation in a backpackers hostel in London. By her third internship at a public relations agency, which paid £10.00 per day, Natasha had begun sofa surfing at a friend's house, who then tried to take advantage of her. As a result, Natasha ended up sleeping in the agency's office each evening until the cleaners arrived at 6am. The agency's reference for Natasha noted that she was 'always tired'.[18]

Although prison work, work within immigration detention centres, workfare, and internships generate economic value for private corporations, and (in many instances) the state, the workers are paid minimal wages, if any wage at all, and are not legally recognized as engaging in employment. One of the central obfuscations as to why this work is classified as 'non-market' work is that it 'benefits' the participants, as opposed to the employing entities, serving to mystify both its economic contribution and the exploitative form of its extraction. A series of intimate connections therefore exist between labour market policies and interventionist forms of governance in areas such as immigration, welfare, and the criminal law, which codify and shape our perceptions of constructs such as 'work', 'employment', and decisions over who should be included and excluded from the allocation of labour rights. This book analyses the legal position of these workers—specifically prison workers, immigration detainees, workfare participants, and interns—and reflects on the growing privatization of state functions, which allows private corporations to profit from state-induced 'unfree' labour. Building on work developed by sociologists and socio-legal scholars,[19] we argue that this labour should be considered 'unfree'

[17] 'Facts: People's Experiences of Workfare' (Boycott Workfare) <https://web.archive.org/web/20220214213259/https:/www.boycottworkfare.org/facts-about-workfare> accessed 6 December 2024. Since this webpage was last accessed, it has been archived, meaning that the URL cited is no longer active.

[18] Simon Doherty, '"We Slept in the Office": Internship Horror Stories|LinkedIn' (*Linked In Pulse*, 1 January 2021) <www.linkedin.com/pulse/we-slept-office-internship-horror-stories-simon-doherty> accessed 12 November 2025.

[19] Katie Cruz, 'Beyond Liberalism: Marxist Feminism, Migrant Sex Work, and Labour Unfreedom' (2018) 26 Feminist Legal Studies 65; Judy Fudge, 'Modern Slavery, Unfree Labour and the Labour Market: The Social Dynamics of Legal Characterization' (2018) 27 Social & Legal Studies 414; Genevieve LeBaron, 'Unfree Labour beyond Binaries' (2015) 17 International Feminist Journal

and explore the ways in which the exploitation of such workers could be reduced through both legal measures, such as the reconceptualization of 'work' and 'worker' status; the expansion of labour rights; the securitization of basic needs outside of the wage–work bargain; and collective labour action.

As an increasing number of underpaid and unrecognized workers perform work within the state sector, this book provides a timely analysis of the ways in which labour law interacts with other areas of law and policy to exclude unpopular minorities from labour law protections—broadening the scope of traditional 'labour law' research. Although a number of the case studies explored in the book are well researched within academia, such as workfare[20] and prison labour,[21] there are few texts that look at the role of the state in facilitating and enforcing unfree forms of labour, particularly in the United Kingdom, notwithstanding Mantouvalou's contribution to the theorization of law as a form of structural injustice.[22] Accordingly, this book forms more than just a presentation of case studies but is rather an assemblage and analysis of the contemporary neoliberal political economy surrounding certain forms of work, to which (we argue) academics, activists, and the political world should give much greater attention. Specifically, we are interested in the role of the state in facilitating 'unfree' labour through privatization, de-regulation/re-regulation, and the historical continuities of exclusion that are reproduced as a result of capital accumulation.

The book has four central objectives. First, it charts a political economy comprised of the state's approach to and engagement with four case studies: prison workers, workfare claimants, immigration detainees, and interns. Applying a jurisprudential approach to employment status derived from case law, the book analyses whether these individuals in these categories would be considered 'employees' or 'workers' if they were not formally denied employment status and rights by the state, at the same time contextualizing their exclusion

of Politics 1; LeBaron and Phillips (n 2); Virginia Mantouvalou, *Structural Injustice and Workers' Rights* (OUP 2023); Robert J Steinfeld, *Coercion, Contract, and Free Labor in the Nineteenth Century* (CUP 2001).

[20] Jamie Peck, *Workfare States* (Guilford Press 2001); Amir Paz-Fuchs, *Welfare to Work: Conditional Rights in Social Policy* (OUP 2008).

[21] Genevieve LeBaron, 'Rethinking Prison Labor: Social Discipline and the State in Historical Perspective' (2012) 15 WorkingUSA 327; F Milman-Sivan, 'Prisoners for Hire: Towards a Normative Justification of the ILO's Prohibition of Private Forced Prisoner Labor' (2013) 36 Fordham International Law Journal 1619; Amy Ludlow, *Privatising Public Prisons: Labour Law and the Public Procurement Process* (Hart Publishing 2015); Hugh Collins, 'The Right to Fair Pay and Two Paradigms of Prison Work' (2024) 15 European Labour Law Journal 445; Rory Kelly, 'Prison Labour as Punishment' (2024) 15 European Labour Law Journal 426.

[22] Mantouvalou (n 19).

through a historical materialist lens. A thorough mapping of state-organized labour which sits outside of traditional labour regulations is yet to be undertaken. This book aims, in part, to fill that gap.

Second, the book charts the boundaries between free and unfree labour, analysing whether the labour outlined in the case studies should be considered 'unfree'. Drawing upon legal and sociological insights, the book draws out the circumstances, structures, and social relations that might compel individuals to agree to perform exploitative work and concludes by addressing the legal, political, institutional, and social changes that could be made to ameliorate labour unfreedoms and the exploitation that arises from unequal bargaining relationships.

Third, the book highlights the ways in which prison labour, workfare, internships, and labour within immigration detention are exploitative. Although numerous studies—academic, journalistic, and non-governmental organization-initiated—have documented conditions of labour within these contexts,[23] there are no academic texts that provide a broad perspective on conditions of state-organized labour and the political economy of the UK system.

Fourth, and finally, the authors are interested in the ways in which private corporations and the state profit from this work, using cheap and unregulated labour to perform work that would otherwise be undertaken by workers entitled to the national minimum wage and employment rights. The implications for the workers themselves, competing sectors, and society at large will also be considered.

The book adopts a socio-legal research methodology to contextualize and better understand the legal instruments that exclude particular populations from recognition and labour law protections, situating labour law as deriving from historical, social, and cultural epistemologies devised to facilitate modern capitalism. Law (as doctrine, interpretation, reasoning, and argument)[24] is thus shaped by complex networks of structural relations that are best understood from a socio-legal perspective to denaturalize a number of the underlying assumptions used to justify the law's rationale. Accordingly, the book draws from different disciplines, including sociology, history, and political economy, to theorize, analyse, and understand contemporary forms of unfree

[23] Katie Bales and Lucy Mayblin, 'Unfree Labour in Immigration Detention: Exploitation and Coercion of a Captive Immigrant Workforce' (2018) 47 Economy and Society 191; Katie Bales, 'Rethinking "Unfree" Labour: The Immigration Industrial Complex' in Eileen Boris and others (eds), *Global Labour Migration: New Directions* (University of Illinois Press 2023); LeBaron (n 21); Ludlow (n 21); Milman-Sivan (n 21); Paz-Fuchs (n 20); Peck (n 20).

[24] Roger Cotterrell, 'Why Must Legal Ideas Be Interpreted Sociologically?' (1998) 25 Journal of Law and Society 171.

labour overseen by the state. Building upon methods used successfully in the authors' previous works,[25] the study comprises library and internet-based research, with a small amount of data gathered from Freedom of Information Act requests. While the book has a conceptual focus, it also draws from a body of primary legal materials as well as political and social records. This includes reference to international instruments and regulations, domestic statutes and case law, parliamentary debates, parliamentary inquiries, and committee reports. In addition, the authors draw from government data and guidance as well as documents detailing the nature and extent of state-organized 'unfree' labour obtained via freedom-of-information (FoI) requests. The authors also utilize (with due caution) evidence produced by campaign groups such as Boycott Workfare and Corporate Watch. While these are not academic research sources, they provide access to workers' testimony and accounts of the work being undertaken.

Over the past few years, there has been a growing unease with the terms deployed by modern legislators to depict labour exploitation, including 'slavery', 'servitude', and 'forced labour', thus leading to a proliferation of research on 'unfree labour'.[26] Unlike forced labour or modern slavery, 'unfree labour' is not a legal concept but offers an additional way of criticizing and conceptualizing consent and the coercive circumstances, structures, and social relations that compel individuals into performing exploitative work. We have chosen to adopt this theoretical perspective, explored more fully in Chapters 4 and 5, as it recognizes that issues are often nuanced and constructed narrowly to suit capitalist agendas, moving away from the liberal 'consent'-based approach used in much legal classification (such as the International Labour Organization Forced Labour Convention 1930, which, arguably, fails to capture many

[25] Bales and Mayblin (n 23); Bales (n 23); Katie Bales, 'Labour as a Component of Carceral Circuitry: The Case of Asylum Seekers' [2024] European Labour Law Journal 597; Paz-Fuchs (n 20); Amir Paz-Fuchs, 'Workfare's Persistent Philosophical and Legal Issues: Forced Labour, Reciprocity and a Basic Income Guarantee' in Anja Eleveld, Thomas Kampen, and Josien Arts (eds), *Welfare to Work in Contemporary European Welfare States* (Policy Press 2020).

[26] Bales and Mayblin (n 23); Bales (n 23); Cruz (n 19); Fudge (n 19); Judy Fudge, 'What Makes Labour Free? (And Why This Question Matters)' (*Futures of Work*, 24 May 2019) <https://futuresofwork.co.uk/2019/05/24/what-makes-labour-free-and-why-this-question-matters> accessed 7 November 2025; Judy Fudge, *Constructing Modern Slavery: Law, Capitalism, And Unfree Labour* (CUP 2024); LeBaron (n 21); LeBaron (n 19); LeBaron and Phillips (n 2); Jens Lerche, 'A Global Alliance against Forced Labour? Unfree Labour, Neo-Liberal Globalization and the International Labour Organization' (2007) 7 Journal of Agrarian Change 425; Jens Lerche, 'The Unfree Labour Category and Unfree Labour Estimates: A Continuum within Low-End Labour Relations' (2011) 11 Journal of Agrarian Change 104; Siobhán McGrath, Ben Rogaly, and Louise Waite, 'Unfreedom in Labour Relations: From a Politics of Rescue to a Politics of Solidarity?' (2022) 19 Globalizations 911; Nicola Phillips, 'Unfree Labour and Adverse Incorporation in the Global Economy: Comparative Perspectives on Brazil and India' (2013) 42 Economy and Society 171.

of the coercive pressures faced by those within our case studies). The use of government approved legal frameworks, such as a human rights, to critique government-induced forms of working (from which the state profits) is thus likely to prove ineffective.

4. Structure and Chapter Overview

Each chapter of this book develops the argument that state-facilitated unfree labour is neither incidental nor anomalous but forms part of a wider logic of legal exclusion, political economy, and social reproduction. The book unfolds across seven substantive chapters, each building on the last to expose how law, policy, and ideology conspire to legitimize exploitation at the core of the liberal labour order.

Following this introduction, Chapter 2, 'Exploring the State's Hidden Workforce', sets the context for the study and introduces the empirical terrain. It explores 'the state's hidden workforce' by examining the case studies of prison labour, the labour of immigration detainees, workfare, and internships, taking into account their associated histories, the conditions of the labour process, the breadth and scale of work undertaken, and available testimony from workers. Importantly, we also scrutinize the involvement of private corporations, taking into account the potential profits being made by both the state and private groups who capitalize on the work performed. The chapter concludes by drawing out the commonalities between each of these forms of work, which provisionally relate to coercion by the state; the involvement of private corporations; and social exclusion based on status, such as immigration status, unemployment, and/or criminality. Although this chapter provides a detailed overview of the case studies, their analysis is not compressed into this single chapter but runs throughout the book, revisited through the lens of unfreedom and exploitation.

Chapter 3, 'Working Without a Job: Why Are They Not Workers?', interrogates the doctrinal exclusions that sustain this regime. It undertakes a legal analysis of the employment status of the workers outlined in the case study sectors. Applying the statutory framework and established case law on employment status, the chapter determines 'who is a worker' and why certain groups are excluded from protection—including those within the case study sectors. It is here that relations of race, class, and gender have special illuminating power. While the chosen schemes are varied, there is scope to argue in all cases that participants should be granted employment status. Case law in the United

Kingdom in these case studies is sparse, so a comparative perspective is applied in certain instances. Such a perspective reveals, for the most part, the striking ingenuity of the courts in carving out exceptions to the granting of employment rights; however, there is notable consensus as to why those within our case study groupings remain excluded from employment recognition as 'non-market' work. Notwithstanding some important differences in the structure and content of employment law protection across jurisdictions, courts noticeably converge in their denial of protection for workers engaged in these practices. The comparative perspective thus supports the thesis that this marginalization is not a consequence of a particular, doctrinal structure but rather stems from arrangements rooted in a particular (capitalist) political economy. The courts' willingness to accept the government's exclusion of such groups from labour regulation and rights reveals not only layers of state complicity but also the flexibility of law in bowing to the public 'collective' interest at the expense of marginalized communities.

A historical materialist perspective is also adopted in this chapter to first reveal where the 'non-market' justification for the exclusion of labour rights and recognition originates and how it has been used in the past to deny and exclude access to the formal labour market by particular populations, such as women and formerly colonized subjects. Drawing upon these histories and critiquing them through the lens of feminist theory and post-colonialism allows us to deconstruct the underlying assumptions used to segregate these forms of labour from the capitalist labour market, instead revealing the intrinsic connections and dependency of capitalism upon these excluded forms of work, past and present. Recognition of worker status is therefore not only about labour law and policy but also about welfare, immigration, citizenship, the criminal law, and social ideas of what is—and what is not—commodifiable. Acknowledging these wider influences provides us with greater critical purchase in understanding why certain groups are endowed with worker status, whereas others remain excluded at the boundaries.

Accordingly, Chapter 4, 'Unfree Labour', begins by setting out the current legal parameters of 'unfree labour'; defining the terms 'slavery', 'servitude', and 'forced labour' in international law; and situating them in their historical contexts. Applying a historical materialist lens is helpful here as it highlights the ways in which legal protections were shaped to serve colonial agendas, reducing the scope and effectiveness of protection against unfree labour and exploitation. The chapter then goes on to explain why the forms of work highlighted in the case studies fail to satisfy the legal requirements of these protective statuses. Addressing why the international legal framing is problematic, the remainder of the chapter explores the theory of unfree labour and posits a Marxist feminist theoretical approach as the preferable lens for identifying and addressing unfree labour practices. Our theoretical framing begins with discussion of the meaning of exploitation, adopting a broader Marxist conception of exploitation as the extraction of surplus value which denotes that workers can only ever be 'formally' free insofar as they have the capacity to sell their labour power as a commodity.[27] We then draw out how certain forms of work are more (or less) exploitative—linking this to the concept of 'unfreedoms': the more 'unfreedoms' a worker experiences, the more likely they are to be subjected to higher degrees of exploitation. Accordingly, Chapter 4 rejects the free/unfree binary, instead construing free and unfree labour as part of a continuum of labour relations based on degree rather than categorical opposition.[28] Adopting this perspective raises other conceptual issues, however, such as how to plot different forms of labour on the continuum; or whether plotting is possible, or indeed, necessary. These issues are critically analysed throughout the chapter, which concludes by providing an unfree labour framework for analysis of exploitative forms of work, drawing from the work of Marx[29] and LeBaron.[30]

The framework attends to three different dimensions of freedom that exist at different scales and levels of governance: (1) at the macro scale, processes of production and reproduction that rely (or relied) on practices of dispossession and appropriation structure our relationship with capital and the labour market, undergirding the systemic compulsion to enter into the labour contract and the (in)ability to leave. (2) On the meso scale is the sphere of circulation and the (in)ability of people and capital to move freely, whether geographically, socially, or economically. Of relevance here are the laws and policies that stem or exclude the flow of mobility. (3) At the micro scale are the conditions involved in, and the workers' experience of, the labour process itself. Whereas the other two scales structure an individual's entry into the labour market and indicate a propensity to exploitation, this final lens is an indicator of the degree of exploitation taking place within the labour relationship.

Chapter 5, 'Positioning Unfree Labour at the Centre of the Labour Analysis', builds on this final lens, bringing discussion of 'unfree labour' into conversation

[27] Jairus Banaji, 'The Fictions of Free Labour: Contract, Coercion, and So-Called Unfree Labour' (2003) 11 Historical Materialism 69; Judy Fudge, 'Feminist Reflections on the Scope of Labour Law: Domestic Work, Social Reproduction, and Jurisdiction' (2014) 22 Feminist Legal Studies 1; Robert Hale, 'Coercion and Distribution in a Supposedly Non-Coercive State' (1923) 38 Political Science Quarterly 470; Karl Marx, *Capital: A Critique of Political Economy, Vol 1* (1st edn, Penguin 1976).

[28] LeBaron (n 19); Lerche (n 26); Phillips (n 26).

[29] Marx (n 27).

[30] LeBaron (n 19).

with labour law. In doing so, it attempts to answer two central questions: first, how does, and how should, our understanding of unfreedom inform our comprehension of labour law and its future development? And second, how do, and how should, well-rehearsed labour law principles and practices enrich our conceptualization of unfreedom? Our conclusion is two-fold: first, that beyond a certain point across the continuum, some cases of unfree labour should not exist, and the law should thus seek to abolish these practices; second, that where examples of unfree labour are not deemed sufficiently 'extreme', and thus allowed to exist, there is a general legal imperative to mitigate the consequences of the unfreedom and, indeed, to move the case further 'down' the spectrum towards less unfreedom. As explored in Chapter 7, 'Power to the Workers', addressing labour unfreedom might take place through simply improving the conditions of the labour process or through addressing some of the underlying structural dimensions that lead individuals into agreeing to undertake exploitative work.

One of the defining traits of all the case studies analysed in this book is the strong involvement of government agencies not only as regulators but also as instigators and managers in the work performed. In addition, in the vast majority of cases, private—for profit—corporations are involved in running the schemes studied and profit in some way from the work performed. The governing rationality for this practice is that of neoliberalism, under which humans are viewed first and foremost, if not solely, as economic actors, and every field of activity is transformed into a market. Unlike classical liberalism, under *neo*liberalism, the state does not withdraw. In fact, it may enhance its activity in a way that serves big business. The case studies considered in our book offer strong evidence to that effect. Accordingly, Chapter 6, 'The Political Dimension: Neoliberalism, Privatization, and State Complicity', analyses the contours of state involvement in the organization of unfree labour—including its initiation, management, negotiation, and regulation of the work. FoI requests and secondary data supply important information regarding the nature of the relationship between national and local government and the corporations involved in the case study sectors, including profits, sanctions on participants, the ability to truly regulate the daily operations, and the implication on other market actors.

Unfree and exploitative forms of work harm the interests of all workers. The final substantive chapter of this book, Chapter 7, 'Power to the Workers', asks how we can ameliorate the unfreedoms experienced by those within our case study sectors and beyond and reduce the unfreedom and exploitation experienced in their working practices. The chapter scaffolds its recommendations along three axes—the micro, meso, and macro—which broadly link back to the dimensions of unfreedom explored within Chapter 4. The micro aspect explores existing legal doctrines and statues to ascertain whether there is any space within current legal practice to address the dimensions of unfreedom identified throughout the book. The meso recommendations are those that relate to existing areas of law and policy that could be amended and altered to help reduce the unfreedom and exploitation of those within our case study sectors, addressing both structural change and improvements to working conditions. The macro changes are those that tend to the structural dimensions of unfreedom, representing a provocation to the reader and policymakers to reconceptualize our current legal order. This includes the reconceptualization of work and employment status, the provision of basic minimum income or services, and the reconfiguration of numerous systems to counter capitals domination of the working classes.

Chapter 8, the concluding chapter of the book, summarizes its key arguments and reflects on the key themes that have transpired throughout the discussion and analysis, including the varying degrees of exploitation experienced by those within the case study sectors and its relation and connection to the different dimensions of unfreedom explored, the insidious creep of privatization, and the probability (or improbability) of positive change in the current political climate. It summarizes the central arguments and reflects on the broader lessons for labour law, social justice, and political economy. It restates the need to centre unfreedom—not as an exception but as a structuring principle of the current labour order.

2
Exploring the State's Hidden Workforce

1. Introduction

For centuries in the United Kingdom, the criminal justice and welfare systems have worked to instil labour market discipline upon poorer populations as well as aiming to create a distinct labour force. Over the past few decades, this has led to an increase in the popularity of penal labour and an emphasis on workfare, which compels welfare recipients to undertake certain tasks, including unpaid labour, in order to access financial support. As noted by Burnett, though both these systems have a long history, the drive to open them up to capital has expanded over the past few decades, meaning that 'through a cocktail of profit and punishment... these labour forms have come to exist as an opportunity for those wanting to extract value from them, or facilitate their use'.[1] This ideology has also seeped into the governance of immigration, particularly the sphere of immigration detention which, similarly to prison labour, uses detainees' labour as a means of cost reduction for private companies facilitating the detention estate as well as cutting down government expenditure.

As will be explored, the majority of workers falling within the case studies of prison labour, workfare, and labour in immigration detention come from poor socio-economic backgrounds and, often, a disproportionate number are non-white and male in comparison to the general population—meaning this work is classed, gendered, and racialized. This chapter juxtaposes these case studies alongside that of internships, which is another growing category of work where labour remains unpaid for the benefit of private corporations and the public sector. Like the other case studies in this book, employment law and regulation specifically exclude internships from the legal category of 'worker' or 'employee', meaning they lack access to rights such as the national minimum wage. Aside from these similarities, however, internships encompass a very different category of worker in terms of characteristics and socio-economic

[1] Jonathan Burnett, 'Work, Capital and the "Administration of Punishment"' (*Brave New Europe*, 15 October 2017) <https://braveneweurope.com/jonathan-burnett-work-capital-and-the-administration-of-punishment> accessed 12 November 2025.

Underpaid and Unrecognized. Katie Bales and Amir Paz-Fuchs, Oxford University Press.
 DOI: 10.1093/9780197910467.003.0002

background. Despite this, the common thread across the case studies outlined above is that the workers involved are excluded from formal labour law protections while generating profit for corporations and/or the state. As well as benefiting financially from the fruits of this labour, the state is also implicated as a facilitator of this broad category of 'hidden' work through the creation of law, policy, and regulation that carves out space for these practices to exist.

Accordingly, this chapter provides an overview of the forms of 'hidden' work being organized by the state. It looks in depth at the case studies of prison labour (section 2) and workfare (section 3), which form part of a long historical narrative in which poor populations have been funnelled into unpaid labour relations for capitalist gain. In addition, we address the case studies of labour within immigration detention (section 4) and internships (section 5) to demonstrate the ways in which different forms of governance and regulation continue to propel different communities into the sphere of unfree labour. Specifically, we chart the forms of work being undertaken, their timelines, numerical data on the number of persons engaged in these forms of work, working conditions, testimony from workers, the involvement of private corporations, and data on the potential profits being made by both the state and private companies. The chapter concludes by drawing out the commonalities between each of these forms of work, which provisionally relate to coercion by the state, the involvement of private corporations, and social exclusion with respect to status.

2. The Prison Industrial Complex and Prison Work

Notwithstanding the long history and prevalence of penal labour across jurisdictions, labour law has consistently excluded workers who are engaged in prison work from status and protection.[2] This is so even while prison work is strongly connected to processes of market exchange via the production of goods and services for sale on the outside or through 'prison housework'-style jobs.[3]

In the United Kingdom, the governance of prisons and imprisonment is a devolved matter, meaning that there is no national UK-wide prison system. The focus of this book is on the prison system in England and Wales, which is

[2] Deirk van Zyl and Frieder Dunkel (eds), *Prison Labour: Salvation or Slavery* (Routledge 1999).

[3] Noah Zatz, 'Working beyond the Reach or Grasp of Employment Law' in Annette Bernhardt and others (eds), *The Gloves Off Economy: Workplace Standards at the Bottom of America's Labour Market* (ILR Press 2008).

governed by His Majesty's (HM) Prison and Probation Services, an agency of the Ministry of Justice. England and Wales have the eighth highest rate of prisoners in the European Union (EU) and the highest among Western European countries.[4] Figures from 2022–23 show that the average cost per prisoner per year was £33,628.00, but including all the additional overheads needed for a prison to function, the cost per prisoner is closer to £51,108.35.[5]

Prisoners are accommodated across 124 prisons, 108 of which are run by His Majesty's Prison and Probation Service (HMPPS), with the remaining 16 run by private companies[6] that have been involved in the sector since 1992. Three different companies are involved: G4S (which operates four); Serco (which operates five), and Sodexo (which operates six).[7] These private prisons tend to be newer and larger than the public prisons,[8] and there is evidence that the United Kingdom detains a greater number of prisoners in private prisons than any other European state or the United States.[9] As of 28 October 2024, the prison population in England and Wales was 85,900,[10] meaning incarceration rates in 2024 were at their highest rate since 2011, creating a capacity crisis as occupancy levels have exceeded 110 per cent.[11] In 2019, the government invested a further £2.5 billion to create an additional 10,000 prison places, which were delivered through the creation of 3 new prisons and the expansion and refurbishment of the prison estate.[12] This capital was freed up by closing and selling off some of the older Victorian prisons. However, the charity and lobby group Corporate Watch suggests that one of the central reasons behind this move is the fact that older prisons are not

[4] Georgina Sturge, 'UK Prison Population Statistics' (House of Commons Library, 8 July 2024) No 04334 <https://researchbriefings.files.parliament.uk/documents/SN04334/SN04334.pdf> accessed 27 January 2025.

[5] ibid.

[6] National Audit Office, 'Increasing the Capacity of the Prison Estate to Meet Demand' (4 December 2024) HC 376 <www.nao.org.uk/wp-content/uploads/2024/12/increasing-the-capacity-of-the-prison-estate-to-meet-demand.pdf> accessed 24 March 2025.

[7] Jacqueline Beard, 'The Prison Estate in England and Wales' (House of Commons Library, 29 June 2023) No 5646 <https://researchbriefings.files.parliament.uk/documents/SN05646/SN05646.pdf> accessed 12 November 2025.

[8] Graham Atkins and others, 'Performance Tracker 2019 A Data-Driven Analysis of the Performance of Public Services' (Institute for Government and the Chartered Institute for Public Finance and Accountancy 2019) <www.instituteforgovernment.org.uk/sites/default/files/publications/performance-tracker-2019_0.pdf> accessed 13 November 2025.

[9] Corporate Watch (Organization: Great Britain), 'Prison Island: Prison Expansion in England, Wales & Scotland' (August 2018) <https://corporatewatch.org/wp-content/uploads/2018/08/Prison-Island-by-Corporate-Watch-Low-Res.pdf> accessed 12 November 2025

[10] National Audit Office (n 6).

[11] Ben Jarman and Helen Fair, 'Working Prisoners in the UK: Laws, Policies, and Practical Realities' (Institute for Crime and Justice Policy Research, July 2024) <https://www.prisonstudies.org/sites/default/files/resources/downloads/working_prisoners_in_the_uk_final.pdf> accessed 12 November 2025.

[12] Baroness Scott of Bybrook, HL Deb 1 December 2020, cW <https://questions-statements.parliament.uk/written-questions/detail/2020-11-17/HL10423> accessed 12 November 2025.

able to accommodate prison industries. In contrast, new 'mega prisons' will have prison 'factories' as their centre point and a greater number of workshops.[13] An increase in prison spaces does not, however, map onto a surge in crime rates as data from 1981 to 2020 reveals that while crime rates in England and Wales peaked in 1995, they have steadily fallen since.[14] Accordingly, the modern expansion of the prison estate is not a direct consequence of increased crime rates or 'explosions in crime' but rather at least partially attributed to motivations tied to capitalist expansion.[15]

The concept of the 'prison industrial complex' accommodates these viewpoints and pushes our understanding of the prison estate beyond simply that of crime and punishment. The term itself was coined in the United States by Mike Davis in 1995[16] and refers to a network of relationships linking private corporations, government, correctional communities, and media, suggesting that prison construction and the drive to keep inmate numbers high is motivated more by racialized control and the pursuit of profit than crime reduction.[17] Accordingly, both private and public prisons generate huge incomes for private companies, as evidenced by the case of Carillion which, prior to its liquidation, was granted a £500 million contract by the UK Government in 2015 to provide 'facilities management' involving services such as cleaning, maintenance, and the management of prison stores. Similarly, all of the food, linens, materials, and other resources relied upon by prisons are provided by private contractors.[18] With reference to the United States, Sjoberg notes that 'the prison-industrial complex . . . serves two functions. It sweeps the "unwanted" (especially members of racial and ethnic minorities) off the streets, and it provides a stable market for producers of a rather wide range of goods and services.'[19] The 'administration of punishment' in the present also creates a labour force that, although marginal in comparison to the labour force as a whole, is nonetheless significant: in 2016–17 around 11,200 prisoners worked

[13] Corporate Watch (Organization: Great Britain) (n 9); Corporate Watch, 'Prison Island: Winter 2021 Update' (31 October 2021) <https://corporatewatch.org/wp-content/uploads/2021/10/Prison-Island-2021-Low-Res.pdf> accessed 12 November 2025.

[14] Office for National Statistics, 'Crime in England and Wales—Office for National Statistics' (23 October 2025) <www.ons.gov.uk/peoplepopulationandcommunity/crimeandjustice/bulletins/crimeinenglandandwales/yearendingjune2025> accessed 12 November 2025.

[15] Loic Wacquant, 'The Prison Is an Outlaw Institution' (2012) 51 Howard Journal of Criminal Justice 1.

[16] Mike Davis, 'Hell Factories in the Field: A Prison-Industrial Complex' (1995) 260 The Nation 229.

[17] Angela Davis, *Are Prisons Obsolete?* (Seven Stories Press 2003).

[18] Corporate Watch (Organization: Great Britain) (n 9).

[19] Gideon Sjoberg, 'Observations on Bureaucratic Capitalism' in JL Abu-Lughod (ed), *Sociology for the Twenty-First Century: Continuities and Cutting Edges* (University of Chicago Press 1999) 33.

for around 16 million hours;[20] in 2019–20 (the most recently available data), this rose to just under 18 million hours.[21]

A further rationale is suggested by LeBaron, who notes that prison labour is a means of disciplining, containing, and exploiting the labouring poor in ways that have 'instantiated and reproduced racialized forms of market discipline'.[22] By compelling deviants and the racialized poor into prison labour, this form of work underpins and reinforces racialized and class-based social relations, which are central to the capitalist order. This perspective is supported by the profile of the typical prison population in the United Kingdom, which reveals an undeniable 'strong social gradient in imprisonment, with people of lower class, income and education much more likely to be sent to prison than people higher up the social scale'.[23] While persons from an ethnic minority background make up only 18 per cent of the general population, they make up approximately 27 per cent of the prison population, meaning that prison is both racialized and gendered as women make up only 4 per cent of the prison population in England and Wales.[24]

The remainder of this section will highlight the case study of prison labour, outlining its history in England and Wales and the ostensible purpose put forward by the government to justify the contemporary regime. We will also address the current legal framework that gives rise to prison labour and enterprise as well as the conditions of work and prison workers' perspectives. Finally, the private profit-making arrangements embedded within the prison estate will be explored, arguing that, ultimately, the carceral state and prison labour industry exploit inmates labour power, using their criminality as a justification to further business interests.

a. A History of Prison Labour

Prison labour in Britain has a long history, dating back to the emergence of systematic detention in sixteenth-century England. While there are differences in

[20] Burnett (n 1).

[21] Ministry of Justice, 'HMPPS Annual Digest 2019/20' (updated 10 June 2021) <https://assets.publishing.service.gov.uk/media/60bdfead8fa8f57ce63f1869/HMPPS-annual-digest-2019-20.pdf> accessed 13 November 2025.

[22] Genevieve LeBaron, 'Rethinking Prison Labor: Social Discipline and the State in Historical Perspective' (2012) 15 WorkingUSA 327.

[23] Richard Wilkinson and Kate Pickett, *The Spirit Level: Why Equality Is Better for Everyone* (Penguin UK 2010) 148–49.

[24] Sturge (n 4).

the ways this work has been organized, the common themes of poverty, industrial development, and capital accumulation persist throughout the centuries to the modern prison industrial complex. A brief history of prison labour is sketched below.

In line with the weakening of traditional feudal bonds, the rise of the Protestant 'work ethic', and the growing demands of mercantile capitalism, sixteenth-century England also saw the establishment of systematic detention through the creation of houses of correction, also known as bridewells (originally intended as penal hospitals). These institutions were sites not only for detention but also for punishment and reformation.[25] As well as the Protestant association of idleness with sin, this type of systematic confinement developed relative to mercantilist requirements for regular, sustained labour to generate surplus value for capital accumulation.[26] Accordingly, the first house of correction was established in London in 1557 by prominent merchants and statesmen to satisfy labour shortages in the locality. The redefinition of property rights during this era, paired with the move from feudalism to capitalism, saw a growth in petty theft as the peasantry were separated from the land and their means of subsistence,[27] leading to their criminalization and detention through vagrancy and petty theft laws. As noted by O'Connell Davidson, there was not enough paid work to absorb all those thrown off the land, resulting in 'masterless' men, women, and children wandering the country relying upon begging, tinkering, horse thievery, prostitution, and any other means of providing subsistence.[28] These 'vagabonds' were seen as a serious threat to the establishment, resulting in a flurry of legislation and attention from Parliament, which sought to control them.

These facilities quickly multiplied so that by the seventeenth century, houses of correction were common throughout Protestant England.[29] Individuals could end up in a correction house for a range of minor offences including being 'idle and disorderly', able bodied and wandering (ie vagrant), and for unlicensed begging. This captured a very specific sector of the population primarily drawn from the ranks of the labouring poor. In addition, many detainees were committed for 'offences' perpetrated against their employers, such as insubordination, leaving work while under contract, or the 'embezzlement'

[25] Joanna Innes, 'Prisons for the Poor: English Bridewells, 1555–1800' in Francis Snyder and Douglas Hay (eds), *Labour, Law and Crime: An Historical Perspective* (Tavistock Publications 1987).

[26] Russell Dobash, 'Labour and Discipline in Scottish and English Prisons: Moral Correction, Punishment and Useful Toil' (1983) 17 Sociology 1, 3.

[27] LeBaron (n 22).

[28] Julia O'Connell Davidson, *Modern Slavery: The Margins of Freedom* (Palgrave Macmillan 2015).

[29] Edward Geoffrey O'Donaghue, *Bridewell Hospital; Palace, Prison, Schools: From the Earliest Times to the End of the Reign of Elizabeth*, vol 1 (Lane 1923).

of goods and materials. Innes maps these offences on to the emancipation of workers from personal servitude to 'free' wage labour in the sixteenth century, a shift that changed the management of work relations from private manorial courts to ordinary state courts.[30] Accordingly, the law of master and servant that governed work relations up until the late nineteenth century facilitated confinement at the behest of employers.[31]

Systematic detention thus served several moral and social purposes: control and punishment of beggars, relief of the poor, prevention of idleness and evil, the disciplining of the workforce, and the development of skills associated with production, instilling the habits of the capitalist order in the minds of the reluctant poor.[32] As well as developing skills for production outside of the houses of correction, some inmate labour was also used to maintain the houses of correction themselves, employing inmates in socially useful tasks such as milling, baking, food preparation, cleaning, and maintaining and repairing the institution. As a reward for demonstrating disciplined labour, inmates would be paid a small wage. Foucault argues that such wages were merely an artifice that, rather than rewarding production, 'function as a motive and measure of individual transformation: it is a legal fiction, since it does not represent the "free" granting of labour power, but an artifice that is presumed to be effective in the techniques of correction'.[33] Work is thus not motivated by wages but rather prisoners work(ed) because the work itself serves (and served) as a disciplinary mechanism.

Throughout the nineteenth century, more rigorous systems of imprisonment were put in place, moving away from evangelical methods of confinement towards more stringent and unified methods of incarceration and labour. Houses of correction, designed to discipline the poor for petty crimes, gave way to prisons developed for the punishment of serious crimes. Yet, despite this change, the number of delinquent poor committed under the Vagrancy Acts was sustained.[34] Though solitary confinement was considered key to instilling social discipline, this had to be moderated by labour to avoid the development of mental and physical deterioration among inmates, which was considered a waste of labour power. In 1853 and 1857, the Penal Servitude Acts resulted in the use of inmate labour in Britain and the colonies, leading to an

[30] Innes (n 25).

[31] Douglas Hay, 'Master and Servant in England: Using the Law in the 18th and 19th Centuries' in Willibald Steinmetz (ed), *Private Law and Social Inequality in the Industrial Age: Comparing Legal Cultures in Britain, France, Germany, and the United States* (OUP 2000) 39.

[32] Dobash (n 26) 4.

[33] M Foucault, *Discipline and Punish: The Birth of the Prison* (Knopf Doubleday Publishing Group 1995) 243.

[34] Innes (n 25).

increase in sentences alongside the establishment of parole as a means of reducing overcrowding.[35] Though the economic benefits of prison labour were obvious in terms of reducing the costs of incarceration, as well as benefiting the military and the commercial market, this work continued to be grounded by the ideology that it was rehabilitative in nature, allowing for the development of training and useful skills. A report from the period suggested, for example, that 'public works is most beneficial in teaching criminals' habits of industry, and training them to such employments as digging, road making, quarrying, building and brick making—work of a kind which cannot be carried on in the separate system'.[36]

Labour within English prisons was further expanded in 1877 when the British Government began to nationalize the local and county prisons, which aimed to standardize discipline, diet, hygiene, staffing, and useful labour. Though penal labour could be implemented by the facilities under the Hard Labour Bill of 1865, this type of labour was not dominant as facilities preferred to use labour that served socially necessary functions. Now that British prisons had a permanent division for producing goods for the private sector via an 'industrial sub-contracting system', Dobash contends that the authorities 'reinstated one of the original goals of confinement . . . : the linking of inmate labour power to capital for the purpose of creating surplus value'.[37]

b. The Purpose of Prison Labour in the Contemporary Regime

There is a rich literature on prison labour and a divergence of opinion on its rationales and driving motivations. Indeed, the law does not define one purpose for prison work to fulfil, though a number of different policy documents provide perspectives on the government's motivations, which have drawn mixed critiques.

One of the narratives surrounding prison labour focuses on the rationale of cost saving for the government, which is considered beneficial to the general public and taxpayer as it 'limits the cost of prison' and 'allows funding to be spent on other priorities in individual prisons, such as security measures or

[35] Dobash (n 26) 16.
[36] Parliamentary Papers, *Reports from Commissioners, Inspectors, and Others*, vol 38, Penal Servitude Acts (1878–79).
[37] Dobash (n 26) 16.

offender behaviour programmes, which tackle the root causes of offending.'[38] Indeed, in 2023–24, HMPPS spent £3.56 billion on the operation of prisons, around 67 per cent of HMPP's total net expenditure.[39] Against a backdrop of worsening living conditions for prisoners,[40] the Ministry of Justice and HMPPS now expect the expansion and delivery of the prison portfolio to cost between £9.4 billion to £10.1 billion, an increase of between £4.2 billion and £4.9 billion, 80 per cent more than initially planned and approved in 2021.[41] Referring to the US context, LeBaron notes that most of the profits and cost savings from prison labour do not go towards private corporations but rather to the state, which offsets the cost of the carceral matrix that anchors the unequal socio-economic order.[42]

For many campaigners, scholars, and policymakers, prison work is considered crucial in preparing prisoners for a positive re-entry into society and life in the outside world, enabling prisoners to reconstruct their complex and often negative relationship with formal employment.[43] This is labelled as 'the most important role of prison work' by the Ministry of Justice,[44] which makes clear that prison work is intended to prepare 'offenders for future employment in modern jobs. We need to provide prisoners with skills for which there is a real demand from employers. Prisoners should use their time in prison productively to gain employable skills.'[45] Within this context, the closer prison work is to 'real work' in the formal economy, the more it enhances prisoners'

[38] Ministry of Justice, 'Education and Employment Strategy' (May 2018) Cm 9621 <https://assets.publishing.service.gov.uk/media/5b05783aed915d7c91f94be8/education-and-employment-strategy-2018.pdf> accessed 12 November 2025.

[39] National Audit Office (n 6) 13.

[40] Peter Clarke, 'Life in Prison: Living Conditions. A Findings Paper by HM Inspectorate of Prisons' (10 October 2017) <https://webarchive.nationalarchives.gov.uk/ukgwa/20240417095859/https://www.justiceinspectorates.gov.uk/hmiprisons/inspections/life-in-prison-living-conditions> accessed 12 November 2025; Michael Savage, 'Three-Quarters of Prisons in England and Wales in Appalling Conditions as Overcrowding Fears Grow' *The Guardian* (London, 5 August 2023) <www.theguardian.com/society/2023/aug/05/three-quarters-of-prisons-in-england-and-wales-in-appalling-conditions-as-overcrowding-fears-grow> accessed 12 November 2025.

[41] National Audit Office (n 6) 19.

[42] LeBaron (n 22).

[43] Roy King and Kathleen McDermott, *The State of Our Prisons* (Clarendon Press 1995); Ann Chih Lin, *Reform in the Making: The Implementation of Social Policy in Prison* (Princeton UP 2000); Alison Liebling and Helen Arnold, *Prisons and Their Moral Performance: A Study of Values, Quality, and Prison Life* (OUP 2004); Penny Green, *Prison Work and Social Enterprise: The Story of Barbed* (Howard League for Penal Reform 2008) 6; Ministry of Justice, 'Breaking the Cycle: Effective Punishment, Rehabilitation and Sentencing of Offenders' (The Stationery Office, December 2010) <https://assets.publishing.service.gov.uk/media/5a74b433e5274a3cb2866813/breaking-the-cycle.pdf> accessed 12 November 2025.; Ministry of Justice, *Transforming Rehabilitation: A Strategy for Reform* (The Stationery Office 2013).

[44] Ministry of Justice (n 38) para 77.

[45] Ministry of Justice, *Prison Safety and Reform* (White Paper, Cm 9350, 2016) para 135.

rehabilitation.[46] This perspective is supported by international and domestic human rights law, which regards prison work as rehabilitative in nature as opposed to a process of market exchange. Article 4 of the European Convention on Human Rights, for example, considers prison work as distinct from forced or compulsory labour when it is undertaken in the 'ordinary course of detention' and is designed to assist with prisoners' reintegration in society.[47] This position is mirrored by the Human Rights Act 1998 and domestic courts.

To further prisoners' connections with the outside labour market, the New Futures Network, which operates on behalf of HMPPS, seeks to establish relationships with private corporations that can provide employment opportunities for prisoners in three distinct ways: for those prisoners serving their sentence, for those released on temporary license, and for prisoners' post-release. The company Census Data, for example, is praised in the Government's White Paper on Prison Reform for running a call centre operation in 7 prisons which, in 2019, had recruited up to 75 prisoners after their release.[48] Yet, research from Jenna Pandeli suggests that, in most cases, prison labour does very little to rehabilitate inmates or reduce the costs associated with incarceration.[49] Instead, she contends that prison labour in the United Kingdom 'primarily functions to increase the profits of private companies—both the private prisons themselves and the private companies utilising prison labour'.[50] This is supported by Bullock and Bunce, who note that any 'institutional provision for rehabilitation is generally perceived by prisoners as self-serving and experienced as ill-resourced, poorly conceived and superficial'.[51] Maycock and McGregor further note that

> with respect to the 'free' granting of labour power, during interviews, numerous mentions were made of the expectation that participants were located in a 'working jail', highlighting a moral compulsion, backed by coercive

[46] Fabrice Guilbaud and Amy Jacobs, 'Working in Prison: Time as Experienced by Inmate-Workers' (2010) 51 Revue française de sociologie 41; Jenna Pandeli and Nicholas O'Regan, 'Risky Business? The Value of Employing Offenders and Ex-Offenders: An Interview with James Timpson, Chief Executive of Timpson' (2020) 29 Journal of Management Inquiry 240; Clara Luísa Oliveira Silva and Luiz Alex Silva Saraiva, 'Alienation, Segregation and Resocialization: Meanings of Prison Labor' (2016) 51 Environmental management 366.

[47] *Case of Van Droogenbroeck v Belgium* (Application No 7906/77).

[48] Ministry of Justice (n 45) 133.

[49] Jenna Pandeli, 'A Money-Making Cycle of Incarceration: The Private Sector and UK Prison Labour' (*Futures of Work*, 30 September 2019) <https://futuresofwork.co.uk/2019/09/30/a-money-making-cycle-of-incarceration-the-private-sector-and-uk-prison-labour> accessed 12 November 2025.

[50] ibid.

[51] Karen Bullock and Annie Bunce, '"The Prison Don't Talk to You about Getting Out of Prison": On Why Prisons in England and Wales Fail to Rehabilitate Prisoners' (2020) 20 Criminology & Criminal Justice 111, 112.

measures, to work, and thus bringing into question the rehabilitative lens through which prison work is often presented.[52]

The ostensibly 'rehabilitative' and 'progressive' nature of prison work is also rejected by a study which argues that, from the perspective of prisoners in the United Kingdom, prison work reinforces the undesirability of mundane, monotonous, and low-paid jobs.[53] This is consistent with theories advanced by, inter alia, Wacquant and LeBaron,[54] which regard prison labour as part of a broader political strategy utilized to instil the market and social discipline needed to sustain the neoliberal order. Prison work is thus conceived as a means to indoctrinate the incarcerated classes into precarious forms of labour that serve the capitalist agenda both inside and outside of prison.[55] This accords with the historical construction of prison labour explored earlier, which suggested that it was a means of 'allowing the habits of the capitalist order to instil in the minds of the reluctant poor'.[56] 'Rehabilitation', then, must be situated within the broader political aims of disciplining the workforce and cultivating a market-based social order.

c. Contemporary Prison Labour

The primary legislation governing prisons in England and Wales is the Prison Act 1952, which empowers the government to operate prisons and to create secondary legislation and policy to regulate prison management, including the 'classification, treatment, employment, discipline, and control of persons required to be detained therein'.[57] The central governance of day-to-day life in prisons is thus contained within the Prison Rules, a form of secondary

[52] Matthew Maycock and Daniel McGregor, '"I Do Enjoy the Work, But I Think the Wages in the Jails Are Shocking": Analysing Prisoner Wages as a Pain of Imprisonment Using Foucault's Artifice' (2023) 4 Incarceration 3.

[53] Jenna Pandeli, Michael Marinetto, and Jean Jenkins, 'Captive in Cycles of Invisibility? Prisoners' Work for the Private Sector' (2019) 33 Work, Employment and Society 596.

[54] Wacquant (n 15); Loïc Wacquant, 'Crafting the Neoliberal State: Workfare, Prisonfare, and Social Insecurity' (2010) 25 Sociological Forum 197; Loïc Wacquant, '"Suitable Enemies": Foreigners and Immigrants in the Prisons of Europe' (1999) 1 Punishment & Society 215; Genevieve LeBaron and Adrienne Roberts, 'Toward a Feminist Political Economy of Capitalism and Carcerality' (2010) 36 Signs 19; Alessandro De Giorgi, *Re-Thinking the Political Economy of Punishment: Perspectives on Post-Fordism and Penal Politics* (Ashgate 2006).

[55] Genevive LeBaron, 'Prison Labour, Slavery and the State' in Julia O'Connell Davidson and Laura Brace (eds), *Revisiting Slavery and Antislavery: Towards a Critical Analysis* (Springer International Publishing 2018).

[56] Dobash (n 26).

[57] Prison Act 1952, s 47(1).

legislation, which have remained largely unchanged in terms of prison work since the 1960s; and through Prison Service Policies, which regulate prison labour in greater detail, mimicking employment-like rights, though importantly they are non-statutory and non-binding and enforced only through a complaints resolution process.

Within the contemporary regime, prison work is implemented in England and Wales via Rule 31(1) of the Prison Rules, which states that a 'convicted prisoner shall be required to do useful work for not more than 10 hours a day'. This provision 'in effect classifies prison work as being separate and different to "ordinary" work, with penological, and not economic, aims'.[58] This is tempered by Rule 31(4), which also states that no prisoner shall work for the benefit of any private person without authority from the Secretary of State. Refusal to work, or intentional failure to work properly, is classified as a disciplinary offence under Prison Rule 51(21), the implication being that work is a duty rather than a right. However, evidence suggests that in practice, those who do not wish to work do not have to do so.[59]

Unlike labour within immigration detention or internships, which we address below, prisoners are therefore legally compelled to undertake prison labour. Their labour derives from their prison sentence as opposed to the traditional employment contract. As a result, in the United Kingdom, section 45 of the National Minimum Wage Act 1998 explicitly excludes prisoners from the national minimum wage. And yet, all prisoners engaging in work are entitled to pay (below the minimum wage), which includes the possibility of earning bonuses to recognize and reward productivity.[60] Prisoners' wage rates are set out in Prison Service Order 4460,[61] which states that the minimum pay rate is £4.00 per week. However, the governors of individual prisons are empowered to set rates of pay for their particular prisons to reflect the regime's priorities. This amount is based on prisoners completing a full working week, which either consists of ten morning, afternoon, or evening sessions or five night shifts.[62] Rates of pay have remained unchanged since their introduction in 2002, and an attempt by the prison service to increase the minimum weekly rate to £5.50 was vetoed by the Prime Minister in 2008.[63]

[58] Jarman and Fair (n 11) 4.
[59] ibid.
[60] HM Prison Service, 'Prisoner's Pay' (2020) Prison Services Order 4460 para 2.1.1.
[61] ibid.
[62] ibid para 2.4.2.
[63] HM Inspectorate of Prisons, *Life in Prison: Earning and Spending Money. A Findings Paper by HM Inspectorate of Prisons* (January 2016) <https://cloud-platform-e218f50a4812967ba1215eaecede923f.s3.amazonaws.com/uploads/sites/19/2025/03/Earning-and-spending-money_2016.pdf> accessed 12 November 2025.

Prison work involves a range of activities, for the benefit of a range of different actors, including

- 'prison housework' or 'prison service'-style jobs, such as cleaning and cooking, which reduces the running costs of the prison estate;
- work in private-sector 'prison workshops' involving the production of commercial goods for sale on the outside;
- community or voluntary work outside of the prison estate;
- work for outside employers where prisoners are released on a temporary facility licence for the primary purpose of undertaking this work. In these instances, where work is not considered to be voluntary or charity work, prisoners must be paid the appropriate rate for the job, at or above National Minimum Wage levels, to avoid undercutting market wages.

Piecework, where prisoners are paid based on the quantity and quality of 'pieces' produced, is also approved, provided it yields at least the minimum prison weekly rate. Broadly, then, this work falls into three categories: prison service work (to support daily operations within the prison), prison industries (where prisoners produce economic outputs and services for consumption outside of the prison itself), and work to prepare them for release (relating to upskilling to increase the likelihood of employment post release).[64] Data on the percentage of prisoners working in these various roles is scant and points to a wider issue of transparency and statistical data on prison work in general, though data suggests that up to 70 per cent of prisoners could be undertaking prison service work, which means that the majority of work in prison is unaccounted for and the extent of compulsion is unclear.[65] Data collected between 2012 and 2020 revealed that approximately 13.8 per cent of prisoners laboured in 'prison industries' during this period for the production of resources for consumption outside of the prison.[66]

If prisoners are willing to work, but there is no work available, they receive unemployment pay at a minimum rate of £2.50 per week[67] and are also able to claim short-term sick pay (£2.50 per week), long-term sick pay, maternity pay, and retirement pay where appropriate (at a rate of £3.25 per week) and should receive an allowance for any authorized absences. In addition, pay may be withdrawn or reduced for disciplinary reasons.[68] Where prisoners reach the

[64] Jarman and Fair (n 11).
[65] ibid.
[66] ibid.
[67] HM Prison Service (n 60) para 2.2.1.
[68] ibid para 2.1.1.

normal thresholds for income tax and national insurance, they will be expected to pay it and are not exempt, further adding to our argument that prison work has economic value and should be recognized as work deserving employment rights. Since 2011, prisoners undertaking paid work in the community on temporary release who earn more than £20.00 per week may be subject to a levy of up to 40 per cent on their earnings, which is paid towards Victim Support (a charity that supports victims and communities affected by crime). Between October 2011 and January 2016, £3.3 million was raised from the levy.

The only money available to prisoners is the amount that they bring with them upon entry, what is sent in by family or friends or what they earn through work. Money sent in or paid to prisoners in the form of wages is held by the prison and transferred electronically to the prisoner on a weekly basis, subject to weekly spending limits. These limits are based on the behaviour of detainees and on the incentives and earned privileges scheme.[69] Basic necessities for prisoners (such as accommodation, meals, toiletries, and/or clothes) are provided where needed, however everything else needs to be paid for by the prisoners themselves. This includes items such as phone credit, TV rental, and additional goods, which can be bought from the prison shop or canteen such as tobacco, snacks and food, stationery, non-prescribed medication, and hobby materials.[70] Prisoners can also purchase clothing and other items or religious artefacts from approved catalogues for which the prison charges an administration fee.

d. Participants' Perspectives on (Prison) Work

In general, prisoners report that prison work is dull and monotonous, undertaken primarily to escape the drudgery of daily confinement within a cell.[71] Pandeli, Marinetto, and Jenkins studied five workshops in one prison, which involved tasks such as breaking down electrical items for recycling; the packing of rubber-coated electrical wires; the packing and shrink wrapping of books, applying sale stickers, and performing quality checks; wrapping straps through a plastic case and rolling and packing them; repackaging small car parts and applying stickers to them; assembling and repackaging different components of household plumbing, such as lavatory flushes; and, finally,

69 HM Inspectorate of Prisons (n 63).
70 ibid 1.5.
71 Pandeli, Marinetto, and Jenkins (n 53); Bullock and Bunce (n 51).

waste management within the prison via waste collection and sorting into recyclable groups.[72] The latter of these jobs received the most positive feedback from prisoners, who felt that they gained valuable skills which could be transferable to a career in waste management 'on the outside'. Yet, frustration is widely documented across a number of studies, where prisoners feel that the work undertaken is not designed to 'rehabilitate' them but rather to benefit the prisons economically.[73] For example, in another study, a prisoner notes,

> you can make money for the prison basically in every direction you're looking, you can mop floors or just mundane things that just drive me mental. If I'm doing something that hasn't got a positive outcome for myself . . . that's not going to do anything for me sort of tomorrow, the next day and the day after that I find it difficult to even do it.[74]

A number of prisoners explain that they feel 'forced' to undertake this work as alternatives to work, such as vocational training classes in skills such as carpentry, were over-subscribed. Accordingly, they were assigned workshop roles, and refusal could lead to the denial of certain privileges such as family visitation, reduced income, or reduced gym time, among other restrictions. In particular, dissatisfaction with the work was mainly due to lack of skills development and job prospects created by the work. Jobs such as putting stickers on bottles and clipping wires can also influence prisoners' perceptions of work on the outside and/or their desire to engage in the formal employment market. Though prison work is designed to establish a positive relationship with formal employment, the respondents in the Pandelli study suggested that the monotony of the work could push them the other way. Jermaine (eighteen) thus noted, 'Clipping wires? . . . Can I ask you the same question and hear your response please? . . . this would not encourage me to do work at all . . . [in] what I was doing before [crime] I was earning more money than what I'm doing now, so why would I ever want to go 'legit' [for this] . . . ?'.[75] This perspective contradicts claims that prison labour is supposedly rehabilitative in preparing prisoners for work in the formal economy and indicates a failure 'to bridge the boundary between legal non-economic work inside prison and an imagining of lawful economic work post-release'.[76]

[72] Pandeli, Marinetto, and Jenkins (n 53).
[73] Susan Craig, 'Rehabilitation versus Control: An Organizational Theory of Prison Management' (2004) 84 The Prison Journal 92S; Bullock and Bunce (n 51).
[74] Bullock and Bunce (n 51) 120.
[75] Pandeli, Marinetto, and Jenkins (n 53) 607.
[76] ibid 609.

Zatz and Boris note that 'prison labor often mimics market forms through payment, supervisory structures, and ultimate sale in competition with or substitution for consumer goods',[77] but they question whether the acute power imbalance and pervasive legal constraint negate the market character of prison labour or exemplify it.[78]

And yet, it is noted that, despite the monotonous nature of the work, prison work remains valued by some prisoners, who enjoy the social aspects of the work, offering forms of social cohesion, inclusion, routine, and belonging among inmates.[79] Certain jobs are also regarded positively, particularly where prisoners acquire skills for vocational jobs on the outside, such as the waste management work, detailed in the Pandeli and colleagues (2019) study, where a number of participants responded positively about the nature of the work. For example Lewis (forty-eight) reflected,

> I like it actually, it's given me a bit of an incentive that I can go out there and get a job in recycling. Yeah, that's where the money is. There's not many jobs out there now, and this recycling thing, it's a big business so I'm hoping I can go into it.[80]

Prisoners' perceptions of work are thereby variable, largely determined by the type of work which they are offered, though the literature indicates that the more valuable forms of work, such as refuse and recycling which are stimulating for inmates give way to the more monotonous forms of work which reinstate feelings of dissatisfaction and exploitation for economic gain.

e. Private Profit

According to a report from HMPPS, one-third of businesses state that they are unable to address skills gaps in their workforce. [81] Although the report does not explain the causes for these labour shortages, HMPPS suggest that 'thinking outside of the box' by recruiting prison labour may help businesses

[77] Noah Zatz and Eileen Boris, 'Seeing Work, Envisioning Citizenship' (2014) 18 Employee Rights and Employment Policy Journal 95.
[78] ibid 100.
[79] Pandeli, Marinetto, and Jenkins (n 53) 605.
[80] ibid 606.
[81] Ministry of Justice, 'Employing Prisoners and Ex-Offenders' (HMPPS 2023) <www.gov.uk/government/publications/unlock-opportunity-employer-information-pack-and-case-studies/employing-prisoners-and-ex-offenders> accessed 12 November 2025.

to overcome such challenges. The relationships between prisons, businesses, and employers are facilitated through the New Futures Network (formerly ONE3ONE solutions), a dedicated unit within the prison service responsible for brokering such partnerships.[82]

In a 2019 study, one prison industries director claimed that prison labour was sourced because the commercial firms involved in its commission struggled to recruit workers from the formal labour market due to the monotonous nature of the work itself. A senior representative of one of the firms also noted that costs were a major factor in choosing to recruit prisoners to undertake the work. Naturally, 'this would suggest that labour could have been found in the external labour market but (unless somehow forced) it would have been at a higher price than prisoners' wages, which ranged from around £15–£25 per week—considerably lower than the National Minimum Wage'.[83] Indeed, HMPPS highlights that hiring prison labour would generate a number of benefits to employers, including reducing recruitment and job advertising costs, diversifying the workforce, resolving skills shortages, reducing staff absences, and increasing staff retention.[84] LMB Textiles, which have been relying on penal labour to support their business since 1995, note that using prison labour 'allowed us to continue manufacturing in the UK, which I don't think otherwise would've been possible. Most of our competitors moved to Eastern Europe about 10 years ago.'[85] Accordingly, LMB expanded its business to four establishments, employing about 150 prisoners.

The most recent figures show that, in March 2023, over 400 businesses and government departments in England and Wales provided employment opportunities to serving prisoners within prison workshops, those released on temporary licence, those on placements,; and prison leavers after their release.[86] Financial data from the New Futures Network[87] reveals that this work is primarily concentrated within the general assembly and packing sector; however, it also includes work within textiles, laundry, engineering, recycling, and woodwork. There are also a wide range of 'customers' involved, including local city councils; charities such as Sue Ryder, Marie Curie, and the Royal British Poppy Legion; construction companies such as Balfour Beatty; call centres;

[82] ibid.
[83] Pandeli, Marinetto, and Jenkins (n 53) 603–04.
[84] Ministry of Justice (n 81).
[85] ONE3ONE Solutions, 'ONE3ONE Solutions: Justice Working for You' <https://mronline.org/wp-content/uploads/2017/09/prospectus.pdf> accessed 12 November 2025.
[86] Ministry of Justice (n 81).
[87] New Futures Network, 'NFN Sales 2021–2022' (New Futures Network) <https://newfuturesnetwork.gov.uk/document/new-futures-network-sales-2021-22> accessed 12 November 2025.

and companies working in manufacturing, textiles, and recycling. Prison work does not therefore benefit the state alone but also private corporations that rely on prisoners as a source of cheap labour in a competitive global economy.

3. Workfare

Modern workfare schemes, developed originally in the United States and Australia, require claimants to 'work for their benefits'. Thus defined, workfare schemes are a subset of the more general welfare-to-work, or Active Labour Market Policy (ALMP) schemes. Although the ALMP is the bureaucratic framework, workfare has been a staple of benefit provision schemes since their inception, in the early days of the seventeenth century Poor Laws. Claimants were sent to labour yards and were required to undertake tasks such as stone breaking, oakum picking, road making, gardening, and boot repairing.[88] Therefore, in one form or another, since the very first organized initiatives to provide social or community assistance to the indigent, this assistance was consistently attached to a demand that the beneficiary provide work of some nature for the community, for a government agency, or for a private corporation. We thus start this section by providing a brief overview of the long history of (putative) justifications for workfare schemes before moving to the contemporary UK domestic scene, with a particular focus on the contested legal framework. The second half of the section will offer some examples of participants' experiences, in their own words, before concluding with information regarding the corporate involvement, and the related profit motivations, for the schemes.

a. The History and Rationales for Workfare

What is the reason for workfare's enduring appeal? Though it is difficult (and possibly overly simplified) to identify one particular reason that animates public discourse and motivates policymakers, it is possible to sketch out four interrelated rationales that have been influential in this respect. These are deterrence, self-realization, enhancing structure and discipline or human capital, and reciprocity.

[88] Desmond King, *In the Name of Liberalism* (OUP 1999) 242.

i. *Deterrence*: the idea here is that workfare is simply a measure to make dependence on benefits as unattractive as possible.[89] Sidney and Beatrice Webb, for example, find that the Poor Law workhouse was designed so that a person would not admit themselves 'except in the direst necessity',[90] while others have identified that labour yard tasks, such as those noted above, were designed 'purely for deterrence'.[91] But despite its long history, it would seem that this rationale is not as persuasive as it used to be and that contemporary programmes are at least partly motivated by other principles.
ii. *Self-realization*: similar to prison labour, this moralistic, and blatantly paternalistic, rationale suggests that work improves the moral constitution of the individual. The workhouse, for example, was seen to infuse 'new life, new energy into the constitution of the pauper; he is aroused like one from sleep; . . . He begs a job—he will not take a denial.'[92] Its religious antecedents are made clear by the fact that contemporary versions of this rationale suggest that welfare institutions have replaced 'Christian morality . . . by affirming right and wrong conduct'.[93] Citing the Scottish Community Development Centre, Lynne Friedli and Robert Stearn note that this feature of conditionality—work as a prerequisite for wellness—is now as significant a feature 'in the lives of those who are poor as going to church once was, and they share a common evangelical language: "something within the spirit of individuals living within deprived communities that needs healed". Unfortunately, the compulsions of positive affect are not confined to Sundays.'[94]

Prominent advocates of welfare-to-work programmes in general, and workfare in particular, routinely view any work as instrumental in improving one's character.[95] These critics do not take into account that jobs in general, and workfare tasks in particular, may be 'routine,

[89] Amir Paz-Fuchs, *Welfare-to-Work: Conditioning Rights in Social Policy* (OUP 2008) 77–80, 103–04.
[90] Sidney Webb and Beatrice Webb, *English Poor Law History: Part I—The Old Poor Law* (Cass88 1963) 243.
[91] MA Crowther, quoted in Desmond King, *Actively Seeking Work* (Chicago UP 1995) 240.
[92] 'Report from His Majesty's Commissioners for Inquiring into the Administration and Practical Operation of the Poor Laws' (1834) [the Poor Law Report] cited in King (n 88) 227.
[93] Frank Field, 'A Rejoinder' in Alan Deacon (ed), *Stakeholder Welfare* (Institute of Economic Affairs (IEA) 1996) 107, 111.
[94] Lynne Friedli and Robert Stearn, 'Positive Affect as Coercive Strategy: Conditionality, Activation and the Role of Psychology in UK Government Workfare Programmes' (2015) 41 Medical Humanities 40.
[95] See eg Charles Murray, *The Emerging British Underclass* (IEA 1990) 23; Lawrence Mead, *Beyond Entitlement* (Free Press 1988) 48.

low-skilled, or mind-numbingly exhausting [and thus] may fail quite dramatically to offer anything close to self-realization'.[96]

iii. *Structure and discipline*, or *human capital*: this may be viewed as the pragmatic version of the previously discussed moralistic rationale. Community leaders hoped that 'disciplinary institutions' like the almshouse and the penitentiary 'would produce industrious workers for the urban economy'.[97] Where long-term unemployed individuals are concerned, there may be a real need to assist their re-integration into the labour market by encouraging them to get out of bed, shave, dress up, and report to work on time. Instilling discipline and structure through workfare requirements would thus be instrumental, if not vital, for future workers. Thus, government documents highlight the advantage of workfare in promoting soft skills such as 'appropriate communication, work attire, punctuality and how to behave generally in a workplace'[98] or 'building overall confidence, motivation and wellbeing'.[99] However, it is not clear that, first, the relevant claimants lack those skills and, second, that those positions do much to enhance them. What is clear, however, is that many of the positions advertised serve functional roles that employers would otherwise need to staff. Moreover, while this is not the place for an extended discussion of this rationale, it is worth noting that many workfare participants have extensive job experience and thus have no need for discipline enhancement measures. In addition, as Noah Zatz explains, while discipline and structure are fundamental for menial tasks, the modern workplace tends to value other traits, such as creativity, spontaneity, flexibility, adaptability, and risk-taking, which may be viewed as freedom from discipline.[100]

The European version of this rationale is couched in the popular terminology of 'human capital'. Here, we find the idea that workfare should be conceived as vocational training and non-paid work experience, which aims to improve the employability of the workfare participant in

[96] Noah Zatz 'What Welfare Requires from Work' (2006) 54 University of California Los Angeles Law Review 373, 436.

[97] Seth Rockman, *Scraping By: Wage Labor, Slavery and Survival* (Johns Hopkins UP 2011) ch 1.

[98] Rowan Foster and others, 'Employer Engagement and Capacity to Support T Level Industry Placements (Department for Education, August 2018) 48 <https://assets.publishing.service.gov.uk/government/uploads/system/uploads/attachment_data/file/737471/Employer_Capacity_Report.pdf> accessed 12 November 2025.

[99] Department for Work & Pensions (DWP), 'Work Experience: Employer Guide' (updated 9 October 2025) <www.gov.uk/government/publications/employers-could-you-offer-work-experience/work-experience-employer-guide> accessed 12 November 2025.

[100] Zatz (n 96) 433.

a more substantive way. This human capital approach to workfare is currently celebrated in welfare state literature.[101] However, the question can be raised as to whether people need months, and perhaps years, of 'on-the-job training' before they are able to perform (very) low-skilled jobs. In addition, the research that exists does not provide evidence of the re-integration into regular paid employment because of a (long-term) participation in workfare.[102]

iv. *Reciprocity and contractualism*: while the positivist language is modern, the instinct that 'something' should be 'given back' when assistance is provided dates back centuries. In his brilliant depiction of the rise of Baltimore through the perspective of working men and women, Seth Rockman notes that many of the city's leading employers came 'to think of working people's labour as the property of the community as a whole'. Therefore, 'when poorer men and women withheld their labor, they should face criminal charges of forfeit freedoms inside public institutions like the almshouse'.[103]

Over the past three decades, political philosophy, social policy, and legal relations have been caught 'in the grip of contractual thinking',[104] sometimes referred to under the heading of 'Reciprocity'. In many cases, workfare schemes are but the foremost derivatives of the contractual paradigm. The first scheme that earned the appellation 'workfare'—the American Community Work Experience Program—was introduced as part of the JOBS programme, justification of which, in turn, was presented in the language of contractual obligation.[105] In Britain, Parliament's Employment Committee indicated its support for workfare measures, declaring it appropriate to expect reciprocal activity from benefit recipients on contractual grounds.[106]

This was apparent in the language chosen: in the United Kingdom, 'A New Contract for Welfare' was the title for a series of consultation

[101] Anton Hemerijck, *Changing Welfare States* (OUP 2013).

[102] Richard Crisp and Del Roy Fletcher, 'A Comparative Review of Workfare Programmes in the United States, Canada and Australia' (DWP 2008) DWP Research Report No 533; Brian Kroch Graversen and Jan C Van Ours, 'How to Help Unemployed Find Jobs Quickly. Experimental Evidence from a Mandatory Activation Program' (2008) Journal of Public Economics 92; Jonas Maibom Pedersen and others, 'Experimental Evidence on the Effects of Early Meetings and Activation' (2012) Discussion Paper Series, Forschungsinstitut zur Zukunft der Arbeit No 6970.

[103] Rockman (n 97) 43.

[104] Virginia Held, *Feminist Morality: Transforming Culture, Society and Politics* (Chicago UP 1993) 193.

[105] King (n 88) 275.

[106] ibid 239.

papers.[107] The political rhetoric relating to welfare reform was—and still is—strikingly contractual, with Tory ministers in charge of welfare, in particular, routinely making the case that conditions must be put in place *in return* for benefits. For instance, in 2008, the Conservatives, in opposition at the time, claimed that they would 'not allow anyone claiming Jobseeker's Allowance over a long period to do nothing'.[108] And in 2013, the Chancellor George Osborne, announcing the new Community Work Placements Programme, reiterated the language, proclaiming that 'there is no option of doing nothing for our benefits, no something-for-nothing anymore'.[109] The language found its way from the speakers' podium to formal government documents. The Mandatory Work Activity Provider Guidance, for example, states that 'A community benefit placement must be of benefit to the community *over and above* the benefit of providing a placement to the individual.'[110] In addition, according to the government's guidance on Mandatory Work Activity (MWA), 'There is no work experience element for the MWA scheme, instead there is a work placement for community benefit.'[111] The wording suggests that the central aim of workfare is not to contribute to the claimant's chances of finding a regular job but rather to coerce them into a reciprocal act for the benefit of the community.

b. Contemporary British Workfare Programmes

Despite its Poor Law antecedents, the United Kingdom entered the post-war workfare arena quite late compared to nations with a similar ethos and public morality. The Welfare Reform Act 2009 introduced a 'Work for Your Benefits' Scheme as a compulsory element for Jobseeker's Allowance, which was piloted from November 2010. The Act directed that regulations could mandate 'work, or work-related activity, during any prescribed period with a view to

[107] Department of Social Security (DSS), *New Ambitions for Our Country: A New Contract for Welfare* (DSS 1998); DSS, *A New Contract for Welfare: Principles into Practice* (DSS 1998); Department for Education and Employment (DEE 1998), *A New Contract for Welfare: Gateway to Work* (DEE 1998).

[108] Conservative Party, *Work for Welfare: REAL Welfare Reform to Make British Poverty History* (Conservative Party 2008) 34.

[109] Francis Elliot and Philippe Naugthon, 'No More "Something for Nothing", Says Osborne on Welfare Scheme' *The Times* (30 September 2013) <www.thetimes.co.uk/tto/news/politics/article3882763.ece> accessed 12 November 2025.

[110] DWP, *Mandatory Work Activity Provider Guidance* (2014) ch 1, annex 1, A1.3 (emphasis in original).

[111] DWP, *Advice for Decision Making* (2013) ch K3, K3037.

improving their prospects of obtaining employment'.[112] The accompanying regulations were passed in April 2010.[113] Subsequently, the Welfare Reform Act 2012 allowed the imposition of a 'work preparation requirement', which may be in the form of 'participating in an employment programme'.[114]

In 2011, the Coalition Government introduced three central schemes that included a workfare element.[115] First, the Work Programme, which began in 2011 and enrolled participants for up to two years, included the MWA scheme. By January 2012, nearly 50,000 participants were placed on MWA placements.[116]

Welfare claimants were now described differently. Reflecting the neoliberal era, the Regulations stated that these '*customers* will be referred to a four week period of activity, with the aim of helping them develop those crucial disciplines associated with full time employment, while at the same time making a contribution to their community'.[117] Second, the Sector-Based Work Academy (SBWA)—a work experience placement for up to six weeks—was introduced under a different set of regulations.[118]

In the 2013 case of *Reilly*,[119] the UK Supreme Court accepted that the 2011 Regulations,[120] which provided the basis for workfare schemes were ultra vires under sections 17A and 17B of the Jobseekers Act 1995 as they did not describe the schemes, prescribe the circumstances requiring a person to participate in the schemes, or prescribe the period of the schemes, as the 1995 Act required.

In response to the judicial decisions, Parliament repealed sections 17A and 17B[121] and later introduced the Jobseekers (Back-to-Work Schemes) Act 2013 and the accompanying 2013 Regulations.[122] The 2013 Regulations followed the Court's instructions by prescribing the necessary details for the workfare schemes which, prior to the Regulations, were left to the discretion of the Secretary of State. They now included details of seven schemes, their extent, and the duties required from participants. A number of schemes (such

112 Introducing the Jobseekers Act 1995, s 17A (col 18).
113 Jobseeker's Allowance (Work for your Benefit Pilot Scheme) Regulations 2010 (SI 2010/1222).
114 Welfare Reform Act 2012, s 16(3)(d) (col 5).
115 Jobseeker's Allowance (Mandatory Work Activity Scheme) Regulations. These replaced the Jobseekers Allowance Work for Your Benefit Scheme Regulations 2010.
116 *Department of Work and Pensions v Frank Zola* [2016] EWCA Civ 758 [2].
117 The Jobseeker's Allowance (Mandatory Work Activity Scheme) Regulations 2011 (Explanatory Notes).
118 Jobseekers Allowance (Employment, Skills and Enterprise Scheme) Regulations 2011.
119 *R (Reilly and Wilson) v Secretary of State for Work and Pensions* [2013] UKSC 68.
120 Jobseeker's Allowance (Employment, Skills and Enterprise Scheme) Regulations 2011 (SI 2011/917).
121 Welfare Reform Act 2012, sch 14, pt 4.
122 Jobseeker's Allowance (Schemes for Assisting Persons to Obtain Employment) Regulations 2013.

as the SBWA, the Community Work Placements,[123] the Work Programme,[124] and the MWA) explicitly required participants to work 'for the benefit of the community'.

Finally, the Community Action Programme was aimed at the long-term unemployed. These were, as the Department for Work and Pensions (DWP) declared when introducing yet another scheme in 2014—the Community Work Placement (CWP)—'new intensive measures to help the long-term unemployed into work'.[125] The explanatory notes for the Work for Your Benefits Scheme outlined the rationale, according to which,

> the scheme will consist of work experience and job search support for up to six months, delivered by organisations through contract with the DWP. This aims to help those furthest from the labour market develop work habits and routines, giving them experience of work in order to increase their employability.[126]

The *direct* form of state-imposed unfree labour, in a manner that paralleled prison labour, was short lived in the United Kingdom (at least, that is the case at the time of writing). Insofar as the Universal Credit (UC—the benefit that was introduced to replace a number of other benefits) is concerned, Regulation 91A of the Universal Credit Regulations 2013 (UC 2013 Regs) empowered the Job Centre to impose mandatory work requirements—a *duty* to work without pay[127]—thus providing the statutory platform for conditioning UC work. However, in 2016, the government responded to a multifaceted, and remarkably successful, campaign of resistance by revoking Regulation 91A.

In 2017, the Work Programme was replaced with the smaller Work and Health Programme (WHP), whose remit was limited, predominantly, to unemployed individuals with disabilities but also to those unemployed for over twenty-four months (the latter are the only group subject to mandatory participation).

[123] SI 2013/2548.

[124] Regulation 3(8).

[125] DWP, 'Help to Work: Nationwide Drive to Help the Long-Term Unemployed into Work' (Gov.uk, updated 27 May 2014) <www.gov.uk/government/news/help-to-work-nationwide-drive-to-help-the-long-term-unemployed-into-work> accessed 12 November 2025.

[126] DWP, 'Explanatory Memorandum to the Jobseekers Allowance (Work for Your Benefit Pilot Scheme) Regulations 2010 (Explanatory Notes)' (House of Common Library 2010) <www.legislation.gov.uk/ukdsi/2010/9780111493496/pdfs/ukdsiem_9780111493496_en.pdf> accessed 12 November 2025.

[127] Anja Eleveld, 'The Duty to Work without a Wage: A Legal Comparison between Social Assistance Legislation in Germany, the Netherlands and the United Kingdom' (2014) 16 European Journal of Social Security 204.

For a period of time, there was some confusion as to the voluntariness of this scheme. The 2017 draft explicitly mentioned the provider's authority to mandate work placements as part of the 'compliance conditions'. Thus, in chapter 8 ('Raising a Compliance Doubt'), the Guidance prescribes: 'When a [Long Term Unemployed] participant is undertaking community benefit work placements they will have been mandated to do so using the normal mandation process.'[128] In addition, an early version (April 2018) of the Advice for Decision Making (ADM) regarding Low Level Sanctions included the example of 'Nicky', who 'fails to turn up to start the placement as she says she didn't fancy working in a supermarket. She didn't think it would be for her. The DM [Decision Maker] believes Nicky does not have a good reason for refusing the work experience and imposed a low level sanction.'[129] The Guidance states that the work experience in question may last two to eight weeks and may include 'working in an office, warehouse, retail store or restaurant', where duties may include 'customer service, stock management, or administrative duties'.[130]

However, the final version of the WHP, which included reference to 'placements' arranged in collaboration with third parties, also clarified that the provider 'cannot mandate to work experience [*sic*] for this programme'.[131] Moreover, the current version of the Guidance clarifies that 'Participation in a work experience opportunity is on a purely voluntary basis and a low-level sanction cannot be imposed where the claimant fails to comply for no good reason with a work experience opportunity unless the claimant is dismissed for gross misconduct.'[132] It also removed the example of Nicky, suggesting that the earlier Guidance no longer represented the current state of affairs.

Another indication of continuity between the past, mandatory nature of the scheme and its present, voluntary nature is the contractual paradigm. As part of the WHP, claimants are required to sign a 'Claimant Commitment', which replaced the Jobseeker's Agreement, as a condition for receiving benefits.[133]

[128] DWP, 'Work and Health Provider Guidance—Draft' (updated 30 July 2018) <www.gov.uk/government/publications/work-choice-provider-guidance-post-april-2017> accessed 26 March 2025.

[129] DWP, 'ADM Chapter K5: Low Level Sanctions' (no date) <https://assets.publishing.service.gov.uk/media/677fb6fe99c93b7286a39843/admk5.pdf> accessed 12 November 2025.

[130] DWP, 'Back to Work Schemes' (updated 10 March 2025) <www.gov.uk/guidance/universal-credit-and-jobseekers-allowance-jsa-back-to-work-schemes> accessed 12 November 2025.

[131] DWP, 'Chapter 5a: Mandation to Activity Attracting a Low Level Sanction' (updated 16 January 2026) para 28 <www.gov.uk/government/publications/work-and-health-programme-including-jets-provider-guidance/chapter-5a-mandation-to-activity-attracting-a-lowlower-level-sanction> accessed 12 November 2025

[132] DWP (n 129).

[133] DWP, 'Commitment Not Accepted' (DWP Guidance 2018) <http://data.parliament.uk/DepositedPapers/Files/DEP2018-0759/CC_-_Commitment_not_accepted_v1.0.pdf> accessed 12 November 2025.

We will postpone to Chapter 5 the discussion of the importance that Western governments place on the ceremonious signing of a contract, supposedly a symbolic empowering of claimants but often 'an abuse of power in an abuse of language'.[134] For now, it is important to emphasize that a refusal to commit to 'voluntary work' (in the language of the guidance) cannot be grounds for sanction. And yet, refusal to sign a 'reasonable' Claimant Commitment, which may include required preparation activities, can lead to reduced payments and even a decision that the claimant is not eligible for UC. However, 'voluntary' work experience may be encouraged and—if agreed—incorporated into the Claimant Commitment. If the claimant agrees to take part but then fails to complete the pre-employment training and interview, sanctions may follow.[135]

c. Participants' Perspectives on Workfare

A recent ethnographic study of the Work Programme in the United Kingdom, conducted by John David Jordan, revealed a stressful administrative regime willing to levy major sanctions for minor infractions, such as 'lateness, failing to apply for enough, or appropriate (ie that staff thought that participants could achieve) jobs, bringing children into the centre, forgetting an appointment time, or not completing some minor activity or general aspect of mandatory paperwork'.[136] Jordan refers to 'Sue', a participant who voiced a common concern, stating, 'So you're thinking if you turn up one minute late your kids won't have anything to eat. You won't be able to heat the house.'

The charity and lobby group Corporate Watch interviewed participants on these schemes. A 21-year old, Joe Wilson, worked for four days a week, unpaid, at the Asda store in Harrogate, Yorkshire:

> There were about 15 of us on placements. The manager said they had overspent on stocking Christmas stuff so they'd got people in on placements [to save money]. The paid staff told us they were being asked to leave before they'd ended their shift as we could do the work. I worked Christmas Eve and New Year's Eve. They arranged it so everyone came in those days . . . The Jobcentre had got a group of us in for CV writing training. It was really obvious stuff—don't use a crayon and so on. When we were there, they said

[134] Paz-Fuchs (n 89); Peter Vincent Jones, *The New Public Contracting* (OUP 2006).
[135] DWP (n 129) para K5055.
[136] John David Jordan, 'Welfare Grunters and Workfare Monsters? An Empirical Review of the Operation of Two UK "Work Programme" Centres' (2018) 47 Journal of Social Policy 583, 591.

> some people had come to speak to us about a work experience programme. Then, a few days later I got a letter saying that, as I'd expressed an interest they'd be organising a work placement. The letter said if I didn't go they'd stop my JSA [Job Seeker's Allowance]. I'd never said I wanted to do a placement in Asda.[137]

The same piece also reported the experience of another claimant, who was assigned to a three-month placement in Booker Wholesale in Bath. His hope of moving from unpaid workfare to paid work was not realized:

> I asked the manager about jobs and he said: 'keep working as you are and you will be fine'. The turning point came for me about two months in, when two part-time employees were laid off for stealing some alcohol. I thought there would be a job for me but they hired the brother of an employee already working there. I went to see the manager and he said that there were no positions. He suggested I could continue doing four days a week unpaid.
>
> I left in disgust and took my last two days off. They had the nerve to say: 'what if we are counting on you to be there?' Then hire me! You're supposed to help me find a job, not turn me into a slave.[138]

The association between workfare and slavery is not a surprising one, perhaps, but it merits further discussion in light of its ubiquity. In a recent book,[139] Erin Hatton interviewed American workfare participants, prison labourers, graduate athletes, and graduate students and found that analogy to be repeated time and again, perhaps most prominently by workfare participants. The 'closeness' of workfare to paid work and the fact that, notwithstanding protestations to the contrary and its unlawful nature, workfare participants do replace paid workers, amplify the claimants' (and others') feelings that this *type* of work should be paid for. For example,

> It's just crazy, how we got to do this, and they're supposed to be having the city doing this. . . . Because, like, we were planting flowers over there at that circle, and I was like, 'Why are the [city workers] not doing it?' I was like, 'That's slave work.' And cutting grass and doing that stuff behind [this building],

137 Anon, 'To Pay or Not to Pay: Asda and Argos Choose Workfare over Work' (*Corporate Watch*, 17 February 2020) <https://corporatewatch.org/to-pay-or-not-to-pay-asda-and-argos-choose-workfare-over-work> accessed 12 November 2025.

138 ibid.

139 Erin Hatton, *Coerced: Work under Threat of Punishment* (University of California Press 2020).

> that's slave work. . . . I think it's slave work because the city supposed to be doing this. Not us.[140]

A clear example of this experience was evident in the United Kingdom when John McArthur, whose position as a temporary worker was not extended, found himself in the same position, 'working' for the same business as a participant in a back-to-work scheme, at no cost to the employer, for a six-month period.[141]

d. Private Profit

As noted, workfare is implemented through a partnership between state agencies and public, non-profit, and for-profit organizations. In late 2011, journalists began to document the range of employers who were involved in workfare programmes. These included retailers such as Asda, Primark, TK Maxx, and Matalan; local councils (Newham Council filled an administrative role for six months—a position that would have included a basic wage of £17,000 at the time—with a workfare placement); major public companies, such as the London Underground which, after cutting 800 posts on the London Underground, accepted 200 wardens from A4E (a Work Programme provider) to staff North London stations;[142] and charities such as Barnardo's, Age Concern, the British Heart Foundation, and Cancer Research.[143] Indeed, local councils were found to have benefited from more than 500,000 hours of unpaid labour from a back-to-work scheme in a variety of areas, including cleaning, waste collection, parks maintenance, and library support.[144] Though councils denied that the participants in the scheme were deployed at the expense of employees, it was found that jobs were lost during the same period. In some cases,

[140] ibid 183 (Felisha); Kim offered the same sentiment: 'I feel like a slave. I feel like a slave, because—for one—it's not a job . . . [Workfare workers are performing labour that others are] actually getting paychecks for . . . which is not fair'—ibid 184.

[141] Shiv Malik, 'DWP Orders Man to Work without Pay for Company That Let Him Go' *The Guardian* (London, 3 November 2014).

[142] Anon, '"It's Exploitation and It's Repellent": Retailers, Councils and Charities Benefiting from Workfare' (*Corporate Watch*, 25 September 2011) <https://corporatewatch.org/its-exploitation-and-its-repellent-retailers-councils-and-charities-benefiting-from-workfare> accessed 12 November 2025.

[143] Anon, 'Charitable Exploitation: Workfare at Barnardo's' (*Corporate Watch*, 22 December 2011) <https://corporatewatch.org/charitable-exploitation-workfare-in-barnardos> accessed 12 February 2025.

[144] Sarah Marsh, 'UK Councils Found to Benefit from Half a Million Hours of Unpaid Labour' *The Guardian* (London, 4 January 2014) <www.theguardian.com/local-government-network/2014/jan/04/councils-uk-benefit-unpaid-labour> accessed 12 February 2025.

as in the United Kingdom, privatization and outsourcing are deeper, as even the commissioning, procurement, and operational design are outsourced to a small number of large-scale, for-profit companies, such as G4S, Ingeus, A4e, and Serco.[145]

As of writing, workfare and work experience schemes remain voluntary. As a result, the numbers of participants on the scheme have dropped dramatically. In response to a freedom-of-information (FoI) request made by the authors, the Department of Work and Pensions revealed that in 2019, the first full year of the WHP, 416 participants took part in work placements. In 2020 and 2021 (up to May 2021), which were impacted by the COVID-19 pandemic, the numbers were 253 and 75, respectively.[146]

These numbers stand in stark contrast to participation levels prior to the removal of the option to make workfare compulsory. We find these data to be important because welfare policy is highly changeable, and the possibility of a resurgence of mandatory workfare, in line with the practice in countries as varied as the United States and the Netherlands, is very real. Indeed, the continuation and expansion of workfare schemes in the vast majority of capitalist welfare states lends a sense of urgency to the analysis.

A DWP publication from July 2018,[147] which includes data up to November 2017 (the last year for which data is available), reveals that, since 2011, there have been 730,130 work experience starts, with 84,990 over the previous year (December 2016 to November 2017). Of those, 330,090 took part in the SBWA scheme, with 36,510 starts over this period. In terms of benefit schemes, since 2011, 78,910 were UC claimants, but over the past year, those constituted about 40 per cent of claimants overall.

A notable subset within that cohort involves the use of unpaid work through workfare claimants within the DWP itself. In response to a question in Parliament in February 2018, the Secretary of State provided a breakdown of the number of people who have undertaken unpaid work experience (up to eight weeks, usually four to six weeks) within the DWP since 2011.[148] The numbers range from 834 in the first year to 7,428 in the peak year (2015–16). In total, nearly 28,000 individuals provided the DWP with unpaid work.

[145] Friedli and Stearn (n 94) 41.

[146] FOI2021/36425 from DWP to Katie Bales (3 June 2021, copy with authors).

[147] DWP, 'Employment Scheme Official Statistics' (11 July 2018) <https://assets.publishing.service.gov.uk/government/uploads/system/uploads/attachment_data/file/731504/employment-schemes-statistics-to-november-2017.pdf> accessed 12 November 2025.

[148] HC Deb (22 February 2018) <www.parliament.uk/business/publications/written-questions-answers-statements/written-question/Commons/2018-02-19/128345> accessed 12 November 2025.

4. Labour within Immigration Detention

Although not widely recognized, labour within immigration detention involves thousands of hours of work that are carried out by detainees in immigration removal centres throughout the United Kingdom who are paid a fraction of the national minimum wage. In the UK context, this form of work remains relatively underexplored, notwithstanding scholarly critiques in the United Kingdom[149] as well as a burgeoning literature in the United States.[150] Below, we briefly set out the United Kingdom's immigration detention framework before turning to the history of labour within immigration detention, its purpose, and the contemporary programme in the United Kingdom. We then examine the private sector's role in operating both the detention estate and the labour regime.

a. The Immigration Industrial Complex

The United Kingdom has one of the largest immigration detention estates in Europe with an estimated capacity of 2,200 beds in mid-2024.[151] Redolent of the 'prison industrial complex', the immigration detention estate can be conceptualized as an 'immigration industrial complex',[152] comprising a system of mutually beneficial relations linking corporations, government, and media to the incarceration industry. Accordingly, the use of the term 'immigration industrial complex' challenges the assumption that the number of detainees is increasing as a consequence of rising migration. Instead, this conceptualization suggests that the construction of the detention estate and the drive to keep

[149] Jon Burnett and Fidelis Chebe, 'Captive Labour: Asylum Seekers, Migrants and Employment in UK Immigration Removal Centres' (2010) 51 Race and Class 95; Katie Bales and Lucy Mayblin, 'Unfree Labour in Immigration Detention: Exploitation and Coercion of a Captive Immigrant Workforce' (2018) 47 Economy and Society 191.

[150] Anita Sinha, 'Slavery by Another Name: "Voluntary" Immigrant Detainee Labor and the Thirteenth Amendment' (2018) 6(1) Stanford Journal of Civil Rights and Civil Liberties 1; Nancy Hiemstra and Diedre Conlon, 'Captive Consumers and Coerced Labourers: Intimate Economies and the Expanding US Detention Regime' in Diedre Conlon and Nancy Hiemstra (eds) *Intimate Economies of Immigration Detention. Critical Perspectives* (Routledge 2017) 123–39.

[151] Stephen Shaw, 'Review into the Welfare in Detention of Vulnerable Persons. A Report to the Home Office by Stephen Shaw' (Home Office, January 2016) Cm 9186 <https://assets.publishing.service.gov.uk/government/uploads/system/uploads/attachment_data/file/490782/52532_Shaw_Review_Accessible.pdf> accessed 25 January 2016; The Migration Observatory at the University of Oxford, 'Immigration Detention in the UK' (12 December 2024) <https://migrationobservatory.ox.ac.uk/resources/briefings/immigration-detention-in-the-uk> accessed 11 February 2025.

[152] Tanya Golash-Boza, 'The Immigration Industrial Complex: Why We Enforce Immigration Policies Destined to Fail' (2009) 3 Sociology Compass 295.

inmate numbers high is driven by a combination of racism and the pursuit of profit.[153]

The Immigration and Asylum Act 1999 sets the basic statutory provisions governing removal centres and empowers the Secretary of State to make rules for their regulation and management. The power to detain was further expanded by the Illegal Migration Act 2023, which also restricted judicial challenge. Detention centres are regulated and managed in accordance with the Detention Centre Rules 2001, Detention Services Orders, and the Detention Services Operating Standards Manual. Rule 3 of the Detention Centre Rules 2001 states that the purpose of detention is to provide secure but humane accommodation for detainees in a relaxed regime with as much freedom of movement and association as possible. It also states that detention centres should encourage detainees to 'make the most productive use of their time'. In connection with this aim, in 2006, the government introduced 'paid activities' within immigration removal centres in the United Kingdom, ostensibly 'to prevent instances of boredom and frustration among detainees'.[154] The 'paid activities' regime, which equates to labour within immigration detention, is explored in more detail below.

In the year ending September 2024, 19,335 people entered immigration detention,[155] 79 per cent of whom were non-European Economic Area (EEA+) nationals.[156] In tandem with increased asylum applications from these countries, the most common applications were from Albanian nationals.[157] This form of detention is regarded as 'administrative' as migrants are detained to deter entry and manage their presence within the state. Within the United Kingdom, detention is justified for a number of reasons: to verify a person's identity, to effect their removal, where there is reason to believe that a person will fail to comply with the conditions attached to their grant of temporary admission or release, and where Home Office officials are deciding whether to grant temporary admission.[158] While the majority of those detained are asylum seekers and failed asylum seekers,[159] a number of other status groups

[153] Davis (n 17).
[154] Tony McNulty, Hansard, 16 November 2005 (col 1016).
[155] Home Office, 'How Many People Are Detained or Returned?' (28 November 2024) <www.gov.uk/government/statistics/immigration-system-statistics-year-ending-september-2024/how-many-people-are-detained-or-returned> accessed 11 February 2025.
[156] The Migration Observatory at the University of Oxford (n 151).
[157] Home Office (n 155).
[158] Immigration Act 1971, sch 2, para 16(2) and sch 3, para 2; Nationality, Immigration and Asylum Act 2002, s 62; UK Borders Act 2007, s 36.
[159] All-Party Parliamentary Group (APPG) Refugees and APPG Migration, 'The Report of the Inquiry into the Use of Immigration Detention' (House of Commons 2015).

are subject to immigration detention, including newly arrived migrants who have been refused permission to enter the United Kingdom, visa overstayers, those in breach of visa conditions, those likely to fail to comply with conditions attached to their admission or release, and those who have committed a crime and have been issued with a deportation order.

Unlike its European counterparts, the United Kingdom does not have a statutory time limit on the length of detention for immigration purposes. As a result, detainees have been held within immigration detention for significant periods. Government statistics for 2023 reveal that of the people leaving detention in 2023, 35 per cent were detained for over twenty-eight days; 2 per cent were detained for between six months and one year; and 1 per cent of people were detained for over a year.[160] In 2015, the (then) immigration minister, James Brokenshire, stated that the power to detain, though not subject to statutory limitation, is subject to the *Hardial Singh* principles which, alongside judicial oversight, protect against the arbitrary use of detention. The *Hardial Singh* principles prescribe that detention can only be used where deportation is intended; that the length of detention must be 'reasonable'; and where deportation is no longer likely within a 'reasonable period', the detainee should be released.[161] There are, however, a number of detention powers to which the *Hardial Singh* principles are irrelevant, including the now-inactive, detained fast track procedure and where persons are detained at ports of entry in order to establish permission to enter.

Concerns have been raised regarding the inconsistent application of the *Hardial Singh* principles by caseworkers[162] and of the varied interpretation of what constitutes a 'reasonable' period by the judiciary, which impacts upon the effectiveness of judicial review as a protective measure.[163] For example, in the case of *Giwa*,[164] a detention period of fifty-three months pending deportation for an 18-year-old (at the start of the detention) was considered reasonable, given the length of the appeals process, the genuine difficulties in proving the applicant's nationality, and the continuing prospect of achieving his removal within a reasonable time. In 2023, the Illegal Migration Act gave further powers to the Home Secretary to determine what is 'reasonable'.[165] Ruben Andersson

[160] The Migration Observatory at the University of Oxford (n 151).
[161] *R v Governor of Durham, ex p Hardial Singh* [1984] 1 WLR 704.
[162] HM Chief Inspectorate of Prisons, 'Report on an Unannounced Inspection of Harmondsworth Immigration Removal Centre, 5–16 August 2013' (Her Majesty's Inspector of Prisons (HMIP) 2013); HM Chief Inspectorate of Prisons, 'Report on an Unannounced Inspection of Yarl's Wood Immigration Removal Centre, 17–28 June 2013 and 30 September—1 October 2013' (HMIP 2013).
[163] APPG Refugees & APPG Migration (n 159).
[164] *R (on the application of Giwa) v Secretary of State for the Home Department* (2013) EWHC 3189.
[165] Illegal Migration Act 2023, s 12.

argues that this usurpation of time limits is part of a management technique that uses detention as a form of collective punishment as well as disrupting mobility and the flow of capital.[166] He situates this within a wider 'economics of illegality', which consumes migrants' mobility, 'deposes their bodies in a show of deterrence', and 'stretches their experience of time'.[167]

At present, there are 7 immigration removal centres in the United Kingdom, with plans to add a further 3, creating an extra 1,000 spaces.[168] Primarily, these centres are run by private corporations, the exception being Morton Hall, which remains under the control of His Majesty's Prison Service (HMPS). The companies running the detention estate are Mitie, Serco, and G4S. As well as managing the immigration detention estate, all three of these corporations have commercial government contracts to provide prison services and police custody. In this context, Bacon writes that it is necessary to 'question a system in which private companies have a vested interest in keeping the immigration detention population as high as possible'.[169] She also connects the privatization of immigration removal centres to a growth in the use of detention, a willingness among immigration officers to detain, the growing secrecy and lack of accountability present in the detention estate, and the move towards increasingly harsh detention practices.

b. Labour within Immigration Detention

The use of detainee labour within the immigration industrial complex began in the United States in the 1950s via 'voluntary work programmes', which were implemented to reduce the running costs of the immigration detention estate. The labour of immigration detainees is now understood as one iteration of a historical narrative of exploitation through incarceration which began in the United States following the abolition of slavery and the introduction of convict leasing, chain gangs, and 'black codes' in former slave states. It is not the focus of this book to re-examine this argument, which is well traversed in US academic prison literature, but rather to highlight its significance in the context of labour within immigration detention. Michael Flynn places the United States

[166] Ruben Andersson, 'Time and the Migrant Other: European Border Controls and the Temporal Economics of Illegality' (2014) 116 American Anthropologist 795.
[167] ibid.
[168] The Migration Observatory at the University of Oxford (n 151).
[169] Christine Bacon, 'Evolution of Immigration Detention in the UK: The Involvement of Private Prison Companies', Refugee Studies Centre (RSC) Working Paper No 27 (University of Oxford 2005).

at the centre of the proliferation of immigration detention globally, noting its instrumentality in initiating policy innovation, imitation, and implementation, which has led to the immigration industrial complex phenomenon.[170]

Following the US lead, the United Kingdom's 'paid activities' regime was introduced in 2006 via Rule 17 of the Detention Centre Rules 2001. The central justification for the regime was to maintain 'control and order' while enhancing detainee welfare. Although the rules maintain that these activities are designed to tackle boredom, it has been noted that, in contrast to prisons, immigration removal centres are not *obliged* to provide educational or therapeutic activities such as arts and crafts, English language classes, or training in IT support, which might also go towards 'preventing boredom'.[171] 'Paid activities' were further justified in the 2018 Secretary of State's report, 'Review into the Rates of Pay within Immigration Removal Centres', on the grounds that the regime allows detainees to earn extra money before departing the United Kingdom and also, in some cases, provides training and certification (such as food hygiene and catering certificates), which can be used in their home countries.[172]

Linking back to our earlier discussion of workfare, the themes of 'structure and discipline' and 'self-realization' persist throughout the paid activities regime. Yet, unlike prisoners or benefits claimants, immigration detainees are prevented from engaging in formal work in the United Kingdom as they have no right to work and, as a result, can be prosecuted for the criminal offence of 'illegal working', which results in a fine and/or a six-month prison sentence.[173] Accordingly, any new skills acquired while detained via paid activities are not designed to be used within the United Kingdom but rather within detainees' countries of origin. However, the statistics demonstrate that only 44 per cent of detainees released from detention in 2025 were returned to their country of origin, meaning that the remainder were released back into UK society, subject to work restrictions and unable to utilize their developed 'skills'.[174] The alternative, overarching narrative, which is denied by the UK Government, is that 'paid activities' were introduced to reduce the staffing costs of the detention centre estate. As we later explore, notwithstanding its denial, it is difficult to reconcile this response with the number of hours worked and the jobs

[170] Michael Flynn, 'How and Why Immigration Detention Crossed the Globe', Global Detention Project (April 2014) Working Paper No 8 <www.globaldetentionproject.org/wp-content/uploads/2014/04/How-and-Why-Immigration-Detention-Crossed-the-Globe-GDP-WP8-1.pdf> accessed 12 November 2025.

[171] Mary Bosworth, *Inside Immigration Detention* (OUP 2014).

[172] *Morita v Secretary of State for the Home Department* [2019] EWHC 758.

[173] Immigration Act 2016, s 34.

[174] Home Office, 'Immigration Statistics, Year Ending December 2020' (25 February 2021) <www.gov.uk/government/statistics/immigration-statistics-year-ending-december-2020> accessed 4 May 2021.

undertaken. Between January 2014 and July 2016, over 1,955,000 hours' worth of work were undertaken by immigration detainees performing 'paid activities'.[175] Ironically, this means that the UK Government and the associate corporations running immigration detention sites are the single biggest employer of irregular migrants in the country—despite them having 'no right to work' via the Immigration Act 1971.

Those engaging in work within immigration detention are paid at a rate of £1.00 an hour for 'routine work' and £1.25 an hour for specific projects as authorized by the removal centre's manager.[176] This involves 'prison housework'-style jobs[177] as cleaners, laundry workers, gardeners, litter pickers, kitchen assistants, waste disposal workers, barbers, librarians, decorators, and gym orderlies.[178] Concerned that detainees would be considered employees and entitled to the national minimum wage, the government excluded detainees from protection under the National Minimum Wage Act,[179] embracing a neoliberal, contractual narrative by stating that granting detainees the national minimum wage 'would not be viable financially, nor reflect the true economic value of the work likely to be carried out' in debate over detainees' exclusion under section 153A of the Immigration and Asylum Act 1999.[180] This position conflicts with the recommendations set out in the review conducted by Stephen Shaw, a former prisons and probation ombudsman, which recommends that 'the Home Office reconsider its approach to pay rates for detainees in light of my comments on the benefits of allowing contractors greater flexibility'.[181]

Though detainees are able to 'voluntarily' put themselves forward for 'paid activities', eligibility to work is dependent upon detainees helping UK Visas and Immigration resolve their case. Non-compliant or violent behaviour (such as failing to attend an interview or causing disruption) will also automatically exclude individuals from paid work opportunities, linking back to the overarching narrative of control.[182] The Shaw Review criticized this aspect of the programme as 'redolent of the prison system' and an unnecessary limitation on the eligibility to work.[183]

175 Bales and Mayblin (n 149).
176 Detention Services Order 01/2013, ss 4–6.
177 Zatz (n 3).
178 Bales and Mayblin (n 149).
179 Immigration and Asylum Act 1999, s 153A as inserted by Immigration, Asylum and Nationality Act 2006, s 59.
180 McNulty (n 154).
181 Shaw (n 151) 195.
182 Detention Services Order 01/2013, s 10.
183 Shaw (n 151).

In general, detainee work appears to be formally organized. Detainees are restricted to working a total of thirty hours per week (increased from fifteen hours) and are provided with: timetables; an 'Employment Job Description', which confirms their title, responsibilities, pay, hours of work; and a 'Resident Pay Policy', which specifies a pay scheme for sickness and absence consisting of £1 per day for 'acceptable' absences. The pay policy also contains information regarding the consequences of 'sub-standard performance' such as poor timekeeping and absence, which can result in the detainees' removal from paid activity. Training (such as manual lifting) is also provided, depending on the job role.

In many ways, then, labour within immigration detention is highly regularized and holds many of the key features of traditional employment. It is legal, and workers have contracts, use time sheets, and are not (as workers) thought to be subject to arbitrary violence, the threat of violence, or to be working in dangerous conditions absent of health and safety considerations. Yet, despite its 'voluntary' nature, detainee accounts (recorded in the media) reveal that detained workers feel voiceless, exploited, and subjected to slave labour.[184]

c. Perspectives on Work

'Do they think we just got off a slave ship?' This is the voice of a detainee participating in an investigation conducted by Corporate Watch into the paid activities regime.[185] He received £17 per week for serving breakfast, lunch, and dinner over four days at the canteen in Harmondsworth Detention Centre.[186] Though the work in detention is 'voluntary', a number of pressures and coercive factors undermine the ability to establish true consent in the 'paid activities' regime. Detainee accounts explain that they feel compelled to engage in work because they need the money rather than simply as a way of passing the time. 'John', a former detainee held in Brook House Immigration Removal Centre in the United Kingdom, recalls:

[184] Brian Whelan, 'Detainees Paid Pin Money to Paint, Clean and Serve Food' (*Channel 4 News*, 22 August 2014) <www.channel4.com/news/detainees-detention-centres-pay-private-contractors> accessed 12 November 2025.

[185] Phil Miller, 'True Scale of Captive Migrant Labour Revealed' (*Corporate Watch*, 22 August 2014) <https://corporatewatch.org/true-scale-of-captive-migrant-labour-revealed> accessed 12 November 2025.

[186] ibid.

> I spent about £10 per month on phone credit so that I could speak to my family and solicitors. I also needed money to buy food because what we were served in the centre was not healthy or nice to eat . . . I also went to the gym so I bought energy drinks. I know this does not sound like much, however, to have the option of what to have for dinner or to be able to buy an energy drink is a small luxury which made life in detention more manageable. The Home Office would only give us 71p per day so I could not have afforded this had I not been working in detention.[187]

Detainees have their liberty, agency, and property removed upon entrance to the detention estate. The detention centre shops (stocking goods such as toiletries, tobacco, phone cards, snacks, drinks, writing materials, and postage stamps) profit from this privation as complaints about lack of goods such as extra clothing, food, and games results in purchases. Evidence suggests that the cost of goods sold within the detention centres is vastly inflated in comparison to those sold on the outside, meaning that a process of dispossession and accumulation takes place on a micro scale within detention. As noted by Hiemstra and Conlon, 'detainees are spatially fixed as both captive consumers and coerced labourers in ways that generate important transfers of wealth'.[188]

Many accounts also explain that detainees need to work to send remittances home to family members. As one detainee stated in the *Working Illegally* documentary, 'I'm working here not for me. I'm not working for myself, I'm working for my daughter.'[189] Here then, we see a form of social reproduction, that being 'the labour of individuals to sustain, care for, and attend the survival of, well-being, and reproduction of themselves and each other',[190] which is also one of the most common pressures leading to exploitative work among asylum seekers and those refused asylum outside of detention.[191] Yet, because this work is considered 'consensual', and the low wages given to detainees are authorized by law, there are few legal avenues to challenge exploitative conditions. The issue of employment status and rights is explored further in Chapter 3.

[187] John, 'Working for a Pound an Hour: An Immigration Detainee's Perspective' (*Futures of Work*, 30 September 2019) <https://futuresofwork.co.uk/2019/09/30/working-for-a-pound-an-hour-an-immigration-detainees-perspective> accessed 12 November 2025.

[188] Hiemstra and Conlon (n 150).

[189] Anonymous interviewee, immigration detainee, Standoff Films, *Working Illegally* [Documentary Video] (Standoff Films 2015).

[190] Kate Hardy, 'Uneven Divestment of the State: Social Reproduction and Sex Work in Neo-Developmentalist Argentina' (2016) 13 Globalizations 876, 880.

[191] Louise Waite, 'Asylum Seekers and the Labour Market: Spaces of Discomfort and Hostility' (2017) 16 Social Policy and Society 669.

d. Private Profit

As evidenced above, millions of hours' worth of detainee labour have taken place in immigration detention centres since 2016. It is likely that millions more have taken place since these practices began in 2008. As highlighted in the case of *Morita*,[192] such services 'confer a benefit on the removal centre and its occupants, including detained persons and staff'.[193]

If we accept that these working arrangements displace citizen workers who would be paid the national minimum wage, then companies such as G4S could be saving millions in costs by engaging cheap detainee labour. Based on the FoI figures for 2014 to July 2016, these companies would have saved approximately £15,092,600 in costs. As well as constituting the raw materials processed by for-profit private corporations involved in the immigration industrial complex, inmates are also directly exploited as a source of cheap labour.[194] The proposition that detainees are replacing paid workers in detention centres has been refuted by the Home Office, which maintains that paid work practices are 'not intended to substitute the work of trained staff'.[195] This is also supported by Stephen Shaw, who claimed that nothing he saw during his review of immigration detention supported the view that paid work is used by contractors to increase their profits.[196] Yet, if labour in detention is intended primarily as a means of alleviating boredom, why focus on activities that render detainees complicit in the maintenance of their own incarceration (as cleaners, cooks, and handymen) at the expense of expanding activities such as sports or language lessons? Perhaps because, by offering jobs in detention, those running the centres receive cheap labour and save money on extra staff paid at the minimum wage, while expanding the provision of leisure activities would *cost* money. Burnett and Chebe note that, in this way, 'a core rationale of detainee labour is to reduce expenditure on essential aspects of the day-to-day running of the detention estate'.[197]

Outside of detention, detainees are prevented from engaging in paid work for reasons of deterrence and as a means of protecting British workers and business from illegitimate competition.[198] Detention centre practices in which

192 *Morita* (n 172).
193 ibid 93.
194 O'Connell Davidson (n 28) 98.
195 Miller (n 185).
196 Shaw (n 151) 136.
197 Burnett and Chebe (n 149) 98.
198 Bridget Anderson, 'Migration, Immigration Controls and the Fashioning of Precarious Workers' (2010) 24 Work, Employment & Society 300; Katie Bales, 'Universal Credit: Not So Universal? Deconstructing the Impact of the Asylum Support System' (2013) 35 Journal of Social Welfare and Family Law 427; Lucy Mayblin, 'Colonialism, Decolonisation, and the Right to Be Human: Britain

detainees work for low pay, potentially displacing British workers, conflicts with the Home Office's position that immigrants who 'end up in shadowy jobs in the grey economy undermine the terms and working conditions of British workers'.[199] However, these concerns are waived once the detainee enters the dominion of the detention centre.

5. Internships and Traineeships

a. Concepts in Flux

Over the past decade or so, the status of trainees, apprentices, and interns within the labour market has attracted increased attention. This is presumably due, in part, to the increase in their number within the labour market. A 2010 UK Government report, relying on data obtained by the Chartered Institute of Personnel Development (CIPD) estimated that 50,000–70,000 internships are published each year in the United Kingdom, of which at least one in five is unpaid.[200] However, it is estimated that the following decade saw a rise of at least 50 per cent,[201] with another report suggesting that at least 200,000 placements and 100,000 internships are taken up every year,[202] and a more recent report finding that 70 per cent of internships are unpaid and that over 27 per cent of graduates completed at least one unpaid internship.[203] The disparity may be attributed to a significant rise in the popularity of internships or, indeed, the sense that they are necessary. Alternatively, at least part of the explanation

and the 1951 Geneva Convention on the Status of Refugees' (2014) 27 Journal of Historical Sociology 423; Lucy Mayblin, *Asylum after Empire: Colonial Legacies in the Politics of Asylum Seeking* (Roman & Littlefield International 2017).

[199] John Reid, 'Enforcing the Rules: A Strategy to Ensure and Enforce Compliance with Our Immigration Laws' (Ref 280123, Home Office 2007).

[200] HM Government, 'Annex C—Information to be Released' (HM Publishing Service, 15 July 2010) <https://assets.publishing.service.gov.uk/government/uploads/system/uploads/attachment_data/file/200302/supporting-doc-foi-130498-annex-c.pdf> accessed 12 November 2025.

[201] Carys Roberts, *The Inbetweeners: The New Role of Internships in the Graduate Labour Market* (Institute for Public Policy Research (IPPR), 16 April 2017) <www.ippr.org/articles/the-inbetweeners> accessed 12 November 2025.

[202] David Docherty, Rosa Fernandez, and Inga Sileryte, 'Increasing the Offer of Work Experience in STEM Subjects: Can Demand Match Supply?' (National Centre for Universities and Business, October 2015) 13 <www.ncub.co.uk/wp-content/uploads/2015/10/Increasing-the-offer-of-work-experience-in-STEM-subjects-can-demand-match-supply.pdf> accessed 12 November 2025.

[203] Carl Cullinane and Rebecca Montacute, 'Pay as You Go: Internship Pay, Quality and Access in the Graduate Jobs Market' (Sutton Trust 2018) 21 <www.suttontrust.com/wp-content/uploads/2019/12/Pay-As-You-Go-1.pdf> accessed 12 November 2025.

may be attributed to definitional issues, that is, disparities in categorizing some work experiences.

Indeed, unlike the other case studies, in the case of internships, we encounter a very basic and fundamental set of questions, namely, what *are* internships, how are they similar, and where do they differ from other similar categories, such as apprenticeships and trainees? This question is important because, while these terms are quite often used interchangeably, and the respective schemes involved derive from the same (or, at least, from very similar) rationales, there are serious implications for the differing categories.

First, it is important to note that there is no universal—and in the United Kingdom no legal—definition of, or even reference to, internships.[204] In this respect, internships differ from traineeships and apprenticeships.[205] And so, unsurprisingly, the confusion and conflation between the three terms reigns supreme, even in situations where one expects a degree of care and caution. Thus, in 2010, the European Parliament's Committee on Employment and Social Affairs noted that, as the economic crisis caused a significant rise in unemployment rates in EU Member States across the board, and as there are fewer opportunities for young people to find stable employment, 'employers seem to be using traineeships and internships more frequently to replace regular employment, thereby exploiting the obstacles to entering the labour market faced by young people'.[206]

Two years later, a European Commission Staff Working Document expressed concern that

> traineeships and apprenticeships in some cases do not play the role they should: for several years now, concerns have been raised about their quality... traineeships may be abused as a source of cheap or free labour by employers who in many cases fail to provide the first step towards decent and sustainable work.[207]

[204] ibid 10. In fact, one of the report's recommendations is to call for establishing a 'common, legally protected definition of internships'—43.

[205] Those are referred to in the Employment Rights Act 1996, the National Minimum Wage Act 1998, s 54(3), and the National Minimum Wage Regulation 2015, reg 53.

[206] Committee on Employment and Social Affairs, 'Report on Promoting Youth Access to the Labour Market, Strengthening Trainee, Internship and Apprenticeship Status' (European Parliament 2009/2221(INI) 2010) <www.europarl.europa.eu/sides/getDoc.do?pubRef=-//EP//TEXT + REPORT + A7-2010-0197 + 0 + DOC + XML + V0//EN#title1> accessed 12 November 2025.

[207] European Commission, *Commission Staff Working Document—Quality Framework for Traineeships* (2012).

A similar conflation is observed in the UK domestic context. Take, for example, the 'Modern Apprenticeship/National Traineeship Framework', which was at issue in *Rinaldi-Tranter*.[208] In that case, the employment tribunal referred to the 'Learner' (in the terminology of the scheme) as an apprentice, a categorization that the Employment Appeal Tribunal (EAT) rejected, finding her to be a 'trainee', while immediately clarifying that 'Fortunately', in this case, 'this was a distinction without a difference'.[209] We note, then, that in the course of accounting for concerns regarding the prevalence of free labour (here, in the sense of 'unpaid') as a motivation for the different schemes, the documents refer to 'trainees', 'interns', and 'apprentices' interchangeably, sometimes (as in the title for the European Parliament's Committee Report) noting all three, sometimes two of the three, and sometimes just one, with no apparent rationale.

And yet, there are crucial differences between the three. The International Labour Organization (ILO) identifies 'people in unpaid *trainee* work' as 'all those of working age who, during a short reference period, performed any unpaid activity to produce goods or provide services for others, in order to acquire workplace experience or skills in a trade or profession'. There are three important elements to this definition. First, the period of activity is one that is not only fixed but also short. The British Government defines traineeships, for example, as 'work-based education and training programme with work experience for young people who want to find an apprenticeship or job but lack the skills, experience, and behaviours to make that next step' and that 'can last between 6 weeks and 12 months'.[210] In contrast, it identifies apprentices as ranging between one and six years, during which an apprentice is entitled to at least a reduced minimum wage (about 50 per cent of the national living wage). Similarly, the British EAT rejected claims for apprenticeship status even when that was the formal arrangement, deciding instead that it is a 'combination of training and job experience'.[211] There is also a clear hierarchy, as traineeships may *lead to* apprenticeships. And yet, even with this, more circumscribed, institution, there is a long history of capitalists presuming to show young apprentices into the trade only to exploit them for their labour. In *Scraping By*, Seth Rockman writes,

208 *HMRC v Rinaldi-Tranter* [2007] UKEAT 0486-06-1309 (13 September 2007).
209 ibid [6].
210 Department of Education (DoE), 'Traineeships: Framework for Delivery 2022–2023' (updated August 2023) <www.gov.uk/government/publications/supporting-young-people-to-develop-the-skills-for-apprenticeships-and-sustainable-employment-framework-for-delivery/traineeships-framework-for-delivery-2020-to-2021-web-accessible-version> accessed 12 November 2025.
211 *Thorpe v Dul* (2003) EAT 630/03/TM [65]; *Dunk v George Waller & Sons* [1970] 2 All ER 630.

> By 'sweating' production, relying on workers outside the craft tradition, and turning their eyes toward distant markets, artisan masters became capitalist manufacturers. Working from their own homes, adult women stitched 'slop', a derisive term for cheap, ready-to-wear shirts and pants. Apprentices in the shoemaking trade lost access to the 'art and mystery' of their craft and instead found themselves exploited for their labour.[212]

Before we conclude the definitional section of this introduction, we should note that of the three, the contours of apprenticeships are most easily recognizable. Stewart and colleagues explain that the term 'apprentice' originated in the context of medical training and education, with reference, then as now, to a period of postgraduate, clinical training in hospitals, under supervision and for relatively low pay.[213] Therefore, it is relatively straightforward to state that in what follows, we will *not* discuss apprenticeships. On the other side of the continuum, the concept of the intern is the most open-ended, particularly in the United Kingdom where, as mentioned, no legal definition exists. The result is that an individual who accepts an 'internship' may (retrospectively) be categorized as an (unpaid) trainee or volunteer, a (moderately paid) apprentice, or even as a (fully paid) worker or employee.[214] Therefore, we will use and focus on the institution of internships, predominantly due to its open-ended nature. At times, however, this will require reference to documents and writings that refer to trainees and traineeships, which may be subsumed under the broader umbrella concept of internships.[215]

Even after excluding apprenticeships from the focus of our inquiry, we encounter a vast terrain. A European Commission report recognized the great diversity of the field and distinguished between types of schemes.[216] We list them here in an order of low to high intensity of regulation and state involvement:

i. Traineeships in the open market: these are taken up by young people as a way to acquire work experience. The Commission notes that these schemes have 'attracted most criticism since they tend to be unregulated and associated with reports of questionable employer practices including low quality, poor terms and conditions, including low or no pay'.[217]

[212] Rockman (n 97) 120.
[213] Andrew Stewart and others, 'The Regulation of Internships: A Comparative Study' (ILO 2018) Working Paper No 240, 1 <www.ilo.org/media/415746/download> accessed 12 November 2025.
[214] Paul Rudd, 'All Work and No Pay: Establishing the Standard for When Legal, Unpaid Internships Become Illegal, Unpaid Labor' (2015) 63 University of Kansas Law Review 451.
[215] See eg European Commission (n 207) 56.
[216] ibid 4–5.
[217] ibid 5.

ii. Transnational traineeships: these are increasingly popular for work experience across the EU, organized through EU mobility programmes such as Leonardo da Vinci and Erasmus.
iii. Traineeships linked to educational programmes: these are part of a vocational or higher education programme.
iv. Traineeships as part of mandatory professional training, where there is a legal requirement to undertake a compulsory traineeship as part of a professional training: examples in the United Kingdom include health (medicine, nursing, pharmacy, dentistry, psychology, psychotherapy, and veterinary medicine); law and accountancy; and social work, engineering, education, architecture, media and journalism, tourism, and hospitality.[218]
v. Traineeships linked to Active Labour Market Policies: these are a form of 'workfare' designed specifically for unemployed young people.

The whole range of internships and traineeships cannot be examined in full within this context. Since category [v] is a subset of workfare, and can be seen to have been addressed within the confines of that case study, we will concern ourselves here with internships and traineeships in categories [i] and [iv]. Schemes in both categories thus rely on a state-constructed legal framework that not only allows employers to make use of free, or extremely cheap, labour but also sets these internships as formal preconditions for entry into the occupation. In the United Kingdom, this legal framework is characterized by a *lack* of direct, national regulation. Instead, insofar as it exists, such regulation is left to the initiative of educational institutions (for category [iii]) and by professional bodies (for category [iv]), leading to growing concerns regarding abuse and exploitation.[219] Moreover, where such frameworks are in place, as is the case with the CIPD's *Code of Best Practice for Quality Internships*, those were found to be

> more effective at helping organisations who 'want' to provide quality traineeships . . . than they are in stimulating good practice in organisations where bad practices are more entrenched. For example, quality frameworks are unlikely to have much impact on organisations deliberately using trainees as a source of cheap labour.[220]

218 ibid 61.
219 ibid 47, 62.
220 ibid 847–48.

Furthermore, it should be highlighted that the United Kingdom is an outlier in this regard. The outstanding example on the other end of the spectrum is France, which passed a number of laws between 2006 and 2011 to explicitly regulate traineeships and to guarantee that they live up to their stated aim.[221] This was done by mandating that *all* traineeships, including those in the open market, must be part of a learning environment and in partnership with an educational institution. In turn, this objective was secured by requiring a signed tripartite agreement between the training provider (eg a university), the host organization (eg a business), and a trainee.

One might object, at this stage, suggesting that, unlike prison work, labour in immigration detention, or even workfare, one does not *have* to choose to pursue a particular occupation that includes implicit or explicit expectations to take part in unpaid internships. Thus, if one chooses to be a teacher or a nurse, for example, such a person should be fully aware of the preconditions for entering this occupation and could avoid the choice of occupation wholesale if it does not fit one's priorities. We will discuss the concept of choice in more detail in Chapters 4 and 5, but for now, we can say the following: first, even with the more rigorous contexts of prison work and workfare, for example, one can 'choose' not to take part in the relevant scheme and suffer the consequences. And with respect to internship requirements and expectations, an individual who turns away from an occupation because they cannot *afford* to take on unpaid internship is an individual whose life choices have arguably been constrained in ways that are structurally unjust. This is not solely a theoretical response. Internships create one of the highest barriers to social mobility.[222] In 2012, in the United Kingdom, the Panel on Fair Access to the Professions noted that internships (here probably in their 'trainee' variety) exclude entrants who are unwilling or unable to take unpaid work.[223]

An example to that effect was made apparent in 2017, when the following petition was submitted to the UK Government website: 'Pay healthcare students for placement hours'. The details of the petition were quite revealing:

> Healthcare students who started in September 2017 do not receive a bursary. We have to do 23000 hours over 3 years and work 37.5 hours a week during our placements with no pay which is basically free labour. It is very hard to

[221] ibid 42–43.

[222] Cullinane and Montacute (n 203).

[223] Cabinet Office, *Fair Access to Professional Careers: A Progress Report by the Independent Reviewer on Social Mobility and Child Poverty* (2012).

> keep a healthy lifestyle, do our placements, keep a part time job and complete university work.[224]

The government's response stated that this new policy followed the 2015 Spending Review, and was justified because

> We know that whilst undertaking their courses, healthcare students are required by the Nursing and Midwifery Council (NMC) to complete 2,300 hours of clinical placements during their degree in order to obtain their professional registration. This compulsory training in a clinical setting makes healthcare students unique in the student population.
>
> The NMC provide guidance on the requirement for students to have supernumerary status during clinical placements. The NMC state that 'Programme providers must ensure that students are supernumerary during all practice learning. Supernumerary means that the student will not, as part of their programme of preparation, be contracted by any person or body to provide nursing care.' It is our view that students' completion of high-quality clinical placements is essential to having a well-trained workforce for the NHS.[225]

The supernumerary schemes are sometimes referred to as 'passive'. And yet, in one case, the British EAT declined to distinguish between 'passive' and 'active' training schemes for the purposes of the Race Relations Act 1976 but did find that while that the Act covers ten-day training schemes (even if 'passive') with a programme, it does not cover one-day visits for prospective applicants.[226]

b. Why Intern?

Internships are seen as addressing both the significant rise in youth unemployment in some countries and, more generally, the transition of young people from school to work. With respect to the former, in the United Kingdom, of an estimated 987,000 young people (aged sixteen to twenty-four), 13.4 per cent of that cohort were not in education, employment, or training (NEETs) from

[224] Petition, 'Pay Health Care Students for Placement Hours' (2017) <https://petition.parliament.uk/petitions/201548> accessed 12 November 2025.

[225] ibid.

[226] *Treasury Solicitor's Department v Chenge* [2007] IRLR 386, EAT.

October to December 2024.[227] The percentage of those who were NEETs in the age group of eighteen to twenty-four is 15.8.[228] The latter aim is understood to be realized by introducing trainees to real-life work environments, channelling their theoretical knowledge into applicable skills, exposing them to prospective employers, and facilitating the building of networks that will provide a gateway to future employment.[229]

A 2018 report by the Sutton Trust, for example, indicated that almost one-half (46 per cent) of employers offer graduate internships, with large employers twice as likely to do so as small businesses.[230] It also found growing recognition that internships are becoming an informal prerequisite: 46 per cent of 21–23-year-olds report they have completed one, compared to 37 per cent of 27–29 year olds. Of these, 70 per cent of internships were unpaid.

Despite the value of the ideal internship, questions have been raised regarding the quality, supervision, and learning environment (on the one hand) and the working conditions and terms of work (on the other). In other words, the concern focused on whether a growing number of interns feel 'obliged' to offer cheap or free labour, while gaining very little by way of introduction to a work environment. Instead of providing a stepping stone to stable and decent work, internships may serve as a 'vehicle for channelling youths into the precariat'[231] since, as the European Commission notes, they 'often trap young people in a vicious cycle of precarious employment and insecurity'.[232]

This trend was noted by the 2017 Taylor Report commissioned by the UK Government to review 'modern workplace practices'.[233] The report recommended that 'the Government should ensure that exploitative unpaid internships, which harm social mobility in the UK, are stamped out. The Government should do this by clarifying the interpretation of the law and encouraging enforcement action taken by HMRC [Her Majesty's Revenue and Customs] in this area'.[234] The government responded to the report with admirable rhetoric,

[227] Office for National Statistics, 'Young People Not in Education, Employment or Training (NEET) UK: February 2025' <www.ons.gov.uk/employmentandlabourmarket/peoplenotinwork/unemployment/bulletins/youngpeoplenotineducationemploymentortrainingneet/february2025> accessed 15 March 2025.

[228] ibid.

[229] European Commission (n 207) 23, 111; Lee Harvey and others, 'Work Experience: Expanding Opportunities for Undergraduates' (Centre for Research into Quality, University of Central England 1998) <www.qualityresearchinternational.com/Harvey%20papers/Harvey%20et%20al%201998%20Work%20Experience.pdf> accessed 12 November 2025.

[230] Cullinane and Montacute (n 203).

[231] Guy Standing, *The Precariat: The New Dangerous Class* (Bloomsbury 2011) 16.

[232] European Commission (n 207) 24.

[233] Matthew Taylor, *Good Work: The Taylor Review of Modern Working Practices* (Department for Business, Energy and Industrial Strategy 2017).

[234] ibid 91.

noting that 'Exploitative unpaid internships should not exist and we will work to eradicate these.'[235]

c. Perspectives on Internships

Some placements are, one would assume, rewarding and even important for professional development. Others are less so, as students are asked to take on menial tasks that do not support their learning, are not supervised, and feel exploited. A European Commission report noted that open market internships have attracted the most criticism as they are associated with

i. poor or non-existent learning content, which relates to trainees' developmental needs;
ii. poor terms and conditions, including lack of social security coverage and/or health insurance, low or no compensation, no sick or holiday entitlement, and/or pay, etc;
iii. trainee exploitation, including heavy workload and/or long working hours;
iv. replacement of regular staff by trainees who are used as cheap or even free labour;
v. lack of transparency in the recruitment process;
vi. lack of equity of access due to poor terms and conditions, including no or insufficient remuneration.[236]

When turning to personal reports, one intern reported that 'with unpaid internships . . . they just wanted someone to do the admin—and this way they didn't have to pay anyone, they didn't have to get anyone in permanently'.[237] As we note in Chapter 3, a central test used to deny interns rights and status assesses—and, in some cases, assumes—that the intern benefits more than the employer. However, notwithstanding the questionable normative and legal status of the test itself, there is reason to believe that it is often not realized. As two interns suggest,[238]

[235] HM Government, *Good Work: A Response to the Taylor Review of Modern Working Practices* (HM Government 2018) 46.
[236] European Commission (n 207) 89–90.
[237] Roberts (n 201) 20.
[238] ibid.

> It was like it was just for paper—so I can write I've done this, and they can write we have given them the opportunity for this. But it wasn't real practice for the real world or working with projects and people.

and

> I think I was mismanaged quite heavily. They didn't get the best out of me at all because stretched resources at the start meant a larger workload for me. But then the onus was on me so much that it flattened my productivity because I was overworked. Then when I brought that up it was met with hostility.[239]

In Chapter 4, we note that one indicator for the identification of work and 'unfree' relates to the terms and conditions of employment and another to the degree of control and discipline that may be exerted over the worker. As with previous case studies, both indicia may suggest that, in some cases, unfree labour may be found. One intern noted that 'My work definitely expects you to stay for three hours extra without pay. If there is a deadline coming up, you stay weekends, you stay there all night. There are people who have stayed there for 48 hours straight.'[240]

One intern in the film and media industry, Keri Hudson, stands out as a rare case in which she succeeded in a claim for worker status and consequent rights (minimum wage and holiday pay) before the employment tribunal.[241] She told *The Guardian* that she worked from 10am to 6pm, eventually 'managing six other unpaid interns who were all crammed on to a desk meant for two'. She exclaimed, 'I'd done ridiculous amounts of work for them.... I'd practically run the site.'[242]

A medical student testified that, after seeing a corpse for the first time, she was left alone to cry in a toilet. She said, 'Placement is just so exhausting... I get that staff are stressed and busy, but if you're going to choose to be a mentor for a student, you have to actually check on them when there's a distressing situation.'[243] Another mentioned that she sometimes feels that she's 'fulfilling the

239 ibid.

240 ibid 19.

241 *Keri Hudson v TGP Publishing Ltd* (unpublished 2011); another rare success is *Vetta v London Dreams Motion Pictures* (unpublished 2009), both noted in European Commission (n 207) 816.

242 Shiv Malik, 'Unpaid Website Intern Celebrates Court Victory' *The Guardian* (London, 7 June 2021) <www.theguardian.com/media/2011/may/23/unpaid-website-intern-court-victory> accessed 10 March 2025.

243 Flora Carr, 'Student Nurse Horror Stories: The Reality of Working within an NHS Stretched to Breaking Point' *The Telegraph* (London, 23 January 2017) <www.telegraph.co.uk/education/2017/01/23/student-nurse-horror-stories-reality-working-within-nhs-stretched> accessed 12 November 2025.

job of an HCA [Healthcare Assistance]'.[244] Along with the cuts to bursaries, which make it extremely difficult for some students (particularly those who have care duties of their own) to make ends meet, the reality of the conditions within NHS placements has led to a drop of 20 per cent in applications for nursing.[245] Another expressed a similar sentiment, stating that

> I wouldn't mind the NHS paying me this (£450 a month) if it wasn't for the fact that every day I go to 'train' I feel as if I'm used as a cheap way to keep the NHS running, I feel as though I'm just cheap labour to them. The nurses do not get allocated time or pay to train me and therefore are totally unenthusiastic and impatient.[246]

Social work students are in a similar situation as they are required, as a condition for qualification, to undertake 200 days of practice over the course of their degree, of which 30 days may be allocated to develop their skills.[247] Placements may be taken in 'statutory' or 'non-statutory' settings. Under the Social Work England Placement Guidance, a 'statutory' placement is one that requires students to carry out tasks which involve high-risk decision-making and legal interventions and which take place in a local authority setting or settings delivering delegated statutory functions on behalf of the local authority. It involves a sufficient amount of work on cases where there are children in need or on delivering requirements of the Care Act 2014 and Mental Capacity Act 2005 and requires case records to be updated by the student, under appropriate supervision.[248] A non-statutory placement takes place in the private, voluntary, and independent (PVI) sector. It involves statutory work taken by an organization in the PVI sector that has been delegated the function by a local authority, provided that there is opportunity for students to be directly involved in cases comparable to those taken by statutory placements. In addition, such work may involve carers' charities, which have been commissioned by the local authority to undertake carers' assessments; advocacy organizations, which employ individuals to work as independent mental capacity advocates;

[244] ibid.
[245] ibid.
[246] Anon, 'I'm a Student Nurse—the NHS Exploits Us as Cheap Labour' *The Independent* (London, 7 July 2017) <www.independent.co.uk/voices/letters/nhs-student-nurse-doctor-midwife-cuts-g20-theresa-may-justin-trudeau-a7829236.html> accessed 12 November 2025.
[247] Social Work England, 'Practice Placement Guidance' (27 April 2023) 4 <www.socialworkengland.org.uk/standards/practice-placements-guidance> accessed 12 November 2025.
[248] ibid.

hospices, which require individuals to undertake Mental Capacity Act assessments; and/or court-ordered work or offender-related work.[249]

In 2013, the Department for Health initiated a consultation to revisit the funding scheme (established as the Education Support Grant in 2003) for social work placements, which focused on compensating employers for their supervision costs and higher education institutions for their administrative costs.[250]

We have now moved slightly beyond the original remit mentioned earlier for this section, namely, to occupations that include placement or apprenticeship as a formal requirement for entry. This is because, it is worth assessing the social and legal situation for trainees on national traineeship programmes. Unlike 'open market internships', which may be initiated and managed by private companies, with very 'light-touch' regulation, national traineeship schemes are heavily regulated, funded, and monitored by the state. A government agency supervisor oversees the programmes and visits the employer to assure that standards are upheld. Thus, we find that these schemes share much in common with others that are of interest to us in the current context, namely, cooperation between the state and private corporations, the provision of free or cheap labour, and the legal cover for this arrangement. A further impetus for the introduction of this matter in the current discussion is the sheer number of those subject to these schemes and the financial implications that are involved.

d. Private Profit

One of the most serious, and common, causes for concern in relation to internships concerns the potential for exploitation. A significant portion of internships offer low (below the national minimum wage) or even no pay. This is particularly prevalent in open market internships, with the creative industries, media, public relations, and the third sector frequently cited in this regard. Professor Gower noted, with respect to the legal profession, that 'not all solicitors are conscientious; some, I think not many, regard their articled clerks as cheap labour to be employed on whatever is most profitable to the principal, rather than on what is most instructive'.[251] Much has changed, for better and for worse, since Gower wrote with such tentativeness in 1950. With respect to

[249] ibid 5.
[250] Department of Health, 'Reforming the Education Support Grant—a Paper for Consultation' (September 2013).
[251] LCB Gower, 'English Legal Training' (1950) 13 Modern Law Review 137, 153.

the particular occupation to which he was referring, the Solicitors' Regulation Authority (SRA) now dictates and monitors the manner and quality under which training contracts must be carried out, the areas that will be covered, and the skills that will be developed. In addition, it sets standards concerning pay and working conditions, including adherence to minimum annual leave and the national minimum wage (previously, it prescribed a minimum wage that exceeded the national minimum wage). The Law Society 'recommends' a higher minimum wage of £28,090 in London and £24,916 outside London.[252] Other professional bodies practice a more laissez-faire approach, not mandating standards of quality or terms and conditions of employment and leaving it to the trainee to 'negotiate' these terms with the host provider.[253] Naturally, this approach may, and frequently does, lead to exploitation.

Thus, in its 2010 Annual Report, the Low Pay Commission (LPC) cited the National Union of Journalists, which submitted evidence according to which there was 'an over-supply of people desperate to work in the media industry and employers have built unpaid work placements into their business model'.[254] The LPC concluded that the 'evidence we received on unpaid work experience indicates that there is *systematic abuse* of interns, with a growing number of people undertaking "work" but excluded from the minimum wage'.[255]

To clarify: while compensation is central to the analysis, exploitation extends beyond unpaid status. The vast power disparities in this context, against the background of high and rising youth unemployment, lead to frequent reports of heavy workloads and long working hours, with clear implications for young people's mental health.[256]

Moreover, the lack of quality assurance leads to many occasions in which no real training or education is offered 'in return' for the work as supervision, mentoring, guidance, and monitoring are minimal, if they exist at all. Finally, and perhaps particularly worrying, concerns have been raised about the use of trainees' cheap labour that takes the place of regular, paid staff, even when contracts exist that prohibit the practice.[257]

[252] The Law Society, 'Recommended Minimum Salary for Trainee Solicitors and SQE Candidates' (22 July 2025) <www.lawsociety.org.uk/en/topics/hr-and-people-management/recommended-minimum-salary-for-trainee-solicitors-and-sqe candidates> accessed 12 November 2025.

[253] European Commission (n 207) 817.

[254] LPC, *National Minimum Wage—Low Pay Commission Report 2010* (Cm 7823, The Stationery Office 2010) 109.

[255] ibid 110 (emphasis added).

[256] Thomas Connelly, 'City Law Firm Asks Trainees to Pull All Nighter Days after Promising to Support Lawyers' Mental Health' (*Legal Cheek*, 16 October 2018) <www.legalcheek.com/2018/10/exclusive-city-law-firm-asks-trainees-to-pull-all-nighter-just-days-after-publicly-promising-to-support-its-lawyers-mental-health> accessed 12 November 2025.

[257] European Commission (n 207) 116–20.

Kit Sadgrove, a manager at Etsio, a start-up company that *charges* interns £100 per day for placements, distances himself from extractive practices by explaining that 'Large companies are typically taking advantage of interns. . . . They are replacing paid staff with interns who work for them for six months or longer at a time and they are doing jobs that should be taken up by proper people. We are not doing that.'[258]

6. Conclusion

Whilst the case studies examined vary in description and form, there remain significant parallels. All are created through processes of law and policy to create a reserve army of labour power for the state and private corporations to draw upon as and when workers are needed, offsetting the rising costs of labour and production in a competitive, globalized capitalist market. Although small in number, the workers within these case studies are nevertheless significant, with indications that these sectors will continue to grow into the future, particularly in the case of prisons and immigration detention as the state pursues plans for expansion of the carceral industrial complex. In the case of internships, data reveals that the number of internships undertaken by graduate students has risen by 12 per cent since 2018, with the access gap between working-class and middle-class students rising 20 per cent, up from 12 per cent in 2018.[259] Although the expansion of workfare has been stifled as a result of the resistance from benefit claimants and organizations such as Boycott Workfare, the conviction behind these schemes remains apparent in the conditionality and sanctions regime that characterizes the administration of UC.[260]

As will be explored in Chapter 3, the disposability of these workers is enabled and reinforced by their exclusion from employment status and its associated rights, including the right to the national minimum wage, the right not to be unfairly dismissed, and the right to protection for participating in collective action, which exists to counterbalance precarity and exploitation. As noted by Burnett, in the case of prison work, labour in immigration detention, and

[258] Shiv Malik and Rajeev Syal, 'Internships: The Scandal of Britain's Unpaid Army' *The Guardian* (4 November 2011) <www.theguardian.com/money/2011/nov/04/internships-scandal-britain-unpaid-army> accessed 12 November 2025.

[259] Erica Holt-White and Carl Cullinane, 'Unpaid and Underpaid Internships' (The Sutton Trust, 23 January 2025) <www.suttontrust.com/our-research/unpaid-and-underpaid-internships> accessed 17 February 2025.

[260] Michael Adler, *Cruel, Inhuman or Degrading Treatment? Benefit Sanctions in the UK* (Palgrave Macmillan 2018).

workfare, this labour serves to manage 'recalcitrant populations that have been criminalised or thrust into un-or-under employment', which serves the dual purpose of enforcing labour market discipline upon the workforce themselves while also 'disciplining others through laying bare their potential fate', serving as a deterrent for 'decent' law-abiding citizens.[261]

As this chapter has demonstrated, many of the labour forms within our case studies have long histories that highlight the diffuse and mutable reasoning used by the state to justify the existence of the work itself and workers' exclusion from access to labour rights; this includes labour as a form of punishment and reformation; deterrence; instilling market and social discipline; cost saving and relief; reciprocity; rehabilitation and 'self-realization'; and, importantly, the facilitation of work as a response to changes in the supply and demand of labour within the capitalist market. Yet, despite the ever-changing justifications, these labour forms have endured since at least the sixteenth century.[262] The elasticity of reasoning here also highlights the capricious boundaries of 'work' and who qualifies for the status of 'worker', which we unravel further in Chapter 3.

[261] Burnett (n 1).
[262] Innes (n 25).

3

Working without a Job

Why Are They Not Workers?

1. Introduction

The central legal issue that underpins the predicament of participants in our case studies is the fact that they are not legally recognized as workers. This has consequences for the participants' access to wages and rights as well as social standing and the value ascribed to their labour. Accordingly, the first section of this chapter examines the legal requirements for worker and employee status in the United Kingdom, demonstrating that in all four of the case studies offered, the tests for worker, and even employee status in some instances, are satisfied. Yet, despite this, the workforce in these case studies remains excluded from formal recognition and access to rights, such as the national minimum wage, through to statutory exclusions, supported via common law judgments.

Second, the chapter addresses the socio-political justifications for the exclusion of our case studies from formal employment status. Much like the notion that caregiving is 'natural' (used to validate the non-recognition of domestic labour as a form of employment), these justifications serve to mystify the economic nature of the work performed on the grounds that it 'benefits' the participants as opposed to the employing entities, ostensibly framing it as non-market work. Adams argues that law thus has a 'profound role in shaping the social imaginary, influencing societal perceptions and beliefs about the world'[1] in ways that shape behaviour and our understanding of constructs such as 'work' and its substance as well as the stratification of rights (including labour rights) and who is deemed worthy of inclusion.

Third, we adopt a historical materialist approach to reveal where the arguments used to deny and exclude employment status come from and why the market/non-market distinction is considered plausible, drawing on feminist theory and post-colonial critique to deconstruct these assumptions. We argue

[1] Zoe Adams, *The Legal Concept of Work* (OUP 2022) 339.

Underpaid and Unrecognized. Katie Bales and Amir Paz-Fuchs, Oxford University Press.
 DOI: 10.1093/9780197910467.003.0003

that what gives the market/non-market distinction normative value as a reason for paying or not paying a wage is historically and materially linked to the gendered and racialized social division of labour that emerged with capitalism. This reinforced wage labour as a distinct legal and economic category to which a variety of work relationships, for diverse reasons, did not appear to conform, such as domestic work or indeed, as will be explored, the work within our case studies. A historical materialist lens embodies a Marxist approach to explore what is historically specific about certain modes of production within a particular social formation, taking into account the ways in which economic production and class struggle influence and shape society.[2] By drawing on historical examples, we reveal the intrinsic connections and dependency of capitalism upon forms of ostensibly 'non-market' labour. Recognition of worker status is, therefore, not only about the nature of the work's market character (which leads to a specific construction of employment under labour law) but also about welfare, immigration, citizenship, the criminal law, and social ideas of what is and what is not commodifiable. Acknowledging these wider and historical influences provides us with greater critical purchase in understanding why certain groups are endowed with worker status while others remain excluded at the boundaries.

2. Employment Status

Analysis of the legal definitions of employee and/or worker status reveals that our case studies largely satisfy the common law tests used to afford 'worker' or 'employee' status. Though the employment status framework remains reductive in its construction of work, serving to exclude domestic caregiving and other forms of essential labour, within the boundaries of the capitalist economy, employment status is key to the enjoyment of rights, including those related to wages, job security, working time, and discrimination. The impetus and urgency for employment status protections was made clear by the UK Supreme Court (citing the Canadian Supreme Court): 'The more the work life of individuals is controlled, the greater their dependency and, consequently, their economic, social and psychological vulnerability in the workplace.'[3]

[2] Bertel Ollman, *Dialectical Investigations* (Routledge 1993); Collin L Chambers, 'Historical Materialism, Social Change, and the Necessity of Revolutionary Optimism' (2021) 14 Human Geography 296.

[3] *McCormick v Fasken Martineau DuMoulin LLP* [2014] 2 SCR 108 [23] cited at *Uber v Aslam* [2021] UKSC 5 [75].

Employment rights are thus intended to serve as a counterbalance to inequality of bargaining power and purportedly safeguard those who are most vulnerable against the vagaries of the market. Accordingly, determining whether our case study participants satisfy the tests for employee and/or worker status remains an important aspect of our contribution for four reasons. First, satisfying the test for employee and/or worker status indicates that the work being carried out by our participants falls within the traditional notion of 'productive' or 'market work' that would normally garner a wage, alongside other employment rights. Second, in meeting the requirements of employee/worker status, it becomes clear that our case study participants are excluded from protection on the grounds of their social status—as prisoners, migrants, unemployed claimants, and interns rather than as a result of the work performed. This reflection is important as it underscores the diminished significance of the employment contract and reveals the underlying structural shackles that prevent our case study participants from enjoying labour rights, implemented through statutory and judicial exclusions. In essence, then, the fight for recognition is more likely to be a political battle than a legal one. Third, establishing that employment status is satisfied provides our case study participants with a platform from which they can push for social change and legal recognition. Finally, recognition of employment status has the potential to challenge the paradigm of the market, which is heavily biased in terms of class, race, gender, and migration status. We acknowledge that the long-standing alignment of labour market inclusion with social inclusion has proven to be strained, if not even disingenuous:[4] individuals working in low paid, dirty, dangerous, and demeaning jobs do not, by virtue of their employment, gain access to significant social capital. Yet, there is a stronger correspondence between labour market exclusion and social exclusion, particularly in light of the fact that the categories targeted for exclusion are often populated by women, non-white, and migrant workers—as evident in our case studies.

In this section, we focus on the aspects that militate towards the recognition of our case study participants as 'employees' and/or 'workers'. In the UK context, such a claim begins with the relevant definitions, primarily in section 230 of the Employment Rights Act 1996, but are replicated in other areas of legislation that concern particular rights.[5] Section 230 ERA states as follows:

[4] Amir Paz-Fuchs, *Welfare to Work: Conditional Rights in Social Policy* (OUP 2007).

[5] See eg the Trade Union and Labour Relations (Consolidation) Act 1992; National Minimum Wage Act 1998; Working Time Regulations 1998, s 2(1).

230 **Employees, workers etc.**

(1) In this Act 'employee' means an individual who has entered into or works under (or, where the employment has ceased, worked under) a contract of employment.

(2) In this Act 'contract of employment' means a contract of service or apprenticeship, whether express or implied, and (if it is express) whether oral or in writing.

(3) In this Act 'worker' . . . means an individual who has entered into or works under (or, where the employment has ceased, worked under)—

   (a) a contract of employment, or

   (b) any other contract, whether express or implied and (if it is express) whether oral or in writing, whereby the individual undertakes to do or perform personally any work or services for another party to the contract whose status is not by virtue of the contract that of a client or customer of any profession or business undertaking carried on by the individual.

While section 230 provides a basic framing for the concept of 'employee' and 'worker' status, the wording of the legislation remains vague and in need of interpretation, and that is delivered via the common law tests established by the judiciary. What is clear from section 230 is that, for a participant in any of these schemes to claim employee or worker status, they must first establish that the relationship with the employing entity rests on contractual foundations. Accordingly, we turn to the question of contract before moving on to the common law tests for determining whether our case study participants meet the requirements of 'employee' and/or 'worker' status.

a. The Contract

The contract of employment has been described as the 'cornerstone of the edifice' of employment law[6] and may be express or implied, oral or in writing. Unlike traditional commercial contracts, however, the law recognizes the contractual inequality between employers and the employed by taking into

[6] Otto Kahn-Freund, 'Legal Framework' in A Flanders and H Clegg (eds), *The System of Industrial Relations in Great Britain* (Blackwell 1954) 45. For a critique of the reliance on the contractual model and a proposal for an alternative approach, see Mark Freedland, 'From the Contract of Employment to a Personal Work Nexus' (2006) 35 International Law Journal 1.

account the inequality of bargaining power that separates it from the ordinary principles governing contracts. Consequently, for example, where written terms within the contract do not reflect the reality of the arrangement, the courts will more readily override such terms as a 'sham'.[7] In our case studies, the first question to ask is whether a contract governs the employment relationship. In subsection (b) below, we examine whether the realities of the employment relationships satisfy the common law tests to render them contracts of employment, work, or service.

For a contract to be established, there must be an offer, acceptance, and some form of consideration. Both parties must also enter the contract voluntarily and possess an intention to create legal relations, distinct from an agreement that is 'binding in honour only', as in the case of a volunteer agreement.[8] Though some form of contract is apparent in each case study, applying contractual principles is not straightforward, particularly regarding voluntariness and consideration.

In the case of prison labour, the components of a standardized contract are considered missing due to the involuntary nature of the work itself, which renders it outside the sphere of the employment contract and the traditional 'wage–work bargain'.[9] As Zatz notes, involuntariness 'is a marker of a relationship that arises out of the institutions of punishment, not the institutions of the labour market'.[10] Previous case law considering the employment relationship of prison workers has posited the Ministry of Justice (as an executive agency of the prison service) as the employer rather than the private corporations who utilize prison labour. Indeed, the New Futures Network highlights that contracts with external partners to provide work and training in prisons and training academies are between His Majesty's Prison and Probation Service (HMPPS) and the business or organization that pays HMPPS to utilize the services of detainees.[11] In 1957, *Pullen*[12] established that prison workers were not employees, and thus not subject to the protections of the Factories Act

[7] *Autoclenz v Belcher* [2011] UKSC 41.

[8] *X v Mid Sussex Citizens' Advice Bureau* [2010] ICR 429, confirmed in *X v Mid Sussex Citizens Advice Bureau* [2011] EWCA Civ 28. See the discussion in Mark Freedland and Nicola Kountouris, *The Legal Construction of Personal Work Relations* (OUP 2011) 136–37.

[9] See the Prison Rules 1999 (SI 1999/728) Rule 31(3), which provides that a convicted prisoner shall be required to do useful work for not more than ten hours a day.

[10] Noah Zatz, 'Working at the Boundaries of Markets: Prison Labor and the Economic Dimension of Employment Relationships' (2008) 61 Vanderbilt Law Review 857, 887.

[11] New Futures Network HMPPS, 'New Futures Network Sales 2021–22' (28 October 2022) <https://newfuturesnetwork.gov.uk/document/new-futures-network-sales-2021-22> accessed 19 February 2025.

[12] *Pullen v Prison Commission* [1957] 1 WLR 1186.

1937, as there was no contract of employment between them and the government. In 2016, *Cox*[13] considered the vicarious liability of the Ministry of Justice in relation to an accident resulting in injury that occurred during prison work time. As part of the court's analysis, the nature of the relationship between the prison worker and the Ministry of Justice was assessed, with the Supreme Court upholding the lower courts' decision that the relationship was not akin to that of employee and employer on grounds that the relationship was 'if anything *closer than one of employment*: it was founded not on mutuality but on compulsion'.[14] Though the court found that vicarious liability applied in this case, it rejected the claim that liability derives from an employment relationship but rather on the 'close relationship' between the prison and the prisoner and because the Prison Service derived a 'direct and immediate' benefit from the work being undertaken. Yet, as noted by Mantouvalou, the nature of the close relationship 'should make us question whether it is legitimate to exclude them from basic labour protections' as the element of compulsion makes prisoners more, rather than less, vulnerable to exploitation.[15]

As a result of their exclusion, prisoners are exempt from protection under the Employment Rights Act 1996, the Working Time Regulations 1998, and the Health and Safety at Work Act 1974, which means that they are unable to associate with others or collectively bargain for improvement to working conditions and wages. Despite this, prisons are bound by the common law duty of care, which requires them to protect prisoners from foreseeable injury and harm. If this duty is neglected, then prisoners can make a compensation claim for negligence, which would be handled through the administrative and civil courts rather than the employment tribunal, creating a number of procedural barriers.

In the United States, the obstacle to prisoners' claims to employment status and rights was framed in terms of involuntariness. In a relatively recent case, an Employment Tribunal in England also considered this factor to be crucial. It found that there was no contractual mutuality of obligation because, while 'the claimant could not be physically coerced to work, . . . he was subject to prison discipline if he refused'.[16]

[13] *Cox v Ministry of Justice* [2016] UKSC 10.
[14] *Cox* (n 13) (emphasis added).
[15] Virginia Mantouvalou, *Structural Injustice and Workers' Rights* (OUP 2023) 54; Virginia Mantouvalou, 'Human Rights for Working Prisoners' (*UK Labour Law*, 8 September 2021) <https://uklabourlawblog.com/2021/09/08/human-rights-for-working-prisoners-by-virginia-mantouvalou> accessed 12 November 2025.
[16] Case 3312375/2019 *Pimm v Sodexo Justice Services Ltd and Secretary of State for Justice* (2021) [49].

Even where prisoners are able to voluntarily agree to work, the US courts have ruled that the penal context of their work pushes the work outside of the traditional labour contract as it remains labour 'performed as part of a sentence of incarceration', rendering it non-economic.[17] This reflects an 'exclusive market approach', in which market relations are seen as the essence of economic life and incompatible with non-market institutions. Despite evidence which indicates that prison labour creates economic profit for private and public organizations, prison labour, like many of the case studies within this book, is thus considered 'non-market' and thereby non-economic.

Unlike prison labour, labour within immigration detention centres is regarded as 'voluntary'. Rule 17 of the Detention Centre Rules provides detainees with the opportunity to participate in activities to meet their 'recreational and intellectual needs and the relief of boredom', including 'paid activities'.[18] From a liberal perspective, compulsion or forced labour is not thereby present within this relationship which, within the context of the ruling in *Cox*, means that it could be considered an employment relationship. In fact, prior to 2006, paid activities were not available to detainees out of concern that payment would need to be in line with the National Minimum Wage Act 1998 (which applies only to workers and employees). This risk was removed through statutory exclusion via section 153A of the Immigration and Asylum Act 1999 and section 45B of the National Minimum Wage Act 1998,[19] which disqualified detainees within immigration removal centres from access to the national minimum wage. Without this exclusion, it should be assumed that immigration detainees would be entitled to the national minimum wage, having satisfied the relevant employment status tests, which are explored in subsection (b). Indeed, none of the cases concerning labour in immigration detention are yet to address the nature of the employment relationship and/or who the associate employer would be in light of the tripartite nature of the arrangements involving privately run detention centres outsourced by the Home Office. The contention that detainees are workers or employees is further supported by obiter from the 2019 case of *Morita*,[20] which concerned an application for judicial review of a decision by the Secretary of State not to increase pay rates for 'paid activities'. In this case, Mr Justice Murray confirmed that the Secretary of State did not 'dispute that the paid activity carried out under the paid activity regime is

[17] *Morgan v MacDonald*, 41 F.3d 1291 (9th Cir 1994).

[18] See also *Morita v Secretary of State for the Home Department* [2019] EWHC 758 (Admin), Mr Justice Murray [82].

[19] As inserted by the Immigration, Asylum and Nationality Act 2006, s 59.

[20] *Morita* (n 18).

"work"', noting further that a 'person undertaking such an activity outside a removal centre would be unlikely to undertake such work without payment, unless it was being done for personal, family or charitable purposes'.[21]

A 2019 freedom-of-information (FoI) request provided insight into the internal documentation and guidance relating to 'paid work' at The Verne Immigration Removal Centre and at Morton Hall, both of which are run by HMPPS. Evidence confirmed that detainees are able to put themselves forward for whichever role they desire, while eligibility to work relies on compliance and cooperation with the Home Office in helping to resolve their immigration claims. Non-compliant or violent behaviour (such as failing to attend an interview or causing disruption) will automatically exclude individuals from paid work opportunities.[22] Once detainees are deemed eligible, and they agree to work, they are given timetables that specify their working time and places of work. Formally, such an agreement would constitute a contract, satisfying the first requirement for the existence of an employment relationship.

Turning now to the matter of internships, we find that, all else being equal, the terms and conditions of such a contract could be viewed as emblematic of an employment contract. Therefore, to avoid such a result, courts and tribunals have posited a contract of employment as distinct from, and incongruent with, a contract for learning. The matter of establishing a contract, however, is far less contested. Thus, in the leading case for the status of trainees, *Edmunds v Lawson*,[23] a pupil barrister claimed that she was entitled to minimum wage as a worker under a contract of apprenticeship. She succeeded in the first instance, but the Court of Appeal disagreed.[24] It noted that the 'duties of pupils-masters were specified' and that the chamber's Pupillage Code provided that 'There must be a total two-way commitment between pupil and pupil-master'.[25] This detail, and the importance of the agreement to both parties, led the court to conclude that it would 'be surprising to infer that the parties intended to bind themselves in honour only'.[26] So, while accepting that there was a contract between the parties, Bingham LJ rejected its characterization as a contract of employment on a narrower basis, namely, that it is not expected that pupil barristers will 'render services of value' for their masters.

[21] ibid [36].
[22] Detention Services Order 01/2013, s 10.
[23] [2000] ICR 567 (CA).
[24] *Edmunds v Lawson* [2000] EWCA Civ 69.
[25] ibid [17]–[18].
[26] ibid [21].

The situation of workfare participants (WP) is similar to that of trainees in respect of a clear and detailed contract. Indeed, agreeing to the details of such a contract—with titles such as 'Jobseeker's Agreement', 'Claimant Commitment', or 'Individual Action Plan'—is a prerequisite for receiving benefits,[27] and failure to comply often leads to severe sanctions.[28] The contractual element, however, is intended to establish voluntariness in a context that suggests significant compulsion. One Member of Parliament described it as 'an abuse of language in an abuse of power'.[29] Now, if that is the case, it is worth pausing to ask *why* there is an insistence on the ceremonial signing of a contract[30] in the United Kingdom and elsewhere,[31] where it is abundantly clear that the lack of bargaining power of welfare recipients vis-à-vis the government casts the 'contract' between the two as 'take it or leave it'?[32] The reason is quite clear: framing the relationship between claimants and the government in such a manner places them in a no man's land of statutory protection—removing the parties from a public law (government agency to citizen) relationship while simultaneously avoiding a genuinely enforceable contract. What, then, are the practical consequences of signing such a contract?

A claimant who has signed a Jobseeker's Agreement may then be referred to a scheme provider. As part of the outsourcing agenda, these providers are large, private companies, including Atos, Ingeus, Seetec, and others. A representative from the provider then contacts the claimant and notifies them where and when their placement is to commence. Participants are then required to sign an 'Individual Action Plan' (IAP) with the provider, setting out the mandatory activities to be undertaken during their engagement in the workfare scheme.[33] Failure to undertake any mandated activity may result in the loss of benefits for a certain period. The initiation of the sanction process is delegated to the private provider operating the scheme.[34]

[27] Department for Work and Pensions (DWP), 'Guidance—Universal Credit and Your Claimant Commitment' (updated 12 February 2025) <www.gov.uk/government/publications/universal-credit-and-your-claimant-commitment-quick-guide/universal-credit-and-your-claimant-commitment> accessed 12 November 2025, stating that 'The Claimant Commitment is your record of the responsibilities that you have accepted in return for receiving Universal Credit, and the consequences of not meeting them.'

[28] Michael Adler, *Cruel, Inhuman or Degrading Treatment? Benefit Sanctions in the UK* (Palgrave 2018).

[29] *Hansard* col 600 (26 June 1995).

[30] Joel Handler, *Social Citizenship and Workfare in the US and Western Europe* (CUP 2004) 12.

[31] Under the US programme, claimants must sign an 'Individual Responsibility Plan'.

[32] Vadim Mahmoudov, 'Are Workfare Participants Employees: Legal Issues Presented by a Two-Tiered Labor Force' (1998) 1998 Annual Survey of American Law 349, 378.

[33] DWP, Community Work Placements, s 2.59.

[34] ibid s 3.10.

Against this background, two central objections arise regarding the construction of the IAP or the Claimant Commitment as a contract. First, denying the IAP its status as a contract rests on the lack of genuine voluntariness. The irony here is clear, as this was precisely the argument advanced by opponents of workfare, who claimed that it was akin to forced labour, or at least incompatible with the right to freely chosen work. This claim, it is noted, was rejected by the European Court of Human Rights,[35] by American Federal Courts,[36] by the UK Supreme Court,[37] and by the Dutch Central Appeals Tribunal.[38] In those instances, *proponents* of workfare emphasized its contractual (as opposed to its coercive) nature. Second, one might argue that contracts with administrative bodies should not carry the same legal consequences as those with private corporations. However, the decision to outsource the administration of workfare schemes to private providers—which, again, is frequently criticized by opponents—undermines this objection. If private providers run the schemes, assign responsibilities, are party to the action plans, and initiate sanctions, they are significantly distant from the public administration to undermine this reservation as well.

b. Common Law Tests

Where the contract's central purpose is to form and regulate a work relationship, common law tests are applied to determine if it is a 'contract of employment' (to establish employee status); 'any other contract whereby the individual undertakes to do or perform personally any work' etc (to establish worker status); or a commercial (eg consumer, client) contract, which has the effect of denying employment status. While the boundaries between worker status and employee status are notoriously vague and need not detain us here in detail, two things should be noted: first, the requirements to establish employee status are more onerous than worker status;[39] second, both require, at a minimum, that the work be performed *personally*—that is, individuals cannot use unapproved substitutes.

[35] *Talmon v The Netherlands* (1997) EHRLR 448; *Schuitemaker v The Netherlands* (2010) ECHR 820.

[36] *Brogan v San Mateo County*, 901 F.2d 762 (9th Cir 1990).

[37] *R (Reilly and Wilson) v Secretary of State for Work and Pensions* [2013] UKSC 68.

[38] Central Appeals Tribunal 8 February 2010, LJN BL 1093.

[39] Anne Davies, *Employment Law (Pearson 2015)*, suggests that the tests for worker status may be seen as a 'low-fat' version of the tests for employee status. But cf *Cotswold Developments v Williams* [2006] IRLR 181 and then *Clyde & Co v Bates van Winkelhof [2014] UKSC 32*, in which Lady Hale questions whether 'mutuality of obligations', which needs to be present for employee status, is required at all where worker status is claimed.

With regard to 'employee' status, the irreducible minimum required for a contract of employment is personal service, a sufficient level of control exercised by the employer, and mutuality of obligation between the parties that relates to an obligation upon the employer to provide work and a duty upon the employee to accept and perform that work in return for a wage.[40] The courts will also consider whether there are any other factors indicative of a contract of employment, such as whether an individual is integrated into the business, and will consider factors such as adherence to uniform policies or the provision of equipment.

Given the centrality of personal service to both employee and worker status, it is appropriate to begin with the *personal nature of the relationship*. While this requirement has generated considerable debate in tribunals and courts in a number of interesting cases,[41] they are of less relevance here. This is because the extent to which the work needs to be performed personally by the individual or, conversely, the extent to which the individual can appoint a substitute[42] is completely theoretical in the case of these schemes. It is quite clear, in other words, that participants need to take part in the schemes themselves, and the personal nature of the requirement could not be clearer. In relation to workfare, for example, the personal completion of the activities is central to accessing individual benefits; hence, personal service is satisfied. Similarly, in the case of labour within immigration detention, detainees are given a written job description that requires them to provide their own services with no further details on the issue of substitution.[43]

The personal nature of the relationship is closely related to a second test: that of control. As Mark Freedland notes, the requirement that the contract establish a personal relationship also works to identify what the *character* of the personal relation between the employee and the employer or employing enterprise must be, stipulating that this relationship must be one of personal subordination of the employee to some kind of control exercised by the employer over the work and, indeed, the working life of the employee.[44] Again, there is little point here in delving into the exact nature of the 'subordination' or 'dependence' that the requirement for control exacts on the individual.[45]

[40] *Ready Mixed Concrete v Minister of Pensions* [1968] 2 QB 497; *Autoclenz* (n 7).

[41] *Autoclenz* (n 7); *Aslam v Uber BV* [2017] IRLR 4; *Pimlico Plumbers v Smith* [2018] UKSC 29.

[42] *Ready Mixed Concrete* (n 40); *Express & Echo v Tanton* [1999] ICR 693.

[43] *Express and Echo Publications* (n 42).

[44] Mark Freedland, 'The Legal Structure of the Contract of Employment' in Mark Freedland and others (eds), *The Contract of Employment* (OUP 2016) 28, 32.

[45] Paul Davies and Mark Freedland, *Kahn-Freund's Labour and the Law* (3rd edn, Stevens 1983) 18; Hugh Collins, 'Is the Contract of Employment Illiberal' in Hugh Collins, Gillian Lester, and Virginia Mantouvalou (eds), *Philosophical Foundations of Labour Law* (OUP 2018); John Gardner, 'The Contractualisation of Labour Law' in Collins, Lester, and Mantouvalou, ibid 33; Noah Zatz and Eileen

Studies of the realities of WPs, prison workers, and interns (graduate students and university athletes) in the United States suggest that the degree of control that supervisors have over the lives of participants in the scheme is so extensive that some have compared it to slavery.[46] While such comparisons in contemporary discourse may be rhetorically exaggerated,[47] Hatton documents the harsh reality in which supervisors control not only the 'the power of deciding the thing to be done, the way in which it shall be done, the means to be employed in doing it, the time when and the place where it shall be done'[48] but also matters well beyond the realm of their labour.

In the United Kingdom, even a cursory look at DWP Provider Guidance for the Community Work Programme suggests that WPs sign a contract under which they are required to work, obey orders (as relayed to them by the provider and by the placement employer), and are acutely dependent on performing their duties for their livelihood. Indeed, the Guidance notes that 'work placements must be supervised, with tasks similar to those that a claimant might experience in a normal working environment'.[49] And when instructing the participant, the Guidance states that a participant must 'meet the same standards of behaviour expected of anyone working for the organisation that provides your work placement'.[50] The power to determine whether non-compliance was present, the discretion to sanction for non-compliance, and the effects of the sanction on participants' lives are all unparalleled in the mainstream labour market.[51] In the case of prisoners, the refusal to work or to not work 'properly' is considered an 'offence against discipline',[52] which carries with it consequences including exclusion from work for no more than twenty-one days, deductions or stoppage from earnings, cellular confinement for no more than fourteen days, or an increase in sentencing of no more than forty-two days, among other punishments.[53] These sanctions evoke the traditional master–servant relationship in which punitive responses are imposed for failure to comply with an employer's directions.[54] Similarly, documentation

Boris, 'Seeing Work, Envisioning Citizenship' (2014) 18 Employee Rights and Employment Policy Journal 95, 100–01.

[46] Erin Hatton, *Coerced: Work under Threat of Punishment* (University of California Press 2020); Zatz, 'Working at the Boundaries of the Market' (n 10); Noah Zatz, 'The Impossibility of Work Law' in Guy Davidov and Brian Langille (eds), *The Idea of Labour Law* (OUP 2011) 234, 236.

[47] Amir Paz-Fuchs, 'Badges of Modern Slavery' (2016) 79 Modern Law Review 757.

[48] *Ready Mixed Concrete* (n 40) [515] (Mackenna J).

[49] DWP, 'Community Work Placements: DWP Provider Guidance' (Annex 1, May 2014).

[50] ibid Annex 2.

[51] Hatton (n 46) ch 2.

[52] See the Prison Rules 1999 (SI 1999/728) Rule 1.

[53] ibid Rule 55.

[54] *Ready Mixed Concrete* (n 40).

from Morton Hall Immigration Removal Centre contains information on the consequences of 'sub-standard performance' that can result in the detainees' removal from paid activity. Where necessary, detainees will also be provided with training such as hygiene certificates to perform their roles. With regards to our case studies then, it is clear that the element of control is easily fulfilled.

The final element, 'mutuality of obligation', concerns the reciprocal duty to provide and accept work.[55] This test has gained prominence (and notoriety) within British labour law, with courts often repeating the dictum that 'some irreducible element of mutuality of obligation' is required to establish a contract of employment, and thus, in its absence, no contract of employment could be recognized.[56] In the case of labour within immigration detention, the timetables provided at The Verne Immigration Removal Centre suggest that mutuality of obligation exists as detainees are provided with thirty hours of work each week and must notify the centre of any 'acceptable' absences for which sickness pay will be granted.[57] There is, therefore, an assumption that the work will be provided and performed, satisfying the requirement of mutuality. Again, debates around continuity of work—whether mandated by the employer, requested by the worker, or driven by external forces (eg seasonal work)[58]—are largely irrelevant in the context of these tightly controlled schemes.

The final aspect to consider is the 'business reality' test, concerning the allocation of risk—economic or other—and is similarly unproblematic in the context of our case studies. Here, we ask whether the putative worker can hire others, provides their own equipment or materials, and covers their sickness pay, holiday pay, and taxes.[59] This test is understood to be governed by a rationale of risk because it suggests that by entering a contract of employment, the employee accepts the employer's control (and to their own subordination) as a price for security with respect to job retention and income.[60] Although the application of this test to the relevant schemes is not straightforward, it is

[55] Nicola Countouris, 'Uses and Misuses of Mutuality of Obligations' in Alan Bogg and others (eds), *The Autonomy of Labour Law* (Hart Publishing 2015) 169; Nicola Countouris, 'The Contract of Employment as an Expression of Continuous Obligations' in Freedland and others, *The Contract of Employment* (n 44) 362.

[56] *Clark v Oxfordshire Health Authority* [1997] EWCA Civ 3035, [1998] IRLR 125; *O'Kelly v Trusthouse Forte plc* [1984] QB 90 (CA); *Stringfellow Restaurants Ltd v Quashie* [2012] EWCA Civ 1735, [2013] IRLR 99 [12].

[57] *O'Kelly* (n 56).

[58] Countouris (n 55) 377–79 and references therein.

[59] Brendan Burchell, Simon Deakin, and Sheila Honey, 'The Employment Status of Individuals in Non-Standard Employment' (Department of Trade and Industry1999).

[60] Simon Deakin, 'Interpreting Employment Contracts: Judges, Employers, Workers' [2004] International International Journal of Comparative Labour Law and Industrial Relations 201, 208.

evident that the participants are far removed from any suggestion of operating a business of their own while engaged in these schemes.

In summary, the common law tests provide strong grounds for recognizing participants in these schemes as employees and, at the very least, workers. We now turn to the principal objections to this conclusion. These are drawn from policy documents, statutory instruments, parliamentary debates, and the common law. These objections include, first, the argument that because it is the participant (rather than the employing entity) who benefits from the scheme, the participant should not be granted employment status; and second, that participants are awarded benefits from the government, not wages from an employer. We turn to each of these issues now.

3. Demystifying 'Work': Challenging the Justifications for Exclusion

a. Work 'for Their Own Good'

This argument suggests that if the intern, prisoner, detainee, or welfare claimant benefits from the scheme while the business does not, this alone suffices to negate employment status. British courts typically frame this test as part of the inquiry into the 'type' of contract established; that is, assuming a contract exists between the parties, is it a contract for personal work or for education or training? The seminal case in this regard, *Daley v Allied Suppliers*,[61] resides, interestingly, in the grey area between back-to-work programmes and business-driven internship schemes. In *Daley*, the scheme was administered by the Manpower Services Commission under the Youth Opportunities Programme (YOP). While the claimant was not required to take part in the scheme as a condition of the receipt of benefits, the involvement of the state agencies was far more extensive than in the laissez-faire cases of open-market internships. The Employment Appeal Tribunal (EAT) held that a trainee under the YOP could not proceed in her claim for race discrimination since, even if there was a contract, it was one for training and not a contract of employment. According to the EAT, the key distinction lies in whether the primary purpose of the scheme is to benefit the participant or the employer. At the time, Mark Freedland argued that the administrative YOP and the judicial decisions

[61] [1983] IRLR 14; see reference to *Daley* in eg *Whittaker v Sherdley Hall Garages Ltd* [1994] UKEAT 569-93-2403.

that governed it created 'a kind of second-class employment citizenship in which the young people concerned engage in work for employers without the benefit of the structure of employment protection legislation which applies to other workers'.[62] Similar concerns were later expressed regarding the 1988 Employment Training Scheme.[63]

The reasoning in *Daley* was subsequently followed in the Court of Appeal's decision in *Edmunds*, already noted, according to which the pupillage did not require the pupil 'to do anything not conducive to the pupil's own training and development'.[64] In *Wiltshire Police Authority v Wynn*,[65] a police cadetship was held to be educational rather than economic, despite the fact that the individual carried out what amounted to over forty hours of service each week, involving four days of police work and one day of physical and legal training. Dunn LJ observed that 'the fact that the conditions of engagement are consistent with a contract of service is not decisive if the principal object of the relationship is teaching and learning'.[66] More recently, the Employment Tribunal explicitly embraced the 'primary beneficiary test', stating that a British cyclist was not to be perceived as employed by the British Cycling Federation since the relationship should not be considered one of employment 'where the purpose is training for the benefit of the trainee'.[67] We may also quickly note that this logic has 'spilled over' to the jurisprudence concerning prison labour. In a recent case, the Employment Tribunal noted that 'The purpose of the work was rehabilitative, not commercial'.[68] Interestingly, however, the Employment Tribunal added, 'I accept that in *Cox* . . . that was a material factor in the Supreme Court, and therefore binding on this tribunal. I am cautious about this element, as intent and motivation may be difficult factors in many employment relationships'.[69] The scepticism, we suggest, is warranted, not merely for evidentiary reasons.

Determining whether the contract is one of service or training/education often turns on identifying the primary beneficiary by stating that the participant (or worker) is the person who benefits from the scheme whereas the employing entity does not. In other words, the focus of the test becomes *cui bono*—'Who is the (primary) beneficiary?'[70] The implication is that, unlike a

[62] Mark Freedland, 'Labour Law and Leaflet Law: The Youth Training Scheme of 1983' (1983) 12 International Law Journal 220, 230.
[63] Nick Wikeley, 'Training for Employment in the 1990s' (1990) 53 Modern Law Review 354, 365–66.
[64] *Edmunds* (n 23) [33].
[65] [1981] QB 95.
[66] *Wiltshire Policy Authority v Wynn* [1980] ICR 649, 661.
[67] Case 2404219/2017 *Varnish v British Cycling Federation* (2019) [245].
[68] *Pimm* (n 16) [51].
[69] ibid, referring to *Cox* (n 13).
[70] *Walling v Portland Terminal* 330 US 148 (1947).

traditional employment relationship, it is only, or primarily, the worker who reaps the benefit of the relationship rather than the putative employer.

The source of this doctrine is found in a decision by the US Supreme Court in the context of internships. In this case, *Walling v Portland Terminal Co*,[71] individuals who received a week-long training for a brakeman position were not entitled to minimum wage or maximum hour protection under the Fair Labor Standards Act 1938 (FLSA). The Court's rationale was that the railroad company received no 'immediate advantage' from the work performed by the trainees, whereas the latter were receiving free training for their own benefit.[72] The Court accepted that, all else being equal, the trainees would qualify for employee status but held that the term 'to employ' in the FLSA was 'not intended to stamp all persons as employees who, without any express or implied compensation agreement, might work *for their own advantage* on the premises of another'.[73] The *Walling* decision, and the 'primary beneficiary' test at its core, have remained influential not just in case law.[74] In 2010, its principles were 'codified' through a six-prong test by the American Department of Labor.[75] Moreover, in recent years, the US courts have taken an even more flexible (pro-employer) approach, not requiring an internship to be tailored to benefit the participant; and not insisting that there be 'no immediate benefit' for the employer (in other words, some benefit to the employer would not negate the conclusion that the contract is still one that has training at its core).[76]

Our interrogation of this argument as one that negates employment status is two-fold: first, normatively, we question whether this test has any place in denying employment status where other tests suggest that an employment relationship exists. Second, factually, we would argue that if, for the sake of argument, such a test is deemed relevant, it is actually satisfied in our case studies.

First, then, one may question whether this dichotomy between benefits for the company (= work) and activities for the benefit of the worker (= not work) holds in general. Paul Budd offers the example of Jake, who is hired (in his example, as an unpaid intern) by a record label to perform administrative duties. He doesn't gain much from his role (making coffee and organizing files) but is

[71] ibid.
[72] ibid 152–53.
[73] ibid 152 (emphasis added).
[74] James Brudney, 'Square Pegs and Round Holes: Shrinking Protections for Unpaid Interns under the Fair Labor Standards Act in Stewart' in Andrew Stewart and others, *Internships, Employability and the Search for Decent Work Experience* (Elgar 2021) 163.
[75] Department of Labor, Wage and Hour Division, 'Fact Sheet #71: Internship Programs under the Fair Labor Standards Act' (April 2010).
[76] *Glatt v Searchlight Pictures* 811 F.3d 528 (2nd Cir 2016); *Wang v Hearst Corp* 877 F.3d 69 (2nd Cir 2017).

overjoyed by his weekly, five-minute encounters with Mick Jagger, when the latter comes into the office for his daily meetings.[77] Would that be a sufficient 'benefit' to Jake to remove him from the scope of employment law protection? We can offer an additional example: Daniel, straight out of law school, was hired as lawyer in a major law firm and is trying his best to cope with the magnitude of the work. Unfortunately, Daniel is simply overwhelmed and is, frankly, a poor employee. However, at the end of the first year, he has gained numerous skills, some general (punctuality, proofreading, writing, and research); some related to the sector (eg operating a case management system, attracting and retaining clients); and some related to the particular firm. The firm may decide to discontinue his employment, but would it be reasonable to say that, because he benefited from the work more than the firm, he should be seen as a trainee and be denied employment rights? Such a conclusion would seem far-fetched. More generally, to drive the point home, we can turn to the position of the business sector during congressional hearings prior to the enactment of the FLSA in 1937. Mr Lane, an industry executive, expressed the concern that workers who start off in the furniture business would be paid as much as a seasoned worker, since the 'average beginner . . . is, for the first 3 months, . . . an expense rather than an asset; then the next 3 months he might be worth the room he is taking up, part of which we are paying him, and then after that he becomes valuable to us'.[78] Would that mean that, for the first three to six months, such workers should be viewed as trainees, denied the right to a minimum wage and related rights?

Moreover, does the paradigm of reciprocity continue? In other words, when the employee becomes more proficient, and the employer is able to charge a higher rate of billable hours for the employee's work, should the employee receive compensation that correlates with that increase? It is, after all, quite common that the billable hours are higher than the hourly wages by a factor of over 100. This, one should clarify, is not a Marxist negation of the fairness of the compensation structure. It is, however, a rebuttal of the premise according to which one's compensation should, at any given time, be commensurate to the benefit derived from one's work. The consequences of this type of logic are present in a US case, *McLaughlin*,[79] in which the majority accepted the claim that the men who had to undertake a week of 'exposure to tasks' were entitled

[77] Paul Budd, 'All Work and No Pay: Establishing the Standard for When Legal, Unpaid Internships Become Illegal, Unpaid Labor Comment' (2014) 63 University of Kansas Law Review 451, 478.
[78] Fair Labor Standards Act of 1937: Joint Hearings on S 2475 and HR 7200 before the S Comm on Education & Labor and the HR Comm on Labor, 75th Congress 481 (1937).
[79] *McLaughlin v Ensley*, 877 F.2d 1207, 1209 (4th Cir 1989).

to the minimum wage. During that week, they worked between fifty and sixty hours of labour, loading and delivering food and stockpiling vending machines. It was clear from the evidence that they learned very little and, in essence, performed manual labour, relieving other drivers from work. All routemen who took part in the 'orientation' were then 'hired' as drivers. And yet, the minority judge in the case still sought to deny the claim, reasoning that the fact that the participants learned skills that had 'practically no transferable usefulness' was 'of little significance'.[80] It was enough that they 'learned to interact with store managers' and 'complete some of the paperwork'. This vividly illustrates how far a judge may go to identify a 'benefit' sufficient to deny access to basic rights.

It is thus our strong assertion that this test of *cui bono* has no analytical or normative grounding and should not serve as a further obstacle for employment status. As the EAT noted, unequivocally,

> The regulations do not require *nor even permit* a calculation of whether, having regard to the time and any money expended on the trainee on the one hand, and the time of experienced and paid staff saved on the other, the business makes a profit out of the trainee or not.[81]

That said, even if, *arguendo*, the test of 'who benefits' is applied to our case studies, an objective assessment would find that it is satisfied.

Prisoners' exclusion from employment status is, somewhat ironically, grounded in the 'rehabilitative rather than pecuniary' interests[82] said to 'define its non-economic status'. Prison labour is therefore not legally considered to be work at all, even when undertaken for private-sector employers.[83] Notably, in *Cox*, Lord Reed rejected the Ministry of Justice's argument that 'the relationship between the prison service and prisoners working in a prison is fundamentally different from that between a private employer and its employees' insofar as it rests on the idea that the purpose of prison work was not to advance the business, enterprise, or profits of the prison but rather to support rehabilitation and act in the public interest. Conversely, Lord Reed confirmed that

> Rehabilitation is, however, not its only objective: it has also been an aim of penal policy since at least the nineteenth century to ensure, as it was put in a

[80] ibid.
[81] *HM Revenue and Customs v Rinaldi-Tranter* [2007] UKEAT 0486-06-1309 (13 September 2007).
[82] Zatz (n 10).
[83] Jenna Pandeli, Michael Marinetto, and Jean Jenkins, 'Captive in Cycles of Invisibility? Prisoners' Work for the Private Sector' (2019) 33 Work, Employment and Society 596.

> 1991 White Paper, 'that convicted prisoners contribute to the cost of their upkeep by helping with the running and maintenance of the prison and by providing goods and services in prison industries and on prison farms' . . . More importantly, when prisoners work in the prison kitchen, or in other workplaces such as the gardens or the laundry, they are integrated into the operation of the prison. The activities assigned to them are not merely of benefit to themselves: a benefit which is, moreover, merely potential and indirect. Their activities form part of the operation of the prison, and are of direct and immediate benefit to the prison service itself.[84]

As outlined in Chapter 2, many prison workers question the genuinely rehabilitative nature of prison work, finding it mundane, monotonous, and lacking in opportunities for skills development or promoting job prospects on release.[85] This perspective militates against the classic argument concerning the benefit of the labour being for the worker's 'own good' as opposed to that of the employing entity.

The status of immigration detainees working in removal centres has been challenged in two cases: *Badmus*[86] and *Morita*.[87] In both, the central purpose of paid activities was asserted to be 'for the relief of boredom', drawing on Rule 17 of the Immigration Rules 2001. The government also claims that paid activities offer detainees the opportunity to earn money prior to departure from the United Kingdom and that some types of activities require training and certification (eg in food hygiene), which detainees can use in their home countries. Yet, research shows that a significant proportion of immigration detainees are not deported to their home countries but rather are released back into the United Kingdom, where they are faced with restrictions on working, unable to legally utilize the employable 'skills' acquired during detention.

However dubiously such 'benefits' are measured, it is evident that detainees are not the sole beneficiaries of the work performed. Indeed, evidence shows that immigration detainees may perform 'literally tens of thousands of hours' undertaking work over the course of a year and that, in 2016, nearly 55,000 hours' worth of cleaning were recorded as as performed by detainees at Harmondsworth Immigration Retention Centre. In *Morita*, Mr Justice Murray noted that 'a person undertaking the activities described in paragraph 17 of

[84] Cox (n 13) [34] (references omitted).
[85] Pandeli, Marinetto, and Jenkins (n 83).
[86] *R (on the application of Badmus) v Secretary of State for the Home Department* [2020] EWCA Civ 657.
[87] *Morita* (n 18).

the Pay Review Report outside an IRC would be unlikely to undertake such work without payment, unless it was being done for personal, family or charitable purposes', which again militates against the government's assertion that the work is carried out for the benefit of the recipients.[88] In reality, without payment, the supposed 'benefits' would be insufficient to the carrying out of the work. Evidence submitted as part of the government's pay review consultation also indicated that at least two detention centres reported that they benefited from the work undertaken by detainees.[89] It is clear, then, that there are multiple beneficiaries from the performance of both prison work and labour within immigration detention, which also applies across workfare and internships.

In terms of workfare, the contention that these programmes do not benefit the end users similarly flies in the face of the evidence. In the United Kingdom, an FoI request by Boycott Workfare revealed that local councils benefited from over half a million hours of unpaid labour through back-to-work schemes in areas such as cleaning and waste collection, library services, and the parks department. The councils denied that the placements were used to replace members of staff, despite the fact that jobs were lost during the same time frame.[90] Similarly, in the Netherlands, employers were accused of using WPs for activities to replace paid employees, whose roles were subsequently phased out.[91] In one analogous case (work programmes for homeless people in New York), Judge Sotomayor (as she was then) found that participants substituted for staff who were late or absent and were even required to work overtime or back-to-back shifts.[92] The court also noted that that the programme was 'particularly lucrative' for the council, generating revenue of $840,000 a year.[93] The court concluded that the FLSA and the duty to pay minimum wage applies to the programme participants.

With regard to internships, the beneficiary test was decisive in the case of *Rinaldi-Tranter*,[94] in which the EAT overturned a negative ruling, instead finding that a trainee hairdresser working under a national traineeship was a worker for the purposes of the National Minimum Wage Act. Whereas the ET

[88] ibid.

[89] *Badmus* (n 86).

[90] Shiv Malik, 'UK Councils Found to Benefit from Half a Million Hours of Unpaid Labour' *The Guardian* (London, 3 January 2014) <www.theguardian.com/politics/2014/jan/02/councils-benefit-half-a-million-hours-unpaid-labour-foi-request> accessed 12 November 2025.

[91] FNV, *Werken in de Bijstand. Allesbehalve Gewoon Goed Werk* (2012); FNV, *Beter Zicht op Werken. Vervolg op het FNV Zwartboek 'Werken in de Bijstand'* (2013).

[92] *Archie v Grand Central Partnership*, 997 F Supp 504 (1998).

[93] ibid [138].

[94] *Rinaldi-Tranter* (n 81).

found that Miss Fuicher was given 'mundane tasks to perform . . . to keep her occupied rather than to benefit the business' and that 'she made little or no financial contribution to the business and that almost all of the benefit was to herself',[95] the EAT rejected the assertion that the mundane nature of the tasks are a matter for concern for the tribunal. Instead, it noted that 'it is obvious that having the sweeping up and the washing of customers' hair done by a trainee saved the experienced staff some time'.[96]

The question of 'benefit' also goes beyond the avoidance of payment of wages for employers. Even as an extensive and inexpensive 'graduate recruitment scheme' and training programme, it seems quite clear that internships are a cost-saving mechanism for businesses, avoiding the alternative route of 'taking a risk' with a prospective employee only to find later that they are unsuitable (an incentive that has become prominent in recent years[97]); or training the employee at the business's expense to gain the skills and competence that will enable them to secure the maximum profit for the business. To clarify: if internships serve increasingly as screening mechanisms, one might argue that both parties benefit—the employer finds suitable workers, and the trainee gains a route into employment.

However, the numbers do not necessarily support even that equanimous conclusion: whereas 76 per cent of employers report that they enjoy using traineeships to screen for potential new talent, 83 per cent of trainees reported that the internship did not lead to a job in their preferred sector.[98] In addition, a report based on a survey of over 1,000 employers and over 2,600 interns[99] suggests that either employers seem to benefit more than interns from internships or, at the very least, that there is a strong element of subjectivity to the assessment of 'benefit'. First, 70 per cent of employers responded that interns did 'useful work' in the business.[100] More notably, the survey asked both

[95] ibid [9], citing the ET decision [52].

[96] ibid [16].

[97] ibid 125; Carys Roberts, *The Inbetweeners: The New Role of Internships in the Graduate Labour Market* (Institute for Public Policy Research (IPPR), April 2017) 17, 19 <https://ippr-org.files.svdcdn.com/production/Downloads/inbetweeners-the-new-role-of-internships_Apr2017.pdf> accessed 13 November 2025; cf *Reich v Parker Fire Protection Dist*, 992 F.2d 1023, 1028 (10th Cir 1993): 'although we agree that defendant derived an ultimate advantage by creating a pool of prospective employees trained in its operations, this is the intended result of any employer sponsored training program'; and similarly *Donovan v American Airlines* 686 F.2d 267, 271 (5th Cir 1982), where this advantage was acknowledged but viewed as not sufficiently determinative to sway the balance in the claimants' favour.

[98] European Commission, *Study on a Comprehensive Overview on Trainee Arrangements in Member States: Final Synthesis Review* (Institute for Employment Studies 2012) 125–26.

[99] Carl Cullinane and Rebecca Montacute, 'Pay as You Go: Internship Pay, Quality and Access in the Graduate Jobs Market' (The Sutton Trust, November 2018) <www.suttontrust.com/wp-content/uploads/2019/12/Pay-As-You-Go-1.pdf> accessed 13 November 2025.

[100] ibid 41–42.

employers and interns to assess the quality and outcome of internships based on five indicators set by the Living Wage Foundation. The criteria were adequate training and monitoring, on-the-job rotation, a designated mentor or supervisor, a workplace learning plan, and a post-internship follow-up. The discrepancies in assessment were striking: while 25 per cent of interns viewed their internships as exhibiting *none* of the indicators, the comparable figure was 8 per cent for employers. And while 18 per cent of employers viewed their internships as meeting *all* of the criteria, a mere 2 per cent of interns felt the same way.[101] These results are not altogether surprising. Even with respect to workfare schemes, which are, in general, more heavily regulated, quality assurance supervision is minimal as it is assumed that 'excessive monitoring would put employers off',[102] a nod to the neoliberal paradigm that will be discussed at length in Chapter 6. Against this backdrop, it is unsurprising that open-market internships provide even less in terms of monitoring or quality assurance, and the United Kingdom is a 'particularly interesting' case for its 'voluntaristic quality assurance approach',[103] which includes no formal process or regulation and, instead, a proliferation of quality assurance frameworks and charters.[104]

These negative findings are echoed in research on internship outcomes, which suggests that unpaid internships may not only fail to help but also may actively harm employment prospects.[105] The above report cites findings which indicate that completing an unpaid internship is 'associated with a salary penalty three years later'; while another survey points to very moderate gains for those who took one unpaid internship and, indeed, that those who did more than three unpaid internships ended up with salaries lower than those who did no internships at all.[106] Similar figures are found in other jurisdictions. Thus, the American National Association of Colleges and Employers (NACE) has found that, over a three-year period, 63 per cent of students with a paid internship received at least one job offer, while only 37 per cent of those who took unpaid internships were in the same position, a negligible 1.8 per cent more

[101] ibid.
[102] European Commission (n 98) 104.
[103] ibid.
[104] Gateways to the Profession Collaborative Forum, 'Common Best Practice Code for High-Quality Internships' (Trades Union Congress (TUC), updated 16 May 2024) <https://assets.publishing.service.gov.uk/government/uploads/system/uploads/attachment_data/file/251483/bis-13-1085-best-practice-code-high-quality-internships.pdf> accessed 22 November 2025; Chartered Institute of Personnel and Development (CIPD), 'Internships That Work: A Guide to Employers' (2013) <www.cipd.org/uk/knowledge/guides/internships-guide> accessed 22 November 2025.
[105] Paula McDonald, 'Open Market Internships: What Do Intermediaries Offer?' (2020) 33 Journal of Education and Work 33.
[106] Cullinane and Monticute (n 99) 44.

than those who did not intern at all. And, again, those who performed unpaid internships received *less* pay than those with no internship experience.[107]

Based on the case law outlined within this chapter, it is clear that very little empirical evidence is provided to demonstrate that participants (ie workers) are the 'primary beneficiaries' of the work performed or that their benefit outweighs the benefits afforded to the businesses or public agencies employing them. Instead, we argue that the courts and government simply *assume* that participants benefit far more. The histories of labour exclusion from recognition as 'market work' and thus the wage, explored at the end of this chapter, demonstrate that work exclusions remain bound and central to the functioning of capital despite categorization of this labour as 'non-productive'. The mystification of the work's underlying 'purpose' thereby fosters a legal and social imaginary that conceals the nature of the work undertaken, its value, and the underlying structural compulsions that guide it.

b. Wages (Not Benefits)

A further objection to extending employment protection to participants stems from the foundational premise that the employment relationship, at its core, a *wage*–work bargain. In the workfare context, however, wages are 'replaced' by benefits.

In *Thorpe v Dul*,[108] the EAT held that the contract was one of employment, not apprenticeship, emphasizing that wages were paid directly by the employer and not subsidized by the local council or college. In one US case, a Federal Court of Appeal denied employee status to WPs, inter alia, because 'participants receive their financial assistance checks through the Public Assistance Case Management Information System, not from the state payroll'.[109] It is worth noting that one of the claimants participated in the programme for 10 months, driving a van for the local council for 750 hours, and received $2,765 in benefits.[110] The other claimant worked 413 hours over 3 months, performing maintenance work for a city corporation before falling from a ladder and sustaining injuries that rendered him unable to work.[111] In another case, the New York

[107] Jordan Weissmann, 'Do Unpaid Internships Lead to Jobs? Not for College Students' (*The Atlantic*, 19 June 2013) <www.theatlantic.com/business/archive/2013/06/do-unpaid-internships-lead-to-jobs-not-for-college-students/276959> accessed 13 November 2025.

[108] UKEAT/0041/04 (2004).

[109] *Johns v Stewart* 57 F.3d 1544, 1558 (10th Cir 1995).

[110] ibid 1550.

[111] ibid 1551.

Court of Appeals rejected a claim by WPs who argued that their hours should be determined by dividing their benefits by the prevailing wage, which is the rate guaranteed to employees under the New York State Constitution.[112] The Court explained that, under the Constitution,

> workers protected in this special way are those in the employ of 'contractors or subcontractors' who are also engaged in the performance of 'public work' (NY Const, art I, § 17). There is a manifest reason for this set of prerequisites: the private employer-contractors actually pay the prevailing wage to the employees, not some municipal entity that may ultimately own or acquire the 'public work' . . . These agencies and entities simply do not pay a salary to the Program participants—one of the fundamental requisites that sparks the prevailing wage entitlement.[113]

In an extreme case, illustrated by *Flett v Matheson*,[114] the Court of Appeal found that the very flaw for which the remedy was sought could itself be evidence of the relationship, with LJ Pill stating that 'If . . . the appellant was receiving less than the national minimum wage, it points to the agreement being one of apprenticeship.'[115] Similarly, in *Edmunds v Lawson*, the Court of Appeal opined, 'the fact that the generality of barrister pupils have been unpaid, not just in the distant past but also in modern times, is in our view of significance in determining whether a relationship of or equivalent to apprenticeship exists.'[116] This reasoning is, with respect, blatantly flawed as its logic would ossify and immunize any unlawful and immoral practice merely because 'it has always been thus.'

Arguably, however, a more serious concern relates to the identity of the payor. In other words, should the fact that a public agency pays, for example through welfare payments, for work done in service of a private entity, be relevant when assessing whether an employment relationship exists? Not according to the Court of Justice of the European Union (CJEU), which held,

[112] *Brukhman v Giuliani* 94 NY 2nd 387 (2000).
[113] ibid 394, 396.
[114] [2006] IRLR 281.
[115] ibid 282. A similar logic was employed by a US court in *Klaips v Bergland*, 715 F.2d 477 (10th Cir 1983), concluding that

> although WEAT participants may perform the same functions as regular employees at some of the projects to which they are assigned, they differ from state employees in that they do not receive the same salary, safe working conditions, job security, career development, Social Security, pension rights, collective bargaining, or grievance procedures as do the actual employee.

[116] *Edmunds* (n 23) [34].

in *Birden*, that 'the fact that the remuneration of the person concerned is provided using public funds' cannot 'have any consequence in regard to whether or not that person is to be regarded as a worker'.[117] In that case, the applicant took part in a scheme involving a job sponsored by the state (Germany), and so paid for with public funds, with the intention of enabling him to enter or re-enter the labour market; in short, a situation not dissimilar to that of WPs. The CJEU held (not for the first time) that neither the individual's level of productivity, nor the origin of the remuneration (eg subsidies from public funds), nor the limited amount of the remuneration has any bearing on whether or not the person qualifies as a 'worker' for the purposes of Community law.[118] In 2013, the UK Supreme Court (UKSC) in *O'Brien* endorsed the CJEU's guidance that the 'spirit and purpose' of the relevant directive is to distinguish between the category of 'worker' and that of the self-employed.[119] Hence, provided that public allowances are deemed remuneration (subsidized by a public fund), WPs would fall within the scope of the European Union (EU) directives. While the case did not involve WPs, the Court emphasized that while national law determines whether a person qualifies for statutory protection, it 'may not remove at will, in violation of the effectiveness of a Directive, categories of workers from protection'.[120]

4. The Exclusionary History of 'Worker'

'Work', in its broadest sense, refers to a transfer of energy to achieve a purpose or result—a form of productive activity regardless of its social context. This understanding is broadly reflected within the English language and dictionary definitions of the term, which involves mental or physical effort done in order to achieve a purpose or result. Yet, as Judy Fudge notes, the concept of work has permeable and shifting boundaries contingent on the era in which it is located, the place in which it is undertaken, and its intertwinement with other social relations such as gender, race, class, ethnicity, age, and immigration status.[121] For example, Richard Donkin notes that the Yir Yoront tribe of Aborigines who

[117] *Case C-1/97 Mehmet Birden v. Stadtgemeinde Bremen, [1998] ECR I-7747.*
[118] Case 53/81 *Levin* [1982] ECR 1035; Case 344/87 *Bettray* [1989] ECR 1621; Case C-188/00 *Kurz* [2002] ECR I-10691 [32]; Case C-456/02 *Trojani v CPAS* [2004] ECR I-7573.
[119] *Ministry of Justice v O'Brien* [2013] UKSC 6 [39].
[120] ibid [30].
[121] Judy Fudge, 'Feminist Reflections on the Scope of Labour Law: Domestic Work, Social Reproduction, and Jurisdiction' (2014) 22 Feminist Legal Studies 1, 4. See also Judy Fudge, Shae McCrystal, and Kamala Sankaran, *Challenging the Legal Boundaries of Work Regulation* (Hart Publishing 2012).

live in Northern Australia have a word—'*woq*'—that is used to refer to tasks and chores but does not include hunting. The reason is that *woq* in this society referred to something that they would rather not be doing.[122]

Historical events have thus impacted our perception of what constitutes work, which can be seen through examination of the transition from feudal to capitalist society and the transformation of the status of socially reproductive work which, during feudal times, was considered vital to the household economy. Yet, under the present institutionalized capitalist social order,[123] socially reproductive labour is considered to have little economic value as 'non-market' work, unworthy of a wage. The normative value underlying the market/non-market distinction as justification for not paying a wage can thus be linked both historically and materially to the gendered and racialized social division of labour that emerged with capitalism. The following subsection briefly sketches out these histories, drawing from feminist and post-colonial theory to deconstruct the assumptions that underpin the market/non-market distinction and the construction of wage labour as a distinct legal and economic category.

a. Work: A Divisive History

Discussion of the formalization of work and the wage must return to the origins of capitalism to track the exclusions on which this economic order—*capitalism*—was created. Before doing so, however, it is important to conceptualize what we mean by the term. In line with Marx's theory of capital, we understand the four defining features of capitalism to be (1) the private ownership of the means of production and class division between the owners and producers; (2) the institution of a labour market that is ostensibly 'free' in the legal sense that the workers are not enslaved, enserfed, or entailed; (3) that capital accumulation aims to expand capital and profit rather than satisfy any human needs; and finally, (4) that capitalism uses markets to determine how the society's social surplus will be allocated and seeks to allocate the major inputs back into commodity production.[124] From a critical perspective, capitalism is conceptualized as an institutionalized social order on account of the background structures upon which it relies for functioning, including those

[122] Richard Donkin, *The History of Work* (Palgrave Macmillan 2010) 3–4.

[123] Nancy Fraser, 'Behind Marx's Hidden Abode' [2014] New Left Review 55.

[124] ibid. See also Nancy Fraser and Rahel Jaeggi, *Capitalism: A Conversation in Critical Theory* (Polity Press 2018).

from the social, natural, political, and legal realms. Accordingly, we acknowledge capitalism's history and structural overlap with imperialism, gender oppression, ecological degradation, and class segregation as opposed to defining it as a purely economic order.

The brief historical reflection set out below is not intended to be a detailed account of the transition from feudal to capitalist society but rather draws attention to the ways in which certain contributions were central to the creation and continued existence of capitalism yet were categorized as 'non-market' work on the grounds that they were not accepted as 'productive'. Acknowledging historical legal forms may thus 'provide an important foundation for broadening the base of labour law's hegemonic narrative',[125] which overlooks and thereby reinforces the exclusionary structures delineating valuable and non-valuable work.

Silvia Federici notes that war and land privatization characterized the beginning of capitalism and the immiseration of the working classes. Simultaneously with colonial expansion, land appropriation began in the late fifteenth century within Europe through evictions, rent increases, and heightened taxation, which created debt, forcing the sale of land.[126] In England, land privatization was most commonly achieved via 'enclosures'—associated with the expropriation of workers from the common land and thereby their wealth. In the sixteenth century, the term 'enclosure' was used to signify a set of strategies employed by lords and rich farmers to eliminate communal land and expand their holdings. Prior to the Reformation, over 2,000 rural villages were made extinct, and the enclosures continued into the eighteenth century. These acts were entirely legal as the peasants had no private property rights but rather rights deriving from tradition, which the state then abrogated through the creation of legal structures both encouraged by and benefiting the bourgeoisie.[127] As noted by Perelman,

> primitive accumulation cut through traditional lifeways like scissors. The first blade served to undermine the ability of people to provide for themselves. The other blade was a system of stern measures required to keep people from finding alternative survival strategies outside the system of wage labour. A host of oftentimes brutal laws designed to undermine whatever resistance people maintained against the demands of wage labour accompanied the

[125] Adelle Blackett, 'Emancipation in the Idea of Labour Law' in Davidov and Langille (n 46) 421.
[126] Silvia Federici, *Caliban and the Witch: Women, the Body and Primitive Accumulation* (Autonmedia 2004).
[127] Michael E Tigar and Madeleine R Levy, *Law and the Rise of Capitalism* (NYU Press 2000).

> dispossession of the peasants' rights, even before capitalism had become a significant economic force.[128]

Removal of access to the means of subsistence thereby forced individuals into wage labour, which further fragmented the cohesion of the rural population and deepened the differences between them. During the sixteenth and seventeenth centuries, merchant capitalists took advantage of the cheap and accessible labour force newly available in rural lands: 'As soon as they lost access to land, all workers were plunged into a dependence unknown in medieval times, as their landless condition gave employers the power to cut their pay and lengthen their working day.'[129] As Federici explains, the dominant work relations during the sixteenth to nineteenth centuries (as imposed by the capitalist ruling class) were slavery and other forms of coerced labour. The only restriction on this type of work was the fear of exhausting the workforce and the workers' resistance to it. Workers who attempted to hire themselves out independently or to leave their employment could be labelled 'criminal' and punished with incarceration or even death in some cases. This history is important for our case studies for three reasons. First, it charts the public's severance from the common land, which continues to propel individuals into exploitative forms of employment in their quest to provide for themselves. Second, it reveals the division of the working classes, which was instrumental in reducing wages and weakening the power of labour. In particular, characteristics such as criminality (linked to socio-economic status), gender, and race (soon to be explored) became convenient vehicles upon which to base these divisions. Third, and crucially, it exposes the foundational role played by the legal system—setting the groundwork for rights, responsibilities, and remedies (or lack thereof)—in constructing the power relations and dynamics within the labour market.

As we moved from a subsistence economy in which the aim of production was use, the unity of production and reproduction came to an end. The move to a market economy, whereby goods were produced for the market, signified the divide between market production, seen as a value-creating activity, and production for use and reproduction, which began to be considered valueless from an economic standpoint. As 'productive labour' moved out of the household and into the factories and mills, additional cleavages were established

[128] Michael Perelman, *The Invention of Capitalism: Classical Political Economy and the Secret History of Primitive Accumulation* (Duke UP 2000).

[129] Federici (n 126) 72.

between work and home, and a spatial construction of the 'work place' took hold, pushing women into the category of 'non-workers'.[130] This split is acknowledged within Marx's writings, which distinguish between 'work', referring to the production of things for use, involving some experience of hardship, and 'labour', which is associated with producing for sale on the market and generating surplus value. These concepts, and the market/non-market division, continue to justify the exclusion of certain workers from labour rights. For example, the context of incarceration is seen to remove prisoners from the market economy as here, 'the non-economic sphere is the prison not the family, but the conceptual underpinnings are identical'.[131]

As part of the devaluation of women's labour, women were subjected to an intense process of social degradation, losing ground in every sphere of social life. During this period, the jobs available to women were largely limited to lower-status roles, including domestic servants and farmhands—the assumption was that women should only engage in 'production' within the home for the benefit of their husbands. Indeed, it was argued that any work undertaken by women within the home should be considered non-work and worthless, even if it was done for sale on the market—whereas if a man completed this work, it would be considered 'productive'.[132] 'Such was the devaluation of women's labour that city governments told the guilds to overlook the production that women (especially widows) did in their homes because it was not real work.'[133] The result was that all work undertaken within the home became defined as 'housework', and any work undertaken by women outside the home was paid at a fraction of that earned by men. At this time, reproductive labour was increasingly mystified as a natural vocation, and women were excluded from many waged occupations.

The sexual division of labour, which peaked in the nineteenth century with the creation of the housewife, redefined women's position in society and in relation to men, creating dependency on their husbands' wage for existence. These changes created a class of proletarian women who, in contrast to their male counterparts, had no access to a wage, 'forcing them into a condition of chronic poverty, economic dependence, and invisibility as workers'.[134] Indeed, Adams argues that the result of social reproduction as non-market work

[130] Joanne Conaghan, 'Gender and the Labour of Law' in Collins, Mantouvalou, and Lester (n 45).
[131] Zatz (n 46) 237.
[132] Merry Wiesner, *Women and Gender in Early Modern Europe* (4th edn, CUP 2019) 92.
[133] Federici (n 126) 92.
[134] ibid 75.

renders it 'invisible' and naturalized into non-existence,[135] regarded as something that naturally occurs and is freely available. There are many parallels between the history of the subjugation of women's work and our case studies. For example, outside of detention, the work of immigration detainees is criminalized, meaning that they are not entitled to any enforceable labour rights or the national minimum wage should they choose to work 'illegally', creating enforced dependency upon the state. Inside of detention, the work they perform is not considered to be market work, so paying them a wage is not 'economically viable' despite the fact that, arguably, removal centres would have to pay official members of staff to perform that work if detainees did not complete it. Justifications given for exclusion thus seek to obscure the simple truth that exclusion from formal employment is used as a tool of governance to control and subjugate particular populations marginalized by society.

In addition to the gendered social division of labour, the 'non-market' paradigm was also weaponized against racialized, colonial labour as a means of exclusion from labour rights and the wage. Federici writes that, while Europe responded to the population crisis through the subjugation of women to reproduction, in colonial America, the response was the slave trade, which provided Europe with the commodities necessary to fuel labour power, linking European waged workers with those held in the slave trade as the producers of cheap goods, including sugar and cotton which, ultimately, aided the industrial development of Europe.[136] Much like the labour of women, however, the production of enslaved people was not considered to be 'industrial' and was subject to colonial monopoly.[137] Once colonialism was institutionalized, it restructured the reproduction of labour on a global scale in two ways. First, a global assembly line was created, which cut the costs of consumer goods in Europe. Second, the 'metropolitan wage' became the vehicle by which the products of enslaved workers entered the market and gained surplus value (through purchase). Similarly to female domestic work, enslaved labour thus became an essential facet of social reproduction of the metropolitan workforce, and 'the wage was further redefined as an instrument of accumulation, that is, as a lever for mobilising not only the labour of the workers paid by it, but also for the labour of a multitude of workers hidden by it, because of the unwaged conditions

[135] Zoe Adams, 'Invisible Labour: Legal Dimensions of Invisibilization' (2022) Journal of Law and Society 385.

[136] Jason Hickel, *The Divide: A Brief Guide to Global Inequality and Its Solutions* (Windmill Books 2018).

[137] Eric Eustace Williams, *Capitalism and Slavery* (University of North Carolina Press 1944); Blackett (n 125).

of their work'.[138] Accordingly, a new division of the working class developed 'by which waged-work, rather than providing an alternative to slavery, was made to depend on it for its existence, as a means (like female unpaid labour) for the expansion of the unpaid part of the waged working-day'.[139]

To summarize this discussion, applying a historical materialist lens to the creation and growth of capitalism reveals that this institutionalized social order relied, or relies, on the labour of women and colonized populations for both its creation and regeneration. Yet, despite this reliance, the labour of these groups remains categorized as 'non-market' work. The status of 'worker', and its associated legal protections, including that of the wage, is thus not afforded to these groups, with significant consequences in terms of dependency and social standing. Our case studies represent a continuation of labour exclusion as forms of, ostensibly, 'non-market' work, which sit outside the boundaries of legal and social recognition, where law and social perception serve to mutually reinforce one another in excluding marginalized groups.[140]

b. Beyond the Market Binary

The question then remains: how do we look beyond this idea of market and non-market work that is used to justify distinction and exclusion? Zatz highlights three strands of argument made by feminist scholars that deconstruct and challenge the exclusionary categorization of work as being of 'non-market' character. These scholars argue instead that the work should be reorientated as 'economic' in relation to its circulation, substitution, and incorporation.[141]

Arguments concerning the circulation of labour contend that products of non-market work *circulate* within the market itself. The obvious example here is that social reproduction produces the workers who provide labour within the market, while Eileen Boris also examines examples of industrial home-working where individuals produce goods at home to fit around family life, often involving family members in the production process itself (such as cigar rolling).[142] These goods then circulate in conventional markets alongside

[138] Federici (n 126) 104.
[139] ibid.
[140] Erin Hatton, 'Work beyond the Bounds: A Boundary Analysis of the Fragmentation of Work' (2015) 29 Work, Employment and Society 1007.
[141] Noah Zatz, 'Prison Labor and the Paradox of Paid Nonmarket Work' in Nina Bandelj (ed), *Economic Sociology of Work*, vol 18 (Emerald Group Publishing Limited 2009).
[142] Eileen Boris, *Home to Work: Motherhood and the Politics of Industrial Homework in the United States* (CUP 1994).

those produced in the factory. We see this in the prison case study, where companies co-opt prison labour as a means of producing cheap goods for sale on the outside. The second facet for immersion into the economic realm is where goods may not circulate but are at least *substituted* for the goods and services that would otherwise come from the consumer market. With regards to social reproduction, we can use the example of care work here where, if family members do not undertake the labour of caring, it would have to be performed either through employees of the state or via private companies at a price dictated by market norms. This is likely the case across all four of our case studies, where participants perform the work that would otherwise be undertaken by workers receiving the national minimum wage. Third, non-market work often *incorporates* or enables economic transactions that distribute valuable goods, services, capital, or other media for exchange. The prison and the immigration removal centres exemplify this dynamic, where the work performed enables the purchase of goods and services by detainees within the complex, which are supplied via external companies. Evidence suggests that the goods sold within these centres are vastly inflated in comparison to prices on the outside, revealing that market processes occur at micro levels within the centres themselves.

Adopting a broader construction of economic interactions beyond the traditional boundaries of 'the market' facilitates a better understanding of economic activities as being both structured by (and embedded within) ongoing social relations. One of the central concerns within feminist literature about recognizing traditional 'non-market' relationships as 'economic' is 'commodification anxiety', that is, that in demanding a monetary transaction for the provision of care, we undermine the essence of nurturing. Yet, as noted by Williams, 'turning labor into love preserved men's traditional access to women's work by arguing that any attempt to link such work with entitlements would sully the home sweet home with the market values of a "selfish and calculating world"'.[143] However, it has been rightly noted that justifications like these sentimentalize and serve to mystify the nature of the labour performed, providing a basis for exclusion that prevents many individuals and minorities from enjoying the status of work and the wage. Indeed, research concerning workfare, homecare, and internships (including graduate labour)[144] in the United States have all problematized the categorization of institutions as

[143] Joan Williams, *Unbending Gender: Why Family and Work Conflict and What to Do about It* (OUP 2001).

[144] Hatton, *Coerced* (n 46).

market and non-market orientated, which determines whether someone will enjoy the status of 'worker'. We argue then that the market/non-market justification rests upon a weak binary that fails to withstand critical reflection, revealing that many of the boundaries restricting the recognition of certain labour as 'valuable work' are socially constructed and politically engineered. The consequences of such distinctions facilitate the maximum extraction of surplus value where workers remain unpaid or underpaid as well as providing a tool for discipline and control.

Yet, even if we were to accept that certain work should sit outside the realm of the economic, this does not need to prove fatal to the claims that our case studies represent 'work', nor that they should be remunerated. Rather than absorb certain relations (such as social reproduction) into the market, Nancy Fraser pushes against their inclusion as 'economic', noting that a number of non-economic relations, goods, and institutions have been central to working-class consumerism and the background conditions on which capitalism functions. Fraser terms these the 'background conditions of possibility for exploitation'[145] and includes conditions such as social reproduction, nature, and law in her analysis. Each of these, she argues, is central to the functioning of capitalism, yet does not mirror capitals commodifying logic, instead embodying its own 'distinctive normative and ontological grammars'.[146] One means of recognizing the importance of unpaid socially reproductive labour is through the caregiver parity model, where those providing unpaid domestic work would be given a wage via state allowances to elevate the caregiver model to a similar status as that of the 'breadwinner'.[147] The point here is not to delve into Fraser's theories on the post-industrial family wage but rather to illustrate the different ways in which the state can recognize and support work outside of the private contractual setting. As was explored in section 2 of this chapter, remuneration from a public authority does not also exclude the labour performed from the category of 'work', particularly in relation to EU law.

Though we argue that the economic element and market nature of work within our case studies are clear, not least because of the direct private profits being accumulated by companies exploiting a cheap and available workforce, arguments that rest on the construction of work within our case studies as non-market work should not prove fatal to claims for a decent wage. Whereas remuneration in the case of social reproduction would come from the state, in

[145] Fraser (n 123).
[146] ibid.
[147] Nancy Fraser, *The Fortunes of Feminism: From State-Managed Capitalism to Neoliberal Crisis* (Verso 2013).

our case studies, there are direct private employers who would be responsible for the payment of wages, notwithstanding the responsibility of the state to run detention facilities.

5. Conclusion: 'Law Relies on Certainty until It Does Not'

In recent years, legislation, case law, and scholarship have all been, to different degrees, challenging the strict boundaries that constrict statutory employment protection to some workers but not to others.[148] This path, originally identified by Bob Hepple,[149] was trail-blazed by Mark Freedland,[150] later in conjunction with Nicola Kountouris.[151] The new project posits the 'personal work relation', explored in Chapter 7 of this book, as the central category in labour law, thus doing away with the binary dichotomy between the contract of service and the contract for services and the implication of that dichotomy. A similar approach suggests that, when assessing statutory protection, we must recognize that 'each piece of legislation has its own purpose, which corresponds with the general values that labour laws are aimed to protect and promote'.[152] Following this approach, it may be suggested that equal protection legislation (working time or pay measures, for example) *were intended* to protect individuals *precisely* in the position of participants in these schemes.

It is clear from the preceding analysis that the work performed within our case studies looks and feels like traditional employment in which private companies and the state profit, either through costs reduction or through the production of tradeable commodities. Application of the standard employment tests also indicate that the work performed should lead to categorization of our participants as workers or even, in some instances, employees. Yet, the law specifically excludes these workers from employment status and the panoply of

[148] Folúkẹ Adébísí, *Decolonisation and Legal Knowledge: Reflections on Power and Possibility* (Bristol UP 2023).

[149] Bob Hepple, 'Restructuring Employment Rights' (1986) 15 International Law Journal 69, 74 asking 'whether statutory rights should continue to rest on the foundation of the common law contract of service'.

[150] Mark Freedland, 'From the Contract of Employment to the Personal Work Nexus' (2006) 35 Industrial Law Journal 1; Mark Freedland, 'Application of Labour and Employment Law beyond the Contract of Employment' (2007) 146 International Labour Review 3.

[151] Lord Wedderburn, 'Labour Law 2008—40 Years On' 36 International Law Journal 397, 411 (2007).

[152] Guy Davidov, 'Re-Matching Labour Laws with Their Purpose' in Davidov and Langille (n 46) 180–81; Noah Zatz, 'What Welfare Requires from Work' (2006) 54 University of California Los Angeles Law Review 373, 377; Guy Davidov, 'A Purposive Interpretation of the National Minimum Wage Act' (2009) 72 Modern Law Review 581.

rights that go with it, meaning the workers within our case studies are paid minimal wages compared to that of the national minimum wage.

How then, can we make sense of our case study exclusions? Policy documents, political statements, and the common law advance a number of central arguments as to why these groups should be excluded which, as explored, are often grounded on the concept of benefit. But as addressed in this chapter, ascertaining the tangible benefits of unpaid and underpaid labour is difficult, and in many cases, the government makes no attempt to establish a body of evidence on which these claims rely. On the contrary, there is growing evidence to show the ineffectiveness of these schemes in meeting their intended outcomes and clear dissatisfaction among participants that the wages provided fail to reflect the true value of the labour performed or that the work improves skills and/or job prospects. The so-called 'benefits' of this work are not, therefore, enough to silence the voices of the workers who have repeatedly challenged the work arrangements in which they take part, demanding better pay and rights, which they believe they deserve. The courts' response has, however, been negative. As opposed to a neutral tool, law is therefore better understood as a 'form of power/knowledge that actively constructs [political] desire'.[153] Law should be framed as having 'a certain origin, trajectory, and history; it has alliances with different manifestations of coercive power, embedding within it the interests and desires of the powerful. In this sense, law is not just an abstract tool for regulation, but it also carries within it, its own directions.'[154] Logics of hierarchization based on structures of race, gender, and capital thus influence the application of the legal doctrine and the inclusion and exclusion of subjects within the parameters of rights and protections. Law has thus been central in solidifying capitalism's relationship with and reliance upon the gendered division of labour and the invisibilization and exclusion of other forms of work upon which it relies. This helps us to understand why 'certain activities come to be associated with leisure and consumption, rather than production, and how some capacities come to be seen as innate to particular groups, rather than as productive skills, which devalues them in the process'.[155]

Finally, the judiciary may be playing its part if it is willing to accept that an employer–employee relationship may contain training elements and that the latter does not undermine the former.[156] Since the courts have considerable discretion when asked to apply statutory protection and have adopted, more

[153] JM Modiri, 'Law's Poverty' (2015) 18 African Journals Online 224.
[154] Adébísí (n 148).
[155] Adams (n 1) 342.
[156] *Thorpe v Dul* [2003] ICR 1571 [17]; but cf *M&P Steelcraft v Ellis* [2008] ICR 578.

than once, the approach according to which the scope of statutory protection should be governed by its *purpose*, which is 'to extend protection to workers who are, substantively and economically, in the same position',[157] we argue that general principles and concrete legal analysis support the expansion of such protection to participants in these schemes if not wholesale, then in particular instances.

These exclusions, however, are far from surprising. Our case studies form part of a long history of excluded labour which, as illustrated throughout Chapters 2 and 3, maps closely onto populations marginalized by socio-economic status, race, and gender. The status of those within our case studies as 'criminals', 'irregular immigrants', and 'the unemployed' routinely obscures both the value of their labour work and their entitlement to legal protection. As noted by Adébísí,

> It seems easier to question the legitimacy of people whose 'problems' fall outside the sacred method of our discipline, than to question the method and presumptions that underpin the discipline—the soul of the discipline itself. Because to question the discipline is to question the (vision of the) world (it has created).

The 'discipline' we refer to here is that of law and its pretentions of objectivity, neutrality, and universality.

[157] *Byrne Brothers v Baird* (2002) IRLR 96 [17].

4
Unfree Labour

1. Introduction

The growing appreciation for the need to find an open-ended term that addresses consent and exploitation in contemporary labour markets without the need to refer to every such instance as slavery, servitude, or forced labour, has led to the term 'unfree labour' being discussed increasingly in the literature in recent years. It originated in political economy scholarship, and gained traction in development studies and critical geography.[1] Distinguishing itself from slavery, servitude, and forced labour, it was noted that '"unfree labour" is not a legal concept, nor should it aspire to be'.[2] As such, it allows scholars outside the realm of law to interrogate, conceptualize, and criticize structures and relations that compel individuals into performing exploitative work without the need to attach themselves to rigid, legal doctrines. To an extent, it offers a less intimidating, though still contested, midway stop on the bridge from slavery to common workplace practices and includes discussions of migrant work[3] and temporary work agencies,[4] for example. The likelihood that individuals or groups will be subject to the more exploitative end of the spectrum is related to a broad set of intersecting factors, which exist on different scales and levels of governance, allowing for a more systematic evaluation of the structural hierarchies that give rise to exploitative work, including those of race, gender, and immigration status.

Applying an unfree labour lens allows us to look beyond the factors traditionally identified as coercive within the liberal legal framework and to more thoroughly examine the unfreedoms that shape an individual's entry into,

[1] Jens Lerche, 'A Global Alliance against Forced Labour? Unfree Labour, Neo-Liberal Globalization and the International Labour Organization' (2007) 7 Journal of Agrarian Change 425; Genevieve LeBaron and Nicola Phillips, 'States and the Political Economy of Unfree Labour' (2018) 24 New Political Economy 1.

[2] Cathryn Costello, 'Migrants and Forced Labour' in A Bogg and others (eds), *The Autonomy of Labour Law* (OUP 2014) 189.

[3] ibid.

[4] Judy Fudge and Kendra Strauss (eds), *Temporary Work, Agencies, and Unfree Labour: Insecurity in the New World of Work* (Routledge 2014).

Underpaid and Unrecognized. Katie Bales and Amir Paz-Fuchs, Oxford University Press.
 DOI: 10.1093/9780197910467.003.0004

exit from, and experience of the labour process. As such, in this chapter, we are interested in mapping out the dimensions of unfreedom that shape certain work relations. This is an important perspective for those performing work within our case studies whose circumstances fall short of the requirements needed for legal categorization as slavery, servitude, or forced labour. Accordingly, in this chapter, we explore the concept of 'unfree labour', positing it as a preferred methodology and theoretical framework for analysing the exploitative labour relations addressed in our case studies and, tentatively, beyond.

At present, the international and domestic, liberal, legal frameworks addressing unfree labour such as trafficking, modern slavery, and forced labour represent the more extreme end of the spectrum of coercing individuals into unfree labour. Though the liberal legal framework has purchase, there remain significant issues in both the construction and implementation of labour unfreedom that weaken its effectiveness in identifying, alleviating, and improving instances of labour unfreedom and exploitation. Using liberal, international and domestic law as an exclusive indicator of unfree labour also excludes huge swathes of exploitative and problematic labour relations from analysis on grounds that they do not meet the specific criteria set out in the instruments, many of which are tied to the concept of consent. For example, the labour of immigration detainees in the United Kingdom would not be considered problematic under the International Labour Organization (ILO) Forced Labour Convention on grounds that, in most instances, detainees 'voluntarily consent' to work.[5] Yet, this consent-based approach results from detainees' deprivation of liberty as well as global structures that compel their migration and neoliberal policies and forms of governance within the United Kingdom that shape their bargaining power. The liberal focus on 'consent' overlooks these factors, failing to account for the social realities that shape many immigration detainees' experiences as well as those of prisoners, workfare claimants, and interns.[6] Embracing the idea that labour unfreedom exists on a spectrum, rather than the binary of free/unfree, permits us to move beyond the restrictions found within liberal legal regulations and allows us to fully account for the myriad of unfreedoms and pressures that might lead an individual into highly exploitative work.

[5] Katie Bales and Lucy Mayblin, 'Unfree Labour in Immigration Detention: Exploitation and Coercion of a Captive Immigrant Workforce' (2018) 47 Economy and Society 191.

[6] ibid; Katie Bales, 'Rethinking "Unfree" Labour: The Immigration Industrial Complex' in Eileen Boris and others (eds), *Global Labour Migration: New Directions* (University of Illinois Press 2023).

Accordingly, the chapter begins by addressing the existing legal framework governing unfree labour relations, outlining its shortcomings and explaining why law may not be a useful tool for inquiry when seeking to recognize the dimensions of unfreedom giving rise to exploitation within our case studies and beyond. The chapter then more fully addresses the meaning of 'unfree labour', adopting a three-part framework established by Marx and further developed in the work of LeBaron. This framework takes into account the global systemic compulsions and forms of coercion that underpin people's entrance into the labour market, the social relations surrounding labour within the sphere of circulation, and the conditions of the labour process itself.[7] We interpret this as unpacking unfree labour along three broad dimensions: the distribution of land and resources that compel individuals to sell their labour power (private ownership of means of production and no commons); circulation (including the circulation of labour and goods in the market economy as well as mobility in the geographic, economic, and social sense); and conditions of the labour process.[8] These three dimensions allow us to analyse the factors impacting upon freedom to enter, exit, and remain within the labour relationship. A spectrum allows us to see that even where someone's conditions of labour may be close to 'decent work', their lack of access to productive property or restrictive laws relative to their status (such as immigration control) may inhibit their freedom to freely choose employment.

Utilizing this framework, we explore the coercive pressures within our case study groupings, mapping out a number of unfreedoms and pressures that should be taken into account when addressing unfree labour relations. This mapping is not intended to be exhaustive; indeed, that would be counterintuitive to the freedom of analysis that comes with applying a spectrum, the content of which will change and mutate depending on the modalities of labour studied. Rather, in mapping out the structures and pressures found within our case studies and the existing literature, we hope to add to LeBaron's insights by providing further detail on the ways in which it can be applied and implemented to reveal instances of unfree labour, giving rise to a better understanding of how such pressures could be alleviated, as explored in Chapter 7.

[7] Genevieve LeBaron, 'Unfree Labour beyond Binaries' (2015) 17 International Feminist Journal of Politics 1.
[8] Bales (n 6).

2. The Limitations of the Current Legal Framework for Unfree Labour Relations

The term 'modern slavery' encompasses practices including human trafficking, slavery, servitude, and forced labour, which sit at the extreme end of the unfree labour continuum and which are prohibited under a number of international legal instruments.[9] It remains important to identify these legally prohibited forms of 'unfree' labour as such conceptions inform civil society's construction and understanding of 'free' labour in the capitalist economy, with significant consequences in terms of class formation, class struggle, and class consciousness.

While it remains important that these extreme forms of abuse and labour exploitation are recognized, the liberal, modern slavery paradigm in which legal instruments are situated has been referred to as 'paternalistic, carceral and imperialist',[10] reinforcing the position that unfree labour stands as an exception to the normal functioning of the market and promoting an image of the 'ideal victim' who is identifiable by subjection to individual and intersubjective instances of force, control, and/or deception.[11] The assertion is that the focus on slavery and forced labour overlooks the systemic and institutional features of state policies and practices that create the conditions under which unfree labour relations flourish and tends to reinforce the idea that 'exploitation and unfree labour occur as a result of morally culpable individuals who should be publicly vilified'.[12] Moreover, while the free market behaviour of employers is certainly a key component of unfree labour relations, focusing solely on this overlooks the foundational structures of unfree labour relations. Indeed, Hammoudi argues that international law and its institutions 'produce, structure and justify exploitation',[13] severing the violence of slavery and forced labour from the construct of 'free wage labour', 'veiling the structural unity and totality of the international legal order with racial capitalism'.[14] In this, he follows in the steps of Joseph Schumpeter, who noted in 1942 that 'The capitalist order not only rests on props made of extra-capitalist material but also derives

[9] Amir Paz-Fuchs, 'Badges of Modern Slavery' (2016) 79 Modern Law Review 757.

[10] Siobhán McGrath, Ben Rogaly, and Louise Waite, 'Unfreedom in Labour Relations: From a Politics of Rescue to a Politics of Solidarity?' (2022) 19 Globalizations 911.

[11] Katie Cruz, 'Beyond Liberalism: Marxist Feminism, Migrant Sex Work, and Labor Unfreedom' (2018) 26(1) Feminist Legal Studies 65.

[12] Judy Fudge, 'Modern Slavery, Unfree Labour and the Labour Market: The Social Dynamics of Legal Characterization' (2018) 27 Social & Legal Studies 414, 415.

[13] Ali Hammoudi, 'International Order and Racial Capitalism: The Standardization of "Free Labour" Exploitation in International Law' (2022) 35 Leiden Journal of International Law 779, 781.

[14] ibid 779.

its energy from extra-capitalist patterns of behaviour which at the same time it is bound to destroy.'[15]

In distinguishing 'forced' labour from 'unforced' labour under capital, international law largely ignores the processes of dispossession, accumulation, and exploitation that are fundamental to the existence of the capitalist labour market. The result is that 'forced' labour is thus constructed as normatively unacceptable, legitimizing work relations that fall outside of this strict definition and enabling corporations and states to exploit structural vulnerabilities in labour supply chains, often felt most acutely by workers from the Global South. In many ways, then, laws regarding slavery, servitude, and forced labour contribute to the marginalization of extreme forms of unequal labour relationships, establishing part of a broader political landscape that has allowed capitalism to flourish.[16]

With regards to the legislative modern slavery framing, the form of unfreedom that is most likely to be invoked by the work undertaken in our case study groupings is that of 'forced labour'. Indeed, there have been a number of legal challenges which suggested that workfare, for example, should be construed as unlawful forced labour. These challenges, however, were unsuccessful.[17] Below, we briefly explain why our case studies fall outside the categories of slavery and servitude before examining the shortcomings of the forced labour framework in relation to the labour performed within our case studies and beyond.

a. Slavery and Servitude

Anti-slavery politics were evident in the Berlin Conference of 1884–85 which, under the guise of suppressing the slave trade, legitimized European authority over Africa under international law. This was later transposed into the Brussels Act of 1890, which was the first treaty to target slavery on the grounds of 'native welfare' as a form of 'international responsibility'. While these treaties were non-enforceable, they allowed for colonial expansion and exploitation of Global

[15] Joseph Schumpeter, *Capitalism, Socialism and Democracy* (first published 1942, Routledge 1994) 162.

[16] Susan Zimmerman, 'The Long-Term Trajectory of Anti-Slavery in International Politics: From the Expansion of the European International System to Unequal International Development' in Marcel van der Linden (ed), *Humanitarian Intervention and Changing Labor Relations: The Long-Term Consequences of the Abolition of the Slave Trade* (Brill 2011).

[17] Amir Paz-Fuchs and Anja Eleveld, 'Workfare Revisited' (2016) 45 International Law Journal 29.

South states to operate under the veil of 'anti-slavery' and abolitionism.[18] In 1926, the Slavery Convention codified a legal definition of slavery as 'the status or condition of a person over whom any or all of the powers attaching to the right of ownership are exercised'. As noted by O'Connell Davidson, defining slavery as proprietary responded to a general understanding of chattel slavery, a legal institution abolished by 1926 in most of the 'civilized' European and New World Nations.[19] She draws out a number of contradictions within this definition, including the fact that under pressure from colonial powers, the brutal labour regimes imposed by colonial authorities in the 1920s were removed from the orbit of the Slavery Convention, justified on the grounds that an attack on forced labour would infringe national sovereignty.

In reality, forced labour was not outlawed at the time because of the potential disruption to European infrastructural projects in the colonies, which relied on systems of forced labour to function. The result was that the Slavery Convention had very limited effect and was consequently dubbed a 'paper tiger'.[20] The more pertinent issue of forced labour, discussed immediately below, was thus passed to the ILO to be dealt with separately. Similarly, labour regimes developed after chattel slavery such as 'apprenticeships' in the British Caribbean and the coolie system, where workers laboured under miserable conditions, did not neatly fit the definition of slavery linked to property and the chattel slave trade. Sharma argues that these labour regimes were enacted specifically against immigrants and formerly enslaved people to weaken their demands for justice and their position within the labour market, creating divisions and antagonisms between groups as 'black' or 'migrant', which then enabled the state to impose unfree labour relations on both by exploiting divisions among the labouring classes.[21]

The imprecision of the slavery definition thus 'reflects the political interests of the colonial powers amongst the original signatories to the Slavery Convention'.[22] This aligns with Miers's claim that anti-slavery politics were advanced by European powers to further their own imperial and colonial interests,[23] forming a convenient justification for European dominance over Africa

[18] Suzanne Miers, 'Slavery and the Slave Trade as International Issues 1890–1939' 19 Slavery & Abolition 16.

[19] Julia O'Connell Davidson, *Modern Slavery: The Margins of Freedom* (Palgrave Macmillan UK 2015) 34.

[20] Suzanne Miers, *Slavery in the Twentieth Century: The Evolution of a Global Problem* (Rowman and Littlefield 2003) 102.

[21] Nandita Sharma, 'States and Human Immobilization: Bridging the Conceptual Separation of Slavery, Immigration Controls, and Mass Incarceration' (2021) 25 Citizenship Studies 166, 167.

[22] O'Connell Davidson (n 19) 34.

[23] Miers (n 20).

and other Global South jurisdictions. In enacting anti-slavery as the 'gold standard of civilisation',[24] intervention into the affairs of 'weaker' Global South states was engineered on grounds of 'humanitarian intervention', 'compelling conformity to and co-operation with the global capitalist economy'.[25] The notion of 'free labour' was constructed against its opposite: slavery, the abolishment of which justified European intervention via commerce and trade. Stanley Engerman explains that 'If slavery is regarded as a unique mode of control of individuals, this would seem to make all nonslavery appear as freedom and, therefore, to be regarded as a progressive and desirable development.'[26] And, as Adelle Blackett notes, in the story of capitalist development, slavery was constructed as an 'anathema to capitalism and democracy', whereas the 'free, self-owned, and legally equal workers' were foundational to the virtuous rise of capitalism and democracy.[27] Adopting a broader understanding of unfree labour counters these widely accepted narratives. Countering the traditional version of economic history is not our central aim here; rather, we seek to ensure that, in this case, history does not repeat itself.

Anti-slavery politics thus sharpened the dichotomy between 'free' and 'unfree' labour, which severed the normative link between racialization and colonization from the international legal order. Imperial intervention was thereby justified on grounds of humanitarian intervention, allowing racial capitalism to flourish.[28] This process also endorsed the ideology of 'free wage labour', which was considered civilized and progressive, operating to mask the capitalist exploitation of the labouring classes in the Global South and beyond.

In the modern context, as a legally permitted labour system, traditional slavery has been abolished everywhere.[29] Perhaps unsurprisingly, instances of case law establishing slavery alone are thin on the ground, and indeed, the context of 'ownership' renders our case study workers outside of its remit. Instead, the much broader category of servitude has proven a more successful route for victims seeking legal justice. Servitude 'prohibits a particularly serious form of denial of freedom. It includes, in addition to the obligation to provide certain

[24] Hammoudi (n 13) 787.
[25] ibid 788.
[26] Stanley Engerman, 'Slavery at Different Times and Places' (2000) 105 American Historical Review 480.
[27] Adelle Blackett, 'Emancipation in the Idea of Labour Law' in G Davidov and B Langille (eds), *The Idea of Labour Law* (OUP 2011) 423. See also Seth Rockman, 'The Unfree Origins of American Capitalism' in Cathy Mason (ed), *The Economy of Early America: Historical Perspectives and New Directions* (2006) 335, 338–39.
[28] Hammoudi (n 13).
[29] United Nations Human Rights Office of the High Commissioner, 'Special Rapporteur on Contemporary Forms of Slavery' (Office of the High Commissioner for Human Rights (OHCHR), no date) <www.ohchr.org/en/special-procedures/sr-slavery> accessed 12 November 2025.

services to another, the obligation on the "serf" to live on the other's property and the impossibility of changing his status.'[30] In the 2005 European Court of Human Rights (ECtHR) case of *Siliadin v France*, the servitude element of Article 4 of the European Convention on Human Rights (ECHR) was triggered as the applicant, who arrived in France at the age of sixteen, was put to work for several years undertaking domestic tasks and providing childcare for seven days a week from 7am to 10pm without pay. She was only able to leave the house alone with her employer's permission, restricting her freedom to leave, and was obligated to follow instructions concerning working hours. Accordingly, the ECtHR unanimously held that this was a case of servitude and therefore a violation of Article 4 of the ECHR.[31] In relation to our case studies, the context of detention indicates that only prison labour and labour within immigration detention could possibly be considered under the category of servitude, given the obligation of the worker to live on the 'other's property and the impossibility of changing his status'. However, as will be explored in subsection (b), prison labour is explicitly excluded from the remit of Article 4 of the ECHR, and the issue of consent within immigration detention renders the servitude provisions of little use.

b. Forced Labour and 'Voluntariness'

In relation to forced labour, the ILO's approach is widely recognized as shaping institutional engagement with the concept at international, European, and domestic levels.[32] Accordingly, the ILO's construction of forced labour reflects policy responses more generally.[33] Article 2(1) of the ILO Forced Labour Convention 1930 identifies forced labour as exacted under the menace of penalty and for which persons have not offered themselves voluntarily. This definition is mirrored by Article 4 of the ECHR and the United Kingdom's Modern Slavery Act (MSA) 2015. On the face of it, both prison labour and workfare in the United Kingdom might meet this definition as both are administered under the menace of penalty. However, Article 2(2) of the 1930 Convention

[30] *Silladin v France* [2005] EHRLR 660.

[31] See discussion in Paz-Fuchs (n 9) 763–64.

[32] Jens Lerche, 'The Unfree Labour Category and Unfree Labour Estimates: A Continuum within Low-End Labour Relations' (1 January 2011) <https://soas-repository.worktribe.com/output/341587> accessed 13 November 2025; Hannah Lewis and others, *Precarious Lives: Forced Labour, Exploitation and Asylum* (Policy Press 2015); Nicola Phillips and Fabiola Mieres, 'The Governance of Forced Labour in the Global Economy' (2015) 12 Globalizations 244.

[33] Case No 8919/80 *Van Der Mussele v Belgium* [1983] ECHR 130.

expressly excludes prison labour from its remit, and although this argument has been raised several times in relation to workfare, it was rejected by a range of courts and bodies, including the ECtHR,[34] the UK Supreme Court,[35] the American Federal Courts,[36] the Dutch Central Appeals Tribunal,[37] and also by the European Committee of Social Rights,[38] as we explore briefly later.

Article 2(2) sets out a number of exceptions from protection, including military work or service; work forming part of the normal 'civic obligations' of citizens; work or service arising as a consequence of conviction in a court of law; work or service that arises in cases of emergency (such as war, flood, famine, etc), where the existence or well-being of the population is endangered; and minor communal services performed by members of a community in the interests of said community. These exemptions are again mirrored in the text of Article 4(3)(a) of the ECHR. Hammoudi notes that upon creation of the ILO Forced Labour Convention in 1930, the justification behind the exceptions was that forced labour for a public purpose would have an 'educative' function towards the natives of colonized states—an exception that legitimated the building of roads, bridges, railways, and ports in Africa, opening up the continent to further capital investment and expansion as part of the global economy.[39] As noted in Chapter 3, the contemporary discourse and case-law still invokes 'educative', 'rehabilitative', and 'beneficial' justifications, in which state parties endorse exploitative labour for the benefit of public and private financial gain while employment rights are curtailed and the work is considered to be 'non-productive' and thus 'non-market' in nature.

The forced labour definition is further substantiated by the eleven ILO forced labour indicators, which are designed to help 'front-line' actors, such as criminal law enforcement officials and labour inspectors, to identify individuals that are potentially trapped in situations of forced labour.[40] When analysing whether an individual is subject to forced labour, the assessor should have regard to the recruitment of the individual, their life at work, and their ability to leave employment.[41] The eleven ILO indicators are abuse of

[34] *Talmon v The Netherlands* (1997) EHRLR 448; *Schuitemaker v The Netherlands* (2010) ECHR 820.

[35] *R (Reilly and Wilson) v Secretary of State for Work and Pensions* [2013] UKSC 68.

[36] *Brogan v San Mateo County*, 901 F.2d 762 (9th Cir 1990).

[37] Central Appeals Tribunal 8 February 2010, LJN BL 1093.

[38] Amir Paz-Fuchs, 'Workfare's Persistent Philosophical and Legal Issues: Forced Labour, Reciprocity and a Basic Income Guarantee' in Anja Eleveld, Thomas Kampen, and Josien Arts (eds), *Welfare to Work in Contemporary European Welfare States* (Policy Press 2020).

[39] Hammoudi (n 13) 792.

[40] Bales and Mayblin (n 5).

[41] ILO, 'Hard to See, Harder to Count: Survey Guidelines to Estimate Forced Labour of Adults and Children' (International Labour Office 2012).

vulnerability, withholding of wages, debt bondage, abusive working and living conditions, excessive overtime, deception, restriction of movement, isolation, physical and sexual violence, intimidation and threats, and retention of identity documents.[42] They are further categorized into being either strong, medium, or weak. If two or more indicators are present, with at least one relating to involuntariness and one relating to penalty,[43] as well as one of the indicators falling into the category of 'strong', then the work in question is likely to be considered 'forced labour'.[44]

Reflecting on the indicators, it is clear that a number of them apply in the context of our case studies. For example, with regards to prisoners and immigration detainees, indicators such as the restriction of movement and isolation; withholding of wages; and abuse of vulnerability (such as poor mental health, disability, poverty, experience of violence) are relevant. However, 'there remains an implicit involuntariness within a number of the indicators,[45] which hinges on negative liberties requiring restraint as opposed to positive liberties that could better the conditions for the exercise of choice.[46] Restriction of movement, for example, is explained with reference to being 'locked up' and/or guarded to prevent workers from escaping at work, and the indicator relating to physical or sexual violence refers to the use of violence as a disciplinary measure to force workers into undertaking tasks.[47] In addition, the withholding of wages does not relate to the level of wages provided, nor irregular or delayed payment, but rather a systematic withholding designed to prevent the worker from changing their employer. Consequently, claims of forced labour have consistently been denied in the context of labour within immigration detention on grounds that the work is 'purely voluntary'.[48]

The ILO's comments on consent reveals the centrality of 'voluntariness' to the construction of forced and free labour. From an ILO perspective, an assertion of consent will only be rendered irrelevant and moot where there is evidence of trafficking, such as deception, fraud, or the retention of identity

42 ILO, 'ILO Indicators of Forced Labour' (International Labour Office 2012).
43 ILO (n 41).
44 Klara Skrivankova, 'Between Decent Work and Forced Labour: Examining the Continuum of Exploitation' (Joseph Rowntree Foundation 2010); *Allen v Hounga* [2014] 1 WLR 2889.
45 Bales and Mayblin (n 5) 202.
46 McGrath, Rogaly, and Waite (n 10).
47 ILO (n 42); Bales and Mayblin (n 5).
48 *Morita v Secretary of State for the Home Department* [2019] EWHC 758; *R (on the application of Badmus) v Secretary of State for the Home Department* [2020] EWCA Civ 657.

documents.[49] However, none of these factors apply to the workers within our case studies, who are most often presented with an accurate account of the work to be undertaken before entering the agreement.

Legal claims of forced labour have also been ruled out in the context of prison work under the Article 2(2)(c) exception,[50] which stipulates that for prison work to fall within the state exception, it must be 'carried out under the supervision and control of a public authority' and on the condition that the prisoner 'is not hired to or placed at the disposal of private individuals, companies or associations'. In cases concerning private companies, the ILO has recognized that although prisoners' consent to work is necessarily constrained by their sentence, genuine consent is theoretically possible and should not be pre-emptively rejected. Consent from prisoners is thus considered acceptable where three conditions are met.[51] First, consent should be formal, in the sense of involving a written work agreement; second, the work should be conducted freely without fear of penalty, punishment, or the loss of rights or privileges; and third, the work should be performed under conditions approximating those of free labour, including levels of remuneration and health, safety, and social security conditions.[52]

Given that there are fifteen privately run prisons in England and Wales,[53] the ILO Committee on Forced Labour has asked the UK Government to ensure that formal, freely given, and informed consent is given with respect to the work undertaken by prisoners in privately operated prisons as well as for all work carried out by prisoners for private companies, both inside and outside of prison premises.[54] The UK Government has, thus far, ignored this recommendation and instead contends that private-sector prison work falls within the Article 2(2)(c) exemption. It grounds its position on the following arguments: first, that the primary purpose of prison work is rehabilitative; second, that both public and private prisons and workshops undergo independent

[49] ILO (n 42).

[50] *Van Droogenbroeck v Belgium* (24 June 1982) s 59, Series A No 50, with reference to *De Wilde, Ooms, and Versyp v Belgium* (18 June 1971) ss 89–90, Series A No 12); *Stummer v Austria* (ECtHR, 7 July 2011) (Application No 37452.02).

[51] ILO (2007) Report III (Part 1(B)), 'General Survey concerning the Forced Labour Convention, 1930 (No 29), and the Abolition of Forced Labour Convention, 1957 (No 105)', International Labour Conference, 96th Session, Geneva, paras 115–116.

[52] ibid.

[53] Jacqueline Beard, 'The Prison Estate in England and Wales' (House of Commons Library, 29 June 2023) 5646 <https://researchbriefings.files.parliament.uk/documents/SN05646/SN05646.pdf> accessed 13 November 2025.

[54] Observation (Committee of Experts on the Application of Conventions and Recommendations (CEACR))—adopted 2020, published 109th ILC session (2021).

inspections; third, that a strong legislative framework protects the working conditions of prisoners; and, finally, that prisoners have access to an effective complaints system. The ILO Committee's response is simply to reiterate that the privatization of prison labour exceeds the exceptional conditions set out in Article 2(2)(c) and that consent must be given to avoid compulsion and thereby the charge of forced labour.[55] Those undertaking prison work within private institutions are thus considered to be working under conditions of forced labour under ILO rules; however, these conditions have not been extended to enforceable rights under Article 4 of the ECHR.

In practical terms, the ILO's construction of 'menace of penalty', which is a required component in their forced labour definition, is not related to broader economic needs but rather to the worker's freedom to leave their abusive employment.[56] Involuntariness relates to a lack of freedom of choice, which then coerces consent. Yet, in reality, consent in employment relationships is not a binary concept but 'one of degree and context; the continuum of consent extends between free enthusiastic choice and duress'.[57] Moreover, the factors impeding freedom of choice and consent are subjective, posing difficulties for an objective valuation of individual labour relations.[58] As noted by O'Connell Davidson, 'the meaning of "consent" is not fixed. It is imagined in relation to wider ideas about free will, volition, and responsibility (among others), ideas which, in turn, are shaped by conventions that are not only historically variable, but can also be subject to political and social contestation.'[59] Where individuals are only presented with one choice, devoid of bargaining power and other options, it is also debateable as to whether freedom of choice is truly feasible. The ILO contends that it is 'the worker's ability to revoke the given consent and the premise that the worker's right to free choice of employment remains inalienable at any given point' that distinguishes free from forced labour.[60] Accordingly, from the ILO's perspective, labour that is economically compelled and subject to extremely poor pay and working conditions is not necessarily exploitative or coerced. This is because the

> price of labour and conditions of work are decided by the market and hence represent a 'just' price . . . It is only the deviation from 'free' labour

[55] ibid.
[56] Skrivankova (n 44).
[57] Maayan Niezna and Guy Davidov, 'Consent in Contracts of Employment' (2023) 86 Modern Law Review 1134.
[58] Skrivankova (n 44).
[59] O'Connell Davidson (n 19) 30.
[60] ILO (2007) Report III (n 51) (para 40).

> markets that should be avoided, even if the outcomes from 'free' labour and from labour markets where non-economic force prevails are more or less the same.[61]

The ILO position therefore aligns with the neoliberal perspective whereby the market regime is not regarded as coercive in itself, nor as a construct that impacts upon one's freedom. Yet, this 'consent'-based approach distorts the lived realities of many workers, which are uncomfortably forced into the rigid binary of 'free' or 'forced' labour practices.[62] Within this paradigm, forced labour is regarded as an exception to the normal functioning of the market, promoting the classic, liberal image of 'victims' and 'exploiters' aligned with a politics of rescue narrative.[63] This narrative was used to justify the introduction of the MSA 2015 by Theresa May, who sought to rid the world of this 'barbaric evil'.[64] Yet Mantouvalou notes the irony that many workers experiencing serious labour exploitation who contact the Home Office for help via the MSA end up locked up in immigration detention, where they are instead offered work for substandard pay. [65] Following deportation, there is then a real possibility that they might be re-trafficked and exploited once more, thus exposing the MSA's failures in addressing the underlying structures that create vulnerability to exploitation. The MSA 2015 is, therefore, often used as a tool for deportation and immigration control rather than protection and the elimination of exploitation.

Voluntariness of exchange is thus the distinguishing feature of 'free labour', which is tempered by the labour market, considered to be 'an area of free exchange in which legally equal parties contract to their own mutual advantage' whereby the state occupies a role of a neutral facilitator.[66] As noted, work that falls outside the parameters of slavery, servitude, and forced labour is legitimated by its exclusion, thus justifying the 'generalised capitalist oppression of workers' as well as the state's structuring of labour

[61] Lerche (n 32) 16.

[62] Bales and Mayblin (n 5).

[63] McGrath, Rogaly, and Waite (n 10).

[64] Theresa May, 'My Government Will Lead the Way in Defeating Modern Slavery' *The Telegraph* (London, 31 July 2016) <www.telegraph.co.uk/news/2016/07/30/we-will-lead-the-way-in-defeating-modern-slavery> accessed 13 November 2025.

[65] Virginia Mantouvalou, 'Structural Injustice and the Human Rights of Workers' (2020) 73 Current Legal Problems 59.

[66] Judy Fudge, 'What Makes Labour Free? (And Why This Question Matters)' (*Futures of Work*, 24 May 2019) <https://futuresofwork.co.uk/2019/05/24/what-makes-labour-free-and-why-this-question-matters> accessed 7 November 2025.

exploitation, which often benefits the state itself as well as corporate profits. As Bales notes,

> Using Government approved legal frameworks that partake of the same liberalism, such as those of the UN or ILO, to critique Government induced forms of working (from which the State also profits), are thus ineffective in revealing the myriad of unfree and exploitative labour practices taking place globally.[67]

Instead, an unfree labour approach dispenses with rigid categorization and the liberal focus on consent, allowing us to fully account for the myriad of unfreedoms and pressures that might lead an individual into highly exploitative work.

3. What Does an Unfree Labour Perspective Add?

There are three ways in which the concept of unfree labour can be useful. First, as indicated, limiting unfree labour to the most extreme manifestations of employment relationships—such as those experienced by victims of slavery, forced labour, child bondage, debt bondage, and similar practices—normalizes a wide range of practices that should be problematized. The legal categories, by their very nature, capture the extreme forms of abuse, leaving market and policy structures largely unexamined in the neoliberal political economy. In other words, 'in isolating the worst forms of exploitation from the broad matrix of unfreedom that characterizes the bottom rungs of the global labour market, such accounts leave unfree labour's social, political and economic foundations unquestioned'.[68] In addition, existing concepts carry their own historical baggage, as is evident in the case of forced labour which, as noted, excludes state-enforced prison labour from its scope.

Moreover, and somewhat paradoxically, the paradigmatic instances of unfree labour—which include slavery, forced labour, debt bondage, and child labour—are clearly categorized as 'labour' or 'work'. In contrast, as we saw in Chapter 3, the exclusion of prison work, labour in immigration detention,

[67] Bales (n 6).
[68] LeBaron (n 7) 2.

workfare, and internships from legal recognition as work deserving of status and rights actually rests on the claim that the work involved is predominantly not considered work but rather rehabilitative activity or training. This is not solely an issue that concerns the law or lawyers. Conflating slavery with unfree labour, and thus normalizing all other forms of labour as 'free', supports a version of economic history that demands critical examination. According to this version, economic development

> follows a linear progression towards a 'pure' capitalism in which coercion would prove unnecessary. From this perspective, the persistence of unfree labor in the early Republic merely suggests that the kinks had yet to be worked out of the system. By conceptualising unfree labour as a paradox or a logical inconsistency within capitalism, historians enshrine freedom as the true dynamic of American economic history.[69]

Second, because unfree labour resides between the unlawful (slavery, forced labour, child labour, etc) and the unproblematic forms of market work, it offers a prism through which policy makers can debate, academics can inquire, and activists may object to particular facets of the labour market. These include the schemes assessed here, as well as agency work, zero-hour contracts, and visa regimes that bind migrant workers to employers and thus is more productive. Moreover, because it is acknowledged that such schemes are lawful, they are, arguably, more potent in their effects on the wider labour market. LeBaron and Phillips have even claimed that unfree labour has 'reshaped' the labour market, suggesting that its 'primary form' of prison work enabled the replacement of public-sector workers in occupations as disparate as firefighting and government data entry.[70] A similar phenomenon has been documented with respect to workfare[71] and interns.[72] The conscious effort to deprive vulnerable workers of protections as entitlements in these sectors, as we saw in Chapter 2, creates a legal structure of precarity that is driven by the state.[73]

Third, legal categories inherently require a binary analysis. However, by not confining ourselves to legal analysis, doctrine, and (crucially) legal

[69] Rockman (n 27) 338–39.
[70] LeBaron and Phillips (n 1) 15.
[71] Amir Paz-Fuchs, *Welfare-to-Work: Conditional Rights in Social Policy* (OUP 2007).
[72] Guy Standing, *The Precariat: The New Dangerous Class* (Bloomsbury 2011) 75.
[73] Mantouvalou (n 65).

consequences, we are able to design a spectrum between free and unfree labour and to acknowledge 'the fluidity of actually occurring unfreedoms'.[74] This position has been increasingly accepted. Thus, in 2009, an ILO Report noted that

> There is a continuum including both what can clearly be identified as forced labour and other forms of labor exploitation and abuse. It may be useful to consider a range of possible situations with, at one end, slavery and slavery-like practices and, at the other end, situations of freely chosen employment. In between the two extremes, there are a variety of employment relationships in which the element of free choice by the worker begins at least to be mitigated or constrained, and can eventually be cast into doubt.[75]

Against this background, Strauss is right to argue that '[u]nfree labour is ... a broad category of which forced labour and slavery are subsets'.[76] And yet, Costello warns that while this assertion is 'eminently plausible', the linkage may be 'inappropriate' or perhaps confusing.[77] This is because as the term 'unfree labour' originated in the political economy literature, the 'prohibition of "forced labour" "servitude" and "slavery" belongs in the legal realm'.[78] Our theoretical perspective supports the former approach, which does, indeed, happily conflate the two realms. Generally, as a matter of a wide theoretical approach, while there is something to gain, there is more to lose by insisting on a strict separation of law from the political economy in general and with respect to labour market and labour law in particular.

Offering a detailed account of this argument would take us too far afield, so we shall quickly outline three arguments in favour of a blended approach. First, descriptively, labour law is awash with value-laden terminology, such as 'reasonableness' (eg in the duty to make 'reasonable adjustments' for disabilities or to offer a 'reasonable response' in the unfair dismissal context); 'necessity' (with respect, in particular, to agency work[79]); the extent of the duty

[74] Lerche (n 1) 447.

[75] ILO, *The Cost of Coercion: Global Report under the Follow-Up to the ILO Declaration on Fundamental Principles and Rights at Work* (Report I(B), 98th Session, Geneva 2009) 8–9.

[76] Kendra Strauss 'Coerced, Forced and Unfree Labour: Geographies of Exploitation in Contemporary Labour Markets' (2012) 6 Geography Compass 137.

[77] Costello (n 2)199.

[78] ibid.

[79] Amir Paz-Fuchs, 'It Ain't Necessarily So: A Legal Realist Approach to Agency Work' (2018) 83 Modern Law Review 558.

to maintain 'mutual trust and confidence', and so forth. Political economy, in other words, will not be to blame for undermining clarity in law. Indeed, reliance on social and economic evidence would lead to a *more* objective analysis. Second, when the law, through the courts, accepts the incursion of real-life scenarios into the analysis, it develops in a positive, humanist fashion. One of the most celebrated legal arguments in the history of American litigation—the Brandeis Brief is quite close to our field of inquiry. In 1908, the Brief succeeded in convincing the US Supreme Court to uphold a law protecting women's health in factories[80] by offering two pages of legal argument and ninety-six pages of social research on the lives of working women. In doing so, it provided 'a healthy antidote to highly apologetic forms of discourse and judgment . . . a necessary demystifying step toward the goal of social reform'.[81] The mirror image of this argument should also be stated. When the courts, and the law in general, *ignore* the background structure of the political economy, the results tend to be extremely harmful to the most vulnerable. Thus, a putatively 'doctrinal' approach to employment contracts has led, for more than a generation, to a series of harsh judicial decisions regarding sham contracts[82] and, to this day, to the employment status of agency workers,[83] for example.

Here, we arrive at our third argument as to why we combine a law and political economy approach. This is the crux of the matter as it indicates where the concept of unfree labour could, potentially, reap real rewards. Tests for employment status, which began their development in the late nineteenth century and still affect eligibility to employment rights, remain decades behind changes in the labour economy, from outsourcing and the fissured workplace, through zero-hour contracts, and on to the gig economy. When courts begin, belatedly, to develop criteria to the relevant tests (for control, business reality, mutuality of obligations), employers routinely adapt and construct the employment reality to suit the tests—substitution clauses, payment by a third party, no obligations, work outside the office, etc. Combined with the fact that 'atypical' work is becoming typical, a new perspective, and perhaps a new paradigm, is needed, one that moves away from employment tests and mobilizes a different rationale for securing employment rights. By focusing on the extent of 'freedom' in the relationship, or its mirror image—exploitation and/

[80] *Muller v Oregon* 208 US 412 [1908].
[81] Morton Horwitz, *The Transformation of American Law 1860–1960: The Crisis of Legal Orthodoxy* (Harvard UP 1992) 209.
[82] Alan Bogg, 'Sham Self-Employment in the Supreme Court' (2012) 41 International Law Journal 328.
[83] Paz-Fuchs (n 38).

or dominance, we go to the heart of the matter: the objective consequences, which employers cannot manipulate.

In doing so, we bring not only slavery within the ambit of unfree labour but also other labour practices, which are currently framed as 'free'. Conceptually, then, unfree labour serves as not only an umbrella concept but also a bridging concept, suggesting that

> certain qualities and dynamics typically associated with unfree labour are in fact also present, albeit to a far lesser extent, in so-called free labour. *Our task, then, is to grapple with the distinct forms of coercion, alienation, dehumanisation, constraint and exploitation that characterise the spectrum of modalities of labour involved in the capitalist mode of production.*[84]

So, when we say that we wish to position unfreedom at the centre of labour law analysis, we suggest that, as a concept and normative value, it should not only inform how we assess extreme examples of abuse and exploitation but also, and perhaps more importantly, occupy a place in our consciousness when we assess everyday situations, including contracts of employment, restrictive covenants, agency work and the gig economy, discrimination, and dismissal.

4. What Is Unfree Labour? The Competing Paradigms and Normative Framework

According to Robert Miles, unfree labour refers to 'relations of production where power is distributed, exploited and retained by politico-legal mechanisms and/or physical compulsion'.[85] This framing is useful as it positions the state as a central actor in the development of capitalism, alongside criminal, migration, welfare, and industrial policies, all of which are central to our case studies.

Unfree labour is traditionally conceptualized through either a binary or a continuum approach. The binary approach, which we see adopted within international law, is also evident in the two main philosophical traditions that were interested in unfree labour—Marxism and liberalism—both constructing labour as a binary: free or unfree.[86] Marx characterized free labour

[84] Genevieve LeBaron and Alison Ayers, 'The Rise of a 'New Slavery'? Understanding African Unfree Labour through Neoliberalism' (2013) 34 Third World Quarterly 873, 879 [emphasis added].

[85] Robert Miles, *Capitalism and Unfree Labour? Anomaly or Necessity* (Tavistock 1987) 171.

[86] Fudge (n 12) 416–17; JM Rao, 'Agrarian Power and Unfree Labour' (1999) Journal of Peasant Studies 26.

as occurring when 'both buyer and seller of a commodity, say of labour power, are constrained only by their free will. They contract as free agents, and the agreement they come to, is but the form in which they give legal expression to their common will'.[87] The paradigmatic case of unfree labour for Marx (and for many others, of course) is slavery, in which 'the slave is the property of a particular master'.[88] The difference between the worker and the slave is, crucially, that 'the worker must sell himself to capital, but not to any particular capitalist, and so within certain limitations he may choose to sell himself to whomever he wishes; and he may also change his master'.[89] The powers to choose one's employer and to quit the work distinguish a worker from a slave and, consequently, free from unfree labour. Marx's identification of slavery is remarkably similar to the definition offered by the 1926 Slavery Convention, according to which, as we noted, slavery is 'the status or condition of a person over whom any or all of the powers attaching to the right of ownership are exercised'.

As for the liberal, political economy paradigm, Judy Fudge explains that, in this context, 'unfree labour is distinguished from free labour by virtue of the fact that the worker is coerced by force to threat'.[90] And here we find another parallel, this time with forced labour, as defined by the ILO's Forced Labour Convention 1930. According to the Convention, forced labour is 'all work or service which is exacted from any person under the menace of any penalty and for which the said person has not offered himself voluntarily'.

We find, then, a notable correspondence between unfree labour as slavery (in some Marxist writings),[91] on the one hand, and unfree labour as forced labour (in the liberal's focus on the use of coercion), on the other hand. As such, unfree labour offers an umbrella term, encompassing these practices, as well as others (eg debt bondage and servile marriage, which, in any case, 'may be covered by the definition contained in the Slavery Convention 1926'[92]). If that is the case, what then is the added value of 'unfree labour' as a concept?

From a Marxist perspective, 'freedom' remains a double bind for the proletariat as although the move from feudalism to industrialization 'appears, on the one hand, as their emancipation from serfdom and from the fetters of the guilds' (as workers are able to choose their employer), the workers are also

[87] Karl Marx, *Capital: Critique of Political Economy* (Penguin, 1990) 49.
[88] ibid 50.
[89] ibid.
[90] Fudge (n 12) 417.
[91] But cf LeBaron (n 7) 8, who suggests that Marx's usage of the term 'free labour' as corresponding with wage labour is misunderstood since 'the tone of his writing is overlooked', and that tone is laced with 'scathing irony'.
[92] Supplementary Convention on Slavery 1953.

'free' from the means of production 'and of all the guarantees of existence afforded by the old feudal arrangements'.[93] In order to survive and provide for one's basic needs within capitalist society, the proletariat is thereby forced into selling its labour power in order to live. Accordingly, the proletariat neither own nor form part of the means of production, compelling its members to enter into a wage-labour contract.[94] From this neo-Marxist perspective, '"free" wage-labor is better understood as a legal fiction that mystifies the intrinsic, coercive nature of labor exploitation under capitalism'.[95] As such, we accept the neo-Marxist position that the majority of workers are subject to a degree of economic coercion due to lack of access to land and the means of production, making them vulnerable to exploitation from employers.[96] The 'work or starve' choice is not a product of natural forces but rather of laws that enable or constrain opportunities, that limit or enable mobility.[97] Accordingly, law is central to this relationship as it creates the concept of private property, which reinforces capital's power, placing employers in a position of power and workers in a position of dependency. Within this context, labour law and welfare are putatively designed to ameliorate and protect individuals from market powers, and our case studies suggest that law simultaneously creates vulnerabilities and structures from which people cannot escape[98] and that employers further exploit this within the labour relationship.

As argued by Nancy Fraser, exploitation is central to capitalism as it involves the extraction of surplus labour from the 'free' yet propertyless proletariat. Accordingly, 'this relation defines the essence of capitalism as a mode of accumulation that is simultaneously a system of domination'.[99] It is only through ownership of the means of production and access to property that workers would be truly 'free' in entering employment as their basic needs could be satisfied by other means, redressing the imbalance of bargaining power that is currently present in the majority of labour relationships.[100]

[93] Karl Marx, *Capital, Volume 1* (Penguin Books 1976) 874.

[94] ibid.

[95] Sebastien Rioux, Genevive LeBaron, and Peter Verovsek, 'Capitalism and Unfree Labor: A Review of Marxist Perspectives on Modern Slavery' (2020) 27(3) Review of International Political Economy 709, 725.

[96] Horatio Specter, 'A Risk Theory of Exploitation' in H Collins, G Lester, and V Mantouvalou (eds), *Philosophical Foundations of Labour Law* (OUP 2018) 205; Fudge (n 12) 429.

[97] Rockman (n 27) 352; Stanley L Engerman 'Slavery, Serfdom and Other Forms of Coerced Labor: Similarities and Differences' in M Bush (ed), *Slavery and Serfdom: Studies in Legal Bondage* (Pearson, 1996) 18, 28–34.

[98] Mantouvalou (n 65).

[99] Nancy Fraser, 'Roepke Lecture in Economic Geography—From Exploitation to Expropriation: Historic Geographies of Racialized Capitalism' (2018) 94(1) Economic Geography 3.

[100] Karl Marx, *Capital: Critique of Political Economy, Vol 3: The Process of Capitalist Production as a Whole* (Penguin 1894,1992).

Moving beyond the binary opposition of 'free' or 'unfree', which often distorts empirical analyses by discarding the complexities and ambiguities of most labour relations, we begin with the premise that most labour under capitalism involves some degree of unfreedom and consequently 'a degree of coercion within every employment relationship'.[101] Yet, within this paradigm, individuals experience different degrees of unfreedom, acknowledging 'the fluidity of actually existing levels of unfreedom'.[102] Such a position recognizes that capitalism 'as a mode of production in the historical sense, has involved various modalities of labour, each characterized by distinct layers and degrees of unfreedom'.[103]

Accordingly, we build on LeBaron's approach to establish a spectrum of dimensions giving rise to labour unfreedom,[104] which can be used to analyse degrees of unfreedom rather than binary oppositions. By addressing three axes of unfreedom that make up the 'spectrum', we are able to 'link macro processes, such as global changes in land ownership, to meso-level changes in migration regimes and, in turn, see how these regimes influence the actual conditions'[105] that workers experience. An individual's or a group's placement within this spectrum relies on a broad set of intersecting factors, which exist on different scales and levels of governance.

These factors include, but are not limited to, the background of individual vulnerability (eg disability) and the structure (including racial, physical, and mental) and conditions created by the state and society (including migration status, housing conditions, poverty, and imbalance of power) that apply. With regard to the language of unfreedom or exploitation, we adopt the word 'unfreedom' to denote the coercive circumstances and structures that impact upon an individual's ability to enter, exit, and remain within the labour relationship.

5. The Spectrum of Unfree Labour

Unlike LeBaron, who utilizes the term 'continuum',[106] 'spectrum' is intentionally used within this chapter to convey that a broad set of intersecting factors,

[101] Mark Freedland and Simon Deakin, 'The Exchange Principle and the Wage–Work Bargain' in Mark Freedland and others (eds), *The Contract of Employment* (OUP 2016) 52, 70.
[102] Lerche (n 1) 447.
[103] LeBaron (n 7) 4.
[104] Nicola Phillips, 'Unfree Labour and Adverse Incorporation in the Global Economy: Comparative Perspectives on Brazil and India' (2013) 42 Economy and Society 171; LeBaron (n 7).
[105] Judy Fudge, '(Re)Conceptualising Unfree Labour: Local Labour Control Regimes and Constraints on Worker's Freedoms' (2019) 10 Global Labour Journal 108, 116.
[106] LeBaron (n 7).

which exist on different scales and levels of governance, contribute to the positioning of a group or individual as being subject to the more severe/unfree end of the spectrum. The terms 'spectrum' and 'continuum', which are often used interchangeably,[107] have different meanings, leading to criticism and confusion within the literature on labour unfreedom.[108] Drawing from scientific and psychological literature,[109] we contend that

- a continuum denotes a unidimensional, unidirectional concept that plots differences quantitatively—with two extremes at either end;
- a spectrum plots multidimensional and multidirectional components that include qualitative and quantitative differences.

Considering the three dimensions identified by Marx, the idea that one could condense and plot these components, which remain fundamentally different from one another in content and form across a unidimensional scale, feels conceptually strained. Yet, there remains purchase in knowing that some workers are more vulnerable to poor working conditions than others, and the reality is that some people enter labour relationships under more significant coercive pressure than others, warranting a variety of different solutions.

Accordingly, the term 'spectrum' is preferred as it denotes multiple values, whereas a continuum tends to be unidimensional. Where analysis across the three axes shows that an individual or group is inhibited by multiple dimensions of unfreedom, it is more likely that they occupy a position of subordination to their employer and the state and thus more likely that they will be subjected to poor working conditions and greater levels of exploitation, meaning that access to labour rights (and beyond) is essential. In such cases, there is greater necessity for protective and positive labour regulation (among other solutions explored in Chapter 7).

This contrasts significantly with the current employment status framework, which only affords rights in limited circumstances and, ironically, often withdraws rights where the work performed is undertaken by vulnerable persons. This political choice has, in many ways, 'reshaped' the labour market, replacing, as we saw, public-sector workers in some instances with those devoid of rights as well as developing legal structures of precarity that are easily extended to new unpopular groupings as and when it is considered necessary,

[107] bid.
[108] Fudge (n 105).
[109] Renato Alarcon, Patricia Rippetoe, and William Walter-Ryan, 'A Spectrum Is Not a Continuum' (1986) 143 American Journal of Psychiatry 678.

such as zero-hours workers. At present, law tends to focus centrally on the conditions of the labour process, ignoring the wider implications of the structural dimensions of unfreedom relating to production, reproduction, and circulation. A spectrum allows us to see that even where someone's conditions of labour may be close to 'decent work', their lack of access to productive property or restrictive laws relative to their status (such as immigration control) is a coercive factor that can limit their freedom within, entering, and/or exiting the labour relationship. This is significant as many of the working conditions in the case studies examined appear to be close to acceptable standards, notwithstanding the issue of pay. And yet, the 'freedom' under which this work is entered into should be problematized.

a. The Systemic Compulsions and Coercions Underpinning Entrance into and Exit from the Labour Contract

In the first of LeBaron's dimensions, she addresses three ongoing global processes that might compel an individual to sell their labour power as property: global transformations in land ownership; the shifting relations of production and social reproduction; and, finally, the consequences of neoliberal governance, which have heightened wealth and income inequalities.[110]

i. Dispossession

The entry point to unfree labour relations is lack of access to property and the means of production, which compels individuals to sell their labour power to survive in capitalist society. As a primarily proletarian grouping, the majority of those within our case studies (and beyond) lack these proprietary privileges. As noted in Chapter 3, the historical foundations for this separation can be traced back to primitive accumulation involving land appropriation through imperial intervention and the system of enclosures in England. Hale contends that it is the law of property (including the privatization of basic amenities such as land and water), that ultimately coerces individuals into wage-work under the penalty of starvation.[111] Franklin D Roosevelt went so far as to note that 'Necessitous men are not free men. People who are hungry and out of a job are the stuff of which dictatorships are made.'[112] Gourevitch contested the

[110] LeBaron (n 7) 8–9.

[111] Robert Hale, 'Coercion and Distribution in a Supposedly Non-Coercive State' (1923) 38 Political Science Quarterly 470.

[112] Franklin D Roosevelt, 'State of the Union Message to Congress' (Franklin D. Roosevelt Presidential Library and Museum 1944) <fdrlibrary.org/address-text>.

association of the 'voluntary contract' with 'economic independence' and focused on those who are 'compelled to labor' because of a 'condition of subjection', which could be economic, legal, or social.[113] This is apparent in the context of workfare, where individuals are seeking benefits to provide a livelihood for themselves and their families. Indeed, eligibility to access welfare benefits is predicated on a means test whereby individuals must demonstrate that their income and capital is below a particular level. Accordingly, they enter the workfare contract in poverty, which enables the government to use benefit sanctions and the associate destitution stemming from sanctions as a tool for discipline, ultimately compelling claimants into the workfare contract.[114]

The situation is not so straightforward in the context of prison work and labour within immigration detention, where detainees have their accommodation and basic needs (such as access to food and water) provided by the prison or detention services themselves. Reflections on land ownership and wealth distribution are important, however, both in framing detainees' entrance into detention and in shaping their entry into the labour contract. The demographic profile of prisoners and immigration detainees is such that they are predominantly poor and racialized. Indeed, research published by the Ministry of Justice notes that many prisoners have a history of social exclusion and are more likely than the general population to have grown up in care, poverty, or both.[115] Research from 2016 also observed that 20 per cent of prisoners entered prison with financial concerns,[116] and a sample survey by Unlock reveals that over one-half of prisoners entered prison in debt (which grew during their sentence) and one-third did not own a bank account.[117] It is also worth noting that a significant proportion (12 per cent) of the prison population is composed of foreign nationals, 42 per cent of whom were born outside of Europe, and that over one-quarter of the entire prison population are from minority ethnic groups. As noted in Chapter 3, a high proportion of immigration detainees also come from formerly colonized states or countries with a subordinate economic relationship to the United Kingdom with specific

[113] Alex Gourevitch, *From Slavery to the Cooperative Commonwealth: Labor and Republican Liberty in the Nineteenth Century* (CUP 2014) 79, 103.

[114] Gijsbert Vonk, 'Hunger as a policy instrument? Some Reflections on Workfare Policies and the Prohibition of Forced Labour' in O Hospes and BMJ van der Meulen (eds), *Fed up with the Right to Food?: The Netherlands' Policies and Practices Regarding the Human Right to Adequate Food* (European Institute for Food Law 2009) 79.

[115] Kim Williams, Vea Papadopoulou, and Natalie Booth, 'Prisoners' Childhood and Family Backgrounds: Results from the Surveying Prisoner Crime Reduction (SPCR) Longitudinal Cohort Study of Prisoners' (Ministry of Justice Analytical Services 2012).

[116] HM Inspectorate of Prisons, 'Life in Prison: Earning and Spending Money' (2016).

[117] Chris Bath and Kimmett Edgar, 'Time Is Money: Financial Responsibility after Prison' (Prison Reform Trust and UNLOCK 2010).

histories of accumulation and appropriation. In considering a detainee's ethnic history and country of origin, dispossession as a means of global wealth distribution should not be relegated to the purely historical as these arrangements pervade into the neocolonial and neoliberal ages through structural adjustment programmes and loan conditions imposed by organizations such as the International Monetary Fund (IMF) and the World Bank. Such measures reproduce and perpetuate the coercion and dependency that were key to imperialist systems of control, governance, and wealth extraction. David Harvey, for example, asserts that credit systems are now the main lever for the extraction of wealth by finance capital.[118]

These profiles and their associated histories are significant as they structure the balance-of-power relations in the present. For example, many migrants seek access to the Global North in part due to economic and political insecurity within their own states, which arose as a result of unequal capital distribution following imperial intervention. 'Indeed, modern migration from former colonial states qualifies as a form of decolonization on the grounds that such movements respond to the asymmetrical benefit structure of co-dependence created by the imperial project.'[119] Deportability is also a significant concern here as non-citizens could be returned to their countries of origin, resulting in anxiety and a desire to gain as much financial security as possible before that occurs. Dispossession and economic insecurity shape many individuals' journeys, not only bringing them into the sphere of criminal regulation and immigration control in the United Kingdom (which leads to the detention estate) but also shaping detainees' bargaining power within the labour relationship. As noted by Cross,

> The apparent chaos of migration cannot be sufficiently explained by a single existing theory, nor can we be deterministic about its outcomes. However, the most comprehensive framework of analysis is rooted in modern economic dispossession and in the continual demand for unfree labour, both mediated by the processes and local meanings of capitalist globalisation. Without this demand, migrants would not disappear into the desert and sea in uncountable numbers, with a lesser proportion ultimately entering northern labour markets that are nonetheless essential to the growth of those economies.[120]

[118] David Harvey, *The Enigma of Capital: And the Crises of Capitalism* (OUP 2010).

[119] Bales (n 6); E Tendayi Achiume, 'Migration as Decolonisation' (2019) 71 Stanford Law Review 1509.

[120] Hannah Cross, 'Labour and Underdevelopment? Migration, Dispossession and Accumulation in West Africa and Europe' (2013) 40 Review of African Political Economy 202, 203.

ii. Social reproduction

Social reproduction is another domain to consider when thinking about the systemic compulsions that lead to unfree labour. We understand social reproduction as 'the labour of individuals to sustain, care for, and attend the survival of, well-being, and reproduction of themselves and each other'.[121] The point here is that those with significant caring responsibilities are more likely to accept precarious and exploitative work than those without due to the increased weight of responsibility upon them and the fact that their reproductive and caring responsibilities are often to be carried out in tandem with waged work, which impacts their availability and flexibility within the labour market.[122]

For many of those in receipt of benefits, workfare is a means of securing day-to-day support for their families, although this is not always effective.[123] One of the central critiques of workfare is the failure to recognize that much socially reproductive work, such as the childcare performed by single mothers, is work that is ignored where parents and carers are forced into workfare arrangements to tackle welfare dependency.[124] The fact that social reproduction may have been one of the factors removing an individual from traditional market employment is another factor relevant to claiming welfare benefits. In the United States, prior to 1996, welfare was associated with support for single mothers to care for their children at home. However, this was altered by the Personal Responsibility and Work Opportunity Reconciliation Act (PRWORA) 1996, which implemented a workfare regime that required all able-bodied adults, even parents who have small children under their care, to take part in the labour force.[125] Social reproduction therefore frames the removal of claimants from traditional forms of productive economic labour and necessitates their entry into the workfare contract as a means of providing for their families.

In the context of carceral labour, the 'prison housework'-style jobs are forms of social reproduction in themselves, where detainees seek to maintain the conditions of their own incarceration. Indeed 'John', a former immigration detainee, asserts: 'if I had not cleaned that detention centre wing every day, it would have been in an absolutely disgusting state. My role was critical in

[121] Kate Hardy, 'Uneven Divestment of the State: Social Reproduction and Sex Work in Neo-Developmentalist Argentina' (2016) 13 Globalizations 876, 880.

[122] Ellie Gore and Genevieve LeBaron, 'Using Social Reproduction Theory to Understand Unfree Labour' (2019) 43 Capital & Class 561.

[123] John David Jordan, 'Welfare Grunters and Workfare Monsters? An Empirical Review of the Operation of Two UK "Work Programme" Centres' (2018) 47 Journal of Social Policy 583.

[124] Carole Pateman, 'Another Way Forward: Welfare, Social Reproduction, and a Basic Income' in Laurence M Mead and Christopher Beem (eds), *Welfare Reform and Political Theory* (Russell Sage Foundation 2005).

[125] ibid.

keeping the detention centre hygienic and safe'.[126] Additionally, in a predominantly male carceral environment (only 4 per cent of the prison population was female in 2022),[127] these types of socially reproductive jobs, which are often undervalued and underpaid due to their association with 'women's work',[128] could be considered emasculating, further augmenting the coercive conditions under which the work is performed.[129] As previously explored, the need to provide for oneself undergirds the work relations of the majority of our case studies. However, social reproduction extends beyond the individual towards support for wider families and communities. Insofar as caring for others is concerned, social reproduction is also relevant in the context of detainee labour for two reasons. First, it can frame the circumstances leading to an individual's entry into the detention estate. Second, once detained, it can compel detainees to work to provide income or remittances to family members on the outside. On a macro scale, social reproduction is often one of the central drivers of migratory movements where individuals seek entry to the Global North to send home remittances, bringing them into the sphere of immigration control and the detention estate. This need is also identified by Waite[130] as one of the most common pressures leading to exploitative work relations for asylum seekers and refused asylum seekers outside of detention, which, if caught, leads them back into the realm of carceral circuity.[131] Similarly, a prisoner writing for *InsideOut* magazine explains that people are often motivated to commit (property) crimes 'by a desperate need to provide necessities for members of their families'.[132]

Once incarcerated, the responsibility to reduce pressures on family members outside of detention can further compel detainees to agree to work for minimum wages. A number of studies, for example, indicate that prisoners' families experience extreme financial hardship, which can be worsened by the loss of an additional wage. By working to provide income for themselves, detainees

[126] John, 'Working for a Pound an Hour: An Immigration Detainee's Perspective' (*Futures of Work*, 30 September 2019) <https://futuresofwork.co.uk/2019/09/30/working-for-a-pound-an-hour-an-immigration-detainees-perspective> accessed 14 November 2025.

[127] Georgina Sturge, 'UK Prison Population Statistics' (House of Commons Library, 8 July 2024) No 04334 <https://researchbriefings.files.parliament.uk/documents/SN04334/SN04334.pdf> accessed 22 November 2025.

[128] Joanne Conaghan, 'Gender and the Labour of Law' in Collins, Lester, and Mantouvalou (n 96).

[129] Bales and Mayblin (n 5).

[130] Louise Waite, 'Asylum Seekers and the Labour Market: Spaces of Discomfort and Hostility' (2017) 16 Social Policy and Society 669.

[131] Katie Bales, 'Labour as a Component of Carceral Circuitry: The Case of Asylum Seekers' (2024) 15 European Labour Law Journal 597.

[132] Former Prisoner, 'Poverty and Crime' (*Inside Time Reports*, 31 March 2023) <https://insidetime.org/mailbag/poverty-and-crime> accessed 11 March 2025.

can relieve the financial pressure upon family members to send in income.[133] Ultimately, these factors, alongside a desire to maintain contact with family via phone calls, the expense of which is significantly inflated in detention,[134] compel detainees to undertake work within detention. This is not a voluntary choice among a suite of options but the only means of securing an income and thereby satisfying these needs. Alongside dispossession, social reproduction is then another central dimension to consider when assessing the pressures and 'freedom' under which individuals enter into the labour contract.

Finally, and pre-empting the discussion in Chapter 6, the significance of neoliberal laws and regulations that facilitate the market cannot be overstated. When we reflect on the systemic compulsions and coercions that underpin exploitative labour relations, the neoliberal legal regime often directly impacts upon processes of dispossession, reproduction, and social reproduction.[135] While neoliberalism is largely considered to involve the state's withdrawal on grounds that the market is best placed to allocate resources, prioritization of market rule requires significant legal and policy interventions to increase market efficiency and competition.[136] Our understanding of 'neoliberal governance' accounts for increasing privatization in the Global North and a move away from Keynesian macroeconomics towards market liberalization, the concentration of wealth in the hands of elite financiers and chief executive officers of large corporations, and 'a range of coercive practices that have sought to pressure governments in the Global South into conformity with neoliberal models of economic governance'[137] centred on the broader objective of creating a hospitable environment for foreign capital.[138]

b. Circulation and Mobility

Under this dimension, we consider the circulation of labour and goods in the market economy as well as mobility in the geographic, economic, and social sense. LeBaron[139] lists a number of factors to consider under this category, including globalization and the heightened regulation and deregulation of labour

[133] HM Inspectorate of Prisons (n 116).
[134] ibid.
[135] Bales (n 6).
[136] Honor Brabazon, 'Introduction: Understanding Neoliberal Legality' in Honor Brabazon (ed), *Neoliberal Legality: Understanding the Role of Law in the Neoliberal Project* (Routledge 2017) 1.
[137] Anna Chadwick, *Law and the Political Economy of Hunger* (OUP 2019) 61.
[138] Bales (n 6).
[139] LeBaron (n 7).

markets, the rise of temporary labour migration schemes, decreased rights for workers, the criminalization of illegal work, migration controls, and migrant labour regimes. Notwithstanding their failings, welfare regimes that ostensibly operate to increase social mobility and opportunities for employment are also central to understanding individual mobility within the sphere of circulation and the social relations that impact engagement with such programmes.

As noted by Fudge, 'States structure different modes of migrant labour incorporation through immigration controls that restrict the ability of migrant workers to freely circulate in the receiving country's labour market.'[140] While immigration controls impact any worker without secure immigration status, in the context of our case studies, the law most severely impacts those labouring in immigration detention as it is their insecure migration status that gives rise to detainment on 'administrative' grounds. Stringent border controls, increased conditionality imposed through the United Kingdom's visa regimes, and the expanding remit of the hostile environment have increased the likelihood of immigration offences to be committed, creating countless pathways into the industrial immigration complex. This includes the criminalization of entry to the state without leave to enter;[141] the extension of restrictive bail conditions including restrictions on access to work, welfare, housing, and study;[142] the criminalization of those found working without the right to work;[143] and increased enforcement, detention, and deportation powers for the Secretary of State.[144] In light of recent legislation, such as the Nationality and Borders Act 2022 and the Illegal Migration Act 2023, and the coalescence of both left and right parties in the United Kingdom, it is likely that access to rights for most migrants (particularly those with irregular status) will continue to worsen. Immigration law thus works in tandem with the criminal law to create vulnerability and precarity, limiting opportunities within the labour market and an individual's ability to circulate freely. In the context of labour within immigration detention, these restrictions reduce the bargaining power of migrants both within and outside of detention, making them more likely to accept exploitative work.

Restrictions on welfare and increased conditionality also shape workers' bargaining power and their freedom to circulate within the market. Where

[140] Fudge (n 105). See also Clifford J Jansen and Vic Satzewich, 'Racism and the Incorporation of Foreign Labour' (1993) 18 Canadian Journal of Sociology 467.
[141] Immigration Act 1971, s 24.
[142] Home Office, 'Immigration Bail Version 21.0' (Gov.uk, 12 June 2025) <https://assets.publishing.service.gov.uk/media/679a0ca085c5e43aa3d10dc6/Immigration + bail.pdf> accessed 7 March 2025.
[143] Immigration Act 1971, s 24B, as inserted by Immigration Act 2016, s 34.
[144] Immigration Act 2016; Nationality and Borders Act 2022; Illegal Migration Act 2023.

welfare fails to meet basic needs, this can push people into irregular forms of work, which can lead to exploitation and criminality. Equally, conditionality in accessing welfare directs claimants into accepting precarious and low-paid labour to avoid sanctioning.[145] For example, while the central purpose of workfare is to increase employment opportunities, there is a wealth of research[146] that points to the inadequacies of the workfare programme, which forces individuals into temporary, low-wage jobs from which they are ultimately pushed out, creating a cyclical process of poverty and precarious work that is felt most acutely by women, ethnic minorities, and lower-class communities, particularly at points of intersection between gender, race, and class.[147] The ability to progress beyond workfare into meaningful, long-term, decent work is therefore strained by the inadequacies of the programmes themselves, creating a cyclical process whereby claimants are returned to workfare schemes with limited ability to refuse the conditions imposed. In contrast to the purported aims of the programme, the possibilities for social mobility within this sphere are thus limited.

Labour deregulation and increasing restrictions on rights also reduces the bargaining power of workers and, for many, worsens conditions of the labour process. The limitations of our current employment status framework, for example, has enabled employers to constrain the boundaries over what constitutes a 'worker' (as evident in cases such as *Deliveroo*)[148] and heightened feelings of insecurity for those at the lower rungs of the labour market. Justified by neoliberal constructions of 'flexibility', 'voice', and 'choice',[149] the 'precariat'[150]

[145] Amir Paz-Fuchs, 'Strict Conditionality, Structural Injustice and Welfare Rights' in Helen Carr and others (eds), *Research Handbook on Social Welfare Law* (Edward Elgar 2024) 259.

[146] Gordon Cleveland and Douglas Hyatt, 'Child Care Subsidies, Welfare Reforms, and Lone Mothers' (2003) 42 Industrial Relations: A Journal of Economy and Society 251; Lydia L Blalock, Vicky R Tiller, and Pamel A Monroe, '"They Get You Out of Courage:" Persistent Deep Poverty among Former Welfare-Reliant Women' (2004) 53 Family Relations 127; J Brian Brown and Daniel T Lichter, 'Poverty, Welfare, and the Livelihood Strategies of Nonmetropolitan Single Mothers' (2004) 69 Rural Sociology 282; Vonk (n 114); Luann Good Gingrich, 'Single Mothers, Work(Fare), and Managed Precariousness' (2010) 21 Journal of Progressive Human Services 107; Peter Taylor-Gooby, 'Why UK Welfare Reform Is Trapped in a Cycle of Revolution, Failure and Further Reform' (King's College London 2023).

[147] Krisztián Pósch and others, 'Scale and Nature of Precarious Work in the UK' (April 2020) <https://assets.publishing.service.gov.uk/media/61b72ecfd3bf7f055fce74b4/scale-and-nature-of-precarious-work-in-the-UK.pdf> accessed 14 November 2025.

[148] *Independent Workers Union of Great Britain (Appellant) v Central Arbitration Committee and another (Respondents)* [2023] UKSC 43.

[149] Mark Freedland, 'The Contract of Employment and the Paradoxes of Precarity' (13 June 2016) = University of Oxford Legal Research Paper Series No 37/2016. <https://papers.ssrn.com/sol3/papers.cfm?abstract_id=2794877> accessed 15 November 2025; Katie Bales, Alan Bogg, and Tonia Novitz, '"Voice" and "Choice" in Modern Working Practices: Problems with the Taylor Review' (2018) 47 Industrial Law Journal 46.

[150] Guy Standing, *The Precariat: The New Dangerous Class* (Special COVID-19 edition, IB Tauris 2019).

now make up one in ten workers in the United Kingdom.[151] The widespread growth of precarious work is important when we consider that the central emphasis of our welfare system is based on the idea that employment will solve dependency. As noted by Standing, 'workfare in the United Kingdom will expand the precariat'.[152] Compelling workers into a precarious labour market via workfare programmes and the threat of sanctions further entrenches their vulnerability and the circularity of the unemployment/welfare nexus.

In considering the circulation and mobility of workers, we see that law and policy impact our understanding of 'freedom' within the labour relationship, imbricating labour law, social welfare, trade regulations, criminal law, and migration controls, which are capable of restricting as well as advancing individual mobility and autonomy. While we are all subject to these areas of law, they are experienced most acutely by poorer populations and racialized groups from the Global Majority whose life choices tend to be hindered rather than enhanced by restrictive trade and immigration controls. Evidently, there is a strong connection between structural exclusions, vulnerability, and exploitation. The current legal and policy framework thus reflects a 'paradox of precarity',[153] in which the most vulnerable are the most likely to be criminalized and socially excluded. Yet, these conclusions must be situated within the context of neoliberal governance, which prioritizes market imperatives above protection. These broader political failings are a relevant factor to consider when analysing the nature of work within our prisons and immigration detention centres, and for which we afford welfare benefits, as these are the stark realities that face the communities from which these workers are drawn.

c. Conditions of the Labour Process

Finally, the conditions of the labour process are perhaps the most commonly analysed indicators of 'unfree labour', including (but not limited to) factors such as physical and sexual violence; alienation; limitations on physical mobility; the withholding of labour or the provision of endless, tiresome work; low wages or the withholding of pay; debt bondage; unsafe and/or unclean working environments; emotional abuse; the (in)ability to collectivise and seek union representation; and lack of privacy and/or a social life. Many of

[151] Pósch and others (n 147).
[152] Standing (n 72) 144.
[153] Freedland (n 149).

these conditions are recognized in international provisions such as the eleven ILO Forced Labour Indicators and in the common law arising from cases concerning Article 4 of the ECHR. Chapter 2 set out the details of the work performed within our case studies which, within the United Kingdom at least, is largely well organized, whereby workers are made aware of their roles and responsibilities, meaning that many of the more extreme indicators listed above are lacking. Nevertheless, within each of the case studies examined, pay is withheld or granted at levels way below the national minimum wage, and collectivization is limited, particularly in relation to those who are incarcerated. The conditions of the labour process are more fully explored in relation to our case studies in Chapter 5, which addresses how labour law might respond to the spectrum of factors outlined in this chapter, moving beyond academic analysis towards legal mobilization.

6. Conclusion: Contextualizing Inequality of Bargaining Power

In addressing the different pressures that might compel entry into (and inhibit exit from) a working relationship, we argue that it is essential to look beyond the conditions of the labour process to address the broader structural factors that create and deepen inequalities between workers and the capitalist class. This approach is particularly relevant in relation to processes of production and social reproduction as well as the laws, rules, regulations, and circumstances that inhibit (or enforce) mobility[154] and circulation within the market. In accounting for these dimensions (production/reproduction, circulation, conditions of the labour process), researchers and practitioners seeking to understand the reasons why workers enter and remain in employment relations can better comprehend the panoply of factors that place pressure on workers within and outside of the capitalist labour market. The different dimensions of unfreedom triggered by the three axes that were explored in this chapter warrant different responses if they are to be reduced, ameliorated, or eliminated. These responses span both legal and non-legal realms and involve a range of actors, including the state, employers, and wider social relations, as explored in Chapter 7. Current policy responses, which seek to reduce instances of unfree labour through utilization of the criminal law and labour

[154] Bales (n 133).

law, will always fall short as they ignore the underlying structural conditions underpinning labour.

Pervading all three of the axes explored are the social relations giving rise to structures of class, race, and gender which, as addressed within this chapter, intersect with each other and each of the dimensions in unique and intersectional ways to produce varying degrees of coercion that compel individuals into the labour relationship. Similarly, neoliberalism underscores all three of the highlighted axes. For example, it is a driving factor in the increasing privatization and accumulation of land and resources; it involves the imposition of immigration controls and the withdrawal of social welfare in order to facilitate the market, which impacts upon mobility; and, finally, it shapes the conditions under which detainees, workfare claimants, and interns work, converting their structural vulnerabilities into opportunities for market enterprise.

While these dimensions may seem obviously relevant, many of these factors remain excluded from legal analysis when ascertaining an individual's work status or, worse yet, are acknowledged to the detriment of workers, excluding them from formal employment and the rights that it entails. The remaining chapters attempt to unpick these conundrums, first offering a legal perspective on how to enhance awareness of the dimensions of unfreedom guiding the labour relationship within the current legal framework before moving to assess the pervasive role of neoliberalism in unfree labour and finally proposing alternative forms of action, dissent, and reform that could ameliorate some of the unfreedoms experienced by those working in the case study sectors and beyond.

5

Positioning Unfree Labour at the Centre of the Labour Analysis

1. Introduction

In this chapter, we attempt to answer two central questions: first, how does and how should our understanding of unfreedom inform our understanding and future development of labour law? And second, how do and how should well-rehearsed labour law principles and practices enrich our conceptualization of unfreedom. Our conclusion is two-fold: first, that beyond a certain point across the spectrum, some cases of unfree labour should not exist, and the law should thus seek to abolish these practices; second, that where examples of unfree labour are not sufficiently extreme, and thus allowed to exist, there is a general legal imperative to mitigate the consequences of the unfreedom and, indeed, to move the case further 'down' the spectrum towards less unfreedom or more freedom. These conclusions are set out in Fig. 5.1.

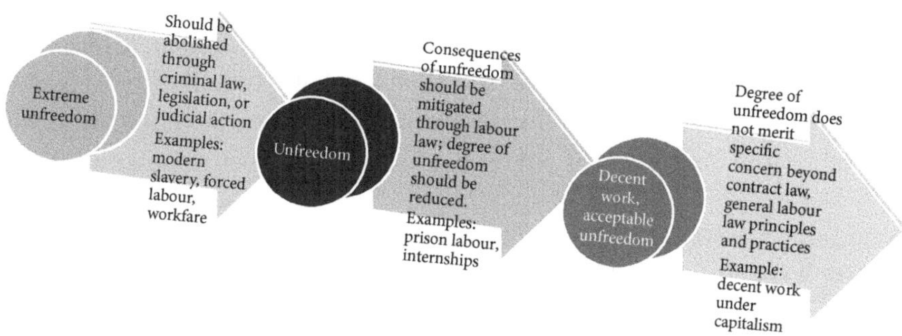

Fig. 5.1 Degrees of unfreedom and their consequences

Underpaid and Unrecognized. Katie Bales and Amir Paz-Fuchs, Oxford University Press.
 DOI: 10.1093/9780197910467.003.0005

2. What Is Unfree Labour? The Competing Paradigms and Normative Framework

a. The Paradigms: Inequality of Bargaining Power, Exploitation, and Domination

Perhaps it is not a coincidence that we enter this realm at a time when it is occupied with important, valuable, and thought-provoking contributions about the very purpose of labour law. In particular, these contributions seek to move labour law away from or at least to supplement the paradigm that has governed it for most of the twentieth century.[1] This, of course, is the position according to which 'the main object of labour law has always been, and . . . will always be, to be a countervailing force to counteract the inequality of bargaining power which is inherent and must be inherent in the employment relationship'.[2] However, given that approximately 60 per cent of the global workforce are located within the informal economy and are thereby excluded from the sphere of traditional 'employee status' and its associated rights, we can question whether labour law is meeting this core objective.[3] More recently, the door has opened to alternative positions regarding the ills that labour law seeks to address and, correspondingly, the cures that it offers, or at least should offer. In other words, this is the search for the rationale for labour law's intervention in or encroachment on freedom of contract.[4]

It can be immediately stated that, from our perspective, the supposed inadequacies of inequality of bargaining power are not, shall we say, resolved by other paradigms. Thus, for example, while the traditional rationale 'has been criticized for its lack of normative precision, i.e. that it is unable to determine who should be covered by labour laws, and what subjects ought to fall within its scope',[5] it is doubtful that alternative theories fare better. After all, these

[1] See eg Guy Davidov and Brian Langille (eds), *The Idea of Labour Law* (OUP 2011); Alan Bogg and others (eds), *The Autonomy of Labour Law* (Bloomsbury 2017); Brian Langille (ed), *The Capability Approach to Labour Law* (OUP 2019); Catherine Barnard, Simon Deakin, and Gillian Morris (eds), *The Future of Labour Law* (Bloomsbury 2021); Guy Davidov, Brian Langille, and Gillian Lester (eds), *The Oxford Handbook of the Law of Work* (OUP 2024).

[2] Paul Davies and Mark Freedland (eds), *Kahn-Freund's Labour and the Law* (3rd edn, Stevens 1983).

[3] International Labour Organization (ILO), 'More than 60 per Cent of the World's Employed Population Are in the Informal Economy' (30 April 2018) <www.ilo.org/resource/news/more-60-cent-world%E2%80%99s-employed-population-are-informal-economy> accessed 13 November 2025.

[4] David Cabrelli and Rebecca Zahn, 'Theories of Domination and Labour Law: A New Conception for Legal Intervention?' 33 International Journal of Comparative Labour Law and Industrial Relations (2017) 339.

[5] David Cabrelli and Rebecca Zahn, 'Guest Editors' Introduction' (2017) 33 International Journal of Comparative Labour Law and Industrial Relations 331, 332.

are normative, abstract theories that are subject to interpretation and application. It is quite obvious that different people would view 'domination' and 'unfreedom' differently in certain situations. However, this is not to say that we reject the quest wholesale. Quite the contrary. As Alan Bogg suggests, labour law must remain 'open to a wide range of different methodological approaches', and part of that exercise will involve harnessing paradigms which can assist us in 'understanding . . . the ways in which labour law is coherent as a field of regulatory activity'.[6] It is within this context that we suggest that freedom and unfreedom should claim an explanatory role.

Moreover, since unfreedom is, as expected, a contested and unclear notion, it is through these competing paradigms and rationales that the meaning of unfreedom gains meaning, coherence, and persuasiveness. Three main paradigms may be noted in this regard. We do so without engaging with their prescriptions in detail, but the overview will be instrumental to inform the doctrinal framework of unfree labour, in section 3.

First, neo-Marxists have found this to be an opportune time to reemphasize the centrality of exploitation in any employment relationship.[7] Unsurprisingly, a Marxist approach would not expect the scourge of exploitation to be remedied through legal, doctrinal reform, even a progressive one. Structural change is necessary to account for structural exploitation. A second approach has been recently offered by scholars who have found Republican philosophy to be appealing and relevant to labour law and labour relations. Here, domination is the matter of the gravest concern. And since unfreedom is identified with domination by all colours of Republican theory,[8] it will assist us in moving forwards. And, finally, scholars of a social justice persuasion have been troubled by the autocratic tendencies that are embedded in the employment relationship,[9] and some now suggest that the capabilities approach may provide remedies.[10]

What are we to make of this wealth of approaches, and where do freedom and unfreedom fit within this assemblage? Before we embark on the inquiry,

[6] Alan Bogg, 'Labour, Love, and Futility: Philosophical Perspectives on Labour Law' (2017) 33 International Journal of Comparative Labour Law and Industrial Relations 7.

[7] Horatio Specter, 'A Risk Theory of Exploitation' in H Collins, G Lester, and V Mantouvalou (eds), *Philosophical Foundations of Labour Law* (OUP 2018) 205; Judy Fudge, 'Modern Slavery, Unfree Labour and the Labour Market: The Social Dynamics of Legal Characterization' (2018) 27 Social and Legal Studies 414, 429.

[8] Elizabeth Anderson, 'Equality and Freedom in the Workplace: Recovering Republican Insights' (2015) 31 Social Philosophy & Policy 48, 52.

[9] Hugh Collins, 'Market Power, Bureaucratic Power and the Contract of Employment' (1986) 15 International Law Journal 1; Guy Davidov, 'Subordination versus Domination: Exploring the Difference' (2017) 33 International Journal of Comparative Labour Law and Industrial Relations 365.

[10] Langille (n 1).

a preliminary issue that needs to be addressed concerns the *purpose* of identifying such a rationale. One can suggest two central motivations in this regard. The first motivation is descriptive or, perhaps, explanatory. In the ongoing (and maybe futile[11]) quest for certainty and clarity, for 'making sense' of a wide range of legislation, statutory instruments, and judicial decisions, scholars sometimes seek to offer a rational for a subset within an area of law (eg unfair dismissal or trade union activity[12]), a legal discipline (eg labour law[13]), or even law as a whole.[14] Where this project is successful, it may take a step further by offering a structure from which a critique may be launched against decisions that fall foul of the stated rationales.

The second motivation seeks to find a normative rationale that, while having strong relevance to the subject matter (for otherwise it would fail to be persuasive), is centrally offered as a platform for reform and development (eg unfair dismissal law, labour law, or law in general). At times, as expected, the two motivations overlap: the author seeks to persuade us that the rationale (enhancing freedom, equality, etc) offers a good explanation for the vast majority of instances covered by the subject matter but is not realized to the fullest extent, as in 'while the aim of law is to enhance efficiency/support equality/ reduce conflict (cross as relevant), this decision/legislation undermines this goal'. This process of conflation was explicitly articulated in a slightly different context (with respect to the role of the judge) by Ronald Dworkin, in which he dubbed the first exercise as the effort to seek 'fit', whereas the second exercise as the aim to seek 'justice'.[15] We believe that while a two-stage or two-pronged approach is clearly legitimate, it is also useful to be clear what we are aiming to do (explain or prescribe) at each stage as we will, quite consciously, be critical of the current state of affairs and suggest that expansion and reform are necessary, particularly with respect to the normative scope, relational coverage, and standards of review.[16]

Now, we may start our enquiry by clarifying that rather than push one against the other, the paradigms noted above complement each other quite

[11] Jerome Frank, *Law and the Modern Mind* (first published 1930, Routledge 2007) 41: 'The genealogy of legal myth-making may be traced as follows: Childish dread of uncertainty and unwillingness to face legal realities produce a basic legal myth that law is completely settled and defined.'

[12] Alan Bogg and Cynthia Estlund, 'Freedom of Association and the Right to Contest: Getting Back to Basics' in Alan Bogg and Tonia Novitz (eds), *Voices at Work: Continuity and Change in the Common Law World* (OUP 2014) 142.

[13] See eg Guy Davidov, 'Articulating the Idea of Labour Law: Why and How' (2012) 3 European Labour Law Journal 130; Hugh Collins, 'Theories of Rights as Justifications' in Davidov and Langille (n 1) 137.

[14] See eg HLA Hart, *The Concept of Law* (3rd edn, OUP 2012).

[15] Ronald Dworkin, *Law's Empire* (Bloomsbury 1998).

[16] Cabrelli and Zahn (n 4) 350, 357.

nicely. Hopefully, this will not seem like a literal and figurative fudge. Thus, we find that for Frank Lovett, one of the most well-regarded scholars currently associated with civic republicanism, inequality of power is one of the three variables constituting domination. Indeed, Chapter 2 of his book—*A General Theory of Domination and Justice*[17]—is not only entitled 'The Imbalance of Power Conception' but also opens with a quote from Orlando Patterson, one of the foremost scholars of slavery, highlighting the links between slavery, domination, and imbalance of power.[18] Philip Pettit and Cecile Laborde, for their part, find non-domination as constitutive of freedom, emphasizing as they do that there is 'no domination without unfreedom ... Freedom involves emancipation from any such subordination, liberation from any such dependency.'[19] This suggests an emphasis not on 'non-interference' or 'freedom from the law' but rather 'freedom under the law' and the public status of the citizen.[20] Finally, Elizabeth Anderson, in her work, connects republican theory with both freedom and equality.[21]

But the juxtaposition of the different rationales encourages us to confront at least two central questions as to the purpose of labour law. First, is labour law concerned with *eradicating* the mischief that we identify (domination, inequality, unfreedom, etc) or solely with *mitigating* its consequences? Second, what should be the level at which we address the remedy—that of the individual or that of society? Focusing on inequality of bargaining power, and of social power more generally, Otto Kahn-Freund, for example, offered clear answers. As to the first question, he noted that 'there can be no society without a subordination of its members to others' and, specifically, that command and subordination are 'necessarily inherent in the employment relationship.'[22] Second, as perhaps implied in the quotes above, while he recognizes the background social structure, Kahn-Freund is clearly interested in the individual employment relationship and the consequences of subordination for which labour law must act as a 'countervailing force.'[23]

[17] Frank Lovett, *A General Theory of Domination and Justice* (OUP 2010).
[18] ibid 55, also 74–78, 120. See also Stuart White, 'The Republican Critique of Capitalism' (2011) 14 Critical Review of International Social & Political Philosophy 561, 565–67.
[19] Philip Pettit, *Republicanism: A Theory of Freedom and Government* (OUP 1997) 5.
[20] Cecile Laborde, 'Republicanism' in M Freeden, L Sargent, and M Stears (eds), *The Oxford Handbook of Political Ideologies* (OUP 2013) 525. Philip Pettit, *On the People's Terms: A Republican Theory and Model of Democracy* (CUP 2012).
[21] Elizabeth Anderson (n 8); Elizabeth Anderson, *Private Government: How Employers Rule Our Lives, and Why We Don't Talk about It* (Princeton UP 2017).
[22] Davies and Freedland (n 2) 14, 18.
[23] ibid 18. See similarly Collins (n 9); Guy Davidov, *A Purposive Approach to Labour Law* 53 (OUP 2016).

For some Republican theorists, at least,[24] the answer to the two questions posed above—'Eradicate or mitigate?', 'Focus on the individual or on society?'—may be slightly different. For Lovett, for example, domination is defined in a manner that is narrow enough to allow arguing for its eradication. In other words, if slavery, but not 'free market' employment, is the example of domination, it is much easier to argue for the elimination of all forms of domination. Such an aim would be much more complicated, realistically, if one were to recognize elements, and perhaps even necessary and inherent elements, of domination *within* an employment relationship. Alternatively, perhaps it is possible to identify *instances of domination* within labour law that could be surgically removed, thus improving the employment relationship at large. Thus, for example, Pettit notes that the unlimited power of US employers to dismiss workers 'at will' is a source of enhanced domination within the employment relationship.[25] In contrast, Alex Gourevitch, whose interpretation of domination is heavily indebted to Marx, unsurprisingly emphasizes 'structural domination', in which 'the unfreedom of the labourer is not a product of his situation vis-à-vis a specific employer, but rather of his dependence on *some* employer or another for livelihood'.[26]

Where does our approach to unfreedom meet this debate? As we saw with the example of Republican theory, a narrow definition of unfreedom (eg akin to slavery) would make it significantly easier to argue for eradication of unfreedom, whereas a wide definition (eg 'any limit on one's ability to live his or her life to the fullest') would necessarily move us to the terrain of 'assessing the ideal' or 'the optimal' rather than a hard-and-fast resolution. As will be clear from our discussion below, our approach to unfreedoms is far closer to the narrow definition of the concept, thus supporting an argument for the eradication of any manifestation. The main reason for choosing a narrow interpretation of unfreedom is that, unlike domination or inequality, writers on both sides of the labour divide (workers vs capital) have expressed their support for 'more freedom'. As is widely familiar, libertarians have spent much effort, with some notable successes over time,[27] seeking to stall and roll back labour law's regulatory structure through reference to 'freedom' in general and freedom of contractin particular. Thus, a wide definition of freedom would be appealing to many, employers and workers alike, but the cost would be a constant balancing

[24] See eg Lovett (n 17); Davidov (n 9) 376–78.

[25] Pettit (n 19) 185.

[26] Alex Gourevitch, 'Labor Republicanism and the Transformation of Work' (2013) 41 Political Theory 591, 602.

[27] *Lochner v New York* 198 US 45 (1905).

of quid pro quo freedoms and the calculus that it entails.[28] Replacing 'freedom' with 'real freedom',[29] which may be achieved through enhancing capabilities,[30] will probably only serve as preaching to the choir and will not persuade those who interpret freedom differently.

At this stage, however, we need to unveil what is meant by exploitation of power and how it is recognized and identified. This is because, notwithstanding the growing, important work which employs unfree labour as a normative concept that is instrumental for a critique of contemporary political economy, the literature tends to spend little time addressing the criteria for identifying unfree labour in practice and even less effort justifying these criteria.

b. [Un]Freedom on the Left, [Un]Freedom on the Right

Before we move to a more concrete analysis, we need to address the fact that scholars of different persuasions understand the concept of freedom, and its consequent ramifications, differently, even with respect to the freedom (or consent) to enter work, Neoliberals, for example (who we discuss in more detail in Chapter 6), do not view the market regime as facilitating coercion or in terms of impacting one's freedom. Friedrich Hayek, for example, explains that 'Even if the threat of starvation to me and perhaps to my family impels me to accept a distasteful job at a very low wage, even if I am "at the mercy" of the only man willing to employ me, I am not coerced by him or anybody else'.[31] And James Buchanan similarly stresses that freedom is distinct from power or ability. Freedom, he insists, is 'negative liberty'—'an individual is at liberty or free to carry on an activity if he or she is not coerced from so doing by someone else, be this an individual or a group'.[32] Indeed, for neoliberals, once the market structure is in place, it becomes impossible to regard any economic transaction as coercive.[33]

[28] Kahn-Freund was well aware of this 'ambiguity', which is inherent and misleading in the word 'freedom'—Davies and Freedland (n 22) 24.

[29] See eg Philippe van Parijs, *Real Freedom for All* (OUP 1995).

[30] Philip Pettit, 'Capability and Freedom: A Defence of Sen' (2001) 17 Economics & Philosophy 1, 17–19; Brian Langille, 'Labour Law's Theory of Justice' in Davidov and Langille (n 1) 111.

[31] Friedrich Hayek, *The Constitution of Liberty* (University of Chicago Press 1960) 137.

[32] James Buchanan, *Liberty Market and State: Political Economy in the 1980s* (Wheasheaf Books 1986).

[33] Rob van Horn and Philip Mirowski, 'The Rise of the Chicago School of Economics and the Birth of Neoliberalism' in Philip Mirowski and Dieter Plehwe (eds) *The Road from Mont Pelerin: The Making of the Neoliberal Thought Collective* (Harvard University Press 2009) 139, 162.

As established in Chapter 4, however, these positions clearly ignore a number of factors, including law's role in creating and enabling the market to function via private property rights, contract, and reduced labour rights as well as policy choices concerning state spending and welfare, which is linked to instances of intense poverty. These overarching background factors create a structure that can, in turn, result in a family sending a child to perform long hours of work and has led men and women to work in factories that are unsafe. Background structures thus work to restrict one's legitimate expectations and choices, thereby *forcing them to choose* to enter into a coercive relationship. Moreover, the premise of 'free' individuals leads to the conclusion that one's circumstances *are* the result of one's choices, thus making autonomy the friendly face of the imposition of personal responsibility.[34]

In contrast, Karl Marx patiently explained that 'The realm of freedom actually begins only where labour which is determined by necessity and of mundane considerations ceases.'[35] And Tawney expanded on this notion, asserting that 'there is no such thing as freedom in the abstract . . . Whatever else the conception may imply, it involves a power of choice between alternatives, a choice which is real, not merely nominal, between alternatives which exist in fact, not only on paper'.[36] Robert Hale develops Marx's perspective by delineating between 'voluntary' and 'volitional' freedom.[37] Whereas the former denotes an understanding of freedom where an individual has no constraints on autonomy or choice, the latter reflects the realities of freedom within the capitalist economy whereby choices are constrained by coercive pressures, much of which is shaped by legal rules that tend to strengthen the bargaining power of capital while reducing that of the workforce.

Contemporary scholarship follows Isaiah Berlin, implicitly Hale's distinction under the headings of 'negative' and 'positive' freedom (or, in Berlin's terminology, 'liberty').[38] Unlike negative freedom, positive freedom requires positive action from the state to enable equality of opportunity so that individuals are able to select the life choices that best suit them. And embracing the

[34] Wendy Brown, *Undoing the Demos: Neoliberalism's Stealth Revolution* (MIT Press 2015) 23–24; Jess, 'Neoliberalism, Family Law and the Cost of Access to Justice' (2017) 39 Journal of Social Welfare and Family Law 246, 249.

[35] Karl Marx, *Capital: Critique of Political Economy, Vol 3: The Process of Capitalist Production as a Whole* (Penguin 1894, rpnt 1992).

[36] Richard Tawney, *Equality* (first published 1952, Allen and Unwin 1964) 228.

[37] Robert Hale, 'Coercion and Distribution in a Supposedly Non-Coercive State' (1923) 38 Political Science Quarterly 470. See also Paddy Ireland, *Property in Contemporary Capitalism* (Bristol UP 2024).

[38] Isaiah Berlin, 'Two Concepts of Liberty' in I Berlin (ed), *Four Essays on Liberty* (OUP 1969) 118.

idea of 'positive freedom' as the true, and relevant, understanding of freedom, Amartya Sen explains that it is concerned 'with the real opportunity that we have to accomplish what we value'.[39]

As ideas for the welfare state crystallized, Karl Polanyi recognized these two types of freedoms, which for him were distinguished as bad and good. The former, associated with negative freedom, included 'the freedom to exploit one's fellows, or the freedom to make inordinate gains without commensurable service to the community . . . or the freedom to profit from public calamities secretly engineered for private advantage'. He explained, however, that the problem is that

> Planning and control are being attacked as a denial of freedom. Free enterprise and private ownership are declared to be essentials of freedom. No society built on other foundations is said to deserve to be called free. The freedom that regulation creates is denounced as unfreedom; the justice, liberty and welfare it offers are decried as a camouflage of slavery.[40]

Herein lies the problem, then. Both sides lay their claim to hold the ideal of freedom in their camp and any challenge to their ideal as slavery and unfreedom. As we expand in Chapter 6, the 'work or starve' choice is not a result of natural forces but rather of laws that enable or constrain opportunities, that limit or enable mobility, to access public lands and to own property, for example.[41]

By focusing on the constitutive elements of *un*free labour, we avoid the treacherous ground of seeking to enhance 'freedom for all'. And just as injustice is not simply a negative, derivative of the main concept (justice),[42] so unfreedom is not understood by offering it as the mirror image of a particular version of freedom.

[39] Amartya Sen, *Inequality Reexamined* (OUP 1992) 31 (emphasis in original). See also Brian Langille and Simon Deakin, 'The Capability Approach and the Economics of Labour Law' in Langille, *The Capability Approach to Labour Law* (n 1) 143.

[40] Karl Polanyi, *The Great Transformation* (Beacon Press 1954) 256–57.

[41] Seth Rockman, *Scraping By: Wage Labor, Slavery, and Survival in Early Baltimore* (Johns Hopkins UP 2009) 352; Stanley L Engerman, 'Slavery, Serfdom and Other Forms of Coerced Labor: Similarities and Differences' in M Bush (ed), *Slavery and Serfdom: Studies in Legal Bondage* (Pearson 1996) 18, 28–34.

[42] Eric Heinze, *The Concept of Injustice* (Routledge 2014).

3. Unfree Labour: The Doctrinal Framework

An intriguing facet of (parts of) legal academia lies in the pursuit of coherence and clarity through the development of doctrine, while simultaneously being captivated by the openness offered by theories and concepts in other fields of humanities and social sciences. The latter is clearly the case with the adoption of 'unfree labour' by legal academics. Praising its non-binary nature, its continuity and flexibility, scholars have found it a useful bludgeon to strike against contemporary structures and practices. However, the advantage of doctrine is a common language within which the debate can develop: is this (workfare, prison labour, internships) an example of unfree labour? What are your criteria? Do I disagree with your criteria or with its implementation? This section advances the discussion along those lines. In doing so, it may have the added, and somewhat surprising, advantage of assisting in disentangling, if not cutting through, some familiar labour law paradoxes.

We identify three such facets to unfree labour: consent, or its reversal—coercion, which affect one's ability to avoid entering an employment contract or their ability to leave; the conditions involved in the labour relationship; and the extent of control and discipline that governs the labour relationship, including the use of arbitrary power to affect the rights outside the labour relationship.[43]

But before we do so, we note and acknowledge a curious distinction between the case studies under examination and other contentious cases, for example, domestic work, gig economy, agency work, etc. This distinction could, perhaps, create challenges for the expansion of our approach beyond the case studies. This is because, as mentioned earlier, in the case studies at focus here, we ask 'who is a worker'[44] against a background in which the employers, the state, and the institutions seek to distance the working individuals from status as a worker, thus disassociating them from normalized recognition in the market and the rights with which they are associated. In contrast, apologists for the latter practices (agency work, etc) seek to highlight the 'normalcy' of existing arrangements in the vein of 'Look away, nothing to see here', while critics highlight facets of unfreedom that characterize the work and argue that these facets militate against viewing such work as distinct from mainstream,

[43] cf LeBaron (n) 9; Amir Paz-Fuchs, 'Badges of Modern Slavery' (2016) 79 Modern Law Review 757.
[44] Rockman (n 41) 7.

free labour, 'where workers could choose their own employers, receive cash wages for their time, quit at will and toil free of physical violence'.[45]

a. Consent to and within the Relationship

Whereas Chapter 4 was concerned with the underlying structural dimensions that may compel individuals to undertake unfree labour—this section is concerned with the labour relationship itself—in which consent is an important factor. As we argued in Chapter 4, consent must be contextualized against the structural dimensions outlined. Accordingly, consent (or lack thereof) is not the definitive feature of unfree labour practices but must be seen within the wider context of the labour relationship. This is already recognized in established labour law principles such as those outlined in *Autoclenz*,[46] whereby the courts are willing to look beyond the terms of the contract itself towards the wider labour relationship to establish the reality of the relationship between the parties.

As noted in Chapter 4, some view the lack of consent to enter employment relations as the defining factor, which distinguishes unfree from paid labour.[47] In particular, we referred to the ILO Convention on Forced Labour, which employs the notion of voluntariness and proscribes work 'under the menace of a penalty'. Later conventions seem even more aspirational in this regard. In the second half of the twentieth century, these aspirations found their axis in the somewhat contested right to work. Thus, Article 6 of the International Covenant on Economic, Social and Cultural Rights (ICESCR) refers to the right of everyone to 'gain a living by work which he freely chooses or accepts'. In Europe, the European Social Charter calls on states to protect workers' right to make their living 'in an occupation freely entered upon'.[48]

[45] ibid 5; Adelle Blackett, 'Emancipation in the Idea of Labour Law' in Guy Davidov and Brian Langille (eds) *The Idea of Labour Law* (OUP 2011) 420; Genevieve LeBaron and Alison Ayers 'The Rise of a "New Slavery"? Understanding African Unfree Labour Through Neoliberalism' (2013) 34 *Third World Quarterly* 873.

[46] *Autoclenz v Belcher* [2011] UKSC 41.

[47] James G Pope, 'Contract, Race and Freedom of Labor in the Constitutional Law of "Involuntary Servitude"' (2010) 119 Yale Law Journal 1474, 1482–86.

[48] Elise Dermine, 'Activation Policies for the Unemployed and the International Human Rights Case Law on the Right to Freely Chosen Work' in Elise Dermine and Daniel Dumont (eds), *Activation Policies for the Unemployed, the Right to Work and the Duty to Work* (PIE–Peter Lang 2014) 139–77; Colm O'Cinneide, 'The Right to Work in International Human Rights Law' in Virginia Mantouvalou (ed), *The Right to Work: Legal and Philosophical Perspectives* (Hart Publishing 2015) 99.

However, labour policy and labour law's engagement with the concept of 'consent to enter an employment relationship' raise not one but two paradoxical conundrums, both of which are intrinsically relevant for our case studies. First, notwithstanding the important liberal emphasis of the right to work, manifested most clearly in the provisions against slavery and forced labour, the right to work tends to sail quite closely to a *duty* to work.[49] The reason is that, as a matter of philosophy, politics, and policy, if the right to work is viewed as important enough to merit calls for full employment (because of work's inherently important value), it is surprisingly easy to make the additional, paternalistic move that suggests that if this is the case, then even those who are work shy should be 'encouraged' to take on work. Indeed, this linkage has been seen to explain why, notwithstanding international proclamations, one can identify ongoing reluctance to view the right to work unambiguously as an integral part of the human rights structure.[50]

Second, the focus on consent in our context leads to a second paradoxical situation since advocates of assigning rights to workers in schemes characterized by unfree labour (eg in the case of prison work, workfare, or internships) often go 'through' the employment contract; that is, they seek to establish that the relationship is an employment relationship, and from that employment relationship rights derive. And, as is well known, the traditional approach (which, of course, has its critics) views the employment contract as a *sine qua non* for the establishment of employment relationships. At the same time, however, these advocates stress the lack of consent embedded in these schemes, which indeed strengthens the case for the work involved to be deemed unfree. However—and herein lies the paradox—the more persuasive the argument that the work involved is not freely chosen, the less persuasive is the argument that a contract, let alone a contract of employment, can be established.

It should be noted that while our case studies present extreme cases of these paradoxes, they are evident in mainstream employment relationships as well. Marx, after all, referred to the worker being 'compelled to sell himself of his own free will';[51] and Kahn-Freund understood freedom of contract to be a necessary fiction, 'not more than the freedom to restrict or to give up one's freedom'.[52]

[49] Amir Paz-Fuchs, 'The Right to Work and the Duty to Work' in Mantouvalou, *The Right to Work* (n 48) 177; Lawrence Becker, 'The Obligation to Work' (1980) 91 Ethics 35.

[50] Paz-Fuchs (n 49); Guy Mundlak, 'The Right to Work: Linking Human Rights and Employment Policy' (2007) 146 International Labour Review 189, 194.

[51] Karl Marx, *Capital: Vol 1* (first published 1867, Penguin 1976) 932; Maayan Niezna and Guy Davidov, 'Consent in Contracts of Employment' (2023) 86 Modern Law Review 1134.

[52] Davies and Freedland (n 2) 18, 25.

As we argue below, we suggest that unpacking the concept of unfree labour and emphasizing its importance can offer a way through these paradoxes. But before doing so, we should ask: when should we find that a person is *coerced* to work, and what constitutes 'freely chosen employment'? Slavery is the paradigm example of coercion to work and, thus, of lack of consent. But even in far less extreme cases, 'there is necessarily a degree of coercion within every employment relationship'.[53] On the other hand, even *within* the extreme context of slavery, we tend to ignore (paternalistically, even if justifiably) the choices made within this context. For example, imagine a rebellious individual who was born or 'sold' into slavery and *refuses* to play their role and to work for their master. As a result, they may suffer extreme physical sanctions, perhaps even risking imprisonment or death. In simple terms, that is a choice.[54] Refusing to recognize the choice as such risks ignoring the agency that is expressed therein and assumes that the blatant, background immorality and illegality override the putative consent.

Indeed, while assessing consent, or lack thereof, one may focus on the action of the coercer to limit free choice. However, of at least equal importance is the ability of the coerced to truly consent, contextualized against (for example) the background structures set out in Chapter 4, which include individual vulnerabilities (such as disability) as well as the social relations giving rise to structures of race, class, and gender and the laws and regulations created by the state and society (including migration status, housing conditions, poverty, and imbalance of power) that apply. And yet, the law is, perhaps unsurprisingly, reluctant to view background structures as facilitating unfreedoms, as such an approach challenges the liberal ideology that values free will and self-sovereignty.[55] That said, courts are willing to identify vulnerability where the actions of a concrete individual are identified as creating the relevant conditions. Thus, in the case of *Kozminski*,[56] two individuals with significant cognitive disabilities worked on the defendants' farm sixteen hours a day, seven days a week. They were not supplied with adequate food, were forbidden to leave the farm to meet friends and relatives, and were routinely beaten. In the US

[53] Mark Freedland and Simon Deakin, 'The Exchange Principle and the Wage-Work Bargain' in Mark Freedland and others (eds), *The Contract of Employment* (OUP 2016) 52, 70.

[54] Robert Steinfeld and Stanley Engerman, 'Labor—Free or Coerced? A Historical Reassessment of Differences and Similarities' in T Brass and M van der Linden (eds), *Free and Unfree Labor: The Debate Continues* (Peter Lang 1977) 118.

[55] Karen Orren, *Belated Feudalism* (CUP 1991) 24.

[56] *US v Kozminski*, 487 US 931 (1987).

Supreme Court, Justice O'Connor stated that 'it is possible that threatening an incompetent with institutionalization or an immigrant with deportation could constitute the threat of *legal coercion* that induces involuntary servitude'.[57]

We find, then, that there is a strong connection between exploitation and vulnerability. Philippe van Parijs contests that since exploiting someone 'consists in taking *unfair advantage* of someone else's work', it 'makes no sense to ask whether there is anything wrong with exploitation. Exploitation is, by definition, unfair.'[58] The pertinent question then becomes: what is an 'unfair advantage'? Here, the identification of vulnerability is helpful since '[e]xploitation thrives in situations where one party is vulnerable'.[59]

As noted in Chapter 4, with respect to prison work, the ILO definition of forced labour excludes mandatory prison labour from its ambit. However, even within the confines of forced labour, Article 2(2)(c) of the Forced Labour Convention 1930 (No 29) stipulates that for prison work to fall within the state exception, it must be established and overseen by a public authority, and thus private entities should not utilize prison labour at their disposal unless such companies are able to obtain 'genuine consent'.[60]

Briefly, the United Kingdom has argued that since private entities provide work opportunities that are rehabilitative and are otherwise in short supply, under certain conditions (such as strict state supervision), prisoners benefit from working for private entities.[61] These arguments notwithstanding, an empirical study of prison work for the private sector have found that

> r*efusal* of such assigned work could result in punishment, such as being downgraded to 'basic' prisoner status, involving restricted access to television, assignment of prison garb, reduced visits from friends and family, less gym-time and less (or no) income. In this context the issue of coercion and the exercise of choice by the inmate was, ultimately, nuanced.[62]

[57] ibid 935, 948 (emphasis added). For further cases, see Baher Azmy, 'Unshackling the Thirteenth Amendment: Modern Slavery and a Reconstructed Civil Rights Agenda' (2002) 71 Fordham Law Review 981.

[58] van Parijs (n 29) 137 (emphasis added).

[59] Jennifer Collins, 'Exploitation at Work' in Alan Bogg and others (eds), *Criminality at Work* (OUP 2020) 97; Allen Wood, 'Unjust Exploitation' (2016) 54 Southern Journal of Philosophy 92, 96.

[60] International Labour Organization, *A Global Alliance Against Forced Labour: Global report under the follow-up to the ILO Declaration on Fundamental Principles and Rights at Work* (ILO 2005).

[61] Faina Milman-Sivan and Yair Sagy, 'On the International Labour Organization and Prison Labour: An Invitation to Recalibrate' (2020) 159 International Labour Review 505.

[62] Jenna Pandeli, Michael Marinetto, and Jean Jenkins, 'Captive in Cycles of Invisibility? Prisoners' Work for the Private Sector' (2019) 33 Work, Employment and Society 596, 604.

Indeed, when one inmate was asked whether he would accept such work outside of the prison context, he replied: 'No . . . I'd avoid it 100%. Because we're in prison we have to do it, we've got no choice.'[63]

Workfare also raises issues of consent. Thus, a European Commission report noted that, in the United Kingdom, concerns have been raised over 'young unemployed people being "forced" into Work Experience placements under the threat of losing unemployment benefits, although the scheme is intended to be voluntary'.[64] Moreover, critical scholars argue that it is this inability to identify a concrete actor that makes these coercive elements so potent since 'power over individuals is increasingly mediated through power over goods until the point is reached where the basic power is largely, though never completely, obscured'.[65] We may also recall that while workfare schemes are designated as 'purely voluntary', once included in the Claimant Commitment, the work must be completed, and if not, sanctions may apply.[66]

Further, consent is not and should not be assessed only at the entry point of the relationship. First, there is the exit point, that is, whether a worker is permitted to leave. Second, there is the matter of consent to demands and changes within the relationship and to what extent those may transform it to one that is 'unfree'. We will address the latter in subsection (b) below. As for the former, there is a long history of cases in England in which workers were punished by imprisonment if they withdrew unilaterally from a contract. The *Ordinance of Labourers* and the *Statute of Labourers* of 1351 mandated imprisonment for a worker or apprentice 'retained in service' if they did so,[67] making the labour contract 'public, long term and unbreakable'.[68] Even after abolition, a servant who left their master prior to the end of the contractual term was subject to imprisonment as one who stole from their employer.[69] It is estimated that during the latter part of the nineteenth century, over 10,000 workers were prosecuted for this offence.[70] This practice continued elsewhere

[63] ibid 606.

[64] European Commission, 'Study on a Comprehensive Overview on Traineeship Arrangements in Member States: Final Synthesis Report' (Publications Office of the European Union 2012) 84–86. <https://op.europa.eu/en/publication-detail/-/publication/19623a37-37ee-4a60-b7ba-14a555260 12f> accessed 13 November 2025.

[65] Orlando Patterson, *Slavery and Social Death* (Harvard UP 1982) 18; see, with particular emphasis on migrant labour, Bridget Anderson and Rutvica Andrijasevic, 'Sex, Slaves and Citizens: The Politics of Anti-Trafficking' (2008) 40 Soundings 135, 144.

[66] Anne Daguerre, 'The Unemployed and the Moral Case for Benefit Sanctions' (2015) 22 Journal of Social Security Law 130, 146.

[67] Robert Steinfeld, *The Invention of Free Labor* (University of North Carolina Press 1991) 28.

[68] Judith Bennett, 'Compulsory Service in Late Medieval England' (2010) 209 Past and Present 7, 13.

[69] Master and Servant Act (1823).

[70] Mark Curthoys, *Government, Labour and the Law in Mid-Victorian Britain* (OUP 2004); Simon Deakin and Frank Wilkinson, *The Law of the Labour Market* (OUP 2005) 74–86.

and well into the twentieth century. In 1944, the US Supreme Court referred to the 13th Amendment, which abolished slavery, and linked the terms and conditions of employment with the constitutional right to exit. It clarified, in *Pollack v Williams*,[71] the 'high watermark case of involuntary servitude',[72] that '[w]hen the master can compel and the labourer cannot escape the obligation to go on, there is no power below to redress and no incentive above to relieve a harsh overlordship or unwholesome conditions of work'.[73]

The legal situation was clarified by the ILO (at least insofar as extreme situations are concerned) when it stated that victims may be in a situation of forced labour even when they enter the situation freely but 'discover later that they are not free to withdraw their labour'.[74] One immediate implication of that decision is found in the place where immigration law and employment law meet. In an effort to 'control our borders', countries have put in place a restrictive immigration regime that limits the freedom that such migrant workers have vis-a-vis their employers. In Britain, when discussing the Modern Slavery Bill, the 2014 Parliamentary Joint Committee on Modern Slavery criticized changes made to the Immigration Rules 2012 (since abolished), which included the removal of the non-EU workers' right to change employers as it subjected domestic workers to 'vulnerability to abuse and exploitation'.[75] It stated that 'tying migrant workers to the employers institutionalises their abuse. It is slavery and is therefore incongruous with our aim to act decisively to protect victims of modern slavery'.[76]

However, beyond these clear instances, how far are we willing to expand the conclusion that unfreedom exists because background conditions limit the ability to exit? For Lovett, Shapiro, and Taylor, exit costs are the key source of dependency and, thus, of domination.[77] While consideration of exit restrictions is necessary for any account of domination, two issues arise. First, practically, exit costs are multifaceted, ranging from the mundane to the severe, and may be self-imposed, state-imposed, or imposed by non-state actors, such as employers. Family concerns, transition costs, insecurities, the need to commute, or financial penalties (eg in the form of non-compete

[71] 322 US 4 (1944).

[72] Noah Zatz, 'Discrimination and Labour Law: Locating the Market in Maldistribution and Subordination' in Collins, Lester, and Mantouvalou (n 7) 156, 172.

[73] *Pollack* (n 71) 18.

[74] ILO, *The Costs of Coercion* (ILO Labour Conference, 98th Session, 2009) 5.

[75] HL Paper 166/HC 1019 (2014) 100.

[76] ibid.

[77] Lovett (n 17) 39, 49–50; Ian Shapiro, *Democratic Justice* (Yale UP 1999) 43; Robert Taylor, *Exit Left: Markets and Mobility in Republican Thought* (OUP 2017).

clauses[78]) could all be 'costs' that lead an individual to stay in a job that they would prefer to leave. Would they all lead to 'dependency' and, moreover, to the conclusion that one's employment is 'unfree'?

Second, one should note the difference between associating lack of exit with unfreedom and domination, on the one hand, and emphasizing the existence of exit as the panacea to freedom and non-domination, on the other. Some (primarily Republican) theorists do, indeed, collapse the two, but while it is clear that the former assertion is sound, the latter is far less so. In other words, a strong exit right may be a necessary condition to escape the conclusion that labour is unfree, but it is not sufficient. This is because, of course, '"Exit" is an exercise in republican futility unless the underlying economic structures of domination are challenged and dismantled.'[79] Similarly, Anderson notes the affinity between Republican and libertarian emphasis on exit and warns that it should function as supplement to worker rights and not as their substitute.[80] It is not enough, in other words, to say, for example, 'freedom to resign is the ultimate guarantee of freedom of conscience' in the workplace, so such (and, presumably other) restrictions are legitimate by default.[81]

The denial of a right to 'exit' from a contractual relationship becomes acutely relevant in contemporary welfare-to-work programmes as well. In particular, the 2012 Welfare Reform Act and its underlying regulations expanded the scope of conditions that could lead to sanctions and introduced a tiered system with longer sanctions for serious violations, including an escalation approach, which increased sanctions for recidivists.[82] For present purposes, failure to participate in a prescribed course, such as a workfare scheme, was perceived as a medium level infraction, leading to a four week sanction for the first time; and thirteen weeks' denial of benefits for a recurring infraction that takes place within fifty-two weeks. Such sanctions, for individuals who rely on these benefits to heat and eat, essentially deprive them of the right to leave a workfare scheme, with all the repercussions noted above. Accordingly, it could be claimed that work is extracted from workfare claimants under the menace of penalty via the threat of benefit sanctions and from a constituency that is

[78] Cynthia Estlund, 'Between Rights and Contract: Arbitration Agreements and Non-Compete Covenants as a Hybrid Form of Employment Law' (2006) 155 University of Pennsylvania Law Review 379.

[79] Alan Bogg, 'Republican Non-Domination and Labour Law: New Normativity or Trojan Horse' (2017) 33 International Journal of Comparative Labour Law and Industrial Relations 391, 414.

[80] Anderson (n 21) 67.

[81] cf *Eweida v UK* [2013] ECHR 37.

[82] Michael Adler, *Cruel, Inhuman or Degrading Treatment—Benefit Sanctions in the UK* (Palgrave 2018) 36–37.

ultimately vulnerable due to its socio-economic position (as well as other possible factors). Yet, the bar set by the courts in assessing threat or penalty in the context of Article 4 of the European Convention on Human Rights (ECHR) is far higher than the threats utilized within workfare schemes. In *Reilly*, for example, the UK Supreme Court focused on the question of *exploitation*, finding that in the context of workfare, a condition (to work) is imposed on the payment of a state benefit. In this sense, the purpose of the condition was viewed as directly linked to the purpose of the benefit. This form of conditional benefit was therefore held as not coming close to the types of exploitative conduct that would trigger protection under Article 4 since 'the threshold for "menace of penalty" has, to date, been placed at a level that is too high to comfortably fit benefit sanctions'.[83]

In summary, it is clear that consent in employment relationships is not a binary concept but 'one of degree and context; the continuum of consent extends between free enthusiastic choice and duress'.[84] As such, it seems to be naturally accommodating to another concept that favours a continuum or 'spectrum' approach, that of unfree labour. It is possible, in other words, that the concept of unfree labour may assist us in resolving the paradox identified at the outset of this section, through the reliance of labour law. After all, labour law recognizes the imbalance of bargaining power and seeks to address its ramifications. Again, a Marxist approach would find the identification of consent in modern employment relationships, against the background of dire necessity, deeply problematic. And yet, labour law moves on, with the aim of mitigating the consequences of that imbalance of power. It would thus be peculiar to suggest that as that imbalance becomes more extreme (but yet not sufficiently extreme to merit the title of forced labour), labour law is unable to assist.

b. Terms and Conditions of Employment

Another interesting issue, which is relevant for our case studies, is the question of payment in relation to freedom. The fact that workfare recipients 'work for their benefits' (and, so their situation as beneficiaries is not improved by their work, that the host provider benefits from unpaid labour) and that many

[83] Amir Paz-Fuchs, 'Workfare's Persistent Philosophical and Legal Issues: Forced Labour, Reciprocity and a Basic Income Guarantee' in Anja Eleveld, Thomas Kampen, and Josien Arts (eds), *Welfare to Work in Contemporary European Welfare States* (Policy Press 2020) 31.

[84] Niezna and Davidov (n 51) 8.

interns in the United Kingdom receive no pay[85] may support the conclusion that such work is unfree. But what of, for example, prisoners, immigration detainees, and interns who receive pay that is below the national minimum wage? Does such pay undermine the case for unfree labour in these contexts?

What is clear is that the levels of pay afforded (if any) to those working within our case studies fall far below the national minimum wage, a matter which has been challenged on numerous occasions by the workers themselves. For example, in a 1968 decision of the European Commission of Human Rights,[86] which addressed the wages of prisoners in relation to Article 4, it was held that Article 4 did not contain any provision relating to the remuneration of prisoners for their work and referred to a long line of case law that rejected as inadmissible claims from prisoners seeking higher payment.

Working without pay or for below minimum wages thus reveals two things: first, that the individual in question is subject to multiple pressures coercing them into agreeing to work, as it is not the level of the wage itself that makes the labour attractive; second, that these individuals have limited mobility in the labour market, meaning there is no suite of employment options to choose from whereby workers can choose the working conditions most attractive to them. Indeed, low income is often used as an indicator of whether work should be considered precarious,[87] which Pollert considers alongside trade union non-membership as indicative of precarity.[88] Yet, Kevin Bales suggests that 'having enough money to get by, receiving wages that barely keep you alive, may be called wage slavery, but it is not slavery'.[89] He was criticized on this by LeBaron and Ayers for seemingly suggesting that *any* pay exculpates from the charge of unfree labour.[90] However, this critique seems unfair on two levels. First, it would appear that Bales simply suggested that low pay, and even very low pay, does not *necessitate* the categorization of slavery; but not necessarily that any pay removes the charge if there are other factors that point to it. Second, and more pertinent for present purposes, it seems that LeBaron and

[85] European Commission (n 64) 89–90.

[86] *Twenty-One Detained Persons v Germany* (Nos 3134/67, 3172/67, 3188–3206/67, *Collection* 27) 97–116.

[87] Krisztián Pósch and others, 'Scale and Nature of Precarious Work in the UK' (London School of Economics, University of Gloucestershire, University College London, April 2020) <https://assets.publishing.service.gov.uk/media/61b72ecfd3bf7f055fce74b4/scale-and-nature-of-precarious-work-in-the-UK.pdf> accessed 14 November 2025.

[88] Anna Pollert, *The Unorganised Worker: Problems at Work, Routes to Support and Views on Representation* (Centre for Employment Studies Research, Bristol Business School, University of the West of England 2005).

[89] Kevin Bales, *Disposable People: New Slavery in the Global Economy* (University of California Press 2004) 5.

[90] LeBaron and Ayers (n 45) 877.

Ayers conflate slavery with the wider category of unfree labour. And while receiving pay could, arguably, remove an individual from the category of slavery, it need not be the conclusion with respect to unfree labour. Thus, predatory working practices could be viewed as a form of unfree labour and/or 'serious exploitation' and would include the failure to pay holiday pay, overtime, or minimum wage.[91]

In *Kozminski*, Justice Brennan stressed that 'oppressive working and living conditions, *and lack of pay* or personal freedom are the hallmarks of that slavelike condition of servitude'.[92] It should be stressed that the first half of the list of criteria (namely, 'oppressive working and living conditions') is not redundant. Thus, individuals who objected to being 'forced' to 'work for free' were unsuccessful in claiming before the European Court of Human Rights that being required to provide free legal aid constitutes 'forced labour'.[93] And a US court reached a similar result when high-school students objected to their school's mandatory community volunteering programme.[94] And yet, it is important to stress, again, that these cases dealt with the higher bar of forced labour, whereas we are concerned with the intermediate range of unfree labour. Indeed, the claim that workfare is 'forced labour' was focussed on the lack of pay, as recipients 'work for their benefits'. That claim didn't succeed in court, but could the argument that lack of pay supports the conclusion that labour is 'unfree', in this case and in the case of our case studies, for example,[95] be more successful? If so, what could be the legal implications? More generally, the paradoxical nature of the claim which focuses on pay as a feature that distinguishes free from unfree labour is the fact that it centres the discussion within the capitalist—and thus productivist—paradigm and is distanced from the critical (eg feminist and environmental) approaches that seek to reduce reliance on market-based criteria. Again, the concept of unfree labour may be of assistance.

We noted, in subsection (a) above, the relevance of consent not only to points of entry and exit but also to conditions and demands within the relationship. As is well known, labour law places some matters beyond the realm of negotiation and, thus, consent. In most countries, a worker cannot agree to

[91] Jennifer Collins (n 59) 97; Wood (n 59) 96; Alan Bogg, 'Sham Self-Employment in the Supreme Court' (2012) 41 International Law Journal 328.

[92] *Kozminski* (n 56) 935, 962–63.

[93] *Van der Mussele v Belgium* (23 November 1983) (Application No 8919/80); *X v Federal Republic of Germany* (1974) 17 Yearbook 148.

[94] *Steirer v Bethlehem Area School District* 789 F Supp 1337, aff'd, 987 F.2d 989 (3rd Cir 1992), cert denied, 114 SCt 85 (1993).

[95] European Commission (n 64) 89–90.

work for a wage that is below a prescribed minimum or to waive their right to a set number of hours of rest per day or per year.[96] However, beyond such statutory minima (and subject to the existence of relevant collective agreements), the worker is deemed to be able to consent to a wide range of terms and conditions, and labour law is putatively uninterested in the result of the negotiation. Recently, Niezna and Davidov suggested revisiting this premise, by offering a series of procedural rules and substantive standards against which such consent will be assessed.[97] The procedural rules would seek to ensure that the consent is informed, by requiring, inter alia, that it is explicit, in clear writing, in plain language, and held in a repository. Perhaps more relevant for present purposes, the substantive standards they suggest 'are designed to invalidate agreements which are deemed to be unacceptable'.[98] This will be done by reference to familiar standards such as good faith, proportionality, reasonableness, and a 'fair exchange'[99] or, in Niezna and Davidov's much more catchy phrase, 'the wage of consent'.[100] Their presumption is parallel to the strong relation law and society accord to an individual's consent to medical treatment and sexual interaction with their age. In the same way that the law assumes that an individual in those contexts has more capacity to understand the actions and implications if they are above a certain age, the assumption in employment contexts would be that a high earner has more *power* to negotiate the terms and conditions and, consequently, to freely agree.

c. Control and Discipline

While labour lawyers have always recognized the subordination embedded within the contract of employment, they have traditionally been concerned with expanding, enhancing, and reforming the contract of employment to mitigate the effects of subordination.[101] The reason they did not opt to throw the baby out with the bath water was because they also noted the advantages that the contract of employment offered the employee, neatly expressed by the quip, 'The misery of being exploited by capitalists is nothing compared to the

[96] Guy Davidov, 'Non-Waivability in Labour Law' (2020) 40 Oxford Journal of Legal Studies 482.
[97] Niezna and Davidov (n 51).
[98] ibid 13.
[99] The latter refers to the suggestion by Freedland and Deakin (n 53) 52, 54–58.
[100] Niezna and Davidov (n 51) 16.
[101] See eg Mark Freedland and Nicola Kountouris, *The Legal Construction of Personal Work Relations* (OUP 2011) 433–46. For a critical perspective, see Joanne Conaghan, 'Work, Family and the Discipline of Labour Law' in Joanne Conaghan and Kerry Rittich (eds), *Labour Law, Work, and Family. Critical and Comparative Perspectives* (OUP 2005) 19.

misery of not being exploited at all.'[102] Indeed, that is why many labour lawyers show frustration with tribunal and court decisions that deny, on particular occasions, the existence of the contract of employment, and our case studies offer examples to that effect. The contract of employment offers a bargain of security and stability, on the one hand, for subordination and dependence, on the other. Indeed, the 'paradox of the modern contract of employment is that it emancipates labour at the same time that it subordinates it'.[103] Incorporating political economy into labour law analysis will bring us closer to the understanding that 'Slavery and forced labour present particularly extreme versions of labour law's core concerns with subordination, not outliers relative to the core problems of labour markets.'[104]

Indeed, the importance of paying attention to instances of unfree labour became poignant during the confusing—and to some, traumatic—reinvention of practices during the COVID-19 pandemic of 2020, with the expansion of monitoring and surveillance. However, this process was already moving at an alarming pace with the development of the gig economy, and even in office workspaces. A few months *prior* to the collective move to work from home, one worker notably told the BBC that 'if we stood up or spoke to each other we were constantly watched, it felt like we were in prison'.[105] While the interviewee is associating the workplace with prison practices in a loose fashion, it does require one to think about the open-ended features of the managerial prerogative in 'normal' circumstances.[106] This includes surveillance and monitoring of communication, use of fitness trackers[107] (perhaps analogous to ankle bracelets?), and mandating polygraph tests.[108]

Under this heading of control, we turn now to discuss a strongly related but also importantly distinct facet, which is the control of the worker's right *outside* the physical and substantive work environment. Although slavery was common throughout the ancient world, the Roman Empire's model of slavery is one of the most notable insofar as modern practices are concerned. The master's complete control over the slave's life and, in particular, the power to

102 Joan Robinson, *Economic Philosophy* (Penguin 1962) 46.
103 Bogg (n 79) 407.
104 Zatz (n 72) 171–72. See also Blackett (n 45) 430.
105 Sarah Griffiths, 'We Were Constantly Watched. It Felt Like We Were in Prison' (BBC, 8 July 2019) <www.bbc.com/worklife/article/20190705-we-were-constantly-watched-it-felt-like-we-were-in-prison> accessed 13 November 2025.
106 Gali Racabi, 'Abolish the Employer Prerogative, Unleash Work Law' (2021) 43 Berkeley Journal of Employment and Labour Law 79.
107 Stefania Marassi and Philippa Collins, 'Is That Lawful? Data Privacy and Fitness Trackers in the Workplace' (2021) 37 International Journal of Comparative Labour Law and Industrial Relations 65.
108 Steven Willborn, 'Consenting Employees: Workplace Privacy and the Role of Consent'(2005) 66 Louisiana Law Review 975, 1000.

change one's status from a free person to a slave, were important characteristics of Roman slavery. The latter power was seen as justified since slaves were, primarily, prisoners of war whose lives were spared by military commanders.[109] The corporeal death from which they were spared was replaced with *social* death,[110] a perspective that is applied in the context of irregular migrants by Mayblin,[111] who draws on the literature of necro-politics to elucidate the 'slow violence' to which many migrants, particularly asylum seekers, are subjected within the United Kingdom's immigration industrial complex. In contemporary fiction, Colson Whitehead captures the servant's feeling of being controlled in totality as an evening of revelry can be interrupted at any moment by 'the overseer's cry, the call to work, the shadow of the master, the reminder that she is only a human being for a tiny moment across the entirety of her servitude'.[112]

For Henry Maine, the shift from status to contract was an indicator of 'progressive societies'[113] because, inter alia, of the legal system's willingness to protect an individual's rights regardless of class or status.[114] However, insofar as the employment relationship is concerned, matters become more complicated. The contract, as we saw, could also serve as a mechanism to entrench status and social subordination. Referring to Weber's notion of 'status contracts', Steinfeld explains that the master's control over the slave—and, in many ways, the employer's control over the worker—are more akin to *governance* than to a commercial relationship. For this reason, a slave's murder of their master was considered not only homicide but also treason.[115]

To what extent do contemporary employment practices follow the historical lead? Elizabeth Anderson finds that even for mainstream employment relationships, the authority of employers through the employment contract is 'sweeping' as they exercise legal power to govern the lives of their employees on and off the job.[116] She offers examples of workers losing their job or otherwise sanctioned for having a gay partner, for suing their daughter's rapist,

[109] Robert Cover, *Justice Accused: Antislavery and the Judicial Process* (Yale UP 1984) 11.

[110] Patterson (n 65) 5.

[111] L Mayblin, M Wake, and M Kazemi, 'Necropolitics and the Slow Violence of the Everyday: Asylum Seeker Welfare in the Postcolonial Present' (2019) 54 Sociology 107; L Mayblin, *Impoverishment and Asylum: Social Policy as Slow Violence* (Routledge 2019).

[112] Colson Whitehead, *The Underground Railroad* (Penguin Random House 2018) 28.

[113] Henry Maine, *Ancient Law* (10th edn, John Murray 1884) 172–74.

[114] Otto Kahn-Freund, 'A Note on Status and Contract in British Labour Law' (1967) 30 Modern Law Review 635; Frances Raday, 'Status and Contract in the Employment Relationship' (1989) 23 Israel Law Review 77.

[115] Steinfeld (n 67) 56–58, referring to Max Weber, *Economy and Society*, vol 2 (University of California Press 1968) 674.

[116] Anderson (n 21) 63.

for supporting political candidates who their managers oppose, for refusing to attend political rallies for candidates who they (the workers) oppose, or for refusing to diet or exercise in accordance with corporate wellness programmes.[117] We mentioned that during the COVID-19 pandemic, more attention was drawn to employer's technical and legal capacity to use surveillance technologies. These were not limited to work related issues but rather were used to map their workers' interpersonal relationships, study their conversations, collect data on their health, and track where they travelled on and off the job, as well as monitoring and manipulating their emotional responses.[118]

For the reasons already noted, labour lawyers will not be quick to accept the Republican theorists' association of the contract of employment with unfreedom (and the contrast—freedom that may be gained only outside of the employment relationship).[119] However, Republican theorists' emphasis on arbitrary power and its constitutive role in creating domination should give labour lawyers pause when they consider the legitimate range of the managerial prerogative and the employer's power in matters that are not intimately related to the employment relationship.

A recent Employment Appeal Tribunal (EAT) case, concerning (yet again[120]) a Facebook post that led to dismissal, covers the familiar ground regarding freedom of speech, freedom of religion, and discrimination.[121] In that case, a pastoral teacher shared an alarmist post concerning the teaching of sexual tolerance towards LGBT+ individuals within primary schools. And yet, what is depressingly absent in the analysis of both the employment tribunal and EAT (even while the EAT reversed the decision to deny the claim) is the effort to establish the relevance of the post, troubling as it may be, to the claimant's job as a pastoral tutor in a school.[122] Indeed, not only did the claimant assert that she was misunderstood (she claimed that she was concerned about the messages that her own children will receive in their school, not about the school in which she was employed and does not hold the views attributed to her) but also that the employer did not claim, at any point, that those views were manifest in her treatment of students.

[117] ibid 63–64.

[118] JS Nelson, 'Management Culture and Surveillance' (2020) 43 Seattle University Law Review 631.

[119] ibid; Anderson (n 21) 53.

[120] Virginia Mantouvalou, '"I Lost My Job over a Facebook Post: Was That Fair?" Discipline and Dismissal for Social Media Activity' (2019) 35 International Journal of Comparative Labour Law and Industrial Relations 101; *Obst v Germany* (23 September 2010) (Application No 425/03) Merits and Just Satisfaction.

[121] *Higgs v Farmor's School* [2023] EAT 89.

[122] Amir Paz-Fuchs, 'From Belief to Speech and Back Again' (2025) 16 European Labour Law Journal 62.

Moving now away from mainstream employment relations, Hatton identifies the *main purpose* of the control exerted across each of the four 'labor regimes' that she studied (workfare participants, prison inmates, graduate students, and student athletes) as distinct from each other.[123] In all the cases, domination and exploitation undergird the motivation for control and discipline, but not to the same extent. In particular, she finds that exploitation (in the sense of extracting surplus value from labour) is the main purpose of the subjugation of students, in a manner that is similar (if more pronounced and extreme) to that of workers in the mainstream labour markets. This position can arguably be applied in a straightforward manner to our analysis of interns. In contrast, while exploitation exists in the cases of inmates and workfare participants, the driving purpose is *domination*: the workers are 'surveilled and regulated, they are degraded and abused, and they are routinely dehumanized in an effort to exert (racist) disciplinary control over them'.[124]

Indeed, indications to that effect can be found by reference to workfare participants, and the power to deny participants benefits for minor infractions. Moreover, as Hatton highlights, the fact that employment rights do not apply to participants correspondingly expands the scope of instances that could lead to sanctions. Thus, a woman complied with her workfare assignments until her son became gravely ill and hospitalized.[125] A single parent was denied benefits for four months after a year of complying with requirements because his shift changed overnight, and he was not able to arrange for his son to be taken to school.[126] Finally, other participants were penalized because they objected to unhealthy and unsafe working conditions, including heavy dust, bedbugs, and other environmental hazards.[127]

This discretionary power which, contrary to predictions, has not abated, offers street-level bureaucrats the opportunity to control participants' behaviour and to determine what activation policies actually mean.[128] As Deguerre and Etherington conclude, with respect to workfare,

[123] Erin Hatton, *Coerced: Work under Threat of Punishment* (University of California Press 2020) ch 3.

[124] ibid ch 3.

[125] ibid 62–99.

[126] ibid.

[127] ibid ch 3.

[128] Joel Handler, 'Social Citizenship and Workfare in the US and Western Europe: From Status to Contract' (2003) 13 Journal of European Social Policy 229; Jorunn Jessen and Per Arne Tufte, 'Discretionary Decision-Making in a Changing Context of Activation Policies and Welfare Reforms' (2014) 43 Journal of Social Policy 269.

> What emerges under the [Work Programme], the escalating sanctions regime, is the image of an authoritarian workfare state which delegates much of its sanctioning powers to contracted out welfare to work providers, while at the same time eroding some of the support services that are at the heart of active labour market policies. Welfare beneficiaries are being subjected to increased monitoring and surveillance, in what appears to be an unbalanced welfare contract.[129]

Turning to the case studies, we find that such violence is sublimated and attenuated and yet is clearly apparent. As outlined in Chapter 2, the conduct of prisoners and immigration detainees while in detention is monitored outside of the labour relationship, giving rise to their removal from labour opportunities if they display violent, non-conformist, or non-compliant behaviour. Somewhat ironically, one can point to the very rationale that led to the exclusion of these workers from the protection of rights and status as the same rationale that facilitates their complete control. We refer here to the configuration of this type of work and labour as educative, rehabilitative, and motivated by a desire to train and prepare for the vagaries of the employment market. In part, this was referred to there as the 'self-realization' rationale. While clearly grounded in historic (at times religious) origins, this rationale has found new life in the positive psychology discourse, which

> coproduces and validates the core mythologies of neoliberalism while simultaneously . . . shift[ing] attention away from the social patterning of unemployment and from wider trends: market failure, precarity, the rise of in-work poverty, the cost of living crisis and the scale of income inequalities.[130]

The approach is thus simultaneously individualistic and holistic. It is individualistic by virtue of its tendency to identify the worker's barriers to productive labour as such that they can overcome; and it is holistic in that, in addressing these barriers, complete access must be granted to complete their 'makeover'—their motivation, attitude, capacities, inclinations, are all subject to revision to fit a particular mould. Failure to overcome one's traits, of course, is

[129] Anne Deguere and David Etherington, 'Workfare in 21st Century Britain—the Erosion of Rights to Social Assistance' (November 2014) 82 <http://workfare.org.uk/images/uploads/docs/Workfare_in_21st_century_Britain-Final.pdf> accessed 13 November 2025.

[130] Lynne Friedli and Robert Stearn, 'Positive Affect as Coercive Strategy: Conditionality, Activation and the Role of Psychology in UK Government Workfare Programmes' (2015) 41 Medical Humanities 40, 42, 45.

attributed to 'not trying hard enough' and, thus, justifiably subject not only to sanctions—as in the case of participants who were too shy to speak during role-playing activities[131]—but also to the 'grotesque daily practices of condemnation and disenfranchisement of those who are the most socially and economically disadvantaged'.[132]

4. From Unfree Labour to the Labour Market: Lessons from Institutional Theory

We have hinted above that focusing on unfree labour is important because it provides a prelude, a trial balloon, to trends that have become, are becoming, and will become, more prevalent in the labour market at large. For decades (and, in some countries, for over a century), workers' rights have become increasingly entrenched. Political scientists who focus on institutional theory would explain this entrenchment in the language of 'path dependency' and 'feedback policy'. Path dependency suggests that 'critical junctures' are shut down due to cultural, political, and economic legacies that make some options far less feasible or attractive. Everyday examples abound, making it very difficult to change rules and behaviours that are entrenched. Feedback policy is closely related as it explains that past policies reinforce and then reproduce future decisions as they 'force and facilitate' the pursuit of particular strategies that past policies advanced.[133] However, notwithstanding the traditional focus on institutions as stable in themselves, and facilitating stability in society (partly as a consequence of path dependency and feedback), more attention has been directed, particularly since the turn of the century, to the way institutions 'evolve and change over time'.[134]

It would be useful, perhaps, to clarify that contemporary approaches not only view traditional agencies, such as national banks or state agencies, as 'institutions' but also broaden the scope of the concept to regimes that involve '*mutually related rights and obligations for actors*, distinguishing between appropriate and inappropriate, "right" and "wrong", "possible" and "impossible" actions and thereby organizing behaviour into predictable and

[131] ibid 43, 44.
[132] ibid 45.
[133] Kathleen Thelen, 'Historical Institutionalism in Comparative Politics' (1999) 2 Annual Review of Political Science 369.
[134] ibid 396.

reliable patterns'.[135] Moreover—and crucially, unlike informal rules and customs, such as shaking hands when entering a room—the formalized rules that underpin institutions may be enforced by calling upon a third party.[136] This ability to enforce the rules brings us closer to the socio-legal realm by creating legitimate expectations in law and in society at large. Against this background, it is clear that policies in general (such as early retirement policies), and labour market policy in particular, may be considered 'institutions' if they stipulate rules that assign rights and responsibilities, backed by third-party enforcement.[137]

Within the range of institutional theories (ie theories that are interested in the development and impact of institutions), we find that historical institutionalism (HI) is most interested, and thus best placed, in identifying how and why institutions *change*. In particular, rather than focusing on identifiable, 'crisis' moments, which lead to a 'puncturing' of an existing equilibrium,[138] HI understands that the very mechanisms that explain the stability and persistence of particular institutional arrangements are those that identify their vulnerability and prospects for change.[139] Moreover, this vulnerability may be exposed and exploited gradually, over significant periods of time, leading to the eventual change of the institution itself.

We conclude here by suggesting that HI shows how the proliferation of unfree labour, from the margins to the centre, is already chipping at labour status and labour protections, not just at the fringes and margins, thus expanding the atypical and the precariat at the expense of the 'typical' and protected and

> normalis[ing] the idea that certain groups of people are not entitled to payment for their labour and that lengthy periods of unpayment (internships or 'volunteering') are a precondition for employment . . . It is important to understand the extent to which activities that until very recently would have been classified as 'work' are now rebranded as 'work preparation' and are hence both unpaid and characterised in terms of 'psychological preparation'.[140]

[135] Wolfgang Streeck and Kathleen Thelen (eds), *Beyond Continuity: Institutional Change in Advanced Political Economies* (OUP 2005).
[136] ibid 11.
[137] ibid 12.
[138] Avner Greif and David Laitin, 'A Theory of Endogenous Institutional Change' (2004) 98 American Political Science Review 633, 639.
[139] Kathleen Thelen and James Conran, 'Institutional Change' in Orfeo Fioretos, Tulia Falleti, and Adam Sheingate (eds), *The Oxford Handbook of Historical Institutionalism* (OUP 2017).
[140] Friedli and Stearn (n 130).

This is done through a number of strategies that have already been documented in other realms, some closely related to labour policy, some more remote. We address those that are relevant to the matter at hand.

The first strategy is *layering*. A classic example of this strategy concerns the US social security system that was considered, precisely because of path dependency and feedback, as 'politically unassailable'.[141] And yet, as Jacob Hacker has showed, those who targeted the system managed to add a layer of individual, market-based, pensions to supplement the existing system.[142] Similarly, in Israel, 'Sick Funds', which provide universal health care under a social insurance-based platform, added the option of subscribing to individual health plans for an additional fee, which would allow patients to choose their physician, have access to better facilities, and (controversially) jump queues.[143] Here, the mechanism is not to move individuals from one system to another but rather to allow new entrants to make use of the additional system, on occasion or more frequently, until it gains popularity and undermines the support for the original, public system.

Turning to the case at hand: unfree labour, as a regime that allocates rights and responsibilities, has existed for thousands of years, even in the most extreme versions of slavery and forced labour. However, its contemporary 'challenge' was to resurface against the background of the welfare state and, particularly, labour law protections that were established during the course of the twentieth century. Adding a layer of exception within existing labour law and policy so that existing rules of the regime do not apply to designated sectors, for designated individuals (eg prisoners) creates the option of placing new entrants (eg workfare participants or interns) within this less attractive category. The role of the courts in this regard is central as they have been devising rules, in the form of doctrines, that facilitate these exceptions and exemptions, which can later be applied widely.

The second strategy is *drift*, which refers to a situation in which the rules remain stable, but the background environment changes, whether by design (eg active political engagement) or not (eg changes in gender roles in the family). As such, drift can supplement rather than be independent of layering. After new rules are in place, structural changes may lead to institutional changes in a

[141] ibid 63.

[142] Jacob Hacker, 'Privatizing Risk without Privatizing the Welfare State: The Hidden Politics of Social Policy Retrenchment in the United States' (2004) 98 American Political Science Review 243.

[143] Aeyal Gross, 'The Right to Health in Israel between Solidarity and Neo-Liberalism' in Colleen Flood and Aeyal Gross (eds), *The Right to Health at the Public/Private Divide: A Global Comparative Study* (CUP 2014) 159.

way that wouldn't have existed otherwise. Thus, Hacker's example above, concerning pension schemes in the United States, is supplemented by the fact that active sponsorship by politicians, policymakers, and private entities encouraged individuals to sign up to the new schemes.[144] With respect to unfree labour, the recession following the 2008 financial crisis placed young people in a particularly vulnerable situation, with youth unemployment reaching extraordinary heights of close to 30 per cent in Greece, Italy, and Ireland, over 40 per cent in Spain and a staggering 52 per cent in the United States.[145] In response, governments began to promote internship schemes as a way to hide unemployment, businesses and public-sector bodies began to use them as form of unpaid or low-paid labour, and courts relied on legal doctrines (see *layering*) to rubber-stamp the drift. Unpaid internships thus 'crept into labour market policy'.[146]

Each of these strategies can bring about significant institutional change in its own right. However, they may also serve as stepping stones towards a further strategy, that of *conversion*. Conversion takes place when institutions are '*redirected to new goals, functions or purposes*', so existing institutions 'adapt to serve new goals or fit the interests of new actors'.[147]

5. Conclusion

Now place the split screen before your mind's eye: on the right you have prison labour, workfare, migrants in detention centres, and interns. In all these cases, workers are subject to low or no pay; are not entitled to labour protections; have limited choice as to entering or existing the employment relationship or its terms and conditions; and suffer from excessive control, exploitation, and discipline over their life within and outside of work. But they have also undergone a process of 'othering', in which 'their' toil is considered unrepresentative of the median, average, or representative worker.

But now, on the left screen of your mind's eye, see the collage of domestic workers, gig economy (Uber and other) workers, agency workers, workers on zero-hour contracts, in call centres and in warehouses, all of which experience a working reality that bears something—at times, much—in common with the

[144] Jacob Hacker, 'Policy Drift: The Hidden Politics of US Welfare State Retrenchment' in Streeck and Thelen (n 135) 40.
[145] Guy Standing, *The Precariat: The New Dangerous Class* (Bloomsbury 2011).
[146] ibid 75.
[147] Streeck and Thelen (n 135) 26 (emphasis in original).

paradigmatic cases of unfree labour noted above. Excessive instances of coercion, harassment and exploitation, control, and invasion of privacy should not be seen to reflect a perversion of governing norms any more than slavery and forced labour should have been seen to reside 'outside' of capitalism. Instead, they should be understood and conceptualized as warning signs to a growing trend in which forces at play are seeking to change the institution of work and to expand, entrench, and legitimize unfree labour through the courts and through social approval.

6

The Political Dimension

Neoliberalism, Privatization, and State Complicity

1. Introduction

One of the defining traits of all the case studies analysed in this book is the strong involvement of government agencies not only as regulators but also in initiating, facilitating, and implementing the work performed. In some cases, government arms, such as agencies or local councils, are also the main beneficiaries of the work extracted from participants in these schemes. In other cases, for-profit corporations are involved in running the schemes and profiting from the work performed. The extent of these collaborations, and the particular forms that they take, have yet to be identified and analysed, particularly in the United Kingdom. A focus on unfree labour that receives direct support and resourcing from governments illuminates the role of the state, which may play a direct and formal role, while at other times 'lurking in the background', preferring to enjoy a certain 'invisibility'[1] rather than being acknowledged as a key structure or agent driving unfree labour.

The governing rationality for the practices identified is currently referred to as neoliberalism, under which humans are viewed, first and foremost, if not solely, as economic actors. Unlike classical liberalism, under neoliberalism, the state does not withdraw but rather reappears and even enhances its activity in a way that serves corporate interests and guarantees *their* freedoms.[2] As Loïc Wacquant has noted, '[W]hat is "neo" about neoliberalism [is] the reengineering and redeployment of the state as the core agency that sets the rules and fabricates the subjectivities, social relations and collective

[1] Genevieve LeBaron and Nicola Phillips, 'States and the Political Economy of Unfree Labour' (2018) 24 New Political Economy 1, 2; Frederick Mayer and Nicola Phillips, 'Outsourcing Governance: States and the Politics of a "Global Value Chain World"' (2017) 22 New Political Economy 134.

[2] Rob van Horn and Philip Mirowski, 'The Rise of the Chicago School of Economics and the Birth of Neoliberalism' in Philip Mirowski and Dieter Plehwe (eds), *The Road from Mont Pèlerin* (Harvard UP 2009) 139, 157.

Underpaid and Unrecognized. Katie Bales and Amir Paz-Fuchs, Oxford University Press.
 DOI: 10.1093/9780197910467.003.0006

representations suited to realising markets.'[3] Mirowski (translates and) quotes Foucault, who observed in 1978 that 'Neoliberalism should not be confused with the slogan "laissez-faire", but on the contrary, should be regarded as a call to vigilance, to activism, to perpetual interventions.'[4]

For those who are curious as to why we noted that these practices are '*currently* referred to' under the banner of neoliberalism, we permit ourselves to point to earlier chapters in which the long history of the schemes was described. After all, practices from past centuries, in which states mobilized quickly to sacrifice workers' and protect capital's interests would clearly be understood as part of a neoliberal regime if they were to occur today. This is especially the case if such state initiative would even render 'free market' principles as insignificant in the process. A well-known example followed the Black Death of the fourteenth century. After it decimated between a third and a half of Europe's population, manual workers found that their labour was in high demand in a way that could increase their bargaining power. Responding to that 'threat', Edward III's Council legislated, first, the Ordinance of Labourers 1349 and then, more famously, the Statute of Labourers 1351 to restrict workers' freedom of movement. These laws prescribed that every man or woman, 'free or unfree, aged sixty years or younger . . . must serve whoever required his labour', for wages set out in the 1351 Statute and under the threat of imprisonment.[5] In a similar vein, Robert Miles emphasized the articulation of pre-capitalist forms of unfree labour, such as bonded labour, to provide a supply of labour for emerging capitalist production regimes. He also highlighted the coercive power of the state in reproducing unfree labour.[6]

And yet, while the past may seem prologue on some occasions, the cooptation of past practices by current ideological paradigms is both interesting and notably prevalent. The revolutions, emancipations, and changes in mindset would have suggested that rationales on which initiatives such as the Statute of Labourers were founded could not see the light of day in this century. And yet, the fact that they not only resurface in myriad instances but also acquire 'conspicuousness, *extensive development and legitimacy*' is important.[7]

[3] Loic Wacquant, 'Three Steps to a Historical Anthropology of Actually Existing Neoliberalism' (2012) 20 Social Anthropology 66.

[4] Philip Mirowski, 'Postface: Defining Neoliberalism', in Mirowski and Plehwe (n 2) 417, 434, citing Michel Foucault, *Naissance de la biopolitique: Cours au Collège de France 1978–9* (2004).

[5] LR Poos, 'The Social Context of Statute of Labourers Enforcement' (1983) 1 Law and History Review 27, 29–30.

[6] Robert Miles, *Capitalism and Unfree Labour: Anomaly or Necessity* (Tavistock 1987).

[7] Michal Tabibian-Mizrahi and Michael Shalev, 'Precarious Employment in the Public Sector: How Neoliberal Practices Preceded Ideology' in Asa Maron and Michael Shalev (eds), *Neoliberalism as a State Project: Changing the Political Economy of Israel* (OUP 2017) 139, 149 [emphasis added].

The latter, italicized segment is important for our purposes because, while the success of neoliberalism has spawned extensive literature, including some efforts to decipher the reasons for its success, its clear failures have not led to its demise.[8]

In particular, insofar as the analysis of the impact of neoliberalism on labour and the labour market is concerned, the focus is routinely on deregulation, privatization, market flexibility and new public management, and the ensuing effect on workers.[9] This is unsurprising and legitimate. And yet, Chapters 4 and 5 have shed light on practices that, while marginal when compared to the overall labour force, are more extreme and, thus, more dangerous. It is our claim that the forces that are driven by the neoliberalism paradigm to create precarity are the same forces that expand the realm of unfree labour.

2. The State and Freedom under Neoliberalism

There is a story about the role of the state with respect to free labour that isn't necessarily articulated explicitly as such but goes something like this: initially, the state facilitated and perpetuated unfree labour. It instigated slavery and enforced it, either directly or through third parties (eg the East Indian company[10]). However, at some point (which varies for different countries), the state took on an emancipatory role. This role was first evident with the abolition of slavery *strictu sensu* (ie the legal ownership of people), but increasingly, it enacted a wider array of protections that enhanced *freedoms from the market* or from third party actions. Thus, the state, incrementally but consistently, legislated to safeguard health and safety, job protection, wages, a decent work/life balance, protection from unmerited discrimination, and so forth. Where the state was not successful or, alternatively, was slow to succeed, the explanation tended to be that other forces—predominantly 'big business'—were more effective at mobilizing the political and legal resources to counter the benevolent forces and interests that the state advances. The state, therefore, is not only part of the *response* to unfree labour but also, moreover, may even be construed as one of its victims.[11]

[8] Colin Crouch, *The Strange Non-Death of Neoliberalism* (Polity 2011).

[9] David Harvey, *A Brief History of Neoliberalism* (OUP 2005) 75–76, 169.

[10] William Dalrymple, *The Anarchy* (Bloomsbury 2019).

[11] LeBaron and Phillips (n 1) 3, referring to International Labour Organization (ILO), 'Profits and Poverty: The Economics of Forced Labour' (International Labour Office 2014) <https://doi.org/10.54394/JJJE9035>.

Two conclusions derive from this story. First, the state has always been involved in the construction of freedom and unfreedom. We will endeavour to show how this is indeed the case. But there is a second conclusion in this story, according to which it is a (Whig) story of linear progress, a move from unfreedom to freedom in which the state is a central actor. This conclusion leads many to considerable frustration when they find that the power of the state is used to retract individual freedom rather than enhance it. But the reason for this disappointment is simple: high expectations. The linear progression story was always a false—or, at least, a more complicated—one. Before we move on from this narrative, it is worth quickly reflecting on its power and pull. In important ways, this position is not only naïve but also logically peculiar. One need not adhere to libertarian, or anarchic, positions to concede that, under a narrow understanding of freedom (ie to operate without restriction) the state—be it the 'welfare state', 'the administrative state', or the 'regulatory state'—is quite active in *limiting* freedoms rather than enhancing them. One cannot build a house, open a shop, or breed cattle without adhering to myriad restrictions on one's otherwise free ability to do so. If that is the case, why would the modern state be perceived as *enhancing* freedoms?

The source of this peculiar vision of the state, then, seems to owe much to the appeal (in some circles) of the welfare state. In particular, it recognizes that the freedom espoused by libertarian and anarchists (ie the idea that people are truly free without the state) is poor freedom indeed. It is, to paraphrase Anatole France, the majestic freedom to sleep under the bridge and to beg in the street or, conversely, to sleep at the Ritz. Notwithstanding Isaiah Berlin's protestations in support of a strict, binary opposition of 'negative' liberty (freedom from . . .) and 'positive' liberty (freedom to . . .),[12] which we referred to in Chapter 5, it seems clear that 'real freedom' enmeshes both.[13] If one wishes to be 'free' to become a lawyer, one needs to live in a jurisdiction in which one's sex, belief, or the colour of one's skin will not be a barrier (negative freedom); but one will also need to be lucky enough to be able to take part in an education system that is accessible, of high quality, and caters for individual needs; be serviced by a health system in which a family illness does not transform into a debilitating economic factor (all positive freedoms); and so on.

Some suggest that the role of the state should be judged differently with respect to the overstated divide between civil and political (CP) rights, on the

[12] Isaiah Berlin, 'Two Concepts of Liberty' in I Berlin (ed), *Four Essays on Liberty* (OUP 1969) 118.

[13] Philippe van Parijs, *Real Freedom for All: What (If Anything) Can Justify Capitalism?* (OUP 1997) 18.

one hand, and social and economic (SE) rights, on the other. With respect to the former, state actions will tend to limit rights. More state involvement in the sphere of speech or religion, for example, would mean less freedom to speak or practice religion. On the other hand, insofar as SE rights are concerned, their existence relies on realization through state action. Thus, the right to health or education cannot be said to truly exist if the state does not build hospitals and schools, train doctors and teachers, and pay the wages of those involved.

And yet, this distinction goes only so far (and not very far). Even with respect to central cases of CP and SE rights, the ideal role of the state cannot be stated in technical, value-neutral, terms as interventionist or non-interventionist.[14] Thus, the right to vote, a paradigmatic political right, is rendered moot without significant state intervention. Conversely, women's health in many countries is impacted severely not only by what the state does not do (eg build enough clinics) but also by what it does decide to do (eg restrict women's choices). President Roosevelt, in addressing the US Congress in 1935, was perhaps conscious of the rhetorical challenge posed by this divide when he framed his cry for a social justice platform in the language of freedom, asserting that 'necessitous men are not free men' and that 'freedom *from* want' was one of four foundational freedoms grounding his political vision. But even if this binary distinction were to hold—though, as mentioned, it does not—it is difficult to place the right to work within a framework that intersects with the role of the state. Thus, work would exist (or would not even struggle to exist) even without state intervention. It has in the past, and in some places, it still does. Some Law and Economics adherents routinely argue that not only employers and the inanimate 'marketplace' but also workers would benefit if government intervened less in the workplace, including in areas such as equality and discrimination.[15] As such, work may be 'free' in a way that health and education simply cannot be. However, the lack of state intervention is not inconsequential. In fact, it tends to create room for coercion, exploitation, and indeed unfree labour. Indeed,

> Advancing the paradigmatically liberal conception that the state is a neutral actor that responds to various interest groups in the context of formal equality, it appears in this literature that . . . states have played no role in fostering the conditions that have given rise to an acceleration of unfree labour. . . . this

[14] Amir Paz-Fuchs, *Welfare to Work: Conditional Rights in Social Policy* (OUP 2008) 18–29.

[15] Friedrich Hayek, *The Road to Serfdom* (University of Chicago Press 1944); Milton Friedman, *Capitalism and Freedom* (University of Chicago Press 2002); Richard Epstein, *The Classical Liberal Constitution: The Uncertain Quest for Limited Government* (Harvard UP 2014).

> paradigm thus overlooks a central mechanism of power deeply imbricated in the rise and expansion of these relations.[16]

So, where a state does not make child labour illegal, it flourishes—and often not because it is the wish of children and their families. If sports' teams are allowed to include a term in their contracts with professional athletes according to which the player cannot move to another team even after *the original contract has ended*, then those contracts will be drafted and signed. If health and safety standards are not codified and enforced, disasters will happen. It may be worth recalling, in this context, that the US Supreme Court decided, in *Lochner v New York*,[17] that a federal statute which provided that no worker would be required to work in a bakery for more than sixty hours per week or ten hours per day was deemed to be an 'unreasonable, unnecessary, and arbitrary interference' with the individual's (both the employer's and the worker's) right to freedom of contract.[18]

As explored in Chapter 5, neoliberals 'extol freedom as trumping all other virtues; but the definition of freedom is recoded and heavily edited within their framework'.[19] Whereas they clearly view taxation and regulation as emblematic of *un*freedom, they also resort to authoritarian tactics to advance neoliberal goals. The latter insight is less obvious, and less discussed, and thus merits some elaboration.

It is clear that, in contrast to mainstream, traditional liberalism, neoliberals are deeply suspicious of democratic governance. The reason for this is found in their unwavering trust in the market, which will always surpass the state's ability to process information.[20] What is less obvious is that neoliberals seek not to destroy the state but rather to redefine its shape and functions to make them subservient to market logic and institutions. To achieve this goal, they advocate strengthening the role of unaccountable institutions, such as the central banks and international financial institutions like the International Monetary Fund (IMF). From the 1980s, neoliberalism became the reigning paradigm as states advanced an 'open-ended and contradictory process of politically assisted market rule'.[21] According to Mirowski, Hayek felt that 'a strong

[16] Genevieve LeBaron and Alison Ayers, '"The Rise of a 'New Slavery"? Understanding African Unfree Labour through Neoliberalism' (2013) 34 Third World Quarterly 873, 873, 878.
[17] 198 US 45 (1905).
[18] ibid 54–55.
[19] Mirowski (n 4) 437.
[20] ibid 435.
[21] Jamie Peck, *Constructions of Neoliberal Reason* (OUP 2010) xii.

state was necessary to neutralize what he considered to be the pathologies of democracy'.[22] He explains,

> The contradiction that the neoliberals constantly struggle against is that a strong state can just as easily thwart their program as implement it; hence, they are inclined to explore new formats of techno-managerial governance that protect their ideal market from what they perceive as unwarranted political interference. . . . One implication is that democracy, ambivalently endorsed as the appropriate state framework for an ideal market, must in any case be kept relatively impotent, so that citizen initiatives rarely change much of anything . . . Hence, the neoliberals seek to restructure the state with numerous audit devices (under the sign of 'accountability') or better yet, convert state services to be provided on a contractual basis. One should not confuse marketization of government functions with shrinking the state, however: if anything, bureaucracies become more unwieldy under neoliberal regimes. In practice, 'deregulation' cashes out as 're-regulation', only under a different set of ukases.[23]

We expand on the importance of the 'contractual basis' at some length below. For now, however, this insight suggests that the well-known linkages between Chicago and Santiago (de Chile), and the heavy influence of prominent neoliberals on the authoritarian regimes in South America, were more in line with neoliberalism's general approach than an historical aberration.[24] Indeed, the neoliberal state supports intense state interventions, 'sometimes repressively, *thus denying the very freedoms it is supposed to uphold*'.[25] Karl Polanyi deftly captures this dualism:

> [T]he road to the free market was opened and kept open by an enormous increase in continuous, centrally organized and controlled interventionism . . . Administrators had to be constantly on the watch to ensure the free working of the system. Thus, even those who wished most ardently to free the state from all unnecessary duties, and whose whole philosophy demanded the

[22] Mirowski (n 4) 443.
[23] ibid 436.
[24] Karin Fischer, 'The Influence of Neoliberals in Chile before, during, and after Pinochet' in Mirowski and Plehwe (n 2) 305, 326–28.
[25] Harvey (n 9) 69.

> restriction of state activities, could not but entrust the state with new powers, organs and instruments required for the establishment of *laissez faire*.[26]

Harvey explains that 'This was precisely Polanyi's fear: that the [neoliberal] utopian project could only ultimately be sustained by resort to authoritarianism. The freedom of the masses would be restricted in favour of the freedoms of the few.'[27] In other words, the authoritarian streak in neoliberalism can be explained by reference to the difficulty in sustaining a system that so clearly skewed in favour of the few. As resistance grows and failure mounts, stronger coercive tools become necessary to preserve the illusion of market rationality and individual responsibility. The apparent contradiction between a philosophy of liberty and a reality of control is reconciled in the neoliberal mindset by declaring all state interventions that support markets and discipline labour as enhancers of freedom. Focusing this issue on the workplace as an instance of private government, Elizabeth Anderson asks, 'Why do workers in capitalist societies work under a dictatorship, rather than a democracy or some less authoritarian form of government?' and swiftly explains, 'the answer is *not* that workers accept it because they can get better pay and benefits . . . It is because state laws make it so.'[28]

Harvey, Polanyi, and others knew that their fears were merited because the intellectual foundations of neoliberalism, and the political involvement of its protagonists, were never too far from an authoritarian streak. A study of the work of early neoliberal thinkers reveals a heavy reliance on Italian and German scholars from the interwar period. Most prominent among them was, in Hayek's words, 'Adolf Hitler's crown jurist Carl Schmitt, who consistently advocated the replacement of the "normative" thinking of liberal law by a conception of law which regards as its purpose "concrete order formation".'[29]

This quote leads us to the final stage of this introductory overview and to a discussion of the role of law in the construction of freedom in general and under neoliberalism in particular. After all, barring exceptional circumstances, in which state authoritarianism is manifested through brute force and violence, in the vast majority of cases, such power is mediated through law and through enforcement agencies. This did not escape the neoliberals. As Simon Deakin

[26] Karl Polanyi, *The Great Transformation: The Political and Economic Origin of Our Times* (Beacon Press 1944) 140.

[27] ibid 70.

[28] Elizabeth Anderson, 'Equality and Freedom in the Workplace: Recovering Republican Insights' (2015) 31 Social Philosophy and Policy 48, 61.

[29] Friedrich Hayek, *Studies in Philosophy, Politics and Economics* (Simon & Schuster 1967) 169.

notes, under the Hayekian view of the market, 'property law identifies the subject of the exchange, contract law enforces voluntary agreements, and tort law ensures protection of the person and of property'.[30] As Robert Hale explained a century ago, there is no 'market' in the abstract, a *tabula rasa* against which relationships develop.[31] The state decides, for example, to protect the right to property and contractual obligations, and when it does so, it correspondingly puts in place a wide range of relationships. The owner of property will dictate terms, which a prospective worker can (supposedly) accept or reject. However, Hale continues, the worker must eat. And while there is no law against eating, or refraining from eating, there is a law against taking food that is seemingly accessible in public, and that is the law of property. Therefore, unless the non-owner of property can produce his own food, 'the law compels him to starve if he has no wages, and compels him to go without wages unless he obeys the behest of the employer'.[32] Elsewhere, he explains the implications of this analysis to our understanding of the voluntariness of the contract:

> It will not do to say that the party to a contract is a voluntary agent merely. He makes the contract in order to acquire certain legal rights he does not now possess, or to escape certain legal obligations with which he is now burdened. Were his liberty not restricted by these obligations imposed by the law and enforced in the ordinary courts, he might never submit himself to the new obligations of the contract.[33]

To offer a more contemporary, and poignant, example, this book's genesis developed over the course of the COVID-19 pandemic of 2020 as the tragic situation of workers in the Leicester fashion sweatshops was unfolding. It transpired that, in late 2020, workers in England were paid around £3 per hour (the minimum wage was £8.72 at the time), exposed to extremely poor health and safety conditions, and forced to work even when they were sick. Their 'choice' to work there, inasmuch as it existed, was constructed and dictated by the background immigration structure to which many of these workers were subject and, in particular, the 'hostile environment' that included the No Recourse to Public Funds (NRPF) policy. Hale pre-empted this scenario in terms that

[30] Simon Deakin, 'Conceptions of the Market in Labour Law' in A Numhauser-Henning and M Ronnmar (eds), *Normative Patters and Legal Developments in the Social Dimensions of the EU* (Hart Publishing 2013) 141, 146.

[31] Robert Hale, 'Coercion and Distribution in a Supposedly Non-Coercive State' (1923) 38 Political Science Quarterly 470, 472.

[32] ibid 473.

[33] Robert Hale 'Law Making by Unofficial Minorities' 20 Columbia Law Review 451, 452–53.

are even more familiar to a modern reader of labour law. He explains that one's freedoms in the market, as well as *the strength of his bargaining power*, are the result of 'legal rights with which the law endows him, and the legal restrictions which it places on others'.[34] Property is then both a bundle of rights and a social relation, granting people power not only over things but also over other peoples' access to things.[35] Particularly through its construction and defence of property and contract rights, the law opens some avenues and limits others, thus creating a seemingly neutral baseline from which 'freedom' is wrongly judged. The neoliberals, peculiarly like Marxists and unlike those with whom they are wrongly confused (the anarchists and the libertarians), were acutely aware of this feature of rights and viewed the transformation of rights as central to their project. Walter Lippmann, who was among those formulating the early neoliberal creed, explained,

> Only by recognizing that legal rights are declared and enforced by the state is it possible to make a rational examination of the value of any particular legal right. The latter-day liberals did not see this. They fell into a deep and confusing error when they failed to see that property, contracts, corporations, as well as governments, electorates, and courts, are creatures of law, and have no existence except as bundles of enforceable rights and duties.[36]

Hayek was also acutely aware of the role that law plays in the constitution of powers of the relevant actors as well as the construction of the idea of freedom itself. Speaking about the potential and actual role of trade unions, for example, Hayek wrote, 'if there is to be any hope of a return to a free economy, the question of how the powers of trade-unions can be appropriately delimited by law as well as in fact is one of the most important of all the questions which we must give our attention'.[37] Hayek did not settle for raising the 'question' of trade unions. In contrast to other founding members of neoliberalism, who considered the possibility that collaboration between employers and unions would mitigate the true threat of *state* power, Hayek viewed unions as a clear threat not only to the 'spontaneous order' of the market but also to the rule of law itself.[38] Identifying them as a threat to the constitutional order and a form

[34] Hale (n 31) 625.
[35] Wesley Hohfeld, 'Some Fundamental Legal Conceptions as Applied in Judicial Reasoning' (1913) 23 Yale Law Journal 16; Paddy Ireland, *Property in Contemporary Capitalism* (Bristol UP 2024).
[36] Walter Lippman, *An Enquiry into the Principles of the Good Society*, quoted in P Dardot and C Laval, *The New Way of the World: On Neoliberal Society* (Verso 2013) 59.
[37] Friedrich Hayek, '"Free" Enterprise and Competitive Order' in Friedrich Hayek (ed), *Individualism and Economic Order* (Routledge 1949) 107, 117.
[38] Yves Steiner, 'The Neoliberals Confront the Trade Unions' in Mirowski and Plehwe (n 2) 181, 192.

of 'legal coercion',[39] he thus advocated trade unions' *legal disenfranchisement* as a vehicle to restore the rule of law which, in turn, is indistinguishable from the market.

Unlike mainstream legal scholars, then, both advocates and critics of the neoliberal agenda recognized that the law never

> simply provides neutral rules of the game and the state's role should be to ensure a 'level playing field' between market actors . . . The creation of a labour market and free wage labour in the metropole depended upon state power—the creation of private property and the 'right' to alienate one's labour power.[40]

Therefore, it may be useful to reconstruct the seminal formulation according to which the role of labour law is meant to balance the inequality of bargaining power insofar as one understands that inequality of bargaining power as the creation of the 'free' market. Instead, a more sombre, and accurate, understanding would be that the inequality of bargaining power is the creation of the law and, thus, an extension of the state. Consequently, what the law giveth with one hand (severe and manifestly unfair inequalities of bargaining power) the law can taketh away through labour protections.

3. State Involvement in Unfree Labour: Three Layers of Contract

LeBaron and Phillips outline a range of ways in which states may exercise power in direct and indirect ways that facilitate unfree labour.[41] Most clearly, in the former, the state would directly impose unfree labour, at times (as in the case of workfare) through primary legislation,[42] in a manner that harks back to the Statute of Labourers 1351, which was noted above. Indirect strategies that do so include policies which distribute social and labour rights and protections unequally (as in the case of prison work, internships, and labour in immigration detention); the non-enforcement of labour legislation and regulation

[39] ibid.

[40] Judy Fudge, 'Modern Slavery, Unfree Labour and the Labour Market: The Social Dynamics of Legal Characterization' (2018) 27 Social & Legal Studies 414, 418–19.

[41] LeBaron and Phillips (n 1) 3.

[42] Anja Eleveld, 'The Duty to Work without a Wage: A Legal Comparison between Social Assistance Legislation in Germany, the Netherlands and the United Kingdom' (2014) 16 European Journal of Social Security 204, 209.

against abusive labour recruitment practices; and policies that facilitate the concentration of private ownership of land, food and water, as explored earlier in this book.

This section purports to show how the state is implicated in the rationales, philosophy, institutions, and implementation of the case studies of unfree labour on which we focus by reference to the most foundational construct in the neoliberal arsenal, that of the contract. As Virginia Held proclaimed in 1993, when neoliberalism was in its ascendancy, 'Contemporary Western society is in the grip of contractual thinking.'[43] And, indeed, enhancing 'contractual thinking' is a perfect example of the neoliberal project, which viewed 'the "heart of the contract" as a *sine qua non* of freedom.'[44] The contract facilitates the expansion of market transactions, through which neoliberalism advances 'economization's enlarged domain—it reaches to practices and crevices of desire heretofore unimaginable ... [the] homo economicus approaches everything as a market and knows only market conduct; it cannot think public purposes or common problems in a distinctly political way.'[45]

The contractual mindset can be described by reference to three distinct, but interrelated, layers: the ideological (or 'philosophical'), the institutional, and the field level. We refer to them as the macro, meso, and micro levels. While distinguishable, the three layers are also interrelated. Thus, the first layer drives and rationalizes actions in the second and third layers, allowing actors to judge their actions against its tenets and to justify their actions if necessary. In addition, actions and perceptions in the micro level may lead policy makers and politicians to revisit their ideological positions.[46]

a. The Macro Level of Contractualism: Philosophical and Symbolic Aspects

i. The social contract revisited

At the most abstract level of contractualism, we find the reference to the effort to change nothing less than the relationship between the state and its citizens, often through reference to the 'social contract'. Early social contract theorists,

[43] Virginia Held, *Feminist Morality: Transforming Culture, Society and Politics* (University of Chicago Press 1993).
[44] van Horn and Mirowski (n 2) 143.
[45] Wendy Brown, *Undoing the Demos: Neoliberalism's Stealth Revolution* (Zone 2015) 32.
[46] Francis Fox Piven and Richard Cloward, *Regulating the Poor* (2nd edn, Vintage 1993).

such as Thomas Hobbes,[47] John Locke,[48] and Jean-Jacques Rousseau,[49] referred to the hypothetical or theoretical 'social contract' to justify the existence of the state and for the moral requirement for obedience. Twentieth-century social contract theorists, such as John Rawls[50] and David Gauthier,[51] sought to revive its relevance by using it to justify (some) state institutions and to argue for what they viewed as the justifiable distribution of resources. And, indeed, this level of contractualism, at times via reference to 'reciprocity', is employed when seeking to justify the schemes of the type examined in this book to taxpayers, on the one hand, and to those subject to them, on the other.[52]

For present purposes, it will be helpful to focus on the modern deployment of the (social) contract in the search for a grand principle through which one can derive institutions, rights, and criteria for redistribution. In particular, it is interesting that both the political left and the political right make reference to the metaphor of the contract as a vehicle to achieve individual dignity and social equality. Famously, John Rawls asks us to imagine ourselves behind the 'veil of ignorance' before we come together to decide on the principles of justice that should govern society. Behind that veil, one does not know one's sex, gender, skin colour, disability, intelligence, wealth, etc. The reason is obvious: while our positions are heavily influenced by these factors, they shouldn't be. And so, the only way to think about principles of justice is to disregard these factors. At this point, if people are rational and at least risk-neutral (and perhaps even risk-averse) when they come together to think about the social contract principles, they will arrive at two principles: first, the liberty principle, which requires that all social goods should be distributed equally. The second principle includes two strands, one that focuses on equal opportunities and a second—the difference principle—that allows for deviation from strict, equal distribution of resources only if the unequal distribution will leave those who are worst off in a situation that is (Pareto) superior to their previous (equal distribution) situation. Ronald Dworkin pointed out that the role of equality is so central in Rawls's social contract theory that, while the theory

[47] Thomas Hobbes, *Leviathan* (Cambridge University Press 1992). For Hobbes's role as the first to clearly articulate the social contract theory, see Michael Lessnoff, *Social Contract* (MacmillanHampton 1986) 13; Jean Hampton, *Hobbes and the Social Contract Tradition* (Cambridge University Press1986) 3.

[48] John Locke, 'The Second Treatise' in Peter Leslett (ed) *Two Treatises of Government* (Cambridge University Press 2000).

[49] Jean-Jacques Rousseau, *The Social Contract* (Wordsworth 1998).

[50] John Rawls, *A Theory of Justice* (Harvard University Press first published 1971, rev edn 1999).

[51] David Gauthier, *Morals by Agreement* (OUP 1984).

[52] Mark Freedland and Desmond King, 'Client Contractualism between the Employment Service and Jobseekers in the United Kingdom' in Els Sol and Mies Westerveld (eds), *Contractualism in Employment Services: A New Form of Welfare State Governance* (Kluwer 2006).

may be criticized for a variety of reasons, 'it cannot be denied in the name of a more radical concept of equality, because none exists'.[53] Similarly, Tim Scanlon argues that Rawls's acceptance of equality as the first solution to the problem of justice suggests that the difference principle marks the limits of acceptable inequality.[54] As equal participants in a system of social cooperation, members of society have a prima facie claim to an equal share of the benefits that society creates.[55] A serious onus is thus placed on those advancing a structure that exhibits non-egalitarian foundations.

Unsurprisingly, neoliberals have also found the idea of the (social) contract attractive for the formulation of and justification for their positions. But whereas Rawls's position finds its historical antecedent in the writings of Immanuel Kant, neoliberals refer to those of John Locke. Locke imagines a 'state of nature' in which all are equal, and people come together to agree on a system that will protect life, liberty, and property. From here, neoliberals and their fellow travelling libertarians find that if this is assumed to be an accurate historical description of the distribution of resources (ie property was transferred through consensual exchange), then the current allocation of resources is justified, and any 'takings', in the form of taxation or otherwise, is suspect. The reference to natural equality of all people leads to the conclusion that, for Locke, if 'virtuous citizens seem to prosper; the poor, then, must be mostly vicious'.[56] As Brian Barry quipped, this starting-gate equality 'cloaks the status quo with legitimacy through a process of mystification'.[57] In particular, and with relevance to the schemes studied here, if the poor require something from society, the axiomatic equality would show its harsh side, requiring that responsibilities be levelled equally too.[58] The emphasis on obligations and duties throughout made this final theoretical phase possible.

If we are to refer to Locke, we should also note his candid approach to the English Poor Laws of the seventeenth century. While few social contract writers published manuscripts on welfare programmes, there is reason to view Locke's 1697 'Proposal for Reform of the Poor Laws' as more representative than anecdotal. The document, referred to as 'appalling'[59] and 'draconian'[60] by modern

[53] Ronald Dworkin, 'The Original Position' (1973) 40 University of Chicago Law Review 500, 532–33.
[54] Tim Scanlon, 'Rawls's Theory of Justice' (1973) 121 University of Pennsylvania Law Review 1020, 1064.
[55] Tim Scanlon, *What We Owe to Each Other* (Harvard UP 1998) 228.
[56] AJ Simmons, *The Lockean Theory of Rights* (Princeton UP 1992).
[57] Brian Barry, *Why Social Justice Matters* (Polity Press 2005) 40.
[58] John Dunn, *The Political Thought of John Locke* (CUP 1969) 227.
[59] Maurice Cranston, *John Locke* (Longmans 1957) 425.
[60] Geraint Parry, 'Individuality, Politics and the Critique of Paternalism in John Locke' (1964) 12 Political Studies 163, 175.

Locke scholars, blames poverty on 'the growth of the poor' and 'the relaxation of discipline and corruption of manners'. The proposal adds that provision for able-bodied poor should be granted only after children over the age of three have been separated from their families to allow both mothers and children to work. Locke's view of poverty as connected to moral depravity, as opposed to economic causes, may be seen as a precursor to some contemporary views.[61]

And yet, neoliberals also emphasized their support for equality. Milton Friedman, for example, explains the 'liberal' (as it was known at the time) vision:

> The liberal will therefore distinguish sharply between equality of opportunity, on the one hand, and material equality or equality of outcome on the other . . . He will welcome measures that promote both freedom and equality—such as measures to eliminate monopoly power and to improve the operation of the market.[62]

It is thus important to understand the way the ideas of contract and equality interact at the level of political theory. For Rawls (and Scanlon, etc), the social contract is discarded once one leaves the hypothetical thought experiment and enters the state; it is then that the principle of equality gains importance and relevance, serving as a default position and, thus, as a baseline for assessing and criticizing policies and practices. Conversely, neoliberals discard the idea of equality at the starting gate of the hypothetical situation, simply assuming that it existed under the social contract, whereas the mechanism of the contract (in the form of reciprocity) takes centre stage. The following, simple table may serve as a useful illustration:

	Equality	**Contractual relations**
Rawls	Throughout	Only as a hypothetical start
Neoliberals	Only as a hypothetical start	Throughout

The table illustrates the reversal in normative emphasis. While, for Rawlsians, the social contract is a tool to achieve equality, for neoliberals, it is a mechanism to presume it. Where Rawlsians deploy the contract to *interrogate* inequalities, neoliberals deploy it to *legitimize* them. This divergence has important

[61] CB Macpherson, *The Political Theory of Possessive Individualism* (OUP 1962) 222.
[62] Friedman (n 15) 195.

implications when applied to social and labour policy. By perceiving social relations as contractual, neoliberals discard social power as an explanation for an individual's situation, and social solidarity is discarded as a motivation for action. This is clearly seen in the following, striking quote, from David Gauthier:

> The rich man may feast on caviar and champagne, while the poor woman starves at his gate. And she may not even take the crumbs from his table, if that would deprive him of his pleasure in feeding them to his birds. Distressing as this situation may seem, we must not be misled by it. We think of rich and poor in a social context, and we think that his wealth and her poverty are in some way related.[63]

The implications should be clear insofar as social welfare programmes are concerned. The principle of reciprocity would dictate that no one is entitled to 'something for nothing' and that assistance should be conditional on performance. Moreover, the concept of rights has changed.

ii. Contractual rights

Here, we find one of the most significant, and least discussed, impacts of neoliberalism. By making rights themselves contractual, or conditional, neoliberalism uproots the most important role of rights in society: to safeguard an individual's or a minority group's interest even when the cumulative aggregation of interests may, perhaps, point in a different direction. Instead, neoliberalism, true to its authoritarian foundation, has managed to transform the rights of workers and the indigent to placeholders and 'negotiated claims'[64] within social policy and not as independent considerations that may have an effect on its formulation.[65] In doing so, it creates a 'confusion that threatens to destroy the concept of individual rights'.[66] This is not coincidental. As noted above, neoliberalism has traditionally been suspicious of what we would now term 'liberal democracy'. Worried that by exercising (liberal-type) freedom, 'we would be certain to create a stagnant society with all the characteristics of unfreedom',[67] it was asserted that 'citizens must learn to forget about their "rights" and instead be given the opportunity to express themselves through the greatest information conveyance device known to humankind, the

[63] Gauthier (n 51) 218.
[64] Robert Cox, 'The Consequences of Welfare Reform' (1998) 27 Journal of Social Policy 1, 12.
[65] Raymond Plant, 'Citizenship and Social Security' (2003) 24 Fiscal Studies 153, 155; Amy Wax, 'Something for Nothing' (2003) 52 Emory Law Journal 1, 3.
[66] Ronald Dworkin, *Taking Rights Seriously* (Duckworth 1977) 199, and also 92.
[67] Friedrich Hayek, *The Constitution of Liberty* (University of Chicago Press 1960) 32.

market'.[68] Anthony Giddens, therefore, was clearly right when he observed that, in the introduction of conditionality to the basic foundation of rights, we are witnessing a 'redefinition of rights and responsibilities'.[69] However, it is important to note that the *sole* example that Giddens offers is that which concerns the right to support and the corresponding duty to work.[70] Interestingly, two other liberal writers, Amy Guttman and Denis Thompson, also find workfare to be the paradigm example of legitimate reciprocity.[71] Clearly, then, this approach does not pervade the jurisprudential spectrum. The right to property, and the right to freedom of contract, are constructed as 'natural' and far from conditional or contingent on the performance of duties.

To suggest that rights are given only in return for the fulfilment of a duty hollows them out: it would mean that 'our rights would extend only up to the point where our actions ceased to make a net contribution to the collective project: our rights, when conceived as a safeguard for private project pursuit, would in fact be illusory'.[72] And, indeed, where the right to welfare is concerned, courts tend to subject the interests of the individual to general SE interests. The European Court of Human Rights, for example, denied claims for assistance in the preliminary stage as 'manifestly ill-founded' on a number of occasions;[73] the Canadian Supreme Court found that denying young adults under thirty the same support as those who are older is justified in light of the state's interest in encouraging young people to enter the workforce;[74] and the Israeli Supreme Court denied a petition challenging the reduction of benefits by 30 per cent because 'all systems of support' must be assessed before it is possible to conclude that a right to welfare has been impacted *at all*.[75]

In summary, it is worth highlighting the link between subsections (i) and (ii) here. The transformation of rights in the legal sphere could not succeed

[68] Mirowski (n 4) 444.

[69] Anthony Giddens, *The Third Way* (Polity Press 1998) 65.

[70] ibid. See similarly Alan Gewirth, *The Community of Rights* (1996) 223, 231–35.

[71] Amy Gutmann and Dennis Thompson, *Democracy and Disagreement* (Harvard UP 1996) 276.

[72] Nigel Simmonds, 'Rights at the Cutting Edge' in Nigel Simmonds, Matthew Kramer, and Hillel Steiner (eds), *A Debate over Rights* (OUP 1998) 113, 145; Joseph Chan, 'Raz on Liberal Rights and Common Goods' (1995) 15 Oxford Journal of Legal Studies 15.

[73] *Skorkiewicz v Poland* (Application No 39860/98) ECHR 1 June 1999; *Domalewski v Poland* (Application No 34610/97) ECHR 1999-V 573; *Goudswaard-Van Der Lans v The Netherlands* (Application No 75255/01) ECHR 22 September 2005. Discussed in Eva Brems, 'Indirect Protection of Social Rights' in Dafna Barak-Erez and Aeyal Gross (eds), *Exploring Social Rights: Between Theory and Practice* 135, 155–56.

[74] *Gosselin v Quebec* 4 SCR 429 (2002). See Patrick Macklem, 'Social Rights in Canada' in Barak-Erez and Gross, *Exploring Social Rights* (n 73) 213, 237–38.

[75] HCJ 366/03 *Commitment for Peace and Social Justice v Minister of Finance* PD 60(3) 464 (2005). See Dafna Barak-Erez and Aeyal Gross, 'Social Citizenship: The Neglected Aspect of Israeli Constitutional Law' in Barak-Erez and Gross, *Exploring Social Rights* (n 73) 243, 250–52.

without a cultural transformation that is manifested in political rhetoric and symbolic gestures. Here, we find the prominence of 'personal responsibility' or 'responsibilization'. The latter is defined as the 'moralization of economic action that accompanies the economization of the political' that is driven by neoliberalism.[76] Brown explains that responsibilization 'tasks the worker, student, consumer or indigent person with discerning and undertaking the correct strategies of self-investment and entrepreneurship for thriving and surviving; it is in this regard a manifestation of human capitalization'.[77] In less academic circles, a related theme is 'something for something' and the negation of 'something for nothing'. Hence, welfare reform programmes were introduced in the United States as a *Contract with America* and in the United Kingdom as *A New Contract for Welfare* to 'sell' the fairness that underlies the schemes. However, as one British MP proclaimed at the time, the use of contractual terminology in this context is 'an abuse of power in an abuse of language'.[78] As we move to the next section, we may pause and ask: even if we are to accept the contract as the reigning paradigm for the construction and analysis of state and society, is it clear that we are in agreement as to the identity of the parties to the contract? We have seen reference to the state, society, the taxpayer, and the indigent individuals subject to the scheme. Conspicuously absent, to this stage, are the most prominent actors under the neoliberal regime in theory and within these schemes in practice: state agencies and major corporations.

b. The Meso Level of Contractualism: Institutional and Structural Issues

This level of contractualism concerns the consequences that neoliberal discourse has on the form and operation of institutions which carry out the schemes that are the focus of our attention here. 'Contractual governance' pervaded British institutions via reforms initiated by Conservative governments in the 1980s but then enthusiastically picked up by the New Labour government from 1997, particularly through the (tellingly entitled) New Deal framework.[79]

[76] Ronen Shamir, 'The Age of Responsibilization: On Market-Embedded Morality' (2008) 37 Economy and Society 1.

[77] Brown (n 45) 132–33.

[78] Hansard col 600 (26 June 1995).

[79] Mark Freedland and Desmond King, 'Contractual Governance and Illiberal Contracts: Some Problems of Contractualism as an Instrument of Behaviour Management by Agencies of Government' (2003) 27 Cambridge Journal of Economics 465, 473–74.

Here, we address the implications of neoliberal contractualism, first on the role of law and judicial review and, second, on the justifications and impact of privatization, outsourcing, and new public management, which are central to any neoliberal reform and, correspondingly, are embedded into the structure of these schemes.

i. Between conditional rights and judicial review

The law has become a prominent instrument for governing labour relations, most evidently through the legislature and the judiciary but also, less conspicuously, through agencies such as ministries of government and processes of audit and enforcement. The 'process of "juridification", alluding to the legal tool that enshrines a large part of the state's policy, compensates for the decreasing impact of social partners'.[80] Moreover, as we noted earlier, neoliberal thinkers have been conscious, from the start, of the central role that law must play in advancing their agenda. In their Draft Statement of Aims, from 1947, they state that

> The preservation of an effective competitive order depends upon a proper legal and institutional framework. The existing framework must be considerably modified to make the operation of competition more efficient and beneficial. The precise character of the legal and institutional framework within which competition will work most effectively and which will supplement the working of competition is an urgent problem.[81]

But what role did and does law have in promoting and entrenching neoliberalism as a rationality and logic? Surprisingly, the answer to this question has been 'entirely ignored as a subject of research and debate'.[82] And yet, neoliberalism operates not only as an amalgamated confluence of policies such as deregulation, privatization, and new public management but also as 'a peculiar form of reason that configures all aspects of existence in economic terms'.[83]

When turning to the judicial realm, the implications of this insight may explain the conundrums discussed in Chapter 2: how is it that the 'clear' tests for employment status yield seemingly indefensible conclusions (that no status

[80] Guy Mundlak, 'Contradictions in Neoliberal Reforms: The Regulation of Labor Subcontracting' in Maron and Shalev (n 7) 153, 167; Harvey (n 9) 164, 176–80.

[81] Cited at Dieter Plehwe, 'Introduction' in Mirowski and Plehwe (n 2) 1, 23.

[82] Honor Brabazon, 'Introduction: Understanding Neoliberal Legality' in Honor Brabazon (ed), *Neoliberal Legality: Understanding the Role of Law in the Neoliberal Project* (Routledge 2016) 1.

[83] Brown (n 45) 17.

is recognized), which are explained through categories of exception? This curiosity is enhanced when the power of neoliberal reasoning is recognized in full. Traditional legal categories and tests are swept aside in favour of judicial stamps of approval for a particular state of affairs as the 'neoliberal agenda can be realised to a significant degree by *twisting, stretching and creatively interpreting* the ordinary legal framework'.[84] Moreover, it is here where the reliance on Carl Schmitt's teachings, which were also noted, receive an additional layer. One of the seminal insights of his theory is the idea that sovereignty is defined and identified by the ability to determine the exceptions to the rule of law: 'Sovereign is he who decides the state of emergency.' Embracing this approach, neoliberal jurisprudence relies on one of the fundamental insights of legal realism, namely, that of *doctrinal indeterminacy*, the idea that the 'there is less possibility of accurate prediction of what courts will do than the traditional rules would lead us to suppose'.[85] Moreover, it is '[b]y falsely presenting (often intuitive) value judgments made by judges as inevitable entailments of predetermined rules and concepts, [that] formalism obscures these choices'.[86] Legal realists further argue that, as courts rarely engage in an 'impartial application of determinate existing rules . . . "doctrine *qua* doctrine is radically indeterminate"'.[87]

To focus on the matter at hand, the judicial vision of the employment relationship, after all, has changed over time due to shifts in ideological or policy-based paradigms.[88] We find here, then, evidence to the fundamental insight of the realist approach to judicial discretion: though not absolute (as the caricature of realism may suggest), it is far wider than what is suggested by the linguistic boundaries between the 'core' and 'penumbra' of a concept.[89] In particular, where the judiciary reconfigures rights as conditional, it necessarily limits its own role in regulating administrative overreach. When rights

[84] Ntina Tzouvala, 'Continuity and Rupture in Restraining the Right to Strike' in Brabazon, *Neoliberal Legality* (n 82).

[85] Karl Llewellyn, 'Some Realism about Realism: Responding to Dean Pound' (1931) 44 Harvard Law Review 1222, 1241; Frederick Schauer, 'Legal Realism Untamed' (2013) 91 Texas Law Review 749, 752; Hanoch Dagan, *Reconstructing American Legal Realism and Rethinking Private Law Theory* (OUP 2013) 18–24.

[86] Dagan (n 85) 22; Frederick Schauer, 'Formalism' (1988) 97 Yale Law Journal 509, 511.

[87] Hanoch Dagan, 'Doctrinal Categories, Legal Realism and the Rule of Law' (2015) 163 University of Pennsylvania Law Review 1889, 1891.

[88] Mark Freedland, 'The Legal Structure of the Contract of Employment' Relations' in M Freedland and others (eds), *The Contract of Employment* (OUP 2016) 28, 35–36; Douglas Brodie, 'The Autonomy of the Common Law of the Contract of Employment from the General Law of Contract' in *The Contract of Employment* 124, 130.

[89] cf HLA Hart, 'Positivism and the Separation of Law and Morals' (1958) 71 Harvard Law Review 593, 607–08; and see the discussion in Schauer (n 85).

are operative (whether or not as 'trumps'[90]), they offer their holder 'leverage', allowing them to state, 'You can push me only so far, until the point where my rights are unduly impacted.' Thus, if freedom of speech (or religion, or privacy) is 'truly' recognized, then when their core is affected by government actions, those government actions would be deemed unlawful. Therefore, if an individual is penalized for criticizing the government on social media, for example, this would justifiably be viewed as a clear violation of their rights.

In contrast, if the rights are transformed to 'negotiated claims', there is very limited room for intervention on the basis that the 'bargain' that has been struck is unfair. Thus, a party (including the state) may make a 'take-it-or-leave-it' offer, to which the other party may 'consent', even if that includes forgoing her rights. And so, in a prison environment, a prisoner does not have an unconditional 'right' to daily activity, for example. Rather, that 'right' is conditional on good behaviour, broadly conceived. If you want your hour outside, behave properly; if you don't behave properly, you lose your 'privileges'. But what if this 'conditional' approach seeps into more traditional rights? One of the implications, which is of interest here, is that the neutral arbiter, such as the judiciary, has no role. The terms have been set in advance: good behaviour leads to time outdoors, and vice versa. It is a contract. Thus, Stuart White noted that the welfare contract, in which 'rights are balanced by responsibilities', may lead to a situation in which 'politicians will exploit this indeterminacy and rhetorical ambiguity to rationalise whatever sorts of coercive behavioural modification they happen to be interested in at the moment, for example, in relation to drug use, procreation, marital status, and so forth.'[91]

To make matters concrete: if the individual is in need of money for subsistence, and the right to welfare does not exist, then the state can demand, as a condition for assistance, that she first seek assistance elsewhere, accept any job offer, 'volunteer' in the community, marry the father of her children, refrain from living with a man who is not the father of her children, agree to vaccination treatments and so forth.[92] Similar examples may be construed with regards to demands from prisoners, migration detainees, and interns. As one of the proponents of the integration of the reciprocity paradigm to social programmes explained, 'recipients . . . need not accept the grants, but neither may they demand them without conditions . . . This strong conditional position has

[90] Dworkin (n 66).

[91] Stuart White, 'Social Rights and the Social Contract: Political Theory and the New Welfare Politics' (2000) 30 British Journal of Political Science 507, 512.

[92] For a discussion of such cases, see Paz-Fuchs (n 14).

meant that requirements like work tests are difficult to challenge in court.'[93] If the indeterminacy of law explains *how* the courts are able to find the room to navigate away from set doctrines to deny participants in these schemes the relevant rights, the construction of welfare rights as conditional reveals *why* they find the path that leads them to reject the challenges.

Prison work offers a strong example in this regard. Where countries, including the United Kingdom, were criticized for falling foul of the ILO Convention on Forced Labour because of the involvement of private entities (discussed further in subsection (ii)), the response stemmed from macroeconomic jargon: the rehabilitative benefits outweigh the associated harms and so, notwithstanding the clear Convention language to the contrary, the practice should be found to be fully in line with the aims of the Convention.[94] The example of workfare is also instructive in this regard, particularly because it simultaneously offers the example of a successful judicial challenge and of the boundaries of such challenges. In the 2013 case of *Reilly*,[95] the UK Supreme Court accepted that the 2011 Regulations,[96] which provided the basis for workfare schemes, were ultra vires sections 17A and 17B of the Jobseekers Act 1995 as they did not describe the schemes, prescribe the circumstances requiring a person to participate in the schemes, or prescribe the period of the schemes as the 1995 Act required. In response to the judicial decisions, Parliament repealed sections 17A and 17B[97] and later introduced the Jobseekers (Back-to-Work Schemes) Act 2013 and the accompanying 2013 Regulations.[98] The 2013 Regulations followed the Court's instructions by prescribing the necessary details for the workfare schemes which, prior to the Regulations, were left to the discretion of the Secretary of State. They included details of seven schemes, their extent, and the duties required from participants. A number of schemes, such as the Sector-Based Work Academy (SBWA) scheme, the

[93] Lawrence Mead, *Beyond Entitlement* (1980) 170–71. See also Richard Epstein, 'The Uncertain Quest for Welfare Rights' (1985) Bringham Young Law Review 201, 212; Ingwer Ebsen, 'Contracting between Social Services and Their Clients in the German Concept of "Fördern und Fordern"' in Sol and Westerveld (n 52) 239.

[94] Ben Jarman and Catherine Heard, *Labouring Behind Bars: Assessing International Law on Working Prisoners* (Institute for Crime and Justice Policy Research, 2023). <https://www.prisonstudies.org/sites/default/files/resources/downloads/labouring_behind_bars_web_final.pdf> accessed 24 March 2026

[95] *R (Reilly and Wilson) v Secretary of State for Work and Pensions* [2013] UKSC 68.

[96] Jobseeker's Allowance (Employment, Skills and Enterprise Scheme) Regulations 2011 (SI 2011/917).

[97] Welfare Reform Act 2012, sch 14, pt 4.

[98] Jobseeker's Allowance (Schemes for Assisting Persons to Obtain Employment) Regulations 2013.

Community Work Placements,[99] the Work Programme,[100] and the Mandatory Work Activity (MWA) required participants to work 'for the benefit of the community'.

The MWA is of particular interest because, following the government's swift enactments in 2013 (in response to the Supreme Court decision in *Reilly*), the MWA scheme was challenged by a participant on grounds similar to those presented in *Reilly*.[101] This challenge, however, was not successful, Hickinson J distinguishing the Supreme Court ruling and determining that 'the MWAS Regulations do adequately prescribe the description of the MWA Scheme, and are thus not *ultra vires*'.[102] On appeal, the Court of Appeal accepted the conclusion that the administrative flaw was properly addressed but went further to add its acceptance to a witness statement provided by the Department of Work and Pensions (DWP), which emphasized the importance of granting 'flexibility' to the DWP and to the 'providers' (which are private corporations).[103] The Court of Appeal rejected the argument that this flexibility contravenes the principle of legal certainty, stating that 'the fact that the description is wide does not mean that it is uncertain'.[104] Perhaps that is so, but the problem arguably lies elsewhere: granting flexibility to private providers means that participants' rights are left in the balance. The greater one side's 'flexibility', the narrower the opportunities to object to the type of work that is mandated, the type of supervision and training that are offered, and the discipline and sanction being enforced.

ii. Privatization

Bearing in mind our interest in the role of the state in initiating and governing unfree labour schemes, it is quite striking, and yet not surprising, that all the schemes discussed as part of our case studies involve private companies in a multitude of ways. Take, for example, the facts governing the case of *Reilly*, noted above. Caitlin Reilly graduated with a degree in geology from Birmingham University and aspired to work in the museum sector. Towards that end, she volunteered at a local museum in Birmingham and simultaneously claimed Jobseeker's Allowance. In October 2011, an advisor at the Jobcentre Plus informed her that she was assigned to a training scheme

[99] SI 2013/2548.
[100] Regulation 3(8).
[101] *R (Smith) v Secretary of State for Work and Pensions* [2014] EWHC 843.
[102] ibid [26].
[103] *Smith v Secretary of State for Work and Pensions* [2015] EWCA Civ 229 [26].
[104] ibid [27].

at the Poundland retail store, following which she was required to work for five hours a day, five days a week, with no rights as a worker, including minimum wage. During that time, she was to report to a supervisor from Seetec, a 'Business Service Provider'. It may be added here that Ms Reilly was joined in her challenge by Mr Jamieson Wilson, who worked as lorry driver and, over the summer, as a landscape gardener from 1994 to 2008. While his 'job readiness' did not seem lacking, he was referred to Ingeus, a British-Australian provider of 'training and skills support' and from there to an organization that collects, renovates, and distributes disused furniture for thirty hours per week, for twenty-six weeks. Needless to say, at this stage, the Jobseeker's Allowance would be the compensation for the work. Ms Reilly and Mr Wilson were, obviously, two individual cases in a grand scheme. The Work Programme, which was discussed in Chapter 2, was centrally controlled by the UK Government, but franchised to eighteen 'prime' contractors, of which sixteen were for-profit corporations. These contractors, known as 'primes', subcontracted service delivery to about 900 smaller 'providers'.[105]

The reason that this involvement is not surprising is because, from the late 1970s, governments began to reduce their role in the provision of services and to shift activities to the private sector. As an umbrella term, this shift—arguably the most fundamental institutional shift in public service provision in the modern era—is referred to as 'privatization'.[106] Under this umbrella, privatization may take on different forms.

The first iteration, implicit privatization, is the most complicated. This occurs when government ceases to take part in a particular activity and reduces its role, thus making space for private actors to enter. This process is sometimes referred to as 'privatisation by attrition'[107] and is complicated by the fact that to identify privatization in a particular case, one needs to assume that government involvement is expected or is even the default norm. Thus, if government disengages from the health or education realms, allowing private companies to provide the services, the attribution of privatization would seem obvious. This may not be the case, however, if the government stands by while private companies develop technologies to facilitate locating stolen phones or cars. Other manifestations of privatization are more straightforward by comparison. The

[105] National Audit Office, *The Introduction of the Work Programme* (HM Government 2012) 4; John David Jordan, 'Welfare Grunters and Workfare Monsters? An Empirical Review of the Operation of Two UK "Work Programme" Centres' (2018) 47 Journal of Social Policy 583, 584.

[106] Emanuel Savas, *Privatization: The Key to Better Government* (Chatham House Publishers 1987) 3.

[107] Paul Starr, 'The Meaning of Privatization' (1988) 6 Yale Law & Policy Review 6, 16.

second form of privatization is 'explicit' in that it includes the sale of ownership and the transfer of management from the state to the private sector. Third, privatization may take the form of contracting out or outsourcing, when the government decides to continue to fund a service but to do so through the private sector. This trend has been so pronounced that the phrase 'the contract state' was attributed specifically to this policy.[108] And, finally, deregulation (and even the privatization of regulation itself[109]) is also assessed under the heading of privatization as it involves the clear reduction of the role of government.

Covering such a wide range of scenarios, it is clear why the current age has been dubbed the 'era of privatisation'.[110] Corresponding with the rise of neoliberalism as the reigning paradigm, within which it is a central tenet,[111] privatization has become 'a national obsession. Hardly any domestic policy issue remains untouched by dispute over the scope of private participation in government',[112] and the UK governments since 1997 have been associated with its most extreme versions.[113] While the Conservative Government of the mid-1990s set the country on the path of compulsory tendering, New Labour quickly picked up the mantle with the *Better Quality Services* framework guidance.[114] Under this framework, government departments were instructed to consider five alternatives to the current provision of service within their organizations: abolition, internal restructuring, contracting out, market testing, and privatization since 'maintaining the status quo was no longer an option'.[115] In particular, the two preferred options—contracting out and market testing—both involved opening bidding to external providers. The difference between the two was that within the latter, the in-house team would be permitted to compete against the external providers. In this specific context, privatization is used in the narrow sense, signifying the fact that the public agency will not only distance itself from the operation of the service (as in the other two variations) but also will no longer be responsible for its funding.

[108] Christopher Hood, 'Which Contract State? Four Perspectives on Over-Outsourcing for Public Services' (1997) 56 Australian Journal of Public Administration 120.
[109] LeBaron and Phillips (n 1) 14ff.
[110] Symposium, 'Public Values in an Era of Privatization' (2003) 116 Harvard Law Review 1211.
[111] Crouch (n 8) 21; Plehwe (n 81) 7–8; see the Mont Pelerin 'Draft Statement of Aims' from 7 April 1947: 'Only the decentralization of control through private property in the means of production can prevent those concentrations of power which threaten individual freedom'—quoted in Plehwe (n 81) 23.
[112] Gillian Metzger, 'Privatization as Delegation' (2003) 103 Columbia Law Review 1367.
[113] Crouch (n 8) 83.
[114] The Stationery Office, *Better Quality Services Handbook* (1998).
[115] Peter Vincent-Jones, *The New Public Contracting: Regulation, Responsiveness, Relationality* (OUP 2006) 51.

Within the analysis of public-sector reform, which includes significant privatization and outsourcing initiatives, it is often tempting to speak of the withdrawal of the state.[116] There is an obvious element of truth to that assessment as the state intentionally seeks to 'steer' rather than 'row' and to remove itself from the business of provision, implementation, and (in some cases) funding. However, if we are to bring the discussion here within the general framework of neoliberalism, we find a more complex movement at play. Vincent-Jones finds an 'apparent paradox of devolution combined with increased bureaucratic control over strategy and policy', which he terms 'centralised decentralisation'.[117] In keeping with neoliberalism's affinity to a strong state for the central purpose of protecting property rights and freedom of contract, New Public Management techniques (eg payment by results and creating competitive markets where none existed, as in the case of the Work Programme[118]) were put in place to *centralize* power away from local government, the NHS, hospital trusts, schools, and other public bodies and then enforce performance indicators to threaten closure, demotion, or takeover by private contractors or management consortia.[119] Studies have suggested that under neoliberalism, state regulation has actually increased.[120]

Even bearing in mind that outsourcing, contracting out, and privatization were and are a sign of the times, it seems that implementing reforms in the sectors assessed here demands further justification for at least two reasons, first, because of the nature of the services involved. Whereas privatization in the form of, for example, the Public Finance Initiative (PFI—as in the case of building a hospital or a bridge, for example) raises considerable difficulties,[121] it can nonetheless be captured by a (complex) articulation of features, goals, and spatial constraints, and (importantly) is time-limited. In contrast, social services of the nature discussed here are open-ended; necessarily subject to change; and expected to raise unexpected challenges (influx of migration or unemployment (or lack thereof), a sudden spike in drug abuse, etc) and require expertise in 'soft' skills, such as communication, training, and rehabilitation that cannot be supervised in an obvious manner. Such contracts are usually referred to as 'incomplete' as the public authority cannot predict, and

[116] See eg Amir Paz-Fuchs, Ronen Mandelkern, and Itzhak Glanoor (eds), *The Privatisation of Israel: The Withdrawal of State Responsibility* (Palgrave 2018).

[117] Vincent-Jones (n 115) 57–58.

[118] Jordan (n 105) 588.

[119] Vincent-Jones (n 115) 59–60.

[120] Andreas Palacios Lleras, 'Neoliberal Law and Regulation' in Brabazon, *Neoliberal Legality* (n 82) 73.

[121] See eg Mark Freedland, 'Public Law and Private Finance—Placing the Private Finance Initiative in a Public Law Frame' [1998] Public Law 288.

consequently cannot dictate, all the parameters of the contract, thus leaving much to the discretion of the agent, the private company.[122]

The second reason why this particular privatization demands justification relates to the fact that conventional liberals, and even early neoliberal writings, tended to be advocates of *markets*, not necessarily of *corporations*. Underlying this preference was a belief (which carried its own flaws) that the market has the innate ability to process and convey information in a manner that is inherently and will always be superior to that of the state.[123] But, contrary to a common misperception (then and now), privatization does not lead to competition in the market. Liberalization is the process of creating and opening markets, thus increasing competition (for better, at times, or for worse). But privatization and liberalization are concepts that may have some overlaps and yet are importantly distinct.[124] Privatization in the cases of a natural monopoly (the cases of British Rail, British Gas, and British Telecom come to mind) creates private monopolies where public monopolies existed, with no liberalization or market creation. Initially, a stream of neoliberal writers, which included Milton Friedman, focused on the prime importance of market creation and facilitating competition and feared any concentration of power, whether public or private. Friedman wrote that 'the state must police conditions favourable to competition and prevent monopoly'.[125] His colleague at the University of Chicago Department of Economics, Henry Simons, wrote even more explicitly that '[t]he great enemy of democracy is monopoly, in all its forms: gigantic corporations, trade associations and other agencies for price control, trade-unions—or, in general, organization and concentration of power within functional classes'.[126]

Within a few years, however, the intellectual and personal force of Friedrich Hayek led Friedman to reconsider, and to view private monopolies, *sans* competition, as innocuous because, as he (and generations of economists who are wedded to 'idealistic thinking') notoriously surmised, 'I have become increasingly impressed with how wide is the range of problems and industries for which it is appropriate to treat the economy *as if* it were

[122] Hugh Mosley and Els Sol, 'Contractualism in Employment Service: A Socio-Economic Perspective' in Sol and Westerveld (n 52) 1, 4–5; Jordan (n 105) 589.

[123] Mirowski (n 4) 435, 444.

[124] Crouch (n 8) 79–81. Christoph Hermann and Koen Verhoest, 'The Process of Liberalisation, Privatisation and Marketisation' in Christoph Hermann and Jörg Flecker (eds), *Privatization of Public Services: Impacts for Employment, Working Conditions, and Service Quality in Europe* (Routledge 2012) 6.

[125] Milton Friedman, 'Neoliberalism and Its Prospects' (1951) 17 Farmand 89, 92.

[126] Henry Simons, *Economic Policy for a Free Society* (University of Chicago Press 1948) 43.

competitive.'[127] Harvey thus suggests that as the competition rationale disappears in the background, we find that the 'corporatization, commodification and privatization of hitherto public assets has been a signal feature of the neoliberal project. Its primary aim has been to open up new fields for capital accumulation in domains hitherto regarded off-limits to the calculus of profitability.'[128] Similarly, Colin Crouch documents the development of the neoliberal approach over the course of the twentieth century, arguing that while its proponents like to pose the central dilemmas as one that posits (the limits of) government intervention against competition, they 'glibly' assume that the 'giant firms' are part of the market.[129] And Mirowski suggests that a central neoliberal tenet is that 'corporations can do no wrong, or at least they are not to be blamed if they do.'[130]

At the same time, economic and legal theorists, primarily at the University of Chicago, led the development of new principles that abandoned the need for 'actual competition' and favoured large, market-dominant firms.[131] Relatedly, the role of the consumer, or customer, which drives market-based dynamics and rationalities and can signal through their market choices, does not exist in the case of privatization of public services. Instead, we have a 'purchaser–provider split' in which public agencies supposedly interact with corporations *on behalf* of consumers.[132] The public agency, rather than the individual client-citizen, then, is the recipient of the service. The individual is solely the 'beneficiary', in the case of privatization of education, health, or care. With respect to prisoners, detainees, and workfare recipients, the situation is even more complex as their productive labour could be, for example, 'fundamental to the prison's economic viability and a market exchange exists between contracting organisations, from which inmates are excluded'.[133]

To bring decades of theory to present-day practice, we note that existing, long contracts that govern the schemes discussed here limit, and perhaps even eliminate, the role of markets, demonstrating again that the neoliberal shift is designed to serve, and is serving, concrete firms rather than abstract markets. Insofar as they exist, the markets can be located only at the point of contract negotiation. But even here, government flexibility to choose between competitors is limited.

127 Friedman (n 15) 120.
128 Harvey (n 9) 160.
129 Crouch (n 8) 53.
130 Mirowski (n 4) 438.
131 ibid 54.
132 Vincent-Jones (n 115) 204.
133 Jenna Pandeli, Michael Marinetto, and Jean Jenkins, 'Captive in Cycles of Invisibility? Prisoners' Work for the Private Sector' (2019) 33 Work, Employment and Society 596, 603.

Moreover, as in other cases, privatization in prison work is manifested across a number of layers. Most conspicuous in public debates and in academic literature is the matter of work in private prisons. Far less attention, however, is directed at work for private providers within public prisons.[134] This focus is problematic, as the ILO report on forced labour suggests that 'of the approximately 8 million recognized prisoners worldwide . . . only some 150,000 are in private prisons, and no figures are available as to those who might be working for private employers'.[135] This focus has been criticised as 'myopic' and a consequence of 'institutional fetishism'[136] as it assumes that while private corporations are driven by profit, public-sector agencies are immune to such concerns and thus may be absolved from the strict constraints on prisoner remuneration that, for example, the ILO applies where the work is organized by private providers. In doing so, this focus ignores the impact of New Public Management strategies and philosophies, which have required public agencies to apply market logic and constraints as a matter of course.[137] Reflecting the degree of fluidity on the public/private distinction, and how deeply the private sphere permeates traditional state functions, the United Kingdom claims that private bodies which perform state functions in connection to prison labour should be considered public authorities.[138]

As explored in Chapter 2, from the perspective of political economy, the privatization of prison labour performs two mutually reinforcing functions for capital: direct profit-making capacity and a surplus population management tool and wage pressure device. Mass imprisonment hides substantial unemployment,[139] while also benefiting capital by adding labour market competition via an alternative labour source. Lloyd and Whitehead argue that mass incarceration continues the legacy of the slave trade and has become, through the generation of insecurity and precarity, an endogenous feature of neoliberalism.[140] Finally, LeBaron argues that prison labour has been

[134] ibid.

[135] International Labour Office (ed), *A Global Alliance against Forced Labour: Global Report under the Follow-Up to the ILO Declaration on Fundamental Principles and Rights at Work, 2005* (International Labour Office 2005) [116].

[136] Faina Milman-Sivan and Yair Sagy, 'On the International Labour Organization and Prison Labour: An Invitation to Recalibrate' (2020) 159 International Labour Review 505, 516. 'Institutional fetishism' is defined by Roberto Unger as 'the belief that abstract institutional conceptions, like political democracy, the market economy and a free civil society have a single natural and necessary institutional expression'. *What Should Legal Analysis Become?* (Verso 1996) 7.

[137] Noah Zatz, 'Working at the Boundaries of Markets' (2008) 61 Vanderbilt Law Review 857.

[138] Milman-Sivan and Sagy (n 136).

[139] Bruce Western and Katherine Beckett, 'How Unregulated Is the US Labor Market? The Penal System as a Labor Market Institution' (1999) 104 American Journal of Sociology 1030.

[140] Anthony Lloyd and Philip Whitehead, 'Kicked to the Curb: The Triangular trade of Neoliberal Polity, Social Insecurity and Penal Expulsion' (2018) 55 International Journal of Law, Crime and Justice 60.

tactically used both to replace public-sector workers and break strikes as part of a broader range of strategies through which capital has pushed down real wages and sped up and intensified the work process.[141]

In the workfare realm, section 20E of the amended Jobseeker's Act 1995 enables the Secretary of State to authorize private providers to require participants to attend interviews and provide information at designated times; and to enter agreements with participants which determine their obligations (see more on this in subsection (c)). Deguerre and Etherington write that the Work Programme was 'emblematic of the governmental strategy of opening up the public sector to the market',[142] but continue to explain that 'the choice of contractors and contracting framework involves negotiating with "prime" contractors (*to last for a period of 5–7 years*) who are deliberately chosen in terms of their size, turnover as well as their "capacity to deliver"'.[143]

In the United Kingdom and elsewhere, the role of employment relations, and the change that they undergo following the shift from the public to the private sector, is unavoidable as a major drive towards outsourcing. This notion has been phrased in stark terms: 'Privatization is fundamentally a labor policy: an overt challenge to public employment defended in the language of efficiency.'[144] In particular, reducing and eliminating the power of trade unions is apparent, and outsourcing seeks to 'remove that workforce from the ambit of public sector bargaining.'[145] Margaret Thatcher even proclaimed that she viewed privatization as creating a path to weaken trade unions and 'reverse the corrupting effects of socialism.'[146] Unions, for their part, shared her assessment of the potential implications of outsourcing, stating that 'among the tactics that the . . . government employs to attack British workers, privatization seems to be the most fatal.'[147] These predictions and assessments are supported

141 Genevieve LeBaron, 'Rethinking Prison Labor: Social Discipline and the State in Historical Perspective' 15 (2012) Working USA 327.

142 Anne Deguerre and David Etherington, 'Welfare and Active Labour Market Policies in the UK: The Coalition Government Approach' in Hugh Bochel and Martin Powell (eds), *The Coalition Government and Social Policy: Restructuring the Welfare State* (Policy Press 2016) 203, 210.

143 ibid (emphasis added).

144 Craig Becker, 'With Whose Hands: Privatization, Public Employment, and Democracy' (1988) 6 Yale Law & Policy Review 88.

145 Paul Davies and Mark Freedland, *Labour Legislation and Public Policy: A Comparative History* (OUP 1993) 622; Christopher McCrudden, *Buying Social Justice* (OUP 2007); Rolph van der Hoeven and Gyorgy Sziraczki, 'Privatization and Labour Issues' in Rolph van der Hoeven and Gyorgy Sziraczki (eds), *Lessons from Privatization: Labour Issues in Developing and Transitional Countries* (ILO 1997); Vincent-Jones (n 115) 20.

146 Margaret Thatcher, *The Downing Street Years* (HarperCollins 1993) 676.

147 Rodney Bickerstaffe, 'Foreword: Keep Our Services Public' in Sue Hastings and Hugo Levie (eds), *Privatisation* (Spokesman 1983) 7.

by the evidence. Union membership in formerly public and now privatized entities has fallen by over 50 per cent in some industries.[148] Relatedly, studies have reported significant job losses, of between 25 and 50 per cent, following privatization as well as a significant shift towards part-time employment and increasing levels of work intensity, worse working conditions, and the creation of two-tier workforces.[149] In many cases, outsourcing of tasks that require expertise leads to the loss of institutional knowledge and institutional memory that is critical for maintaining and developing an effective service.[150] Decades of privatization and outsourcing have hollowed out the civil service, rendering it captive to the dictates of private-sector consultants who not only advise but also design policies and, at times, draft the calls for which their firms bid.[151] Within the UK context in particular, management consultants have been found to be 'agents of change'[152] who drove outsourcing and privatization policies and transformed the public sector.

Finally, it is curious that one of the main justifications put forward in favour of privatization and outsourcing refers to the distribution of information to the public and enhancing transparency. Public accountability can drive public engagement and action, according to this position, where information concerning the terms and conditions of the operations and their costs, performance, and accountability are extracted from the dark corners of public bureaucracy and exposed to the light of the procurement process, contracts and litigation, where relevant. Somewhat ironically, however, it is actually the privatization process that creates a veil of secrecy behind the legal doctrine of commercial confidentiality, thus inhibiting public accountability.[153] This lack of transparency has a clear impact on the instant subject matter. In the collection of primary data in institutional settings such as prisons or immigration removal centres, the lack of transparency and lengthy, complex processes required to navigate access can make meaningful data collection difficult to obtain.[154] For example,

[148] Christoph Hermann and Richard Pond, 'Concentration and Disintegration: Company Responses in the Electricity Sector and Consequences for Employment' in Hermann and Flecker (n 124) 33, 46.

[149] Jorg Flecker and Christoph Hermann, 'Company Responses to Liberalisation and Privatisation' in Hermann and Flecker (n 124) 109; Wieslawa Kozek, Beata Radzka, and Christoph Hermann, 'Privatisation and the Impact on Employment' in Hermann and Flecker (n 124) 124.

[150] Ellen Dannin, 'Counting What Matters: Privatization, People with Disabilities, and the Cost of Low-Wage Work' (2008) 92 Minnesota Law Review 1348, 1372.

[151] Reut Marciano, '"Penny for Your Thoughts": Outsourcing Public Policy Formulation, the Israeli Case' in Paz-Fuchs, Mandelkern, and Galnoor (n 116) 255, 258.

[152] Irvine Lapsley and Rosie Oldfield, 'Transforming the Public Sector: Management Consultants as Agents of Change' (2001) 10 European Accounting Review 523.

[153] Vincent-Jones (n 115) 220.

[154] Shannon Silva and Ceema Samimi 'Social Work and Prison Labour: A Restorative Model' (2018) 63 Social Work 153.

academics researching inmates' work in a private-sector prison in the United Kingdom that contracted firms noted that obtaining the relevant information was a complex process that took over a year.[155] Bales and Mayblin were denied a freedom-of-information (FoI) request to the UK Home Office to study paid work in an immigration detention centre.[156] Private corporations who operate these facilities, such as G4S, Mitie, GEO, and Serco, deliver a significant proportion of detention services, but they are not bound, as public institutions are, to the dictates of the Freedom of Information Act 2000.[157]

c. The Micro Level of Contractualism: Field-Level Implementation

Like many '-isms', it would not have been surprising if contractualism had been confined to the minds of academics and theorists, who tend to 'identify' and conceptualize abstract phenomena. And yet, somewhat curiously, the age of contractualism is also characterized by very concrete, everyday manifestations in the signing of contracts between public agencies (or private companies that are delegated authority) and individuals whose behaviour is judged to require change and control.[158] Now, bearing in mind the institutions that we discuss here, this insistence on the 'myth and ceremony'[159] of signing a contract is peculiar. After all, in most cases, the power disparities between multi-billion-pound corporations, acting on behalf of governments, and the most vulnerable individuals would be sufficient to simply force cooperation. This is especially the case when we are cognizant of the sanctions that may be applied for refusal. Thus, Peter Vincent-Jones refers to 'social control contracts' and is clearly right when he explains that while 'the use of contractual mechanisms . . . both draws upon and reinforces these notions of agency and choice . . . contracts render individuals responsible for their predicament . . . in ways that differ significantly from the governance of relations by hierarchical authority'.[160] But as we are concerned, in this chapter and in the book as a whole, not only with abstract ideas and unattributable trends in the reign of policy but also with the role of the state, it is important to note that 'it has been British *government policy* to

[155] Pandeli, Marinetto, and Jenkins (n 133).
[156] Katie Bales and Lucy Mayblin, 'Unfree Labour in Immigration Detention: Exploitation and Coercion of a Captive Immigrant Workforce' (2018) 47 Economy and Society 191.
[157] ibid.
[158] Freedland and King (n 79) 465–66.
[159] Joel Handler, *Social Citizenship and Workfare in the United States and Western Europe: The Paradox of Inclusion* (CUP 2004) 12.
[160] Vincent-Jones (n 115) 233; Freedland and King (n 79) 470.

cast these relationships in a contractual or contract-like mode. The impulse to do so has, in these cases, come wholly or mainly from central government rather than from the more local or sectional policy formation process of the professional workers.'[161]

Since we have now approached the concrete, field level of the contract, we must speak of the real-life consequences. And here, the peculiar use of the contract within the context of a very clear manifestation of power enables the state and its corporate conduits to have their proverbial cake and eat it. Hugh Collins has suggested that these should be understood as 'quasi-contracts' or 'contractual metaphors' since their role is solely 'to provide a framework of reference for the orientations of the parties' conduct within a system of bureaucratic control'.[162] On the one hand, public (administrative and constitutional) law may be (arguably) irrelevant because of the contractual construct. On the other hand, as we saw earlier, the state's involvement, and its putative motivations (training, education, rehabilitation) are 'portrayed as inhospitable to contract'[163] and consequently sufficient to deny the contractual relationship and employment status:

> The form of enterprise organization that replaces the work contract by a commercial contract with a service provider makes it possible largely to *brush aside the constraints of labour law* ... The increase in proportions of 'negotiated rights' vis-à-vis 'legislated rights' has thus itself accentuated the disparity in rights between workers [and] the fragmentation of labour law.[164]

As such, the third, micro level of the contract supports the purposes identified in the second, meso level: the undermining of the regulation that was put in place to protect vulnerable individuals precisely in the position of participants in these schemes. Mark Freedland and Desmond King rightly argue that, if no safeguards are put in place, the use of the putatively 'liberal' mechanism of the contract may lead to an illiberal process that, moreover, may veer towards 'authoritarianism ... [and] permit the arbitrary exercise of authority by the state or its administrators because of the absence of a sufficiently defined requirement on the administrator's part to demonstrate that sanctions were applied with appropriate justification'.[165]

161 Freedland and King (n 79) 466.
162 Hugh Collins, *Regulating Contracts* (rev edn, OUP 2004) 318–19.
163 Zatz (n 137) 885.
164 Luc Boltanski and Eve Chiapello, *The New Spirit of Capitalism* (Verso 2007) 243–44.
165 Freedland and King (n 79) 471.

In addition, the contractual relationship with the individual complements other institutional dimensions noted above, which are associated with New Public Management. David Nelken, for example, identifies the move to 'task oriented social work' as (supposedly) a more effective strategy for behavioural change,[166] the incorporation of private and voluntary sector actors, and measurable achievements—all as facilitating the use of contractual mechanisms.[167] But it also buttresses the messages conveyed at the most abstract, macro level identified above. In particular, we noted that public and elected officials explained the schemes as governed by the understanding that the claimant signed a 'formalised contract with the *taxpayer*'.[168] Some academics have gone so far as to blend the most abstract with most concrete by suggesting that participants take on the responsibilities associated with the benefits by 'signing the social contract'.[169] In this respect, Nelken identifies a preference for contract as a social work technique that is a consequence of disillusionment with 'treatment philosophy' (ie addressing the needs of individuals) and replacing it with an approach that supposedly celebrates the individual's freedom of choice and sense of personal responsibility.[170]

Workfare may be viewed as the avant-garde of social programmes to adopt the lexicon of reciprocity and contractualism as 'relief-giving is partly designed to enforce work'.[171] Through primary legislation, a number of countries have incorporated the requirement that a claimant sign a 're-integration agreement' (Germany), 're-integration plan' (the Netherlands) or, as noted, the 'Claimant Commitment' (United Kingdom).[172] At the time, Freedland and King viewed it as 'the most coercive form of the potentially illiberal contractual programmes'.[173] We see, then, the significant mileage that the concept of the social contract has made from a thought experiment to an actual contract that the poor are assumed to have signed. As noted in Chapter 2, the British

[166] David Nelken, 'The Use of "Contracts" as a Social Work Technique' (1987) 40 Current Legal Problems 207, 209.

[167] ibid 212.

[168] See text to n 52ff; Employment Committee, *Second Report: The Right to Work/Workfare* (House of Commons Sessions 1995–96, HMSO, 1996) cited in Desmond King, *In the Name of Liberalism* (1998) 248.

[169] Eugene Bardach, 'Implementing a Paternalist Welfare' in Lawrence Mead (ed), *The New Paternalism* (1991) 251, 259.

[170] Nelken (n 166) 210.

[171] Piven and Cloward (n 46) xix.

[172] Eleveld (n 42) 209. The UK Government Guidance to Universal Credit claimants clearly states that 'When you claim Universal Credit you will need to accept your Claimant Commitment': Department for Work & Pensions, 'Universal Credit and Your Claimant Commitment' (updated 12 February 2025) <www.gov.uk/government/publications/universal-credit-and-your-claimant-commitment-quick-guide/universal-credit-and-your-claimant-commitment> accessed 13 November 2025.

[173] Freedland and King (n 79) 472.

Government decided, formally at least, to abandon the blatantly authoritarian imposition of workfare in favour of the paradigms of negotiation, reciprocity, and consent. This has led the idea of the contract to lie at the heart of the workfare arrangement.

The workfare contract corresponds with the neoliberal image of participants as active entrepreneurs who are engaged in training (and hence closer to interns), which would allow them to participate productively in the market. The message of moral authoritarianism that is cloaked in the veil of contract and reciprocity is advocated by Amy Wax, who claims that governments cannot run welfare programmes without making 'convention based judgments . . . grounded in how most ordinary people are expected to behave and how they do behave'.[174] So 'reciprocity', for Wax, is a proxy for the imposition of mainstream majority moral values. And if it wasn't clear enough, she writes elsewhere,

> perhaps potential welfare recipients are *finally getting the message* that they are expected to do anything they can to lift themselves out of poverty, which includes entering the workforce, forswearing drugs and crime and avoiding potentially costly childbearing.[175]

This message, in other words, should be long term and not solely for the duration of participation in the programme:

> The unemployed must be trained to accept the low wages of the labour in which workfare recipients mostly find themselves; they must learn that they are individually responsible for their predicaments—whether these are positive or negative; and they must conceive of themselves as competitors and life as a competition. Whatever one's views of the merits of those different ways of conceptualising workfare, what is clear is that the features identified by both are indelibly characteristic of neoliberalism and the neoliberal state.[176]

All the while, this construct manages to obscure the coercive power of the state through the double-pronged mechanism of the contract: first, by deploying private companies to engage with the individuals; and second, by insisting that

[174] Amy Wax, 'A Reciprocal Welfare Programme' (2001) 8 Virginia Journal of Social Policy 477, 500.
[175] Amy Wax, 'Rethinking Welfare Rights: Reciprocity Norms, Reactive Attitudes, and the Political Economy of Welfare Reform' (2000) 63 Law and Contemporary Problems 257, 285.
[176] Kenneth Veitch, 'Law, Social Policy and the Neoliberal State' in Brabazon, *Neoliberal Legality* (n 82) 71.

those individuals sign contracts that supposedly signify personal choice and consent and work to obfuscate control and power.

4. Conclusion

This chapter sought to illuminate the ways in which neoliberalism, rather than retreating from the domain of labour regulation, actively reconfigures it to serve the interests of capital. The notion of the state as a neutral arbiter in the formation and maintenance of labour relations has been exposed as illusory not only in historical examples but also in its contemporary manifestations. As demonstrated, far from withdrawing, the neoliberal state has redeployed itself in ways that are deeply interventionist—restructuring markets, reshaping legal regimes, and constructing new forms of coercion under the guise of contract and choice.

What emerges from this analysis is a paradox: a state that professes a commitment to individual freedom, yet systematically constructs conditions in which certain forms of unfreedom proliferate. This paradox is particularly acute in the labour schemes examined, where the language of autonomy and entrepreneurship masks the reality of compulsion, subordination, and dependency. Whether in workfare, prison labour, internships, or migration detention, the ideological insistence on contractualism serves to render coercion invisible, transforming the state's role from a coercive agent to a facilitator of 'voluntary' agreements in which refusal is not a meaningful option.

A key insight of this chapter is that neoliberalism does not merely tolerate unfree labour; it actively generates and legitimizes it. The erosion of workers' bargaining power, the increasing precarity of employment, and the strategic use of privatization to obscure responsibility all contribute to an expanding domain of coercive work relations. This is not incidental but structural. The state's involvement in unfree labour operates on multiple levels: it is an ideological project, a policy framework, and a material reality. The regulatory choices made—whether in the privatization of prisons, the outsourcing of workfare schemes, or the selective enforcement of labour protections—serve to reinforce the power of capital while diminishing the autonomy of those who must sell their labour under increasingly constrained conditions.

The operation of the legal framework sustaining these schemes is particularly revealing. Rather than providing a safeguard against exploitation, the law is mobilized to sustain and legitimize forms of coercion that, in other contexts, might be deemed unacceptable. Judicial reasoning that upholds workfare requirements, sanctions exploitative internship arrangements, or permits the privatization of prison labour reflects not the inevitable application of neutral principles but the conscious deployment of legal doctrine to entrench neoliberal rationalities. As this chapter has shown, legal indeterminacy provides fertile ground for judicial discretion, allowing courts to navigate around established worker protections in ways that reinforce the neoliberal project.

Crucially, this analysis invites a reassessment of the dominant narratives of progress in labour law and social policy. The tendency to depict the state as a force that has moved, however imperfectly, towards the expansion of freedom and the protection of workers' rights must be critically examined. As we have seen, state interventions to restrict worker mobility, limit collective bargaining, and enforce work obligations have a long history. What is distinct about the neoliberal era is not the existence of coercion but its justification in the language of markets, contract, and individual responsibility. The moralization of economic hardship—framing poverty and unemployment as failures of personal conduct rather than structural conditions—serves as the ideological linchpin of policies that create, rather than alleviate, economic precarity.

If unfree labour is to be meaningfully addressed, it requires more than technical reforms or stronger regulatory oversight. It necessitates a fundamental rethinking of the role of the state, the meaning of freedom, and the structures that sustain economic coercion. The prominence of neoliberal rationality, which casts work as a moral duty, contractualism as a proxy for consent, and market participation as the sole route to social legitimacy, ensures that the conditions for unfree labour will persist. Addressing this challenge requires not merely resisting specific policies but challenging the deeper logic that sustains them.

Chapter 7 turns to the question of reform, offering legal and policy interventions that might counteract the structural drivers of unfree labour. Recognizing the limitations of regulatory fixes within a neoliberal framework, it explores strategies that go beyond mere mitigation, aiming instead to dismantle the conditions that allow unfree labour to flourish. Central to these discussions is the role of law—not simply as a mechanism of enforcement but as a tool that can reconstitute labour relations in ways that foreground worker autonomy, collective agency, and genuine economic security. In doing so, the chapter considers whether the very legal constructs that have facilitated unfree labour might also hold the key to its undoing.

7
Power to the Workers

1. Introduction

Law and lawmakers have a significant role to play in creating structures of vulnerability that lead to exploitation through, for example, specific statutes and common law doctrines that exclude individuals from particular rights and entitlements or that criminalize their work.[1] In particular, law is central in the creation and shaping of the market economy and, thus, the allocation of property and market-based distributions, which affect the relative freedom and bargaining powers of workers within the labour market.[2] Indeed, Adams asks us to reconceptualize the underpinning justifications of labour law from being a 'correction to market failures' to 'a necessary qualification or restriction' on the market, which prevents 'individuals from pursuing their autonomous self-interest, out of recognition that, in capitalism, their doing so is liable to lead to socially detrimental effects' that would be harmful to capital's reproduction.[3] Law must therefore be understood within this dichotomy, as a system that creates while also attempting to redress exploitation. This dichotomy redirects us away from law as a revered solution to unfree labour relations and makes clear that significant social and political change must take place to address outdated laws regarding what constitutes work and who is entitled to protection. While reform of the employment status framework is key to addressing a number of the unfreedoms that contribute to exploitative and problematic working conditions, broader structural changes concerning social welfare and immigration control must also be implemented if we are to tackle the deep inequality of bargaining power that coerces the working classes into unfree labour. As Blackett eloquently writes, 'emancipation demands structural unshackling from a status that is the basis of subjugation, disenfranchisement, commoditization'.[4]

[1] Virginia Mantouvalou, *Structural Injustice and Workers' Rights* (OUP 2023).
[2] Robert Hale, 'Coercion and Distribution in a Supposedly Non-Coercive State' (1923) 38 Political Science Quarterly 470.
[3] Zoe Adams, *The Legal Concept of Work* (OUP 2022) 336.
[4] Adelle Blackett, 'Emancipation in the Idea of Labour Law' in Guy Davidov and Brian Langille (eds), *The Idea of Labour Law* (OUP 2011) 420.

Underpaid and Unrecognized. Katie Bales and Amir Paz-Fuchs, Oxford University Press.
 DOI: 10.1093/9780197910467.003.0007

For those looking to effect immediate change through law, proposals concerning socio-political action and structural change highlight a gulf between academic theorization of unfree labour and legal practitioners working in the field. The question, then, is whether law, and specifically labour law in its current format, can provide new grounds for challenge or legal redress for those currently excluded from protections? This chapter addresses some of these questions, exploring recommendations and legal avenues that might ameliorate the dimensions of unfreedom addressed in Chapters 4 and 5, which lead to exploitative work relations. It is worth noting, however, that while the case studies share important common features that justify joint analysis, they are also clearly distinct with respect to the populations subject to the schemes, the measures used, and in some cases the particular consequences. For this reason, some of the proposals in this chapter will be more relevant to some of the schemes than to others, and we will endeavour to highlight this when and where relevant.

Our proposals are introduced here through a framework of implementation relating to law and policy: the micro, meso, and macro—attending to the distinction in Marxist theory between a reformist orientation that oscillates within the parameters of the existing legal framework to immediately advance the interests of a particular group and radicalism, which seeks to transcend 'those co-ordinates with a view to advancing the strategic interests of the entire working class'.[5] Accordingly, the micro level explores existing legal statutes and doctrines to ascertain whether there is room for progress within the parameters of law as it stands and whether we can hope for 'incremental judicial development within formal doctrinal constraints'.[6] The meso level addresses reforms specific to our case studies, involving fairly minor changes to areas of law and policy that might help to alleviate the exploitation experienced by workers in those sectors. These reforms largely address conditions of the labour process rather than broader structural changes. Macro changes are more radical, aiming for wide-reaching impact on the structural drivers that lead to instances of unfree labour, acting as a provocation to reconceptualize our current legal order.

[5] Zoe Adams, 'Legal Mobilisations, Trade Unions and Radical Social Change: A Case Study of the IWGB' (2023) 52 Industrial Law Journal 560; Honor Brabazon, 'The Power of Spectacle: The 2012 Quebec Student Strike and the Transformative Potential of Law' (2021) 33 Law and Critique 1.

[6] Alan Bogg, 'Labour Constitutionalism: Effective Judicial Protection as a Constitutional Principle in UK Labour Law' (2023) 43 Comparative Labor Law and Policy Journal 45, 47.

2. The Micro

While much of this book has critiqued legal structures, we believe that there is value in analysing whether there is space within existing statutes and common law principles to expand protections to those who work at the margins to effect immediate change or relief. The question then is whether law, and specifically labour law, can provide additional grounds for challenge or legal redress for those currently excluded from protections.

a. The Doctrine of Illegality

The law of illegality rests upon the principle of '*ex dolo malo non oritur actio*'—that 'no court will lend its aid to a man who founds his cause of action upon an immoral or illegal act'.[7] This doctrine presents issues for informal and irregular workers who wish to make legal claims arising from or in connection with the labour relationship.

Though the work within our case studies is largely formalized and endorsed by the state, illegality remains an important dimension of unfreedom in relation to workers' entry into the labour relationship. For example, the work of immigration detainees is largely criminalized outside the detention estate due to their insecure immigration status.[8] Where irregular migrants undertake 'illegal' work outside of detention, the doctrine of illegality is very likely to mean that they cannot hold their employers to account for the fulfilment of labour rights, including the national minimum wage and back pay,[9] encouraging exploitation and insecure economic status. Upon entry into the detention estate, irregular migrants' lack of access to labour rights outside of detention furthers their inequality of bargaining power as detainees often enter detention in poverty.[10] The doctrine of illegality can also be used by employers as leverage to impose poor working conditions or pay levels on those engaged in informal work as well as weaponizing illegality as a threat to manipulate workers and prevent them from exiting the labour relationship. Accordingly, the courts

[7] *Holman v Johnson* (1775) 1 Cowp 341.

[8] See the Immigration Act 2016, s 34 (which inserts s 24B into the Immigration Act 1971).

[9] Alan Bogg, 'Irregular Migrants and Fundamental Social Rights: The Case of Back-Pay under the English Law on Illegality' in Bernard Ryan and Rebecca Zahn (eds), *Migrant Labour and the Reshaping of Employment Law* (Bloomsbury 2023).

[10] Katie Bales and Lucy Mayblin, 'Unfree Labour in Immigration Detention: Exploitation and Coercion of a Captive Immigrant Workforce' (2018) 47 Economy and Society 191; Katie Bales, 'Rethinking "Unfree" Labour: The Immigration Industrial Complex' in Eileen Boris and others (eds), *Global Labour Migration: New Directions* (University of Illinois Press 2023).

must strike a delicate balance, implementing the public policy of illegality to the extent that enforcement, while not encouraging illegal behaviour, should not 'compromise the integrity of the legal system' by motivating unscrupulous employers to enter into 'illegal' contracts of employment on grounds that labour rights will not be enforced against them.[11]

Traditionally, the strictness with which the illegality doctrine has been enforced has depended on whether the illegality arose as a consequence of statute or the common law and dependent on the claims being brought forward, for example, as matters of contract or tort. Significant developments have taken place over the past decade as a result of judicial interpretation, which has led academics to consider whether there is scope for further progress in the direction of worker protection and the minimization of the doctrine's operation. Here, we examine the operation of illegality and assess whether there is, indeed, scope for progress and the expansion of rights or whether, as contemplated by Bogg these developments constitute a false dawn.[12]

Illegality can occur where an individual's work is expressly or implicitly prohibited by statute (which may include section 24B of the Immigration Act 1971 criminalizing irregular working); where workers enter a contract with the intention of committing an illegal act (as was the case in *Patel v Mirza*);[13] or where the contract is entered into legally but then, knowingly, illegally performed (as per *Hall v Woolston Hall Leisure Ltd*).[14] Whereas the first instance is a case of statutory illegality, the latter two are instances of common law illegality. In relation to common law illegality, the law has developed positively, so the doctrine of illegality is not a block on protective claims. Instead, a balancing methodology is applied, weighing the public policy that founds the defence against any other aspect of public policy to which the defence of illegality might run counter[15] and then applying the principle of proportionality.[16] This provides scope for the consideration of protective human rights, including labour rights, against the illegality doctrine to temper its impact. And yet, to date, in the context of irregular work, judicial interpretation has favoured only those with experience of slavery, servitude, and/or forced labour,[17] where the workers' vulnerability offsets the 'knowledge and participation' elements of

[11] *Hounga v Allen* [2014] ICR 847, SC.
[12] Alan Bogg, 'Okedina v Chikale and Contract Illegality: New Dawn or False Dawn?' (2020) 49 Industrial Law Journal 258.
[13] [2016] UKSC 42.
[14] [2001] ICR 99 LJ.
[15] *Hounga* (n 11).
[16] *Patel* (n 13).
[17] *Hounga* (n 11).

the defence, casting them more as accessories to the illegality than as principal orchestrators.[18]

We argue that, to extend the protective balancing exercise towards other forms of exploited and 'unfree' labour, greater significance should be placed on the innate structural vulnerability of the worker who is economically compelled to enter 'illegal' work in order to survive. Given the centrality of work as a form of social reproduction, a protective approach and the enforcement of labour rights should always be favoured in any balancing exercise regarding illegality. Otherwise, the doctrine reinforces the innate inequality of bargaining power between employers and workers which, in turn, encourages exploitative labour relations. This contravenes the purposive approach of labour law—to minimize the inequality of bargaining power between employers and workers[19]—and disregards the impact of criminal sanctions, such as those relating to a summary conviction or a fine for 'illegal work', which currently act as a counterbalance. By removing labour rights and enforcing the illegality doctrine in addition to criminal sanctions, workers are punished twice, and the balance in terms of bargaining power between capital and labour is severely weighted in favour of the exploitative employer, which further encourages exploitative labour practices.[20] Indeed, as noted by Lord Toulson in *Patel*, in considering whether the denial of a protective claim would be proportionate, the courts must bear 'in mind that punishment is a matter for the criminal courts'.[21]

Further issues arise in the context of statutory illegality, to which we now turn. The effect of section 24B of the Immigration Act 1971 may be an example of an implied statutory illegality (though no case has yet been heard on these grounds), preventing irregular workers from accessing contractual employment rights. This applies broadly to anyone with insecure immigration status who has not been afforded the right to work as a condition of entry. Davidov[22] and Bogg[23] have, however, argued that the courts should take a purposive approach to labour law in general and in the context of illegality in particular. The implication would be that, in deciding whether an implied statutory prohibition exists, courts should consider the underlying purpose of the statute in light of existing constitutional principles. This could, in some cases, create

[18] A Bogg, 'Illegality in Labour Law after Patel v Mirza' in S Green and A Bogg (eds), *Illegality after Patel v Mirza* (Hart 2018); *Robinson v Sheikh Khalid Bin Saqrr Al Qasimi* [2021] EWCA Civ 862.

[19] *Autoclenz Limited v Belcher* [2011] UKSC 41.

[20] Katie Bales, 'Immigration Raids, Employer Collusion and the Immigration Act 2016' (2017) 46 Industrial Law Journal 279.

[21] Lord Toulson [120] in *Patel* (n 13).

[22] Guy Davidov, *A Purposive Approach to Labour Law* (OUP 2016).

[23] Bogg, 'Okedina v Chikale and Contract Illegality' (n 12); Bogg (n 6).

space for the prioritization of labour rights over the doctrine of illegality. A purposive approach to labour law assumes that statutory terms should advance the purpose or goals of the legislation, in a manner analagous to the approach that 'laws should be interpreted in light of the mischief they seek to cure'.[24] Of course, the intention of section 24B is clear: to punish and deter those who have no right to work from working. However, the drafting of section 24B does not prohibit the existence of an employment contract in and of itself, nor the provision of labour rights and protections. It is helpful here to draw on the High Court of Australia in the case of *Yango*,[25] which has been influential on our domestic jurisprudence on the issue of illegality and implied statutory prohibition. Here, Gibbs A.C.J states that

> Where a statute imposes a penalty upon the making or performance of a contract, it is a question of construction whether the statute intends to prohibit the contract in this sense, that is, to render it void and unenforceable, or whether it intends only that the penalty for which it provides shall be inflicted if the contract is made or performed.[26]

Given that the wording of section 24B does not expressly vitiate the contract, the question of 'whether or not the statute has this effect depends upon considerations of public policy in the light of the mischief which the statute is designed to prevent, its language, scope and purpose, the consequences for the innocent party, and any other relevant considerations'.[27] Endorsing this approach, Bogg[28] argues that, in deciding whether an implied statutory prohibition should stand, the mischief of the provision should be interpreted in line with the United Kingdom's constitutional principles, one of which is the principle of legality, which requires judges to protect fundamental rights and freedoms. The implication would be that such rights cannot be overridden by statutes that are worded ambiguously. Labour law protections are part of the rights framework, including the right to a fair and decent wage, which is recognized under Article 23 of the Universal Declaration of Human Rights (UDHR), Article 7 of the International Covenant on Economic, Social

[24] *R v Secretary of State for the Environment, ex p Spath Holme Limited* [2000] UKHL 61; [2001] 1 All ER 195 (opinion of Lord Nicholls) as found in Guy Davidov, 'A Purposive Interpretation of the National Minimum Wage Act' (2009) 72 Modern Law Review 581, 581.

[25] *Yango Pastoral Co Pty Ltd v First Chicago Australia Ltd* (1978) 139 CLR 410.

[26] ibid [413].

[27] *Phoenix General Insurance Co of Greece SA v Halvanon Insurance Co Ltd* [1988] QB 216 (9 October 1986) [Kerr LJ, 273].

[28] Bogg (n 12).

and Cultural Rights (ICESCR) and Article 4 of the European Social Charter. Accordingly, the judiciary should consider whether it was part of the legislative intent that contractual claims would be barred by section 24B in light of the competing public policies of which the government should remain mindful when legislating. In practice, the resulting balance of competing policies would depend on the facts of the case at hand.

Comparative case law largely indicates that where individuals act in good faith or where they have been subjected to trafficking, slavery, servitude, and/or forced labour, the courts will give protective instruments greater weight in assessing the prohibitive intent of the statute.[29] This perspective coalesces with earlier recommendations from the Law Commission, which proposed statutory discretion in cases of implied statutory prohibition and common law illegality to limit the scope of the doctrine in light of the harsh consequences.[30] The good faith issue is, however, already addressed in section 24B, which requires the worker's knowledge of the prohibition. If protection is extended only to those 'without knowledge' or in instances of modern slavery, as opposed to those who are economically compelled to enter exploitative labour, then vast numbers of irregular and informal workers who voluntarily enter 'illegal' work will be excluded and subject to the dual penalties of illegality and criminal sanction, allowing employers to profit from their own wrongdoing. Given the distinct nature of employment and labour law's role in tempering the harshness of capitalism, we argue that the illegality doctrine's standard application should be adapted to account for the worker's inherent vulnerability. Indeed, traditional contractual rules such as the signature rule and parole evidence rule have been altered in relation to employment contracts on such a basis.[31] Better still, given the severity of consequences for the worker, statutory illegality should only be activated where there is an express statutory prohibition.

Finally, another area concerning illegality in which there is scope for judicial development is the characterization of statutory rights, such as those relating to unfair dismissal and national minimum wage, as 'contractual' rights. This characterization opens them up to the specific rules on contractual illegality that, as explored, remain largely restrictive. As noted by Bogg, this

[29] *Still v Minister of National Revenue* (1997) 154 DLR (4th) 229; *'ddowlah v Bengal Cabaret Inc* (1977) 399 NYS 2d 854.

[30] Law Commission, 'Illegal Transactions: The Effect of Illegality on Contracts and Trusts' (Law Com CP No 154, 1999).

[31] Alan Bogg, 'Default Norms in Labour Law: From Private Right to Public Law' (University of Bristol 2024) Paper No 002/2024 <https://www.bristol.ac.uk/media-library/sites/law/research/Default%20Norms%20in%20Labour%20Law-%20From%20Private%20Right%20to%20Public%20Law.pdf> accessed 17 November 2025.

development is largely artificial since the rights themselves are contained and based in statutes and largely derive from fundamental social rights upheld in international law, not the employment contract itself.[32] These rights could be treated as statutory torts as opposed to contractual rights. This distinction matters because, as explored above, 'the illegality doctrine tends to operate more harshly for contract claims, perhaps reflecting a judicial concern that the enforcement of the contractual right permits the claimant to profit from her own wrongdoing'[33] whereas tortious rights, such as those concerning discrimination, are considered more leniently in practice, given the current legal criteria.

b. Trade Unionism

One of the traditional ways of ensuring fair terms and working conditions within the paradigm of the market is through collective bargaining, which redresses the inequality of bargaining power between individual workers and employers by allowing workers to stand as a collective so that their bargaining powers, such as the withdrawal of labour, are multiplied. Indeed, the International Labour Organization (ILO) Collective Bargaining Convention 1981 (No 154) asserts that the purpose of collective bargaining is three-fold: to determine terms and conditions of work, to regulate relationships between individual employers and workers, and to regulate relationships between organizations of employers and worker organizations (Article 2). This is generally achieved in the United Kingdom through trade union representation, where unions bargain on behalf of a workforce. In the United Kingdom, by complying with the rules set out in the Trade Union Labour Relations (Consolidation) Act (TULRCA) 1992 and the Trade Union Act 2016, both unions and individual workers gain immunity from certain employer actions, including dismissal. Yet, a significant barrier to enjoying collective bargaining rights and protections is that in the majority of countries, including the United Kingdom, those deemed to fall outside the contractual status of 'employee' or 'worker' (and thus the majority of the global workforce who are considered 'informal') are prohibited from registering their organizations as trade unions.[34] Consequently,

[32] Bogg (n 12).
[33] ibid.
[34] Marlese Von Broembsen, 'Collective Bargaining for the "New" Working Class: Putting "Personal Work Relations" to Work for Street Vendors' [2024] Industrial Law Journal 527.

'[t]hat such a large global workforce is mostly un-unionized deepens and compounds the exploitation of these workers'.[35]

Article 11 of the European Convention on Human Rights (ECHR), the right to freedom of association, includes 'the right to form and to join trade unions for the protection of his interests', as well as the right to trade union representation, collective bargaining, and industrial action.[36] This aspect was recently incorporated in the United Kingdom through the case of *Mercer*,[37] which (1) recognized the right to strike at an abstract level and (2) established that where employers impose detriments short of dismissal for the purpose of preventing or deterring a worker's participation in union-organized industrial action, the employers' actions may fall foul of Article 11, finding that the UK Government failed to strike a fair balance by failing to provide individual strikers with any form of statutory protection.[38] However, Article 11 remains a qualified right, which can be limited for a number of reasons, including 'in the interests of national security or public safety, for the prevention of disorder or crime, for the protection of health or morals or for the protection of the rights and freedoms of others' as per paragraph 2. Despite the wording of Article 11, which states that 'everyone' can enjoy these rights, in the 2023 case of *Deliveroo*,[39] the UK Supreme Court confirmed that the right to be a member of a trade union applied only to workers, not to 'everyone'. The judgment has been critiqued on a number of levels. One critique holds that the Supreme Court's reading of the European Court of Human Rights (ECtHR) decision in *Pastorul cel Bun*,[40] which was foundational to the issue of who could enjoy trade union membership, was 'questionable because it confuses what the Court said was a sufficient condition for falling within the scope of Article 11 (namely, an employment relation) with a necessary condition, an issue that was not before the Court in *Pastorul cel Bun*'.[41] Indeed, it is not clear that the ECtHR intended for the judgment in *Pastorul cel Bun* to define that *only* those awarded worker status might enjoy these rights, an interpretation that would not align with the wider interpretation of the right to collective bargaining by

[35] Cormac Behan and Matthew Maycock, '"Power to the Convicted Class": Re-Assessing Prisoner-Led Movements and Trade Union Organizing' (2024) 65(4) British Journal of Criminology 1, 3.

[36] *Demir and Baykara v Turkey* [2008] ECHR 1345.

[37] *Secretary of State for Business and Trade v Mercer* [2024] UKSC 12.

[38] Alan Bogg, 'Bringing the Right to Strike Home: Secretary of State for Business and Trade v Mercer—Part 1' (*Oxford Human Rights Hub*, 10 May 2024) <https://ohrh.law.ox.ac.uk/bringing-the-right-to-strike-home-secretary-of-state-for-business-and-trade-v-mercer-part-1> accessed 17 November 2025.

[39] *R (Independent Workers Union of Great Britain) v Central Arbitration Committee* [2023] UKSC 43.

[40] *Sindicatul 'Pastorul cel Bun' v Romania* [2014] IRLR 49 (Grand Chamber ECtHR).

[41] Hugh Collins, 'The Right to Fair Pay and Two Paradigms of Prison Work' (2024) 15 European Labour Law Journal 445.

the ILO. This also conflicts with the broader interpretation of the 'employment relationship' within domestic courts, including litigation concerning foster carers, thus rendering applicable the right to join a trade union.[42]

In interpreting Convention rights, the ECtHR often adopts an integrated approach to create consistency among the various human rights treaties, instruments, and institutions. While Article 2 of the ILO's Convention on the Freedom of Association and Protection of the Right to Organize 1948 (No 87) asserts that the right to join unions or organizations for the purposes of collective bargaining applies to workers, this should be read in conjunction with the commentary of ILO supervisory bodies, which notes that this Convention, as well as the Right to Organize and Collective Bargaining Convention 1949 (No 98), 'cover all employers and workers without establishing distinctions based on their contractual status'.[43] This is further substantiated in the ILO *Digest of Decisions and Principles of the Freedom of Association Committee*, which states that

> by virtue of the principles of freedom of association, all workers—with the sole exception of members of the armed forces and police—should enjoy the right to establish and to join organizations of their own choosing. The criterion for determining the persons covered by that right, therefore, is not based on the existence of an employment relationship, which is often non-existent, for example, in the case of agricultural workers, self-employed workers in general or those who practice liberal professions, who should nevertheless enjoy the right to organize.[44]

The ILO commentary thus provides a wider interpretation of who might enjoy collective bargaining rights, and both the ECtHR and Supreme Court have an opportunity to develop the law in this area more expansively to include those individuals engaged in informal work, who do not occupy the legal categorization of 'employee' or 'worker'.

[42] *National Union of Professional Foster Carers v The Certification Officer* [2021] EWCA Civ 548.

[43] ILO, 'Social Dialogue Report 2022: Collective Bargaining for an Inclusive, Sustainable and Resilient Recovery' (1st edn, ILO 2022) 51 <https://researchrepository.ilo.org/esploro/outputs/report/995218817102676> accessed 17 November 2025.

[44] ILO, *Digest of Decisions and Principles of the Freedom of Association Committee* (4th edn 1996) [235].

c. Unfreedom as Dependency: Worker Status and the Purposive Approach

In the 2021 case of *Uber v Aslam*,[45] the Supreme Court continued to embrace the purposive approach in the context of rights-based claims arising from the employment relationship. Accordingly, worker status should be considered in line with the underlying purpose of the statutory provision in section 230(3) of the Employment Rights Act 1996, which is to extend protection to those performing work 'in positions of subordination and dependency'.[46] The notion of subordination and dependency was further elaborated by the Court, identified as control by the employer over the worker's working conditions and remuneration.[47] However, we would argue that a purposive approach must also take into account the historical context of worker status, which was introduced to protect those performing work who were recognized as economically vulnerable and who struggled to fit within the binary statuses of 'employee' and 'independent contractor'. From this perspective, it is vital that the courts acknowledge the multiple and structural dimensions that give rise to dependency and coercion within the labour relationship, perhaps creating space to prioritize rights for the most vulnerable as opposed to the paradoxical arrangement at present whereby those subjected to the greatest coercion and unfreedoms often have the least access to labour rights or legal redress.[48] This creates space for traditionally excluded groups, such as gig workers, to fall within the scope of protection and offers a challenge to 'the existing abstract, decontextualized view of the wage relation more directly'.[49]

3. The Meso

A number of amendments could be made to the current systems of work explored within our case studies that would improve the working conditions of those within these sectors. In particular, exploitation could be reduced by

[45] *Uber BV v Aslam* [2021] UKSC 5.
[46] Joe Atkinson and Hitesh Dhorajiwala, 'After Uber: Purposive Interpretation and the Future of Contract' (*UK Labour Law*, 1 April 2021) <https://uklabourlawblog.com/2021/04/01/after-uber-purposive-interpretation-and-the-future-of-contract-by-joe-atkinson-and-hitesh-dhorajiwala> accessed 17 November 2025.
[47] *Uber BV* (n 45) [75].
[48] Adams (n 3).
[49] ibid 352.

increasing pay levels across the board, allowing workers to retain more of the profit they have helped to produce, in turn reducing the surplus value absorbed by the private corporations benefiting from the work itself.

a. Prison Labour

In line with calls from prisoners themselves, as well as organizations and individuals advocating for their rights, one of the most significant reforms to improve the conditions of prison workers would be to repeal section 45 of the National Minimum Wage Act 1998 so that prisoners would gain entitlement to wages on par with those outside of the prison industrial complex. This aligns with the recommendations of the UN Special Rapporteur on contemporary forms of slavery, who demanded an increase in prisoners' wages to the national minimum wage as a reasonable starting point,[50] explaining that financial insecurity enhances the risks of recidivism and modern slavery post release. It is worth noting that prisoners' minimum weekly wage (£4.00) is equivalent to just twenty minutes of work at the national minimum wage rate.[51] To demand increased wages for prisoners reframes the work undertaken as productive market work, which aids capital enterprise and subverts the notion that this work is for the purposes of rehabilitation and the prisoner's 'own benefit'. Arguments against increasing payments cite increased costs to employers, which could disincentivize businesses from employing them in the first place, instead seeking to outsource cheaper labour from the Global South. However, this overlooks the benefits of utilizing a contained and compliant workforce which is largely reliable, as shown in cases where prisoners released on a temporary facility licence are paid the national minimum wage. Such benefits are highlighted by His Majesty's Prison and Probation Service (HMPPS) as including a reduction in recruitment and job advertising costs, diversification of the workforce, resolving skills shortages, reducing staff absences, and increasing staff retention.[52]

[50] Tomoya Obokata, 'Contemporary Forms of Slavery as Affecting Currently and Formerly Incarcerated People: Report of the Special Rapporteur on Contemporary Forms of Slavery, Including Its Causes and Consequences, Fifty-Seventh Session, 9 September–9 October 2024' A/HRC/57/46 (United Nations Human Rights Council 2024) para 25.

[51] Matthew Maycock and Daniel McGregor, '"I Do Enjoy the Work, But I Think the Wages in the Jails Are Shocking": Analysing Prisoner Wages as a Pain of Imprisonment Using Foucault's Artifice' (2023) 4 Incarceration 26326663231170767.

[52] HM Prison and Probation Service, 'Employing Prisoners and Ex-Offenders. See What's on the Inside' (2020) <https://assets.publishing.service.gov.uk/government/uploads/system/uploads/attachment_data/file/927039/offender-employment-guide.pdf> accessed 17 November 2025.

Payment of the national minimum wage would also not necessarily involve flooding the prisons with cash flow. Rather, wages could be held on trust for prisoners until their release and used for essential expenses like a housing deposit or rent. This would help to address the homelessness crisis facing prisoners upon release, with up to 600 prisoners released each month with only tents and sleeping bags, increasing rates of recidivism.[53] As noted in the report by the UN Special Rapporteur on contemporary forms of slavery, 'access to decent housing is crucial, as formerly incarcerated individuals without family or friends . . . are at a heightened risk of being pushed into homelessness, which in turn can lead to exploitation in contemporary forms of slavery'.[54] Though a current scheme has been set up to provide prisoners with twelve weeks of accommodation post release on the basis that 'getting offenders off the streets and into temporary accommodation provides the necessary foundation to break the cycle of crime and keep the public safe',[55] charities claim that the scheme merely delays homelessness by a few months as individuals are typically evicted once their twelve weeks of accommodation is over. Indeed, prison charity Switchback claims that seven out of ten of its male clients were released into homelessness in 2023.[56] Allowing prisoners to save wages and providing them with a bank account would improve access to the private rental sector and reduce pressure on social housing.[57] Demanding the national minimum wage for prisoners also aligns with calls from businesses themselves, which are finding it difficult to recruit post-Brexit and the COVID-19 pandemic

[53] Lizzie Deardon, 'Homeless Convicts Committing More Crime to Get Back into Prison, Watchdog Says' *The Independent* (London, 8 July 2020) <www.independent.co.uk/news/uk/home-news/homeless-ex-convicts-re-offend-crime-jail-watchdog-a9606391.html> accessed 17 November 2025; Kaya Kannan, 'More Than Six Out of 10 Women Prisoners Homeless on Release—The Justice Gap' (23 March 2021) <www.thejusticegap.com/more-than-six-out-of-10-women-prisoners-homeless-on-release> accessed 17 November 2025; Andy Gregory, '"Cell, Street, Repeat": Prisoners Set Up to Fail with Release into Homelessness' *The Independent* (London, 28 December 2023) <www.independent.co.uk/news/uk/home-news/prison-crisis-homelessness-probation-reoffending-b2461968.html> accessed 17 November 2025.

[54] Obokata (n 50).

[55] Former Prisons and Probation Minister, Damian Hinds, 'Basic Housing to Keep Offenders off Streets and Cut Crime' *GOV.UK* (18 July 2023) <www.gov.uk/government/news/basic-housing-to-keep-offenders-off-streets-and-cut-crime> accessed 17 November 2025.

[56] Switchback, 'Policy Proposal: National Resettlement Framework' (*Switchback.org.uk*, 2023) <https://switchback.org.uk/wp-content/uploads/2024/06/SWITCHBACK-Policy-Proposal-National-Resettlement-Framework.pdf> accessed 17 November 2025.

[57] Melek Bozkina and Nick Hardwick, 'Preventing Homelessness amongst Former Prisoners in England and Wales: A Rapid Review of the Evidence' (Prison Advice and Care Trust; Royal Holloway, University of London; London Housing Foundation, July 2021) <www.prisonadvice.org.uk/media/m4ebyvqm/preventing-homelessness-former-prisoners.pdf> accessed 17 November 2025.

of 2020,[58] as well as calls from Mark Fairhurst, the national chairman of the Prison Officers Association (POA), who argues that

> If you're paying prisoners the minimum wage, a third can go to the Victims' Charter fund, a third to their savings for when they are released, and a third they can spend while they're in prison. Instead of that small discharge grant, with the savings they could go out with a couple of thousand pounds. They're also leaving with a work skill so not only can they get a job, but they can get away from all the negative peer pressure, maybe put a deposit down on a flat in another area and start afresh. We're giving people hope, we're giving people an opportunity to change.[59]

As part of the traditional wage work bargain, *consent* must also be obtained before prisoners undertake work, and Rule 31(3) of the Prison Rules, which imposes up to ten hours of work on convicted prisoners each day, must be repealed. Prisoners are not sentenced to work, so imposing compulsory labour raises issues of autonomy and proportionality of punishment,[60] which, as Mantouvalou argues, aligns such treatment with slavery.[61] Gaining consent to work would also subvert the liberal construction of prison labour as falling outside the traditional wage–work bargain on grounds that it is punitively imposed involuntarily, rendering it closer to compulsion than mutuality.[62] However, this conflicts with the practical realities of prison labour in the United Kingdom, which is largely entered into voluntarily due to the shortage of available work, and would allow prisoners to occupy the status of worker or employee and its associate protections.

If prison work is 'rehabilitative' rather than punitive, as the government claims, then forcing prisoners to undertake work they do not enjoy or find useful is unlikely to be beneficial for rehabilitation. Indeed, if rehabilitation is concerned with respect for human dignity, as the ECtHR indicates,[63] then work

[58] Frances Crook, 'If Prisoners Are to Help with the UK's Labour Shortages, They Must Not Be Exploited' *The Guardian* (London, 26 August 2021) <www.theguardian.com/commentisfree/2021/aug/26/prisoners-uk-labour-shortage-exploited> accessed 17 November 2025.

[59] Inside Time, 'Pay Prisoners National Minimum Wage, Says Union Leader' (*Inside Time Reports*, 4 April 2022) <https://insidetime.org/newsround/pay-prisoners-national-minimum-wage-says-union-leader> accessed 17 November 2025.

[60] Rory Kelly, 'Prison Labour as Punishment' (2024) 15 European Labour Law Journal 426.

[61] Virginia Mantouvalou, 'Work in Prison: Reintegration or Exclusion and Exploitation?' (2024) 15 European Labour Law Journal 409.

[62] *Pullin v Prisoner Commission* [1957] 1 WLR 1186; *Cox v Ministry of Justice* [2016] UKSC 10.

[63] *Life Imprisonment Case* (21 June 1977) 45 BVerfGE 187E; *Vinter v The United Kingdom* (9 July 2013) (Applications nos 66069/09, 130/10, and 3896/10); Edgardo Rotman, 'Do Offenders Have a Constitutional Right to Rehabilitation?' (1986) 77 Journal of Criminal Law & Criminology 1023; Sonja

must be dignified for it to be rehabilitative. Extracting free work under circumstances of extreme coercion is not dignified work. As noted in Chapter 2, evidence suggests that, in some instances, forcing monotonous work on detainees may discourage them from seeking work in the formal economy.[64] Instead, providing labour rights and wages for consensual prison work would bring it closer to the process of 'normalization' that is proposed in the European Prison Rules and the UN Nelson Mandela Rules,[65] encouraging work in the formal economy outside of detention. As argued by Mantouvalou, providing prisoners with access to the national minimum wage and labour rights would promote social reintegration rather than mortification.[66]

In addition to improved conditions of work, including requiring consent and providing the national minimum wage, there must also be a sustained and increased effort to provide meaningful access to education and training for prisoners as well as job opportunities after release. In particular, access to adequate educational opportunities is lacking, as evidenced by a review from Ofsted and HM Inspectorate of Prisons which, out of twenty-two institutions, judged half inadequate, ten as requiring improvement, and one (HMP Bronzefield) as good.[67] Perhaps unsurprisingly, the number of those participating in the prison education system has fallen by half from over 100,000 in 2014–15 to 49,855 in 2021–22,[68] which is not wholly explained by the fall-out from the COVID-19 pandemic. Major issues with staff retention and literacy are identified as key areas for improvement.

In relation to employment, there are currentgovernment schemes in place to help prisoners secure formal work, including one-stop hubs to provide career advice and CV-writing opportunities, as well as the HMP Academy and Future Skills Programme, which provides employers with access to prison labour while also offering vocational skills training to detainees. For prisoners who engage with these schemes, the outcome is a guaranteed job interview for a

Meijer, 'Rehabilitation as a Positive Obligation' (2017) 25 European Journal of Crime, Criminal Law and Criminal Justice 145.

[64] Jenna Pandeli, Michael Marinetto, and Jean Jenkins, 'Captive in Cycles of Invisibility? Prisoners' Work for the Private Sector' (2019) 33 Work, Employment and Society 596.

[65] The European Prison Rules, Rule 5 and the Nelson Mandela Rules, Rules 96–103.

[66] Mantouvalou (n 61).

[67] Ofsted, 'The Annual Report of His Majesty's Chief Inspector of Education, Children's Services and Skills 2021/22' (2022) <www.gov.uk/government/publications/ofsted-annual-report-202122-education-childrens-services-and-skills/the-annual-report-of-his-majestys-chief-inspector-of-education-childrens-services-and-skills-202122> accessed 17 November 2025.

[68] Ministry of Justice, 'Prison Education Statistics and Accredited Programmes in Custody April 2021 to March 2022' (29 September 2022) <https://assets.publishing.service.gov.uk/media/63347ae3d3bf7f34f5e5d7fd/Prisoner_Education_2021_22.pdf> accessed 17 November 2025.

genuine vacancy. Indeed, these schemes notably increased the proportion of prisoners finding work after release: from April 2022, prison leavers finding work within six weeks of release increased from 15 per cent to 19 per cent, and the proportion of those in work after six months jumped from 23 per cent to 30 per cent.[69] Such schemes must continue; however, employers must be encouraged to offer more than just an interview in return for access to prison labour, including opportunities such as mentoring, paid internships, a commitment to recruit staff from the ex-prison population (as is the case with Timpsons), or an agreement to implement best practices such as those set out by the Prison Reform Trust, including, for example, to 'ban the box' by removing the question about prior convictions from application forms and relaxing onboarding processes such as requirements for references, bank accounts, and ID documentation.[70] Improvements to working conditions may reduce the exploitative nature of work in our case studies, though they are unlikely to eliminate exploitation entirely. Nevertheless, such recommendations are an important first step towards helping to reduce the unfree labour of prison work more generally.

b. Labour in Immigration Detention

The authors' position is that immigration detention should be abolished entirely, thereby eliminating the exploitative system of 'paid activities' within it. While this book does not aim to outline the full range of reasons for ending immigration detention, data gathered by Bail for Immigration Detainees over two decades[71] demonstrates that detention creates and compounds barriers to justice; has a devastating impact on the mental and physical health of an already vulnerable population; increases the likelihood of deaths in custody; and enforces family separation on children, with clear and obvious detrimental effects on their mental health and well-being. It further establishes that isolation for those within prison amounts to torture, that the lack of judicial oversight

[69] Ministry of Justice, 'Employment on Release Statistical Release to March 2023' (23 May 2023) <https://assets.publishing.service.gov.uk/media/646b794c382a51000c9fc520/Employment_Ad-Hoc_publication.pdf> accessed 17 November 2025.

[70] The Prison Reform Trust, 'Prison: The Facts. Bromley Briefings Summer 2023' (2023) <https://prisonreformtrust.org.uk/wp-content/uploads/2023/06/prison_the_facts_2023.pdf> accessed 17 November 2025.

[71] Bail for Immigration Detainees, 'BID Research Reports' (*Bail for Immigration Detainees*, no date) <www.biduk.org/pages/62-bid-research-reports> accessed 17 November 2025.

and transparency leaves immigration detainees vulnerable to systemic abuse and mistreatment, and that unlawful detention remains widespread.[72]

Despite repeated calls from charitable organizations to bring an end to immigration detention, it looks unlikely that this demand will be met in the foreseeable future, and on this basis, a number of other recommendations are made. First, there must be stronger judicial oversight and time limits on immigration detention, including a review of the initial decision to detain by a judge within seventy-two hours, and a twenty-eight-day statutory time limit to reduce periods of incarceration and ensure that they are only held for the purposes of examining their immigration status or effecting removal. Liberty reports that such a limit could also save the taxpayer up to £35 million per year.[73] This aligns with advice from the House of Commons Home Affairs Committee,[74] the HM Inspector of Prisons, and the Joint Committee on Human Rights and Detention Action[75] and would bring immigration enforcement closer in line with the criminal law, where an upper limit on detention without charge exists. The lack of certainty concerning an individual's length of detention creates hyper precarity, making detainees more likely to accept exploitative working conditions.[76] Indeed, Andersson argues that 'the authorities engage in an active usurpation of time for the purposes of migration control' which, alongside disrupting the flow of capital and mobility, constitutes a form of collective punishment.[77]

Second, in line with the demands of detainees outlined in the cases of *Badmus*[78] and *Morita*,[79] wages should be increased for those taking part in 'paid activities' to the level of the national minimum wage. Given that the wage is 'one of the most direct expressions of the relation of power between capital and labor and one of the most tangible objects of struggle over its terms',[80]

[72] ibid.

[73] Liberty, 'Immigration Detention' (*Liberty*, no date) <www.libertyhumanrights.org.uk/fundamental/immigration-detention> accessed 17 November 2025.

[74] House of Commons Home Affairs Committee, 'Immigration Detention Fourteenth Report of Session 2017–19' (2019).

[75] Detention Action, 'A 28 Day Statutory Time Limit on Immigration Detention. The Cross-Party Time Limit on Immigration Detention. Amendment to the Immigration and Social Security Coordination (EU Withdrawal) Bill Briefing for MPs with Q&A' (July 2019) <https://detentionaction.org.uk/wp-content/uploads/2019/07/Detention-Action-Time-Limit-Briefing-July-2019.pdf> accessed 17 November 2025.

[76] Bales and Mayblin (n 10); Bales (n 10); Katie Bales, 'Labour as a Component of Carceral Circuitry: The Case of Asylum Seekers' (2024) 15 European Labour Law Journal 597.

[77] Ruben Andersson, *Illegality, Inc: Clandestine Migration and the Business of Bordering Europe* (University of California Press 2014).

[78] *R (on the application of Badmus) v Secretary of State for the Home Department* [2020] EWCA Civ 657.

[79] *Morita v Secretary of State for the Home Department* [2019] EWHC 758.

[80] Kathi Weeks, *The Problem with Work: Feminism, Marxism, Antiwork Politics, and Postwork Imaginaries* (Duke UP 2011).

its fair endowment is essential in helping to redress the levels of exploitation under which immigration detainees labour. As argued throughout this book, there is no justifiable reason why this group should be paid less than their citizen counterparts for jobs that remain integral to the running of the detention estate. Inadequate remuneration is a clear indicator of unfreedom, and an increase in payment would help to reduce the levels of exploitation experienced by workers, though it would not address the structural forces that compel immigration detainees into agreeing to work for £1.00 an hour.

This brings us to our third recommendation for ameliorating the labour unfreedom of immigration detainees which, in line with the longstanding 'Lift the Ban' campaign, demands unlimited access to the labour market for asylum seekers outside of detention. This is justified on grounds that work prohibitions create carceral conditions[81] that plunge the asylum-seeking community into forms of state-enforced poverty and fuel engagement with irregular work which, in turn, props up the detention estate via prosecutions for 'illegal working' via section 34 of the Immigration Act 2016.

c. Workfare

As noted in Chapter 2, the term 'workfare' is often, confusingly, used to denote two different schemes. In the narrow sense, it refers to 'work for your benefits' and, as such, offers a core example of unfree labour that is initiated and facilitated by the state. However, it is also used as a shorthand for 'welfare to work', which is the broader collection of activation schemes of which workfare is a part. It is this form of the term that Peck referred to when he (accurately) quipped that 'workfare is not about creating jobs for people who don't have them; it is about creating workers for jobs that nobody wants'.[82] These could include the basic principle that unemployed individuals should accept job offers on the basis that 'any job is a good job'[83] or even a form of public works scheme,[84] a version of which was adopted by many nations during their socialist periods.

81 Bales (n 76).
82 Jamie Peck, *Workfare States* (Guilford Press 2001) 6.
83 Patricia Evans, '(Not) Taking Account of Precarious Employment: Workfare Policies and Lone Mothers in Ontario and the UK' (2007) 41 Social Policy and Administration 29, 35ff.
84 Zsuzsanna Vidra, 'Hungary's Punitive Turn: The Shift from Welfare to Workfare' (2018) 51 Communist and Post-Communist Studies 73.

Focusing, then, on the narrow definition of workfare, our recommendation here is straightforward and happily, at present day the current state of affairs in the UK. It adheres to the call to 'abolish workfare'. As we noted in Chapter 2, by 2019 workfare schemes in the United Kingdom had ceased to operate, and at the time of writing, no such scheme exists in the United Kingdom. However, it is useful to chart the path to its abolition for two reasons: first, because workfare is still prevalent across the globe, in countries including the United States (in a number of states[85]), Canada,[86] Australia, and Hungary; second, because workfare is never far from the UK Government's toolkit. This was apparent, for example, as recently as 2023, when the chancellor at the time, Jeremy Hunt, declared as part of his Autumn Statement, that benefit claimants who fail to find work for over eighteen months will have to undertake mandatory 'work experience placements'.[87]

One can identify three prongs that combined to lead to the quick demise of workfare in its extreme and direct form—civic engagement, media activism, and legal challenges. First, a grassroots campaign, led by *Boycott Workfare*, *Keep Volunteering Voluntary* and a number of local groups,[88] identified major retail stores and charities through freedom-of-information (FoI) requests, which were effective only following a legal challenge that stretched over four years and culminated in a decision by the Court of Appeal.[89] Indeed, even at this stage, the government revealed some ambivalence towards the scheme or, at the least, awareness that the schemes are not popular. It sought to deny the FoI requests by claiming that disclosing the involvement of the stores and charities would lead to 'possible commercial detriment',[90] and, on appeal, the DWP argued that making this information public 'would have been likely to have led to the collapse of the . . . scheme'.[91]

[85] One of the most studied is the Wisconsin Works scheme. See Richard Crisp and Del Roy Fletcher, 'A Comparative Review of Workfare Programmes in the United Stated, Canada and Australia' (2008) Department for Work and Pensions (DWP) Research Report 533 <https://webarchive.nationalarchives.gov.uk/ukgwa/20081006105522/http://www.dwp.gov.uk/asd/asd5/rports2007-2008/rrep533.pdf> accessed 17 November 2025.

[86] Mark Freedland and Nicola Kountouris, *The Legal Construction of Personal Work Relations* (OUP 2011).

[87] BBC, 'Benefit Claimants Not Seeking Work to Face Mandatory Work Placements' (16 November 2023) <www.bbc.co.uk/news/business-67439675> accessed 17 November 2025.

[88] Vera Weghmann, 'The Making and Breaking of Solidarity between Unwaged and Waged Workers in the UK' (2019) 16 Globalizations 441.

[89] *Department of Work and Pensions v Frank Zola* [2016] EWCA Civ 758.

[90] *Department for Work and Pensions v IC (Freedom of Information Act 2000)* (First-tier tribunal, 17 May 2013) <www.casemine.com/judgement/uk/5b35bf9d2c94e01ed25519b0> accessed 17 November 2025.

[91] *Department for Work and Pensions v Information Commissioner and Frank Zola* (Upper Tribunal, Administrative Appeals Chamber, 15 July 2014) [67]–[68].

While the courts rejected the argument, it seems that there was some truth to them. Thus, the release of the information led to one employer—Holland and Barrett—withdrawing immediately from the scheme after 'employing' 1,000 unpaid workers between 2011 and 2012, citing 'bad press and in-store protests' as the reason.[92] Additional protests led to the (temporary) withdrawal of companies such as Fortnum and Mason, Barnardos, the British Heart Foundation, and Sue Ryder. The *Guardian*'s disclosure that local councils benefited from half a million hours of unpaid work[93] led some councils to cease their participation.[94] In particular, the compulsory element of the scheme was clearly most difficult to defend and drew analogies to forced labour and modern slavery.[95]

In the beginning of 2012, the *Guardian* reported that Tesco, Argos, Superdrug, Matalan, Waterstone's, and Sainsbury's were among several retailers that had decided to suspend their involvement with mandatory workfare schemes, following protests on their doorstep.[96] This confluence of forces led to the disbanding of the Community Work Programme (CWP) and Mandatory Work Activity (MWA) towards the end of 2015.[97] The Work Programme ceased to accept referrals in March 2017, which meant that the last participants took part in this scheme in early 2019.

This brief overview of developments is evidence of the fluid, and perhaps even erratic, nature of schemes and programmes in this context, leading to the caveat that, with reference to the opening of this subsection, it can only be true to the time of writing. With that understanding in mind, we note that, while the government revoked Regulation 91A of the Universal Credit Regulations 2013, the power to mandate work as a condition of benefits is still located in sections 16(1) and 16(3)(e) of the Welfare Reform Act 2012. In particular, read together, these provisions state that a 'work preparation requirement' is a requirement

[92] David Bailey and others, *Beyond Defeat and Austerity: Disrupting (the Critical Political Economy of) Neoliberal Europe* (Routledge 2016).

[93] Shiv Malik, 'UK Councils Found to Benefit from Half a Million Hours of Unpaid Labour' *The Guardian* (London, 3 January 2014) <www.theguardian.com/local-government-network/2014/jan/04/councils-uk-benefit-unpaid-labour> accessed 17 November 2025.

[94] Shiv Malik, 'Holland & Barrett Pulls Out of Jobseekers' Scheme' *The Guardian* (London, 2012) <https://www.theguardian.com/uk/2012/jul/06/holland-and-barrett-jobseekers-scheme> accessed 11 June 2025.

[95] European Commission, 'Study on a Comprehensive Overview on Traineeship Arrangements in Member States: Final Synthesis Report' (Publications Office of the European Union 2012) <http://op.europa.eu/en/publication-detail/-/publication/19623a37-37ee-4a60-b7ba-14a55526012f> accessed 17 November 2025.

[96] Shiv Malik, Patrick Wintour, and James Ball, 'Work Experience Scheme in Disarray as Tesco and Other Retailers Change Tack' *The Guardian* (London, 21 February 2012) <www.theguardian.com/society/2012/feb/21/back-work-scheme-disarray-tesco> accessed 7 April 2026.

[97] DWP, 'Department for Work and Pensions' Settlement at the Spending Review' (*GOV.UK*, 25 November 2015) <www.gov.uk/government/news/department-for-work-and-pensions-settlement-at-the-spending-review> accessed 17 November 2025.

that a claimant take particular action (as a condition for the receipt of benefits), and that action would include 'undertaking work experience or a work placement'. This legal framework is important because it is clear that workfare always has the potential for resurgence.

d. Internships

In March 2024, the European Commission introduced a 'traineeship package', which consists of a 'Traineeship Directive', with the aim of improving the working conditions of trainees,[98] and a Council Recommendation on the reinforced 2014 Quality Framework for Traineeships.[99] The proposed Directive included positive elements such as the principle of non-discrimination (including in pay), ensuring that traineeships are not used to disguise regular jobs, and allowing workers' representatives to engage on behalf of trainees to secure rights. The Council Recommendation complements the Directive by clarifying, crucially for present purposes, that it (the Recommendation) applies to all trainees, regardless of employment status, including those in formal education and in training for a profession. In addition, the Council recommends awarding trainees 'fair pay'; appointing a mentor to a trainee to facilitate the provision of support and advice; and a written agreement to be provided before the start of the traineeship, setting out the terms, ensuring that the traineeship is not too long.

This recent development suggests that there is an awareness that, while traineeships and internships could be a positive force as a bridge to employment, they are currently, quite often, a regulated form of exploitation. The juxtaposition of the Directive and the Recommendation offers an avenue to assess the gaps that exist towards realizing the aforementioned potential and the risks that remain if certain measures are not taken. For example, the European Trade Union Confederation (ETUC) noted that, in contrast to the Recommendations,

[98] 'Proposal for a Directive on *Improving and Enforcing Working Conditions of Trainees and Combating Regular Employment Relationships Disguised as Traineeships*' ('Traineeships Directive') (2024/0068(COD), 20 March 2024) <https://eur-lex.europa.eu/legal-content/EN/TXT/?uri=celex:52024PC0132> accessed 7 April 2026.

[99] 'Council Recommendation on a *Reinforced Quality Framework for Traineeships*' (2024/0069(NLE), 20 March 2024) = <https://eur-lex.europa.eu/legal-content/EN/TXT/?uri=celex:52024DC0133> accessed 7 April 2026.

> The main shortcoming of the proposed Directive lies in the scope and the definitions. The proposal suggests that only trainees who have an employment contract or employment relationship as defined by the law, collective agreements or practice in force in every Member State with consideration to the case law of the Court of Justice [which exclude unpaid traineeships] should be covered by this Directive. However, it does not address all traineeships after graduation (as the EP proposed in their resolution on quality traineeships in the Union), *and it does not cover the most exploitative forms of traineeships, which are unpaid.*[100]

In other words, as the ETUC identifies, the cohort of interns most in need of protection, partly but not solely because they are unpaid, are excluded from these new measures, which address some of the existing concerns. More generally, in the post-Brexit reality in which European Union (EU) Directives will have minimal effect on the UK legal framework, our proposals for reform refer to the Directive and Recommendations as sources of inspiration and evidence to the concerns and conversations already underway.

The first issue that arises from the discussion above, then, concerns the scope of the measures. In particular, the regulation of internships should include paid and unpaid internships in the open labour market; interns who take part in active labour market policies (ALMP), akin to workfare; and schemes that are a mandatory part of professional training. Second, measures must be taken to ensure that trainees are not used as cheap labour to perform tasks normally undertaken by other workers. Where such situations are identified, trainees should have access to all labour and social rights, including those stipulated by collective agreements. Third, the supervision of and, consequently, the quality of internships should be addressed. As noted in Chapter 2, the dual justification for treating interns differently to standard workers lies in the fact that they produce less and are given more. Both aspects of this justification were challenged, empirically and theoretically, in that chapter. Moving to the constructive suggestions, we suggest here that if internships are to live up to their ideal as a bridge from education, or non-work, to work, they must adhere to a set of minimum criteria to ensure their quality. A written contract will set out, explicitly, these criteria, which will include

[100] ETUC, 'The Traineeship Package' (26 June 2024) <www.etuc.org/en/document/traineeship-package> accessed 17 November 2025.

- the (non-renewable) term of the internship: this should be no more than six months and, in exceptional circumstances, one year;
- the remuneration (pay and social security) that will be offered;
- the expectations and learning outcomes;
- mentoring and supervision specified in the contract;
- working time provisions.

Fourth, where internships are subsidized or paid for by the state, through ALMP or otherwise, employers-providers should adhere to a minimum set of conditions, and governments should not enter into partnerships with employers who have exploited trainees; provided unsatisfactory supervision; or failed to respect labour laws, including discrimination and collective bargaining, for example.

4. The Macro

In foregrounding the alleviation of unfreedoms identified in Chapters 4 and 5, we must also consider how changes to other areas of law might alleviate the pressures forcing individuals into exploitative work, such as the introduction of universal basic services as well as solutions outside the law, such as collective organizing and action. In this section, we put forward some of these proposals. Rather than setting out detailed policy proposals, which would be impossible to explore fully in the current chapter, we offer provocations intended to inspire creative thinking about ways in which we could progress to reduce the impetus of engagement with unfree and exploitative forms of work.

a. Work Outside the Employment Contract: Adequate Labour Rights and Protections

As we have explored throughout this book, the current legal framework remains bound to conceptualizing work through the prism of the employment contract or a 'contract for services'. As such, it is abstracted from the capitalist labour relation,[101] meaning that up to 60 per cent of the world's labour

[101] Adams (n 3) 338.

force[102] and over 90 per cent of those working for micro and small enterprises globally are excluded from status recognition and its associated rights.[103] Those who remain excluded from protection include unpaid workers engaged within the private sphere of the home[104] as well as those who work in informal and non-typical arrangements, such as self-employed and gig economy workers, as highlighted in the case of *Deliveroo*.[105] Yet, as we explained in Chapter 3, the legal classification of employee and worker status does more than simply define legal categories. It also naturalizes and legitimizes particular social constructs and discourses that lead to the devaluation of particular types of work where their purpose is considered to be non-productive and thus 'non-market' in nature. Discourses based on 'care' and 'rehabilitation', for example, inform the boundaries between what we consider to be work and 'non-work', the pursuance of which is grounded in ideas such as 'innate' capacities and activities that are primarily 'of benefit' to the worker as opposed to market forces. As noted by Adams, in 'assigning certain capacities to the worker's personality, and others to their work, the law shapes how different capacities are conceived and valued, as well as how their performance comes to be organized'.[106]

Accordingly, we need a different way of conceptualizing work outside of the employee/worker versus self-employed binary, one that identifies the constructed labour unfreedoms that arise through capitalist social relations and recognizes the coercive nature of capitalism that relies on dispossession as the basis for the exploitation and subjugation of workers. Significant social and political change over what is considered to constitute work and who is entitled to protection is thus key to transforming labour relations in the present. This change must include recognizing reprodutive labour as socially valuable work by supporting the 'wages for housework' claims made by feminist theorists in the 1970s,[107] more recently broadened to the idea of a 'care income', which accounts for ecological practices of care.[108]

[102] Matias Golman and Christoph Ernst, 'Future of Work, Emerging Sectors and the Potential for Transition to Formality' (ILO 2022) <https://www.ilo.org/publications/future-work-emerging-sectors-and-potential-transition-formality> accessed 28 January 2026.

[103] ILO, 'More Than 60 per Cent of the World's Employed Population Are in the Informal Economy' (30 April 2018) <www.ilo.org/global/about-the-ilo/newsroom/news/WCMS_627189/lang--en/index.htm> accessed 7 November 2023.

[104] Sandra Fredman and Judy Fudge, 'The Legal Construction of Personal Work Relations and Gender' (2013) 7 Jerusalem Review of Legal Studies 112.

[105] *R (Independent Workers Union of Great Britain)* (n 39).

[106] Adams (n 3) 341.

[107] Mariarosa Dalla Costa and Selma James, *The Power of Women and the Subversion of the Community: A Woman's Place* (Falling Wall Press 1972); Silvia Federici, *Wages against Housework* (Power of Women Collective 1975). See also Federici's more recent work on the 'social wage' in Silvia Federici, *Patriarchy of the Wage: Notes on Marx, Gender, and Feminism* (PM Press 2021).

[108] Selma James, *Our Time Is Now: Sex, Race, Class and Caring for People & Planet* (PM Press 2021).

Rather than expanding the scope of the employment contract, we propose reconceptualizing our understanding of work and the provision of labour rights to include not only those working under formal employment contracts but also those who work informally and irregularly. When considering working conditions under the spectrum of unfree labour, examples of decent work are considered to be at the least exploitative end. The recognition of work and the provision of labour rights can help to secure decent working conditions for those within and beyond our case studies as it provides a legal basis for challenge where standards fall short. Our normative intention is thus to move towards decent work for workers which, consistent with ILO standards delivers

- a fair income,
- security in the workplace,
- social protection for all,
- better prospects for personal development and social integration,
- freedom for people to express their concerns, organize and participate in the decisions that affect their lives, and
- equality of opportunity and treatment for all.[109]

In many ways, the ILO's decent work agenda also encapsulates the aims of Freedland and Kountouris, who push for the recognition of personality in work that seeks to maximize the dignity of workers and to optimize their capabilities in and through personal work relations.[110] Replacing the employment contract as the focus of enquiry, our proposal focuses attention on the workers themselves, recognizing the performance of work in and of itself, before addressing the nature of the work relationship and its attendant rights and obligations.

Within our analysis, the first question we ask is 'Is this work?' If the answer is in the affirmative, then the premise is that the individual should be afforded access to labour rights and protections. Our perspective thus moves away from the multiple categories currently used to describe work, which define individuals according to their roles, such as 'employee', 'worker', or 'independent contractor', and instead centres on the existence of work in reality. The second question concerns the relational dimension and with whom the responsibility lies for affording and enforcing such rights and obligations. The second part of

[109] ILO, 'What Is Decent Work—International Labour Organization' (26 September 2015) <https://www.ilo.org/resource/what-decent-work> accessed 28 January 2026.
[110] Freedland and Kountouris (n 86) 21.

our recognition process thus acknowledges that the imposition of rights and obligations rests on the relational nature of work and that such rights and obligations are designed to temper the relationships emanating from the work performed, the governance of the work itself, and the working conditions and environment. This insight builds upon the important contributions of Freedland and Kountouris, who call for the reconceptualization of labour law as 'personal work relations', which they define as

> a connection or set of connections, between a person—the worker—and another person or persons or an organization or organizations, arising from an engagement or arrangement or set of arrangements for the carrying out of work or the rendering of service or services by the workers personally, that is to say wholly or primarily by the worker himself or herself.[111]

i. Defining work

We define work as follows:

> The undertaking of tasks, activities or thought processes aimed at the production of goods and/or services which link to processes of market exchange; and/or socially reproductive work aimed at sustaining, caring for, or attending to the well-being of and reproduction of others,[112] which the state would assume responsibility for, had the worker not performed the duties. In both instances, individuals performing work include those who have no right to reside, or to work, in the country.

In essence, this definition extends our conceptualization of work worthy of labour rights and protections in three ways.

First, it widens the construct of 'productive work' by linking it to processes of market exchange rather than positioning market exchange as the primary aim, extending worker status to those in industries, such as prison labour, which ostensibly prioritize 'rehabilitation' over production. Indeed, links to the market in all of the case studies explored cannot be denied.

Second, in line with the Gangmasters (Licensing) Act 2004, the 'work' test we propose extends protection to those who work irregularly. In line with the ILO's decent work agenda, we contend that those engaging in work

[111] ibid 339.

[112] Kate Hardy, 'Uneven Divestment of the State: Social Reproduction and Sex Work in Neo-Developmentalist Argentina' (2016) 13 Globalizations 876.

(which we define broadly) should have rights that are owed to workers by virtue of the work performed rather than relying on a particular employment relation.

Third, we extend our understanding of work to include socially reproductive labour on which the state relies to function or for which the state would assume responsibility had the individual not performed the labour themselves. Of course, many forms of caregiving and social reproduction occur outside of this framework, and it is not our intention to account for all acts of care. For example, if parents are unable to provide care at a sufficient level for their children, then the state would have to ensure care providers for their children as per the obligations set out in the Children's Act 1989 concurrent with the rights and dignity of the child. Similarly, local authorities in the United Kingdom have a duty to provide care and support for disabled persons who can demonstrate a need for such care as per Part I of the Care Act 2014. These proposals are not wholly radical in the sense that this labour is already recognized via government payments to parents and carers via Child Benefit and increases to Universal Credit as well as via Carers' Allowance. However, these sums remain nominal, couched in the language of 'benefit', which fails to recognize that these forms of socially reproductive labour are forms of essential work, upon which the country and economy (and thus capital) relies, and for which workers should be afforded a decent wage.

As noted in Chapter 3, while some feminist literature posits 'commodification anxiety' as a block to providing monetary payments for traditional 'non-market' work, the payment of a wage does not have to result in the commodification of labour, which we understand as the extraction of additional value from the work of others beyond the use value created by the worker. The administration of the wage, how it is raised by the government, and the amount afforded to the worker in terms of working time would need to be carefully considered to ensure that the paid work remains uncommodified.[113] Additionally, we return to our previous arguments in Chapter 3, which suggested that sentimentizing these forms of work serves patriarchal agendas that exclude certain minorities from access to a decent wage and that, for many, socially reproductive labour is already commodified, undervalued, and outsourced to the market as a result of financial pressure that fails to recognize the importance of relations of care. Recognizing this labour as work denaturalizes social reproduction as an assumed female role and instead exposes the

[113] Joan Williams, *Unbending Gender: Why Family and Work Conflict and What to Do about It* (OUP 2001) 41.

'natural caregiving' narrative as a social construct that divides working-class solidarities, enabling capitalist domination.[114] Including socially reproductive labour within the construct of work does not push it into capitalist relations because it has never realistically existed outside of them.[115] The recognition of this labour is also not a call for its fulfilment, meaning that such a proposal must exist alongside adequate care payments where there is a desire for it to be outsourced.

Institutionally, the courts have some experience in ascertaining which forms of social reproduction would qualify under our definition of 'work', as demonstrated by the *Datafin* judgment,[116] which tasks the courts with assessing whether organizations are exercising public functions that are governmental in nature, subjecting them to liability for judicial review. The test asks whether the government would need to step in and perform the function itself, if the defendant were not already doing so.[117] The *Datafin* decision demonstrates capability and a willingness on the part of the courts to undertake such assessments, which could be underpinned by statute to provide further clarity.

ii. The work relation

The second element of the test concerns the relationships involved in the work process itself. Here, again, we take inspiration from Freedland and Kountouris and their construction of personal work relations, which impose obligations on additional parties to account for the varied legal relations arising within the world of work. They conceptualize these relations as a nexus, embodying a 'complex network constructed around the worker', which is split into two levels: the macro, which essentially 'zooms out' on the relations, occupying a taxonomical level, which maps all relations that are classified into categories; and the micro, which essentially 'zooms in' and accounts for the structural features of particular personal work relations.[118] Essentially, this opens up the concept of the work relation, making it more transparent and elucidating the complex and interconnected webs that shape our working lives. In the context of our case studies, a range of different relations are apparent.

While the majority of what Freedland and Kountouris would deem 'primary connections' are between workers and the employing entities, such as

[114] Katie Cruz, 'Materialism, Sex Work, and the Law: Doing Feminist Legal Theory Differently' (2025) <https://journals.kent.ac.uk/index.php/feministsatlaw/article/view/1445> accessed 28 January 2026.

[115] Federici (n 107).

[116] *R v Panel on Take-Overs and Mergers, ex p Datafin plc* [1987] QB 815.

[117] *R v Disciplinary Committee of the Jockey Club, ex p Aga Khan* [1993] 1 WLR 909.

[118] Freedland and Kountouris (n 86).

prisons, detention centres, and workfare businesses (ie those who derive benefits and surplus value from the labour performed), secondary connections are also apparent among, for example, workers and the state, which is responsible for framing the labour relation more broadly. From this perspective, the state is a key actor in upholding the decent work agenda and ensuring the provision of social protections that must accompany a fair income if we are to move towards systems of decent work. Understanding work as multi-relational broadens the distribution of risk and cost beyond the traditional bilateral relation between worker and employer.[119] Secondary connections might also involve co-workers, unions, or wage boards, for example, depending on the context in which they are considered.

b. Centring Subordination and Domination

Another way of extending labour rights and addressing issues of domination is to disregard the employment relationship entirely and to focus instead on power structures that result in economic subordination under capitalism, a proposal advanced by Von Broembsen in her recent call to extend labour rights to informal street vendors.[120] This approach is developed by Harry Arthurs[121] in his 'counterfactual' piece that asks us to imagine a world in which labour law was not invented, but instead, the 'law of economic subordination and resistance' had been developed to regulate all relationships in which persons experience economic subordination, including those between worker and employer, creditor and debtor, and individuals and the state. His thesis rests on the idea that those subjected to subordination should have the 'basic right to be protected from the arbitrary exercise of private economic power', which divides the subordinate class into legal categories such as employee or worker, instead imposing obligations upon the superordinate power. The rights that Arthurs sets out include voice and recognition of representatives, collective negotiation, concerted economic action, formal and informal dispute resolution, agreement, minimum standard terms, political action and affiliation, social safety net, and constitutional and human rights.

Arthurs argues that this is not necessarily radical since many of these protections already exist in law—for workers, tenants, mortgagors, and

[119] Fredman and Fudge (n 104).
[120] Von Broembsen (n 34).
[121] Harry Arthurs, 'Labour Law as the Law of Economic Subordination and Resistance: A Thought Experiment' (2013) 34 Comparative Labor Law and Policy Journal 585.

creditors—but what is perhaps innovative is their collectivization under a single legal principle: 'the law of economic subordination and resistance'. Drawing similarities between Roosevelt's National Industrial Recovery Act (NIRA), enacted in America in 1933 and Canada's Combines Investigation Act of 1889, Arthurs charts the ways in which these statutes sought to protect subordinate classes, aligning labour law principles with other legal initiatives. In many ways, Arthurs call is for the recognition of inequality of bargaining power, central to labour law, to be extended beyond the employment relationship to other areas of law in which subordination takes place. In one sense, the risk of implementing such a doctrine is that we reinforce the current political economy rather than thinking outside of it. However, recommendations of this nature address inequalities beyond conditions of work towards a broader structural rationale. While law creates and upholds structures of injustice, the 'law of economic subordination and resistance' helps identify and rebalance the various ways in which these structures disempower people in work, housing, social security, and education.

We note that the position presented here is not immune to critique. Guy Davidov, for example, emphasizes that the expansion of rights can lead to their dilution by losing the original rational for awarding them in the first place.[122] Davidov explains that the employee/worker status is not guaranteed to individuals in the abstract but rather as a response to the need for 'protection in their relationship *vis-à-vis a specific employer* and at least to some extent the employer is seen as responsible for such protection'.[123] While he recognizes the need to rethink the linkage between some rights (eg to equality and protection from discrimination or to health and safety) to employment status and also to expand the scope of the definition to account for changes in labour force and membership, he argues that the 'old distinction can still play a useful role'.[124]

c. Universal Basic Income and Universal Basic Services

One of the solutions to ameliorate the economic pressures coercing individuals into precarious, exploitative, and ultimately 'unfree' labour, is to provide a universal basic income (UBI), which has the potential to redress the power

[122] Guy Davidov 'The Reports of My Death Are Greatly Exaggerated: "Employee" as a Viable (Though Overly Used) Legal Concept' in Guy Davidov and Brian Langille (eds), *Boundaries and Frontiers of Labour Law: Goals and Means in the Regulation of Work* (Hart Publishing 2006) 133.
[123] ibid 134.
[124] ibid 155.

imbalance under which workers must 'work or starve'. As inherently non-conditional forms of benefit and provision, UBI and, to an extent, universal basic services (UBS), have been suggested as natural responses to address the strict conditionality associated with workfare programmes.[125] Clearly, this is true to the extent that UBI and UBS relieve immediate economic pressure (contingent on the generosity of the provision) from welfare recipients by blunting the force of the 'stick' and sanctions levied by the welfare-to-work activation regime in general and workfare schemes in particular. A similar logic would apply with respect to internships. As we saw, an important divide exists between paid and unpaid internships in two respects. First, those who agree to take part in low-quality, unpaid internship schemes gain very little from them when compared to those who are enrolled in well-supervised, paid internships. Here, a UBI and UBS are likely to have little effect. However, that effect may be significant with respect to a second type of divide: that which exists between those who are able to afford to take part in prestigious, unpaid internships that are viewed as pathways to the profession (eg the BBC, Parliament, and some of the regulated professions) and those who cannot afford to do so. Here, a generous UBI and UBS scheme may mitigate that disparity.

Further afield, implementation of a basic income could confront the structural dispossession that often leads individuals into the sphere of the prison or the immigration detention estate. As noted in Chapter 2, the majority of those in prison come from poor socio-economic backgrounds and deprivation which, arguably, can lead to criminality and the sphere of the detention estate. The need to engage in 'illegal' work would also often be relieved if subsistence were provided for by the state via a basic income, allowing irregular migrants to avoid the criminality that arises through these forms of work.

Calls for a UBI can be traced back to the early years of the French Revolution.[126] Interestingly, it gained widespread political support from neoliberals such as Hayek and Friedman, who considered it an opportunity to roll back the paternalistic welfare state,[127] as well as radical thinkers such as Tom Paine,[128] who justified aUBI in the context of natural rights, in addition to its

[125] Amir Paz-Fuchs, 'Workfare's Persistent Philosophical and Legal Issues: Forced Labour, Reciprocity and a Basic Income Guarantee' in Anja Eleveld, Thomas Kampen, and Josien Arts (eds), *Welfare to Work in Contemporary European Welfare States: Legal, Sociological and Philosophical Perspectives on Justice and Domination* (Briston UP 2020) 27.

[126] JE King and John Marangos, 'Two Arguments for Basic Income: Thomas Paine (1737–1809) and Thomas Spence (1750–1814)' (2006) 14 History of Economic Ideas 55.

[127] Jon Cruddas, 'From the End of Work to the Dignity of Labour' (*Futures of Work*, 2 December 2020) <https://futuresofwork.co.uk/2020/12/02/from-the-end-of-work-to-the-dignity-of-labour> accessed 23 November 2025.

[128] Thomas Paine, 'The Rights of Man' in M Foot and I Kramnick (eds), *Thomas Paine Reader* (Penguin 1987) 201–03.

economic, political, and social benefits.[129] It is also a popular recommendation with socialists, who consider a UBI 'as a means of guaranteeing individual freedom in the absence of private property in the means of production'.[130] UBI is also prevalent within the Futures of Work literature as a potential safety net against the rise in automation,[131] and in feminist literature, where it is seen as a means to provide a 'modest but decent standard of life',[132] decoupled from labour market participation,[133] and as a contemporary demand configuring feminist calls for 'wages for housework'.[134]

At its heart, a UBI accommodates an individual adult's subsistence needs through the provision of a basic allowance, granting workers a potential 'exit choice'[135] or the opportunity to refuse undesirable work. Its universal nature means that it would be available to all individuals, regardless of immigration status (debated by some),[136] familial set up, employment status, or income, and proponents call for it to be set at a rate high enough to provide individuals with a genuine choice over whether to engage with work.[137] Like a wage, it would be paid regularly over an individual's lifetime, separating the need for income from work, providing what Weeks terms 'a social wage',[138] countering the idea that work is the only legitimate source of an adequate standard of living. The idea is not that this would provide a wage supplement but rather a wage alternative. The benefit of a universal income is the recognition that people contribute to society in a variety of different ways and that such contributions are not always measurable in monetary terms.[139] In offering a basic income for all, these contributions would be reciprocated. It could also provide individuals

[129] Amir Paz-Fuchs, 'Strict Conditionality, Structural Injustice and Welfare Rights' in Helen Carr and others (eds), *Research Handbook on Social Welfare Law* (Edward Elgar 2024) 263, 274–75.

[130] King and Marangos (n 126) 56.

[131] Lorena Lombardozzi and Harry Pitts, 'Abstract and Concrete Universals: Basic Services, Basic Infrastructure, Basic Income' (*Futures of Work*, 18 December 2018) <https://futuresofwork.co.uk/2018/12/18/abstract-and-concrete-universals-basic-services-basic-infrastructure-basic-income> accessed 28 January 2026.

[132] Carole Pateman, 'Democratizing Citizenship: Some Advantages of a Basic Income' (2004) 32 Politics & Society 89, 92.

[133] Carole Pateman, 'Another Way Forward: Welfare, Social Reproduction, and a Basic Income' in Laurence M Mead and Christopher Beem (eds), *Welfare Reform and Political Theory* (Russell Sage Foundation 2005); Almaz Zelleke, 'Feminist Political Theory and the Argument for an Unconditional Basic Income' (2011) 39 Policy & Politics 27; Katie Cruz, 'Unmanageable Work, (Un)Liveable Lives: The UK Sex Industry, Labour Rights and the Welfare State' (2013) 22 Social & Legal Studies 465.

[134] Weeks (n 80).

[135] Nick Srnicek and Alex Williams, *Inventing the Future: Postcapitalism and a World without Work* (rev and updated edn, Verso 2016).

[136] Guy Standing, *Basic Income: A Guide for the Open-Minded* (Yale UP 2017).

[137] Philippe Van Parijs, Joshua Cohen, and Joel Rogers, *What's Wrong with a Free Lunch? (Beacon Press 2001).*

[138] Weeks (n 80) 139.

[139] Ailsa McKay and Jo Vanevery, 'Gender, Family, and Income Maintenance: A Feminist Case for Citizens Basic Income' (2000) 7 Social Politics: International Studies in Gender, State & Society 266.

with the freedom 'of time and space for invention . . . a postwork alternative in which the structures, relations, values, experiences, and the meaning of work might be substantially refigured'.[140] The feasibility of such an income is not outlandish and has, indeed, already been piloted in Wales by the Welsh Government and in England by the thinktank Autonomy.[141]

Of course, implementing a UBI high enough to allow for work refusals would require the significant redistribution of wealth, most likely raised through increases to taxes, which would help to reduce levels of inequality.[142] Though critics of a UBI argue that it could disrupt the division of labour and leave potential gaps in industries and jobs that are socially necessary and useful (such as engineering or teaching),[143] implementation of a UBI would reduce the coercive nature under which individuals enter the wage–work bargain.

One of the most relevant critiques of a UBI is that as an individualized payment, it contains no collective dimensions to strengthen the infrastructures and institutions that are key to civil society and its relationship with the state. In addition, through the provision of income in monetary form, the links to capital remain, potentially increasing demand for goods and services, increasing inflation as producers and retailers respond by raising prices. One way to address this critique is to embrace UBS, an agenda that proposes decommodifying particular necessities by providing universal access. Developed by the Institute for Global Prosperity in 2017,[144] basic services relate to the 'most fundamental building blocks for life required by every citizen in the 21st century', among which they note health, education, food, shelter, democracy and legal services, transport and information. Of course, two of these services, health care and education, are already provided by the state. However, the universality and adequacy of these services may be questioned, as seen in the cases of services for those with additional needs, such as disability and/or old age, where individuals are required to spend a large portion of their income to address these needs. The foundations of the UBS are built on the satisfaction

[140] Weeks (n 80) 145 and 146.

[141] Cleo Goodman and others, 'Piloting a Basic Income in Wales: Principles, Precedents and Feasibility' (*Autonomy*, June 2021) <https://autonomy.work/wp-content/uploads/2021/06/WALES-UBI_Report-v6.pdf> accessed 9 July 2025; Dahaba Ali Hussen, 'Universal Basic Income of £1,600 a Month to Be Trialled in Two Places in England' *The Guardian* (London, 4 June 2023) <www.theguardian.com/society/2023/jun/04/universal-basic-income-of-1600-pounds-a-month-to-be-trialled-in-england> accessed 23 November 2025.

[142] Anton Jäger and Daniel Zamora, 'Labour's Love's Not Lost: UBI and the Coming Division of Labour' (*Futures of Work*, 16 October 2018) <https://futuresofwork.co.uk/2018/10/16/labours-loves-not-lost-ubi-and-the-coming-division-of-labour> accessed 23 November 2025.

[143] ibid.

[144] Institute for Global Prosperity, 'Social Prosperity for the Future: A Proposal for Universal Basic Services' (University College London 2017).

of basic needs, which are considered necessary for an individual to reach their full capability for participation in social life.

In similarity to the literature on a UBI, theorists propose that UBS would be funded through taxation and provide access to a 'social wage', which covers the cost of basic services that would otherwise be paid out of a market wage.[145] However, UBS are widely considered by its proponents to be less costly than a UBI as the provision of basic services is argued to be 'far more effective at driving down the cost of living than spending the same money on existing services, or on redistribution'.[146] As noted by Gough, a UBI remains in line with market ideology as 'money is fungible', allowing recipients to spend their income on whatever they please, whereas public services deliver specific provisions.[147] UBS thus focuses on the material conditions needed to 'thrive' and not just 'survive',[148] as opposed to giving everyone an equal amount of money, encouraging 'the construction of a new civil society of collective assets through which these opportunities can be realised' and strengthening social institutions and public infrastructure.[149] However, the Institute for Global Prosperity notes that UBS and a UBI should be seen as complimentary, proposing that a small amount of basic income be given in addition to UBS on grounds that 'there are both personal and specific needs that will require some form of monetary distribution to preserve freedom and agency'.[150] Given that the national minimum wage currently fails to provide many individuals with basic access to essentials such as food, 'a platform of basic services makes real the promise that a basic wage pretends to deliver'.[151]

It is not the intention of this book to set out detailed arguments or policy proposals for either a UBI or UBS, as this has been done in great detail elsewhere,[152] but rather to highlight the variety of ways in which our relationship

[145] Ian Gough, 'Universal Basic Services: A Theoretical and Moral Framework' (2019) 90 Political Quarterly 534.

[146] Institute for Global Prosperity (n 144).

[147] Gough (n 145) 534.

[148] Cathy Gregory, 'Faculty of Public Health Briefing: Universal Basic Services' (Faculty of Public Health, no date) <www.fph.org.uk/media/2ambxe1g/fph-briefing-universal-basic-services.pdf> accessed 23 November 2025.

[149] Lombardozzi and Pitts (n 131).

[150] Institute for Global Prosperity (n 144) 13.

[151] ibid 10.

[152] McKay and Vanevery (n 139); Luke Martinelli, 'The Fiscal and Distributional Implications of Alternative Universal Basic Income Schemes in the UK' (Institute for Policy Research, March 2017) <www.bath.ac.uk/publications/the-fiscal-and-distributional-implications-of-alternative-universal-basic-income-schemes-in-the-uk/attachments/ipr-fiscal-distributional-implications-alternative-universal-basic-income-schemes-uk.pdf> accessed 23 November 2025; Lorena Lombardozzi, 'Gender Inequality, Social Reproduction and the Universal Basic Income' (2020) 91 Political Quarterly 317; Institute for Global Prosperity (n 144).

with capital and the labour market could be altered so that the unfreedoms experienced by the majority of people, but especially those who fall outside the realms of 'decent work', might be reduced or even ameliorated. Both a UBI and UBS could help to redress the superior bargaining power enjoyed by employers who are able to 'hold out and live off their capital until the market price of labour is to their liking'[153] by enabling individuals to meet their basic needs outside of market participation and the wage–work bargain. Both a UBI and UBS thus address the socially reproductive dimension of unfreedom that can coerce individuals into exploitative work as well as those dimensions relating to social and economic mobility in the form of a 'social wage'. Nevertheless, both the UBI and UBS are forms of top-down support, which rely on the state as an instantiation of capitalist social relations, reliant on the extraction of taxes gained through the production of income and/or wealth to uphold both systems.[154] Ground-up initiatives must therefore take place alongside the implementation of any form of UBI or UBS, based on collective struggle that could later inform forms of collective action and organization.

d. Labour Organization and Mobilization

Informal workers can make demands on politicians, employers, and the institutions facilitating their work through legal, political, social, and economic strategies to improve their working, living, and material conditions. These strategies can be articulated around claims either for recognition as humans and citizens (seeking access to human rights and entitlements) or status as workers (seeking access to specific labour rights and protections).[155] Formal and informal representative and community-led organizations mobilize in these spaces, often cutting across all four forms of legal, political, social, and economic organizing and action. Mobilization must therefore be framed around what workers themselves want as this shapes the modality of organization and support that arises. While recognizing the importance of legal mobilization and strategic litigation[156] (as well as its institutional

[153] Collins (n 41) 449.

[154] Lombardozzi and Pitts (n 131).

[155] Katie Cruz and Tess Herrmann, 'The Sex Worker Rights Movement and Trade Unionism in Europe: Case Studies from Sweden, Germany and the United Kingdom' Working Paper No 2024.13 (European Trade Union Institute 2024).

[156] Manoj Dias-Abey and Anthony Forsyth, 'Strategic Litigation and Political Lobbying: Antidotes to Declining Worker Power?' in Jeffrey Vogt, Tonia Novitz, and Judy Fudge (eds), *The Right to Strike Reimagined* (Hart Publishing/Bloomsbury Press 2026); Manoj Dias-Abey, 'Mobilizing for Recognition: Indie Unions, Migrant Workers, and Strategic Equality Act Litigation' (2022) 38

limitations),[157] we do not attend to it here as many of the legal cases challenging work categorization have been outlined throughout this book and legal and policy recommendations were noted earlier in this chapter. Instead, we focus on the other three areas of strategic mobilization and organisation: the economic, political, and social.

In the context of our case studies, though all four groups seek access to recognition and fair pay for the work performed, the remaining needs and wants of the groups differ vastly, shaped by the unique circumstances of the work environments and the social, economic, and cultural compositions of the workforce. For example, in the context of internships, research suggests that interns want secure and regulated work experience that is paid at a fair rate.[158] With regard to workfare, abolition of the schemes themselves was one of the primary demands emanating from those enrolled on the schemes. However, in the context of carceral work and detainee activism, their requests are not confined to just working conditions and often encompass broader claims for civil, political, and social rights. 'It is [thus] inevitable, as prisoners live, work and are confined collectively that they raise concerns beyond working conditions, and their organization is shaped in particular ways by the institutional context of imprisonment'.[159]

In realizing the wants and needs of workers, it is necessary to consider the issue of solidarity. In order to understand how active cultures of solidarity and class relations can be fostered, we must look at the particular 'life-world' of the worker(s), influenced by the political, economic, and social dynamics that shape the working environment and their lived experiences.[160] Both solidarity and class are considered to be forms of social relation, embodied in real people and real context. Whereas we understand solidarity as the 'desire for transformation out of the experience of discomfort',[161] Thompson writes that 'the class experience is largely determined by the productive relations into which men are born—or enter involuntarily. Class consciousness is the way in

International Journal of Comparative Labour Law and Industrial Relations 137; Jack Meakin, 'Labour Movements and the Effectiveness of Legal Strategy: Three Tenets' (2022) 38 International Journal of Comparative Labour Law and Industrial Relations 187.

[157] Albena Azmanova, 'The Paradox of Emancipation: Populism, Democracy and the Soul of the Left' (2019) 45 Philosophy & Social Criticism 1186; Brabazon (n 5); Maja Breznik, 'Less or More Labour Law for Social Change?' (2024) 53 Industrial Law Journal 613.

[158] ETUC (n 100).

[159] Behan and Maycock (n 35); Erving Goffman, *Asylums: Essays on the Social Situation of Mental Patients and Other Inmates* (Anchor Books 1961).

[160] Behan and Maycock (n 35) 12–13.

[161] Clare Hemmings, 'Affective Solidarity: Feminist Reflexivity and Political Transformation' (2012) 13 Feminist Theory 147, 158.

which these experiences are handled in cultural terms: embodied in traditions, value systems, ideas, and institutional forms.'[162] Yet, 'class consciousness can also be generated and changed by social action'[163] wherein workers' struggle against capitalism forges solidarity, resulting in the uniting of the masses and the formation of a class in and for itself. Many of those working within our case studies and informal sectors do so in unique, siloed, precarious, and/or penal circumstances that shape the cultures of solidarity that arise and, in some instances, limit mobilization. Class constitution and solidarity thus needs to be considered as active and ever-changing processes, which remain in motion.

Below, we explore some of the ways in which labour organization and mobilization could take place across our case studies and broader forms of informal work, drawing from the literature on alternative and independent labour movements as well as forms of community activism that have been successful in creating class consciousness and solidarity, both internationally and domestically. Though we organize this across three realms of activity—the economic, political, and social—in practice, those pursuing justice for workers' rights often strategize and organize across all three spheres.

i. Economic strategies

Economic strategies include those which may be used by the trade union movement when bargaining with employers, collectively or individually, to improve working terms and conditions.[164] In some instances, this might involve the exercise of structural power, so workers are able to disrupt the broader economic system by withdrawing their labour power or delaying the production process that is utilized as leverage in collective bargaining.[165]

Economic strategies of this nature could be effective in relation to prison labour and/or work within immigration detention centres, given that, arguably, detention sites depend upon the continuation of workers' labour to facilitate their functioning. Indeed, within the context of our case studies, the carceral sphere has a rich history of economic organization and activism, while also highlighting the vulnerabilities of informal workers who participate in action of this nature. For example, strike action took place throughout UK prisons in 1972 facilitated by 'Preservation of the Rights of Prisoners' (PROP), a self-proclaimed prison union led by prisoners and ex-prisoners with '500 associate

[162] EP Thompson 'The Making of the English Working Class' (Penguin Books 1963), 9.
[163] Gordon Marshall, 'Some Remarks on the Study of Working-Class Consciousness' (1983) 12 Politics & Society 263, 288.
[164] Cruz and Herrmann (n 155).
[165] Dias-Abey and Forsyth (n 156).

members and the power to start and stop prison strikes at command'.[166] On 4 August 1972, PROP estimated that 10,000 prisoners (approximately 25 per cent of the prison population across thirty-three separate sites) went on strike, causing the prisons to 'grind to a halt', given they 'depend for their daily reproduction on the labour of the people they incarcerate'.[167] The aims of the action were largely grounded in the discourse of human rights, demanding the right to trade union membership alongside broader civil and political rights, such as the right to vote and free communications with the press and public, as well as socio-economic rights, such as access to full state benefits for prisoners post-release and access to courses on housing, education, marriage, and childcare to assist in reintegration.[168] Despite representing the most significant and widespread prison strike in UK history,[169] PROP suffered retaliation and violent repression from the Prison Officers Association[170] which, paired with the Home Office's refusal to recognize PROP as a representative body for prisoners, led to its eventual demise. PROP's exclusion from the legal framework, however, facilitated the formation of a more revolutionary form of class consciousness that stood in opposition to both capital and the state as the union was not pressurized to pursue action through restrictive legal frameworks.

A more contemporary example of grassroots organizing for those engaged in carceral labour is the Incarcerated Workers Organizing Committee (IWOC), a prisoner-led division of the Industrial Workers of the World which, although global, has a British arm that launched in 2016. Their purpose is to dismantle some of the structural unfreedoms outlined in this book as well as to emancipate detainees from what they term 'the prison industrial slave complex'.[171] Their objectives cut across the economic, political, and social realms, aiming to build 'class solidarity amongst members of the working class by connecting the struggle of people in prison, jails, and immigrant and juvenile detention centres to workers struggles locally and worldwide'.[172] Detainees engage with their own local prison branches and remain in direct communication with members on the outside, who provide 'organizing training, support and

[166] London IWOC, 'PROP '72: The History of a UK Prisoners' Union' (*libcom.org*, 29 September 2019) <https://libcom.org/article/prop-72-history-uk-prisoners-union> accessed 11 June 2025.
[167] ibid.
[168] Cormac Behan and Abigail Stark, *Prisons and Imprisonment* (Palgrave Macmillan 2023); Behan and Maycock (n 35).
[169] Mike Fitzgerald, *Prisoners in Revolt* (Penguin 1977).
[170] London IWOC (n 166).
[171] Jailhouse Lawyers Speak, 'SHUT 'EM DOWN Abolition Demonstrations' (*Jail House Lawyers Speak*, 2024) <https://jailhouselawyersspeak1.wordpress.com/2024/04/13/shut-em-down-abolition-demonstrations> accessed 24 June 2025.
[172] IWOC, 'About' (28 September 2016) <https://iwoc.iww.org.uk/about-us/> accessed 5 June 2025.

guidance in union building, solidarity, and collaborative actions'.[173] Although the British group is yet to organize any form of national action, the US branches have coordinated strikes across prisons and states, including a series of work stoppages and hunger strikes in 2018, which demonstrates that coordinated action is feasible for those who are incarcerated in the United Kingdom and, indeed, is likely to pose a sufficient threat to capital, given that it can be organized outside of the formal administrative processes attached to the TULRCA.

Nevertheless, there remain difficulties in coordinating and undertaking disruptions to work within carceral, and more widely informal, working environments. As noted, those without formal worker or employee status are unable to apply under the TULRCA for their bargaining units to be recognized by employers, either voluntarily or via statute,[174] meaning that access to formal trade union membership and bargaining is limited, as is its associate protections, including trade union immunities from certain economic torts and protection for workers from detriment and dismissal. Economic strategies involving the withdrawal of labour power can thus be problematic as they may result in the application of penalties or sanctions shaped by the context of the work arrangements themselves. For example, deprivations exist within our case studies beyond the withholding of the wage,[175] including benefit sanctions, the withdrawal of work opportunities, systematic isolation, and transfer across work or detention sites, all of which are designed to atomize and neutralize collective association and power. Indeed, segregation and isolation are a common response to complaints and protests within immigration detention centres[176] which, over the past two decades, have been subject to multiple uprisings and 'riots' as a result of poor conditions within detention, revealing the power that detention providers possess over those in their care. While detainees are entitled to rights under Article 11 of the ECHR (assembly and association), if prison or detention centre staff think that actions taken undermine 'good order and discipline' of the detention site, these rights can be limited.[177]

[173] IWOC, 'About Us | Incarcerated Workers Organising Committee' (no date) <https://iwoc.iww.org.uk/about-us> accessed 23 November 2025.

[174] Trade Union and Labour Relations (Consolidation) Act 1992, pt 1, sch A1; *R (Independent Workers Union of Great Britain)* (n 39).

[175] Erin Hatton, *Coerced: Work under Threat of Punishment* (University of California Press 2020).

[176] Corporate Watch, *The UK Border Regime: A Critical Guide* (2018); Corporate Watch, 'UK Border Regime: A Brief History of Resistance to Immigration Detention' (11 October 2018) <https://corporatewatch.org/the-uk-border-regime-a-brief-history-of-resistance-to-immigration-detention> accessed 13 June 2025.

[177] Aimee Emby, 'Human Rights Information Booklet for Prisoners' (Prison Reform Trust 2014) <https://prisonreformtrust.org.uk/wp-content/uploads/2021/11/human-rights-bookletdigital.pdf> accessed 25 June 2025.

However, labour disruption is not the only means of pressurizing to improve workers' rights, as evidenced by the International Union of Sex Workers (IUSW), established in 2002 as a branch of the General, Municipal, Boilermakers and Allied Trades Union (GMB), who successfully engaged and negotiated with employers to establish union recognition in two strip clubs and one brothel. Although 'this did not lead to traditional collective bargaining, IUSW was able to install "minimum industry labour standards" in those venues'.[178] In 2002, Prison Service Order (PSO) 4480 established 'prisoner representative associations' to create communication and feedback channels between prisoners and prison management, yet the PSO is clear that 'the nature of imprisonment cannot allow for representative structures wider than establishment level. Associations therefore have no standing at either national or area level' and the Prison Service is 'under no obligation to enter into dialogue with any association'.[179] The lack of independence and institutional nature thus render these forms of association limited.

A more hopeful development is that of the Prison Council and consultation model established by User Voice, an independent national charity led by ex-offenders, which operates in over forty prisons throughout the country, facilitating over twenty democratically elected 'Prison Councils', which consult with prisoners to develop proposals for change and communication with prison governors, crossing both the political and economic spheres.[180] The charity's focus is advocacy and solution-focused problem-solving, and research suggests that their work has been 'good for everyone', allowing 'constructive dialogue' and 'a sense of collective responsibility' to develop among the prison population.[181] However, it should be noted that the success of the schemes is largely dependent upon buy-in from the prison's specific governor and staff,[182] and while the agenda is broad, their focus on labour-related rights is minimal. Nevertheless, the group works to influence policy in key areas, providing a prospective model for consultation, policy influencing, and mediation. The risk here, however, is the loss of independence that arises through organic, prison worker-led movements where third- sector organizations take their place.[183]

178 Cruz and Herrmann (n 155) 20.

179 PSO 4480 2002, paras 3 and 9.

180 User Voice, 'Transforming Justice Services through Lived Experience: Our Work in Prisons' (2025) <www.uservoice.org/wp-content/uploads/2025/05/Prison-Council-Consultations_2025.pdf> accessed 6 June 2025.

181 Bethany Schmidt, 'User Voice and the Prison Council Model: A Summary of Key Findings from an Ethnographic Exploration of Participatory Governance in Three English Prisons' (2013) (209) Prison Service Journal 12, 12–13.

182 ibid, 17.

183 Behan and Maycock (n 35).

A further significant example highlighting the successful organization of informal workers outside the carceral sphere is the US 'Coalition of Immokalee Workers' (CIW), which represents the interests of tomato farm workers in Florida, labelled among the fifteen 'most important social impact success stories of the past century'.[184] As noted by Dias-Abey, this group is non-traditional, in the sense that it does not bargain with employers on behalf of its members, but rather has established its own private regulatory system known as the 'fair food programme', which governs labour conditions on tomato farms in Florida, including a code of conduct that regulates wages, sexual harassment, and occupational health and safety, which was drafted with input from the workers themselves.[185]

Economic pressure can also be applied to businesses through boycotting, picketing, and protest, which relies on associational power in order to leverage structural advantage,[186] including, in some instances, support from those outside the employment relationship. As noted earlier in the chapter, organizations such as Boycott Workfare boycotted and protested against the companies utilizing the workfare scheme at the height of its implementation, including Holland and Barrett, which later withdrew from the scheme, declaring 'it was no longer prepared to face further bad press and in-store protests and would now pay all its workforce'.[187] These concerns were shared among other providers such as Tesco, Waterstones, and TK Maxx, which threatened to withdraw from the scheme out of fear of retaliation, forcing the then employment minister, Chris Grayling, to drop the imposition of benefit sanctions against young people on the programme where they withdrew from work placements after one week.[188]

Economic actions can thus be operationalized by campaign groups and collectives that do not fit (or remain excluded from) formal trade union recognition. Though this results in the loss of certain protections concerning a lawful 'trade dispute', it also means that such groups are not subject to the complex procedural requirements imposed on formal unions in relation to calling

[184] Susan Wolf Ditkoff and Abe Grindle, 'Audacious Philanthropy: Lessons from 15 World-Changing Initiatives' [September–October 2017] Harvard Business Review <https://hbr.org/2017/09/audacious-philanthropy> accessed 23 November 2025.

[185] Manoj Dias-Abey, 'A Socio-Legal History of the Coalition of Immokalee Workers' in A Blackham, M Kullman, and A Zbysewska (eds), *Theorising Labour Law in a Changing World: Towards Inclusive Labour Law* (Hart Publishing 2019).

[186] ibid; Jane Holgate, *Arise: Power, Strategy and Union Resurgence* (Pluto Press 2021).

[187] Malik (n 94).

[188] Nicholas Watt, Patrick Wintour, and Shiv Malik, 'Government U-Turn on Work Scheme' *The Guardian* (London, 29 February 2012) <www.theguardian.com/politics/2012/feb/29/government-work-experience-scheme-uturn> accessed 11 June 2025.

strike action and restrictions on secondary action and picketing.[189] Indeed, Adams notes that traditional trade unions' operation within state-sanctioned frameworks for dissent takes for granted and arguably legitimizes 'capital's monopoly on the means of production, or even, the existence and generalisation of wage-labour', which also leads to the exclusion of those labouring outside of the traditional status framework from protection.[190] While the further integration and representation of informal workers by traditional trade unions would be a welcome development, the examples above demonstrate that collective bargaining and economic disruption may take place outside of traditional collective bargaining formats. Importantly, these alternative forms of organization provide space for a more radical and revolutionary class consciousness and forms of action.

ii. Political strategies

In instances where economic strategies are difficult to implement and structural power is not easy to harness, organizations may choose, 'rather than seeking to enter into collective negotiation with employers . . . to draw on institutional power to advance their objectives'.[191] By 'institutions', we refer here to the 'informal and formal rules that pattern human action by enabling and constraining social action', including the political and legal framework that enables capitalism to function.[192] Accordingly, political strategies are directed at 'political and legal institutions, decision-makers, and the wider public', seeking to 'influence policy and public narrative by lobbying, campaigning and education';[193] a significant weapon in the artillery of groups seeking better working, living, and material conditions for workers.

In the United States, the term 'alt-labour' has been increasingly deployed, covering organizations such as campaign groups, advice centres, worker centres,[194] and informal worker collectives as well as a variety of other collectives and actions.[195] Unable to participate in traditional forms of collective bargaining, 'alt-labour' organizations often engage in a range of actions to effectuate change, including the lobbying of political parties and lawmakers,

[189] Department for Trade and Business, 'Code of Practice on Picketing' (2024) para 18.
[190] Adams (n 3) 563.
[191] Dias-Abey and Forsyth (n 156).
[192] ibid.
[193] Cruz and Herrmann (n 155) 16.
[194] Janice Fine, *Worker Centers: Organizing Communities at the Edge of the Dream* (ILR Press/Cornell UP 2006).
[195] Dias-Abey and Forsyth (n 156).

media outreach, and establishing communal solidarities for the purposes of legal mobilization—an ecosystem that is mirrored within the United Kingdom in terms of non-traditional organizations. In the context of our case studies, the campaigning that arises tends not to fall within the specific category of 'alt-labour'—yet workers' rights remain part of their wider agenda. For example, with respect to immigration detention in the United Kingdom, a number of campaign groups, research groups, and charitable organizations engage with detainees and irregular migrants generally to lobby and advocate for political change. Though none of these are created with the specific intention to represent workers' rights, the right to access legal work and the process of labour within immigration detention have been raised as areas of concern, generating media coverage, public interest, and mounting political pressure for change. In 2014, for example, the research group Corporate Watch released a report on 'the true scale of captive labour' in the United Kingdom,[196] alongside a film documentary on the same topic,[197] which drew media attention to the plight of labouring detainees,[198] leading to greater analysis within academia[199] and, eventually, unsuccessful legal challenge.[200] The 'Lift the Ban' coalition of more than 300 charities, trade unions, businesses, think tanks, and faith groups is another organization lobbying to reduce some of the structural unfreedoms placed upon immigration detainees: namely, to 'lift the ban' on asylum seekers working in the United Kingdom. Due to sustained and ongoing pressure, in 2021 the House of Lords added amendments to the Nationality and Borders Bill, stipulating that permission to work should be granted to asylum seekers after six months of launching their initial asylum claim (including adult dependants) and that work terms be no less favourable than those granted to refugees, who enjoy working rights on a par with national citizens—removing the requirement that jobs be limited to those on the immigration salary list. Sadly, the amendments failed to gain support in the House of Commons.

[196] Corporate Watch, 'True Scale of Captive Migrant Labour Revealed' (22 August 2014) <https://corporatewatch.org/true-scale-of-captive-migrant-labour-revealed> accessed 13 June 2025.

[197] *Working Illegally* (directed by Standoff Films 2015) <www.standoffilms.com/?fbclid = IwY2xjawK47uNleHRuA2FlbQIxMABicmlkETFMOTB0YTI3TGsyenRZMzdMAR5D2hxa5xZHaCvEPLPwBmczvViG8lY7pI9IFZDRbVIms8qmvrntrwWKlw3foQ_aem_8ECm9TIwC52cdbOZZeBXKw> accessed 13 June 2025.

[198] Kevin Rawlinson, 'Private Firms "Are Using Detained Immigrants as Cheap Labour"' *The Guardian* (London, 22 August 2014) <www.theguardian.com/uk-news/2014/aug/22/immigrants-cheap-labour-detention-centres-g4s-serco> accessed 24 June 2025; Diane Taylor, 'Home Office Backed "Slave Labour" Pay for Immigration Detainees' *The Guardian* (London, 4 September 2018) <www.theguardian.com/uk-news/2018/sep/04/home-office-pay-immigration-detainees-menial-jobs-legal-action> accessed 24 June 2025.

[199] Bales and Mayblin (n 10); Bales (n 10); Bales (n 76).

[200] *Badmus* (n 78).

Nevertheless, these challenges show the potential of community solidarity and pressure in advocating for legal change.

More success was achieved in challenges to workfare by the Boycott Workfare campaign group which, as highlighted earlier in the chapter, drew on institutional power to help bring an end to workfare, timetabling motions in Parliament to acknowledge 'the role of the Government and companies in forcing people to undertake unpaid or low paid work by threatening to disqualify them from benefits' and calling on the government 'to concentrate on providing real jobs and paying a living wage rather than forcing people into no wage or low wage exploitation.'[201] Political pressure and lobbying from the European Trade Union Confederation (ETUC) has also encouraged the EU to take action to 'improve trainee packages' including policies on equal pay and time for interns.[202] Though there is ongoing dialogue and critique as to the extent to which these policies cover the scope of interests expressed in social consultations held by the ETUC, the ETUC's ongoing involvement and activism demonstrate the importance of labour organizations and campaign groups in providing a platform to strengthen the worker voice that shape policies and political agendas.

iii. Social strategies

Social strategies are intended to develop and strengthen community and individual agency, including worker education and leadership development; advice, representation, and service provision to both workers and ethical employers outside of state agencies; mutual aid; the creation of peer networks; and collaborations.[203] Such strategies are considered central to the sex workers' rights movement[204] and are also common in prison work activism, as highlighted earlier.

Claimants' unions representing those who claim social security also arose in the context of workfare 'in response to the disinterest of trade unions in the unemployed.'[205] 'Just as a trade union directly negotiates with their employers for what they feel they deserve, so the claimants' union tried to do with Social Security offices.'[206] Claimant union initiatives involve representing

[201] Boycott Workfare, 'EDM (Early Day Motion)370' (10 July 2012) <https://edm.parliament.uk/early-day-motion/44511> accessed 28 January 2026.

[202] 'Council Recommendation on a *Reinforced Quality Framework for Traineeships*' (n 99).

[203] Cruz and Herrmann (n 155).

[204] ibid 19.

[205] Weghmann (n 90) 445.

[206] Toru Yamamori, 'A Feminist Way to Unconditional Basic Income: Claimants Unions and Women's Liberation Movements in 1970s Britain' (2014) 9 Basic Income Studies 1, 3.

unemployed individuals at social security settings such as Jobcentres as well as raising consciousness and providing moral support within the welfare claimant community.[207] Modern examples include the Kilburn Unemployed Workers Group, Norwich Claimants Union, the Scottish Unemployed Workers Network, Brighton Benefits Campaign,[208] and ACORN, with powerful trade unions such as Unite also establishing a 'community membership scheme'.[209] Indeed, Holgate situates the proliferation of claimants' unions as a response to the decline in workers bargaining power and trade union membership more generally.[210] Community unions (such as Unite's division) include unemployed members students and pensioners, providing a platform and voice to those with shared concerns over issues such as service closures and material living conditions, aiming to mitigate some of the structural unfreedoms (such as welfare and service provision) that coerce individuals into exploitative forms of work.

In the context of prison work and immigration detention, numerous organizations provide advice, mentoring, and advocacy to detainees, though more often than not, this is in their capacity as incarcerated individuals rather than as workers. Shaped by the context of imprisonment, these organizations tend to make demands primarily related to the human rights and material living conditions of detainees. These include, for example, Bail for Immigration Detainees, Detention Action and AVID, which provide visitor services for moral support, advice, signposting, and community support before and after release.

To summarise, , a range of actors and organizations mobilize to further the aims of informal workers and those featured within our case studies. This includes numerous informal trade unions, which 'do not function as typical or traditional trade unions', and can blur the line between trade union activity and broader activism . Ultimately, however, it is not the aim of this book to wade into the debate over the history and purpose of trade unionism, which is explored thoroughly elsewhere.[211] Rather, what our brief outline of worker organization and social campaigning demonstrates is that the form of mobilization, class consciousness, and solidarity that arises in response to capitalism is specific to the social, cultural, political, and institutional context

[207] ibid.
[208] Weghmann (n 90).
[209] Unite the Union, 'Community Membership' (26 November 2025) <https://www.unitetheunion.org/why-join/membership-types/community-membership> accessed 23 June 2025.
[210] Holgate (n 186).
[211] Richard Hyman, *Understanding European Trade Unionism: Between Market, Class and Society* (SAGE Publications Ltd 2001); Adams (n 5).

in which the labour takes place, sometimes referred to as the 'life-worlds' of the workers themselves. Accordingly, there is no one-size-fits-all approach to cultivating solidarity, collective organization, and mobilization. While some of these groups grow out of worker-led movements responding to workers' relationship with capitalist production and reproduction, others, driven by solidarity, coalesce outside the labour relationship. 'In these cases, solidarity is not created on the basis of a shared identity but draws on emotions such as anger and frustration and a shared desire for transformation', demonstrating that 'there is no need to be oppressed in order to be part of transformative politics'.[212]

Similarly, the struggle to ameliorate labour unfreedom is not confined to the economic sphere or to formal collective bargaining. Instead, collective organization and mobilization should (and does) take place through both political and social forms of strategising and action. Building on the 'multiple and diverse agencies of class struggle'[213] strengthens worker movements and must be intensified if the workers within our case studies and beyond are to challenge the multiple facets of labour unfreedom that lead to exploitative work. In spite of existing exclusions from collective bargaining protections, formal trade unions are encouraged to take stock of wider forms of informal work and include these workers within their membership remit—as we have begun to see in the context of more progressive, 'new-style' unions such as the Independent Workers of Great Britain (IWGB).

Alongside this work, however, grassroots and alternative forms of organization and campaigning that sits outside the union model remain essential to advancing progressive change in relation to the working and human rights of those in informal working relationships. These two spheres of rights are co-constitutive and inform one another, shaping the structural unfreedoms under which labour exploitation takes place. While there are challenges to organizing and mobilizing informal workers, these grassroots initiatives are essential to achieving change and realizing rights for those traditionally marginalized and excluded from legal recognition and protection.

[212] Weghmann (n 90) 452–53.
[213] ibid 453.

e. Migration as Decolonization: Access to Citizenship and the Labour Market

A foundational dimension of unfreedom that shapes entry into exploitative labour relations is the process of dispossession and accumulation linked to colonialism and neocolonialism, which has significantly impacted global wealth distribution and security. These processes compel individuals to leave their countries of origin in search of better opportunities or force them to flee—often as a result of the destabilizing political, cultural, and economic effects of colonial intervention. As Cross argues, this has resulted in the Global North's accumulation of labour power from the Global South, alongside the appropriation of land and other resources.[214] Once individuals have made the decision to migrate, their mobility is impacted both geographically and socially by international and domestic laws and policies, including visa restrictions and immigration controls and limitations on access to the formal labour market and welfare state benefits, which further reduce migrants' bargaining power.

Short of significant structural change and the removal of political structures and colonial logics that commodify space, nature, and humanity, we argue that migration should be contextualized against colonial histories that 'entailed the emigration of tens of millions of Europeans and the flow of natural and human resources across the globe, for the benefit of Europe and Europeans'[215] at the expense of Global South populations as well as processes of neocolonialism that have been significant contributors in the continued suffering and economic struggle of those within the 'zone of non-being', in Fanon's terminology.[216] For Fanon, the 'zone of non-being' is understood as a process of dehumanization that differentiates the construct of humanity (and being) from those below humanity (and non-being),[217] existing as a geographical space as well as a disposition[218] and lived reality for many migrants considered to be 'irregular'. It is worth noting that, within the context of migration, nationals from countries with 'high levels of human development' (as per the Henley Passport Index) can travel visa-free to around 85 per cent of all other countries

[214] Hannah Cross, 'Labour and Underdevelopment? Migration, Dispossession and Accumulation in West Africa and Europe' (2013) 40 Review of African Political Economy 202.

[215] E Tendayi Achiume, 'Migration as Decolonisation' (2019) 71 Stanford Law Review 1509.

[216] Frantz Fanon, *Black Skin, White Masks* (Richard Philcox and Anthony Appiah eds, 1st edn, new edn, Grove Press 1952).

[217] Nelson Maldonado-Torres, 'On the Coloniality of Being' (2007) 21 Cultural Studies 240; Charles des Portes, 'Towards a Decolonial Political Theory: Thinking from the Zone of Nonbeing' [2024] Philosophy & Social Criticism.

[218] Charles des Portes, 'Hannah Arendt's Hidden Phenomenology of the Body' (2022) 45 Human Studies 139.

worldwide, whereas those countries with 'low levels of human development' face significant visa restrictions, rendering irregular pathways as the most realistic (if not the only) option for migration, with dangerous and often deadly repercussions in terms of safety. Perhaps unsurprisingly, countries considered to be of 'high development' are largely in Europe and North America, whereas those with 'low development' are primarily in Africa and Asia.[219]

Drawing from the work of Tendayi Achiume, we argue that migration should be reframed as a matter of corrective redistributive justice and as a personal decolonial act on the part of individual migrants who respond to conditions of neocolonial subordination through movement to another state.[220] Migration as decolonization requires granting citizenship status to those who wish to move, along with equal access to socio-economic and civil and political rights, including the right to work. 'For the Zimbabwean Third World migrant whose territorial presence is unauthorized by the British government, the migration as decolonization thesis casts her as a de facto co-sovereign relative to de jure British citizens, and also attributes to her a right to de jure recognition, admission, and inclusion.'[221] Affording access on these terms would transform the narrative and experiences of numerous migrants who work informally, propagated by growing demands for cheap, exploitable, 'unfree' labour, which has become essential to the growth of Global North economies. As a corrective form of distributive justice, this basis of entitlement responds to neocolonial subordination and challenges the near-unfettered power of states to exclude non-citizens from their territory under international law.[222] Accordingly, Achiume notes that eligibility for the claim to migration as decolonization only applies to those who occupy a position of neocolonial subordination, and similarly, the obligations of Global North states depend on 'the extent of exploitative benefit or advantage Country X derives from neocolonial empire and the extent of subordination or disadvantage that a given migrant endures by virtue of being a national of Country Y'.[223]

A politics of incorporation that recognizes migration as a form of decolonization would remove a number of the structural unfreedoms impinging the mobility of irregular migrants in the labour market and recognize that it is

[219] UN International Organization for Migration (IOM), 'Interactive World Migration Report 2024' (2024) <https://worldmigrationreport.iom.int/msite/wmr-2024-interactive/> accessed 23 November 2025.

[220] Achiume (n 215).

[221] ibid 1552–53.

[222] E Tendayi Achiume, 'Reimagining International Law for Global Migration: Migration as Decolonization?' (2017) 111 American Journal of International Law 142.

[223] Achiume (n 215) 1560.

largely systemic and structural forces that shape migration patterns rather than individual desires to leave ones' country of origin. Migration as decolonization thus presents a shift in the norms and discourses that surround migration more generally. Access to socio-economic rights and the labour market could also increase the level of remittances sent back to Global South states, reducing inequalities, though admittedly failing to overturn the enduring relationship of dependency and subordination created by imperial intervention.

5. Conclusion

At present, law is used to tackle the more extreme forms of unfree labour, such as slavery, servitude, and forced labour (via a human rights or criminal law approach), or to protect those who enjoy the protective statuses of 'worker' or 'employee' . As a result of this significant gap within the legal framework, the law fails to protect workers residing in the centre of the unfree labour spectrum, further heightening their vulnerability to exploitation. This chapter has advanced recommendations aimed at closing that gap, ranging from micro reforms that seek to promote social and legal change within the constraints of the constitution and current doctrinal coherence to meso changes involving political and statutory changes to the systems of work addressed within our case studies. While these recommendations seek to improve the conditions of the labour process for those currently excluded from labour law protections, the macro changes outlined towards the end of the chapter focus on addressing deeper structural changes to redress the dimensions of unfreedom that compel individuals and groups into exploitative forms of work in the first place. As noted by Adelle Blackett at the beginning of this chapter, 'emancipation demands structural unshackling from a status that is the basis of subjugation, disenfranchisement, [and] commoditization.'[224] If we are to break the cyclical nature of exploitative work, we must look beyond simply managing the conditions under which we work and, instead, address the broader question of why we enter the labour relationship in the first place.

[224] Blackett (n 4).

8

Conclusion

The State as Facilitator and Benefactor of Labour Unfreedom

1. Introduction

Across the preceding chapters, this book developed a sustained and multidimensional critique of the ways in which contemporary labour law, policy, and political economy conspire to facilitate forms of unfree labour in liberal democratic contexts. This critique has been situated within a broader concern about how legal categories obscure coercion, how neoliberal rationality reshapes the state's role, and how privatization and contractualism enable the diffusion—but not the diminishment—of power. At the heart of the project lies a refusal to accept the marginalization of unfreedom as exceptional, peripheral, or aberrational. Instead, we have insisted that it be placed squarely at the centre of labour analysis.

This concluding chapter takes up three related tasks. First, it revisits the central claims of the book with a view to crystallizing its core contribution to labour law and socio-legal scholarship. Second, it reflects on the broader implications of our analysis for how we understand the state, legality, and freedom in the contemporary moment. Third, it looks forward—cautiously, but deliberately—to consider what it might mean to resist the structures that produce and naturalize unfree labour, and what role law might yet play in that resistance.

Underpaid and Unrecognized. Katie Bales and Amir Paz-Fuchs, Oxford University Press.
 DOI: 10.1093/9780197910467.003.0008

Our knowledge and experience of researching welfare[1] and immigration control[2] naturally drew our eye to the role of the state as both a facilitator and benefactor of labour unfreedom, responding to a call within the academic literature for greater attention to be paid to the state's 'central role in shaping the global conditions that facilitate the emergence and persistence of unfree labour'[3] on grounds that the state is often marginalized as ancillary to labour unfreedom within the labour relationship, as opposed to being central. Building on our previous research, prison labour, workfare, and labour within immigration detention felt like natural case studies for our analysis as each of these labour forms is organized by the state, yet workers lack legal recognition and access to rights such as the national minimum wage, despite garnering profits for both the state and private corporations. As explored within Chapter 2 of this book, the composition of these workforces share many commonalities, with workers often drawn from poorer socio-economic backgrounds and racialized communities. This reflection challenged us to question whether marginalization was a prerequisite for labour unfreedom or whether there were other forms of state-induced 'unfree labour' that defy these common stereotypes. This led us to the issue of internships, which are distinct from our other case studies in terms of who performs the work, yet remain connected through workers' lack of access to the national minimum wage or recognition under the employment status framework. The role of the state is more obscure in these instances and varies depending on the nature of the work undertaken. For example, in internships that are organized by branches of the state, such as NHS and teaching placements, the link between the state and the labour relationship is clear; however, even in instances where the state is not an 'organizer', the

[1] Amir Paz-Fuchs, *Welfare to Work: Conditional Rights in Social Policy* (OUP 2008); Amir Paz-Fuchs, 'Workfare's Persistent Philosophical and Legal Issues: Forced Labour, Reciprocity and a Basic Income Guarantee' in Anja Eleveld, Thomas Kampen, and Josien Arts (eds), *Welfare to Work in Contemporary European Welfare States* (Policy Press 2020); Amir Paz-Fuchs and Avishai Benish, 'Privatising Social Security' (2023) 31(1) Journal of Social Security Law 82; Amir Paz-Fuchs, 'Strict Conditionality, Structural Injustice and Welfare Rights' in Helen Carr and others (eds), *Research Handbook on Social Welfare Law* (Edward Elgar 2024); Katie Bales, 'Universal Credit: Not So Universal? Deconstructing the Impact of the Asylum Support System' (2013) 35 Journal of Social Welfare and Family Law 427; Katie Bales, 'The "Essential Living Needs" of Asylum Seekers: Lessons Learned from R (Refugee Action) v Secretary of State for the Home Department [2014] EWHC 1033' (2015) 37 Journal of Social Welfare and Family Law 247; Katie Bales, 'Hostile and Inept: The Government's Approach to Asylum Support' (2023) 45 Journal of Social Welfare and Family Law 188.

[2] Katie Bales, 'Immigration Raids, Employer Collusion and the Immigration Act 2016' (2017) 46 Industrial Law Journal 279; Manoj Dias-Abey and Katie Bales, 'Migration and Work in Post-Brexit UK' (Institute of Employment Rights 2023) <https://www.ier.org.uk/product/migration-and-work-in-post-brexit-uk/> accessed 23 November 2025.

[3] Genevieve LeBaron and Nicola Phillips, 'States and the Political Economy of Unfree Labour' (2019) 24 New Political Economy 1, 2.

legal regime creates and enables the system of internships to function, creating a thread of accountability that can be traced back to state policy.

Reflecting on the histories of these case studies in Chapter 2, 'Exploring the State's Hidden Workforce', revealed that these systems of labour have always been connected to processes of capitalist accumulation, either through reducing labour costs and producing goods for profit (benefiting both the state and/or private corporations) or through the facilitation of the schemes themselves, where the bodies of the workers as detainees/workfare recipients create income for the corporations to whom the state outsources its responsibilities. The link between the state and private profit is thus an ever-present thread that binds these instances of state-induced unfree labour to capitalist accumulation. Though working conditions vary among the case studies, the most significant commonality is that all groups are paid below the national minimum wage. Over time, a variety of different reasons have been put forward to justify workers' exclusion from the wage and traditional labour rights, including labour as a form of punishment and deterrence, discipline, and cost saving. And yet, the most salient justification in the modern manifestations of these schemes is that the work is 'of benefit' to the worker, often justified through the language of skills development, learning, and rehabilitation. Of course, the overarching context which also links this work, but which is left out of government narratives, is that this work reduces costs for businesses and industries that would otherwise have to source labour from those paid the national minimum wage, or via globalized supply chains, allowing private companies to accumulate greater profits by increasing the surplus of value extracted.

These legal and political mystifications are further contextualized in Chapter 3, 'Working without a Job: Why Are They Not Workers?', which applies the standardized employment law tests to the chosen case studies to reveal that in all of the scenarios studied, workers meet the common law tests for either worker, or both worker and employee. Yet, due to the proposed purpose of work within each of the case studies examined, which centre the relation as being 'of benefit' to the worker, the labour performed is not considered to be 'market work' worthy of the national minimum wage. In order to denaturalize this assumption, the chapter untangles the conceptual underpinnings of this reasoning and reveals the contradictory ways in which constructions of benefit are manipulated within legal reasoning to suit political agendas, revealing that in many of the cases studied, employers derived equal benefit from the labour performed (if not more), and the benefits derived on the part of the workers is of little significance (if any). What this tells us is that 'like any conceptual framing, the paid/unpaid labour distinction is no more than an intellectual contrivance which may or may not correspond at any time or place with the material realities it seeks to represent'.[4] We enforce this argument through application of a historical materialist lens, based on the premise that the nature of society is shaped by the way in which it materially reproduces itself, in other words, how it produces the goods that are central to life.

Accordingly, Chapter 3 traces the normative value underlying the market/non-market distinction as justification for not paying a wage back to the gendered and racialized social division of labour that emerged with capitalism. Though capitalism required and requires processes of social reproduction and imperialism to take place to facilitate production, the labour undertaken by women and colonized populations in the transition to capitalist society was considered separate from processes of production that led to the sale of goods and services on the market, and thereby their labour was/is regarded as valueless, 'non-market' work. When we contextualize this history against the exclusions present within our current labour market, the normative underpinnings concerning 'market work' continue to resonate, giving purchase to labour as a distinct legal and economic category that excludes large swathes of workers from access to rights and the wage. The issue for the workers within our case studies then goes far beyond the simple question of the employment contract or applying the tests for 'worker status'. Instead, it is centrally concerned with the historical ordering of society and the economy which has created the underlying structures distinguishing valued and non-valued work as well as the social standing of those undertaking it. Law has a significant role to play within this context, delineating valuable wage-earning employment from broader categories of 'informal' work via the concept of the employment contract as well as strict regulatory contexts that blur the possibilities of broadening labour law's scope.

In Chapter 4, 'Unfree Labour', we further problematize the labour relations within our case studies by theorizing them as forms of unfree labour, exploited by the state and private corporations for economic gain. As established within this chapter, the legal boundaries of what constitutes unfree labour (ie slavery, servitude, and forced labour) were forged to align with and support colonial interests and further racial capitalism, strategically ignoring the dispossession, accumulation, and exploitation that was (and remains) central to the functioning of the capitalist labour market. As a result, the normative construction of labour unfreedom and what is deemed to be socially unacceptable

[4] Joanne Conaghan, 'Gender and the Labour of Law' in Hugh Collins, Virginia Mantouvalou, and Gillian Lester (eds), *Philosophical Foundations of Labour Law* (OUP 2018).

remains constrained to situations of extreme exploitation or 'modern slavery'. As such, all other work relations that fail to meet these extreme thresholds are considered legitimate, enabling the capitalist landscape to flourish. It is thus of little surprise that the labour within our case studies fails to meet the strict threshold of slavery, servitude, and/or forced labour, despite many workers within our case study sectors feeling that they are unfairly exploited. In rejecting the legal definition of unfree labour, we then had to consider how best to conceptualize labour unfreedom, drawing from a burgeoning literature on the topic that spans the realms of political economy, sociology, law, geography, and philosophy. Our theoretical framework was perhaps the most difficult part of the book to write as the authors diverged in their perspectives, Amir pushing for a more concrete conceptualization, which allows for the plotting of different case studies relative to the amount of labour unfreedom endured so that this can be activated within the existing labour law framework; whereas Katie was more interested in building a framework to reveal the wider structural dimensions of unfreedom (as well as conditions of the labour process) that guide individuals into and maintain unequal and exploitative labour relationships—with the aim of revealing a wider array of solutions to address labour unfreedom beyond the confines of labour law. Rather than positing these two perspectives in opposition to one another, we included both viewpoints, dealing first in Chapter 4 with the underlying structural dimensions of unfreedom that guide individuals into exploitative work, as well as conditions of the labour process, before then asking in Chapter 5 how labour law might respond to this framing, seeking to bridge some of the existing gaps between theory and law. This is further expanded upon in Chapter 7, which puts forward legal as well as political, economic, and social solutions to ameliorating labour unfreedom.

The theoretical framework adopted in Chapter 4 is that of a 'spectrum of unfree labour', building upon LeBaron's use of the Marxist three-part continuum.[5] We interpreted this as unpacking unfree labour along three broad dimensions: the distribution of land and resources that compel someone to sell their labour power; circulation (including the circulation of labour and goods in the market economy as well as mobility in the geographic, economic, and social sense); and conditions of the labour process.[6] Chapter 4 departs from use

[5] Genevieve LeBaron, 'Unfree Labour beyond Binaries' (2015) 17 International Feminist Journal of Politics 1.

[6] Katie Bales, 'Rethinking "Unfree" Labour: The Immigration Industrial Complex' in Eileen Boris and others (eds), *Global Labour Migration: New Directions* (University of Illinois Press 2023).

of the term 'continuum', which is considered to be unidimensional, and instead adopts the term 'spectrum' to show that there are multiple axes guiding labour unfreedom that differ significantly in content and form. Different axes warrant different responses within and outside of law from a range of different actors. Applying this framework to the case studies revealed that multiple structural conditions impact upon the freedom with which workers enter and remain within the labour contract, rendering their work 'unfree'. This explains why, in some instances, workers might 'voluntarily consent' to exploitative labour conditions such as minimal pay below that of the national minimum wage. In particular, workers' socio-economic position and lack of access to productive property was of significance to the majority of those working in prison, immigration detention, and workfare whereby large proportions of the workforce are poor, which has further consequences in terms of social reproduction and the desire to work to ease pressures upon (or provide for) family members and dependants.

Workers' dispossession was traced historically to processes of primitive accumulation in the domestic context and dispossession by accumulation in the colonies, the repercussions of which continue to impact upon global wealth distribution and migration patterns in the present as well as lack of access to productive property in the modern context. Limitations upon the circulation of workers within our case study areas also raised issues regarding immigration control and access to welfare and workers' rights, which impact both geographic and social and economic mobility. Poor working conditions were highlighted and further expanded upon in Chapter 5. Our analysis reveals that while many of the working conditions within our case studies may appear 'decent', broader structural unfreedoms impact upon the construction of the labour as 'unfree'. If we are to truly understand the pressures and forces that compel individuals to undertake exploitative work, we must therefore look beyond the simple narrative of the unscrupulous employer towards the broader structures that diminish agency and choices in entering work relations, creating further imbalances in the bargaining powers between workers and employers. More generally, the paradoxical nature of claims that focus on pay as a feature that distinguishes free from unfree labour is the fact that it centres the discussion within the capitalist—and thus productivist—paradigm and is distanced from the critical approach adopted within this book, which seeks to reduce reliance on market-based criteria. However, as acknowledged by the International Labour Organization (ILO), decent working conditions are crucial to meaningful and fulfilling work within the capitalist economy, meaning that issues such as payment cannot be ignored. Indeed, the ILO considers adequate earnings as central to its decent work agenda.[7] While increasing pay levels would thus reduce the levels of exploitation experienced by those in our case studies (as they would be able to maintain more of the surplus value they produce), this would not render their labour 'free'.

Chapter 5, 'Positioning Unfree Labour at the Centre of the Labour Analysis', asks how our conceptualization of unfreedom and its structural dynamics should inform our understanding and the future development of labour law and, in turn, asks how well-rehearsed labour law principles, such as those concerning control and consent, should enrich our understanding of unfreedom. Two conclusions are put forwards in this regard: first, that beyond a certain point in the spectrum, some cases of unfree labour should not exist and that law should seek to abolish them; second, that where labour unfreedom is allowed to exist, there should be an imperative to ameliorate the conditions leading to labour unfreedom and a mitigation of its consequences, attempting to move the labour relationship closer to one of freedom than unfreedom. The chapter identifies three facets of unfree labour that might help to shape the response of labour law: lack of consent and/or the existence of coercion that impacts an individual's ability to avoid entering the employment contract; conditions of the labour process; and the extent of control and discipline that governs the labour relationship, including the use of arbitrary power to affect rights outside the labour relationship.[8] While consent is acknowledged as an important factor within the labour relationship (applying on entry, throughout the labour relationship, and upon exit), it is problematized within the chapter as subject to coercion, which renders consent a contested concept that, much like our construction of 'unfree labour', cannot be understood devoid of the historical and wider context in which it is given or withheld. Labour law should thus recognize (as it does in the context of bargaining power) that consent exists on a spectrum.

The conditions of the labour process explored within this chapter relate largely to payment of the wage as within each of the four case studies explored, workers are paid less than the national minimum wage which, at the very least, is a strong indicator that the working conditions experienced are 'oppressive'.[9] We acknowledge that the national minimum wage is not necessarily reflective of the costs of social reproduction, and therefore the sustaining of life, but rather designed to prevent employers from reducing wages in response to

[7] ILO, 'What is Decent Work?' <https://www.ilo.org/resource/what-decent-work> accessed 10 April 2026.

[8] cf LeBaron (n 5) 9; Amir Paz-Fuchs, 'Badges of Modern Slavery' (2016) 79 Modern Law Review 757.

[9] Paz-Fuchs (n 1).

implementation of the tax credit regime—ensuring that labour costs are born by employers rather than the state.[10] This explains why there are such high levels of in-work poverty in the United Kingdom and demonstrates that those who are paid even less than the national minimum wage have less power to negotiate the terms and conditions under which they work, or to freely agree to it, upon which labour law should recognize and place greater importance.

Chapter 5 differentiates the control and subordination exhibited within our case studies, separating internships, which are largely driven on grounds of exploitation, and thus the extraction of surplus value from the cases of labour in immigration detention, prison, and workfare, where, while exploitation exists, it is also undergirded by domination often involving routine forms of dehumanization in efforts to exert disciplinary control.[11] Our workers' exclusion from employment status and its associate protections expands the possibilities for domination and control within the relationship, with few avenues for workers to exert their resistance. Domination and control also extends beyond the labour relationship in all of the case studies examined whereby the behaviour of workers outside of work impacts upon their access to the work placements studied, control and domination that is fostered by workers' lack of access to rights. As Judy Fudge explains, 'broadening the scope of labour law provokes us to consider why certain forms of subordination and segregation are acceptable and other forms are not, and how what we consider to be unacceptable forms of subordination and acceptable methods to redress them change over time and across space'.[12]

Chapter 6, 'The Political Dimension: Neoliberalism, Privatization, and State Complicity', puts neoliberalism as central to the expansion of unfree labour practices, within our case studies and beyond. It refutes the common conception that under neoliberalism the state withdraws, instead framing it as a redeployment of state apparatus to establish the market and prioritize market imperatives,[13] primarily secured through the creation and enforcement of property rights, which constitute a form of private government and coercive power.[14] Law does not provide a neutral baseline from which we can

[10] Zoe Adams, 'Understanding the Minimum Wage: Political Economy and Legal Form' (2019) 78 Cambridge Law Journal 42; Zoe Adams, *Labour and the Wage: A Critical Perspective* (OUP 2020).

[11] Erin Hatton, *Coerced: Work under Threat of Punishment* (University of California Press 2020) ch 3.

[12] Judy Fudge, 'Feminist Reflections on the Scope of Labour Law: Domestic Work, Social Reproduction, and Jurisdiction' (2014) 22 Feminist Legal Studies 1, 19–20.

[13] Rob van Horn and Philip Mirowski, 'The Rise of the Chicago School of Economics and the Birth of Neoliberalism' in Philip Mirowski and Dieter Plehwe (eds), *The Road from Mont Pèlerin* (Harvard UP 2009) 139, 157; Loic Wacquant, 'Three Steps to a Historical Anthropology of Actually Existing Neoliberalism' (2012) 20 Social Anthropology 66.

[14] Robert Hale, 'Law Making by Unofficial Minorities' (1920) 20 Columbia Law Review 451; Robert Hale, 'Coercion and Distribution in a Supposedly Non-Coercive State' (1923) 38 Political Science Quarterly 470.

judge 'freedom'; instead, it is central to the distribution of property, both productive and non-productive, and the establishment of the market and the associate bargaining powers accompanying 'free market' exchange. Though labour law ostensibly seeks to redress inequality of bargaining power, law also creates the dispossession and inequality that gives rise to these inequalities and labour unfreedom in the first place. Recognizing that the state is involved in the facilitation of unfree labour in direct (through compelling individuals into work via policy) and indirect strategies (unequal distribution of rights and protections, non-enforcement of labour legislation and regulation, law and policies that facilitate the concentration of private property ownership),[15] the chapter examines the contract and contractual mindset distilled into three distinct yet connected layers: the ideological (or 'philosophical'), the institutional, and the field level.

The ideology of responsibility further compounds this dynamic. Neoliberal discourse has recast social rights—whether to housing, food, work, or care—as contingent on behavioural performance. The language of entitlement gives way to that of conditionality. The social contract becomes not a mutual guarantee of security but a mechanism for testing individual worthiness. In this setting, poverty is moralized, unemployment is criminalized, and dependency is pathologized. The failure to secure work—no matter how exploitative or underpaid—is read not as an indictment of economic structure but of personal character.

Labour law, in its conventional frame, remains ill equipped to confront this ideological terrain. Its instruments are orientated towards regulating the employment relationship—defined in narrow contractual terms—rather than interrogating the broader political economy of work. Even its more progressive aspirations, such as recognizing rights for atypical workers or expanding collective bargaining, often rest on a foundational acceptance of the wage relation as the normative form of freedom. Yet, what this book has demonstrated is that, for many, the wage relation is experienced not as freedom but as constraint, not as empowerment but as survival under duress. To take unfreedom seriously, then, is to ask more of labour law than it has traditionally been willing to offer. It is to challenge its assumptions, unsettle its categories, and expose the ways in which its formalism facilitates real-world harms. This is not to abandon legal strategies altogether. But it is to resist the tendency—sometimes explicit, often implicit—to treat law as a neutral arbiter rather than an active participant in the construction of coercion.

[15] LeBaron and Phillips (n 3).

Our final chapter, Chapter 7, 'Power to the Workers', proposes recommendations that, if implemented, could reduce or remove some of the dimensions of unfreedom that coerce people into accepting and/or remaining in exploitative work. These recommendations are structured by thinking of law and policy in terms of the scale of implementation (the micro), reform (the meso) and reimagining (the macro) and led to some division between the authors, particularly in relation to the macro reforms listed, many of which are written as provocations. Again, rather than removing or prioritizing one perspective over the other, we attempt within the chapter to highlight some of the general critiques that might be lodged against these suggestions, reflecting the conversations to which they gave rise.

Recommendations put forward at the micro level explore whether we could use the existing contours of the legal framework to effect positive change. The three recommendations put forward relate to the doctrine of illegality, contending there is space for 'incremental judicial development';[16] extension of trade union rights beyond the employment relationship, in line with ILO commentary; and a purposive construction of worker status that recognizes the multiple and structural dimensions that give rise to dependency and coercion within the labour relationship, centring the underlying purpose of section 230(3) of the Employment Rights Act 1996, which is to extend protection to those performing work 'in positions of subordination and dependency'.[17] The likelihood of these reforms gaining traction depends on willing from the judiciary to harness the potential of the common law and revisiting the normative grounding of labour law as a means of offsetting the vagaries of capitalism. Whether such judicial activism is likely in a political climate beleaguered by fascism, nationalism, and the constant reassertion of 'sovereignty' in its many guises remains to be seen.

The meso recommendations explore reforms that could be made to law and policy in the specific areas of our case studies to help improve conditions of the labour process. In all cases, this required increasing wage levels in line with the national minimum wage. Further recommendations in relation to prison work included the need to gain consent before prisoners undertake work and repealing the imposition of mandatory working hours each day[18] as well as

[16] Alan Bogg, 'Labour Constitutionalism: Effective Judicial Protection as a Constitutional Principle in UK Labour Law' (2023) 43 Comparative Labor Law and Policy Journal 45, 47.

[17] Joe Atkinson and Hitesh Dhorajiwala, 'After Uber: Purposive Interpretation and the Future of Contract' (*UK Labour Law*, 1 April 2021) <https://uklabourlawblog.com/2021/04/01/after-uber-purposive-interpretation-and-the-future-of-contract-by-joe-atkinson-and-hitesh-dhorajiwala> accessed 15 November 2025.

[18] See the Prison Rules 1999 (SI 1999/728) Rule 31(3).

increasing meaningful access to education and training. Notwithstanding our position that immigration detention should be abolished in its entirety, we put forward additional recommendations on grounds that abolition is unlikely to be embraced or endorsed by the major political parties in this country at any point in the near future. Accordingly, we recommend that stronger judicial oversight is implemented and a twenty-eight-day statutory time limit placed on the use of immigration detention as well as unlimited access to the labour market for asylum seekers outside of detention. With regards to workfare, our recommendation is relatively simple: that workfare should be abolished in its entirety. In line with the European Commission which, in 2024, introduced a 'traineeship package' intended to improve the working conditions of trainees,[19] we suggest that all interns be provided with a written contract that explicitly includes the (non-renewable) term of the internship capped at six months and, in exceptional circumstances, twelve months; the remuneration offered; expectations and learning outcomes; mentoring and supervision within the contract; and working time provisions. We also recommend increased regulation of internships (akin to that of workfare); that all labour rights are afforded to interns where they are found to be performing tasks normally undertaken by other workers, that is, where they are being exploited as cheap labour; and finally, that employers providing internships subsidized by the state should adhere to a minimum set of criteria to manage quality control. Many of the meso recommendations set out in Chapter 7 have been raised by the workers themselves and wider campaign groups seeking to improve working conditions for those who are often marginalized, at times with positive effects whereby proposals have been endorsed in parliamentary Bills.[20] Their implementation is not thus wholly unrealistic but relies on political will and the desire to reduce social and economic inequalities at the expense of capital.

The macro recommendations set out in Chapter 7 are less detailed policy proposals and instead situated as provocations intended to stimulate outside-the-box thinking over how we might reduce the dimensions of unfreedom leading people into unfree and exploitative forms of work. A number of

[19] 'Proposal for a Directive on *Improving and Enforcing Working Conditions of Trainees and Combating Regular Employment Relationships Disguised as Traineeships*' ('Traineeships Directive') (2024/0068(COD), 20 March 2024) <https://eur-lex.europa.eu/legal-content/EN/TXT/?uri=celex:52024PC0132> accessed 7 April 2026; 'Council Recommendation on a *Reinforced Quality Framework for Traineeships*' (2024/0069(NLE), 20 March 2024) <https://eur-lex.europa.eu/legal-content/EN/TXT/HTML/?uri=CELEX:52024DC0133#:~:text=The%20proposed%20recommendation%20aims%20to,laid%20down%20in%20EU%20law> accessed 7 April 2026.

[20] Spearheaded by the House of Lords, eg the Nationality and Borders Bill, s 13 sought to make progressive changes to employment access for asylum seekers, granting permission to work for asylum seekers and their adult dependents six months after launching their initial asylum claim.

recommendations were suggested including, first, the reformulation of 'employment status' to extend recognition and rights to those considered 'irregular' workers as well as those who are excluded on grounds that their labour is not considered to be 'market-work'; second, refocusing our attention away from the working relationship and instead centring subordination and domination to focus on the power structures that result in economic subordination under capitalism; third, the implementation of a universal basic income or a system of universal basic services; fourth, encouraging alternative forms of labour organization and mobilization that exist and operate outside of the traditional trade union, collective bargaining paradigm; and finally, reconceptualizing immigration as a form of decolonization so that those who have suffered economically as a result of imperialism are able to access the resources of those imperial powers on the same terms as its citizens. As noted throughout the chapter, these recommendations are intended to inspire alternative ways of conceptualizing the current capitalist order, and it is not expected that they will be embraced or endorsed by the current neoliberal political class. Indeed, there are many well-rehearsed arguments against each of them in turn, some of which were engaged with by the authors, who disagreed over what should and should not be included in this section. Yet, their inclusion stimulates us to think beyond the confines of liberal legal doctrine and examine theories emanating from feminism and colonial studies, focusing on the voices of groups whose labour is historically and currently marginalized and made invisible.

What has transpired throughout the research and writing of this book is the way in which law and legal reasoning are manipulated to obfuscate the reality of what is right in front of us, designating some persons as worthy of rights and recognition, while others remain excluded, labouring at the margins. As recognized by Hale,

> when the rights and privileges which one party possesses are vastly superior in strategic importance to those possessed by the other (when the restraints on his liberty, in other words, are vastly less burdensome than those on the liberty of the other), the other party may in effect be compelled to submit by contract to almost any terms imposed by the stronger party.[21]

If society truly seeks to ameliorate labour unfreedom, which at present feels aspirational in itself, we must look beyond the conditions of the labour relationship towards the broader economic, legal, and structural arrangements

[21] Hale (n 14) 452.

that allocate and perpetuate unequal property relations, recognizing that 'dominion over things is also imperium over our fellow human beings'.[22] Labour unfreedom will, thus, always exist within a capitalist economy, but we hope that this book demonstrates some of the ways in which we can better understand these arrangements and push against the coercive dimensions that intensify workers' labour unfreedom and exploitation.

2. From Peripheral Concern to Structuring Logic

One of the animating concerns of the book has been the conceptual positioning of unfree labour within legal and policy discourse. Conventionally treated as an aberration to be remedied through stronger enforcement, anti-trafficking laws, or criminal sanctions, unfreedom is too often framed as something that happens 'over there'—in the informal economy, in rogue sectors, or in the shadow of law's presumed neutrality. The chapters here have challenged this framing. Instead, we approached unfree labour as a structuring logic, a recurring effect of broader institutional arrangements, ideological commitments, and legal architectures that are neither accidental nor marginal.

The point is not merely that these schemes exist or that they rely on various forms of duress. It is that they are rendered legitimate through legal, political, and cultural narratives that frame participation as choice, poverty as pathology, and regulation as protection. This triad—choice, pathology, protection—repeats across domains. The individual signs the form. The bureaucratic system deems them work-ready. The labour law doctrine finds no employment relationship. And thus, responsibility is individualized, coercion is obfuscated, and the system continues.

What, then, does this analysis demand of us—not only as scholars or advocates but also as interlocutors in a legal and political system that reproduces these harms? If the preceding chapters have shown anything, it is that the juridical architecture of labour law cannot be assumed to stand outside the systems of discipline and exclusion it appears to adjudicate. Law does not merely respond to labour conditions; it produces them. And it does so through forms and assumptions that are often treated as neutral, inevitable, or apolitical.

Perhaps most revealing in this regard is the category of consent. As multiple chapters have shown, the law's emphasis on voluntariness operates as a kind of blind spot—a mechanism that displaces structural coercion by reframing

[22] Morris Cohen, 'Property and Sovereignty' (1927) 13 Cornell Law Quarterly 8.

it as individual agreement. The individual 'agrees' to work in a mandatory placement to receive benefits. The prisoner 'agrees' to participate in an unpaid work scheme to gain privileges. The immigration detainee 'agrees' to labour in conditions of precarity. The intern 'agrees' to work for free in the hope of a more positive future. And yet, when the terms of refusal are skills wastage, starvation, destitution, deportation, or imprisonment, what is the nature of the choice being made?

The juridical lens, however, remains fixed on the outward performance of consent. Courts ask whether the individual signed the form, whether a contractual relationship can be established, whether mutual obligations are present. Rarely do they interrogate the underlying social and economic conditions in which these 'choices' are made. In this way, the law's own doctrinal commitment to formal equality and procedural fairness becomes complicit in rendering the substantive inequality of these arrangements invisible.

3. Conclusion: The Role of the State Revisited

The book's central argument about the state bears restating here, not for emphasis alone but because it demands a more radical departure from conventional accounts. The liberal imagination has long held the state to be the institution that tempers market excess, protects the vulnerable, and safeguards freedom. But as this book has shown, the state is deeply implicated in producing and maintaining the very conditions of unfreedom it is assumed to prevent.

This is not a story of state absence or retreat. It is a story of state redesign. Welfare institutions have not disappeared; they have been restructured to discipline. Employment protections have not been eliminated; they have been redistributed through fragmented and selective enforcement. Regulatory capacity has not evaporated; it has been redirected to serve capital through mechanisms such as marketized performance indicators, outsourcing regimes, and behavioural compliance systems. In this sense, the contemporary state does not simply enable unfree labour. It engineers it.

Nor is this process accidental. The restructuring of the state along neoliberal lines reflects a conscious set of political and legal choices. It reflects the ascendance of a particular vision of economic and moral order—one in which market participation is equated with social worth, where dependency is a failure of will, and where contractualism displaces solidarity as the governing ethos of public life. As our book makes clear, this vision is not merely economic but constitutional: it reshapes the very terms by which obligations are defined, rights are distributed, and responsibilities are imposed.

This understanding of the state challenges more than policy. It demands a critical reassessment of the frameworks through which we judge legitimacy and justice in public governance. If the state can no longer be presumed to act as a counterweight to market coercion, then the categories through which we articulate legal protection—employment, status, voluntariness, fairness—require fundamental scrutiny. And this, in turn, requires a more ambitious conception of what labour law is for.

To ask what labour law is for is to return, in a way, to first principles. But it is also to move forwards—towards a politics of reconstitution. If law has been central to the production and legitimization of unfree labour, it must also be part of its undoing, not through nostalgic appeals to mid-century welfarism or formal equality but through a radical reconsideration of how legal systems can be made to foreground autonomy, collective agency, and material security.

The final chapter of this book—the one that now begins in legal imagination rather than empirical case—is therefore not about restoration. It is about disruption. It is about resisting the normalization of coercion in the guise of reform, the rebranding of punishment as responsibilization, and the persistence of inequality under the language of market fairness. And it is about reclaiming law—not as the neutral broker it purports to be but as a political instrument whose shape and purpose remain open to contestation.

This task is not just for lawyers. The reconstitution of labour relations must involve organizers, claimants, workers in precarious conditions, and communities for whom the state has long been more carceral than caring. It requires not only doctrinal reform but also ideological rupture. It requires new imaginaries of value, of entitlement, of what it means to work—and what it means to live.

What might this look like? At the institutional level, it means rolling back the architecture of conditionality and responsibilization that has come to define welfare and carceral labour. It means strengthening collective bargaining not merely for recognized employees but for all those who work under compulsion, threat, or necessity. It means expanding legal concepts of employment to encompass the realities of dependency and power and remaking labour protections in light of these conditions.

At the cultural level, it means displacing the dominant moral narrative that poverty is personal failure and work is a civic virtue regardless of its terms. It means replacing market participation as the precondition for social membership with a recognition of shared dependency and mutual care. And at the theoretical level, it means forging a jurisprudence that centres on vulnerability, relationality, and freedom as non-domination.

This is not a modest agenda. Nor is it a utopian one. It proceeds from the recognition, developed across these chapters, that the status quo is not neutral but structured—legally, institutionally, and ideologically—to sustain unfreedom. If that structure is to be undone, it will require nothing less than a fundamental reimagining of labour law's normative commitments and a refusal to accept coercion as an unavoidable fact of work.

In confronting unfree labour, then, the challenge is not to restore a purer past, nor to perfect the mechanisms of liberal legality. It is to build a future in which freedom—real, substantive, collective—ceases to be the exception and becomes the organizing principle of labour law, of the state, and of the social contract itself.

Index

For the benefit of digital users, indexed terms that span two pages (e.g., 52–53) may, on occasion, appear on only one of those pages.